How White Evangelicals Think

How White Evangelicals Think

The Psychology of White Conservative Christians

DAVE VERHAAGEN

CASCADE *Books* · Eugene, Oregon

HOW WHITE EVANGELICALS THINK
The Psychology of White Conservative Christians

Cascade Books
An Imprint of Wipf and Stock Publishers
199 W. 8th Ave., Suite 3
Eugene, OR 97401

www.wipfandstock.com

PAPERBACK ISBN: 978-1-6667-1068-7
HARDCOVER ISBN: 978-1-6667-1069-4
EBOOK ISBN: 978-1-6667-1070-0

Cataloguing-in-Publication data:

Names: Verhaagen, Dave, author.

Title: How white evangelicals think : the psychology of white conservative Christians / Dave Verhaagen.

Description: Eugene, OR: Cascade Books, 2022 | Includes bibliographical references and index.

Identifiers: ISBN 978-1-6667-1068-7 (paperback) | ISBN 978-1-6667-1069-4 (hardcover) | ISBN 978-1-6667-1070-0 (ebook)

Subjects: LCSH: Evangelicalism—21st century. | Evangelicalism—United States. | Evangelicalism—Psychological aspects—United States. | Evangelicalism—Political aspects—United States.

Classification: BR1642.U5 V40 2022 (paperback) | BR1642 (ebook)

08/11/22

To Ellen, my partner in the journey, the love of my life,
the best person I've ever known.

"Wounds from a friend can be trusted."

PROVERBS 27:6 (NIV)

Contents

Acknowledgments

WRITING A BOOK IS mostly a solitary activity. For me, it's late nights after the house is quiet, except for the snoring of an old dog. I've written eight other books, but none as difficult as this one. Wading through hundreds of books and articles, interviewing people, collecting original research, and late nights of writing made for a tough process. That makes it especially gratifying to have people who have joined me in this writing journey.

Madison Bigler served as my senior research assistant, doing much of the heavy lifting with getting all the research and references together. I couldn't have crossed the finish line without her.

My wife, Ellen, gave me time and space to write, encouragement to keep going, and a listening ear when I needed to talk something out loud. She was also immensely helpful in the early editing phases, helping me cut where I needed to cut and keep what I needed to keep. Beyond the book, she has loved me well for over thirty years. I am blessed to have her in my life.

The folks at Cascade Books, including Michael Thomson, Matthew Wimer, and George Callihan understood the book, including what it was and wasn't about, and stood behind it from the beginning. They allowed me the honor of working with Rodney Clapp, a gifted writer himself, who served as my editor.

Adrian Hon, Tyler Huckabee, Daniel Jones, and Danté Stewart each had important and unique vantage points. Their quotes and insights illuminated me. Thanks to each of you for your excellent perspectives.

One of my favorite parts about writing this challenging book was the kindness of strangers, particularly other professionals who were willing to give me their time. Many of these men and women were people I admire and whose work has helped me on this journey. Several of the top experts in the world, outstanding thinkers, and trailblazers gave me their time to provide me with interviews and original quotes. I'm indebted to Dr. Ryan Burge, Dr. Chuck DeGroat, Dr. Agnieszka Golec de Zavala, Dr. Joseph O. Baker, Dr. Jonathan Haidt, Dr. Andrew Whitehead, Dr. Beverly Daniel Tatum, Dr. Robert P. Jones. Dr. Keon West, Dr. Anton Gollwitzer, Dr. Patricia Turner, Dr. Josh Packard, Dr. Robert Brooks, and Dr. Bunmi Olatunji for their generosity and willingness to share their expertise. In some cases, they gave me a few quotes, but several of them gave me in-depth interviews that not only made the book richer, but sharpened my own outlook and understanding of each topic.

Finally, I'm immensely grateful for those who have stood by me and will continue to stand by me, even in the face of criticism and hostility. I admire kindness and authenticity, but I especially admire courage. I'm grateful for those in my life who embody these qualities.

INTRODUCTION

Same Name, Different State

The Beginning of a Journey

IN A TIME BEFORE smart phones and GPS, I unfolded a map on the table and traced the path from Chapel Hill down the North Carolina highways to where I would arrive in Roanoke Rapids, North Carolina a few hours before I was to speak at a conference. I left with plenty of time and drove leisurely to the retreat center. The only problem? The conference was in Roanoke Rapids, Virginia, which was now about two hundred miles away. It wasn't as serious a screw-up as showing up in Arlington, Texas if you were trying to get to Arlington, Virginia or arriving in Gainesville, Florida if you needed to be in Gainesville, Virginia, but it was still a problem. I headed for one place, but I ended up in another place with the same name.

For many of us who grew up in the white evangelical subculture, we've had the same experience. We thought we were going one place, but we ended up somewhere else, somewhere we did not want to be. The name was the same, but it wasn't where we wanted to go.

I signed up to be a Christian when I was seven years old in Vacation Bible School after what must have been one glorious flannelgraph presentation. I was clueless about what being a Christian meant because I was, you know, seven years old. So later during a youth service at the wise old age of fourteen, I raised my hand to proclaim I was going all in. I'm loyal, so I kept my commitment to God through the years: Bible study small group in high school, large group coordinator of a campus ministry in college, volunteer staff during graduate school, Sunday school teacher, elder board

1

chair, Christian book author, adjunct seminary professor, and Christian conference speaker. I was a good little Christian boy.

There's no question I benefited from this immersion in the Christian community. It's where I met many of my friends, business associates, and my wife. It's how I got my first book published, and what opened doors in my business that might have been harder to get through. Over time, though, I realized I had set out for one destination but had arrived somewhere else. I thought being a Christian meant living your life for others, fighting for the powerless and the fatherless and the hopeless, valuing humility and service and mercy, being meek and gentle. With kindness and compassion at its core, authentic Christian faith rejected worldly power grabs and earthly kingdom-building. I had signed up for a faith that loved others when they were unlovable, showed undeserved mercy, and required dying to self and living for others. I thought that's what it was about.

Instead, I found myself as part of a subculture that appeared self-centered, angry, and unattractive, not only to those outside of it, but to plenty of those within it, including me. Instead of being humble, they were arrogant. Instead of being gentle, they were abrasive. Instead of being kind, they were harsh. Instead of valuing the small, they esteemed the big and grandiose. I headed toward one place, but I ended up somewhere hundreds of miles away in a place that shared a name, but little else.

It's no surprise the fastest growing category for religious identity in the United States is the "Nones," those who don't affiliate with any religious group.[1] Political scientist Ryan Burge wrote an entire book full of meaty research data about the who, when, and why of the Nones. Over a third of the millennial generation checked this box in national surveys.[2] In an op-ed for *The New York Times*, Tony Campolo and Shane Claiborne, founders of Red Letter Christians, wrote, "Nones, many of whom grew up within evangelicalism, often still affirm faith in God. They left the church because they gave up on evangelical leadership."[3]

That leadership has been busy over the past four decades. Since the 1980s, the evangelical branch of the church had been busy exerting its influence in local, state, and national elections. They had been amassing political power and championing conservative political positions. Evangelical church membership continued to rise. As a cultural force, evangelicals became a powerhouse, courted by presidential candidates, discussed on major news outlets. All the while, their divorce rate was atrocious and their

1. Burge, *Nones.*
2. Burge, *Nones.*
3. Campolo and Claiborne, "Evangelicalism is Dead," lines 16–18.

moral behavior was no better than anyone else's. For example, a survey of 63,000 "affair-seeking" individuals found the largest group based on self-identification was "evangelical" at 25 percent of the entire sample. (Agnostics and atheists were only 2 percent and 1.4 percent, respectively.)[4] The public perception of them was often that they were harsh, judgmental, and unkind. It was a mess.

In 2016, I expected the true turnaround moment for evangelicals would be when Trump became the Republican front-runner. For many evangelicals, the mental progression had been "a Christian is a conservative is a Republican." Since the 1980s, this had been reflexive and almost unquestioned. Now here was a man who, by any reasonable standard, was not a good man, nor was he a resolute conservative. This would be the moment of reckoning where evangelicals would stand opposed and reject the idea that being a good Christian meant being a loyal Republican.

I'm pathologically moderate in most things, including politics, with positions both liberal and conservative, having voted for Republicans and Democrats at all levels. Each election cycle, even when I was in favor of a candidate, I respected the opposition and regarded him or her as being well-intentioned and decent. Not so this time. There was no way I could regard Trump as a decent or principled man. I was certain a large percentage of my spiritual brothers and sisters felt likewise. So my heart sank when I learned that a full three-quarters were supporting him in the run-up to the election. Still, I imagined seeing Trump's defeat would be the rebuke that brought us to our senses.

Of course, that wasn't to be. Trump pulled off the biggest upset in the history of American politics with the help of 81 percent of voting evangelicals.[5] Many Christian leaders saw this as an affirmation that they were in the right, that God was intervening to help Make America Great Again. In the days following the election, it became clear we had reached a point where most evangelicals were inextricably bound up in conservative politics.

In 2011, only 30 percent of evangelicals said that an elected official could ethically fulfill their public duties even if they have committed immoral acts in their personal lives, but during Trump's campaign, the number reversed and 72 percent of evangelicals said this could be true.[6] It's debatable whether moral behavior affects public service, but when a Democrat was in office, evangelicals considered immoral behavior disqualifying for public service. When Trump, with his affairs, multiple marriages, casinos,

---

4. Taylor, "Evangelicals are the least faithful."

5. Martínez and Smith, "How the faithful voted."

6. Galston, "Has Trump caused white evangelicals to change their tune on morality?"

crude comments, vindictive attacks, sexual assault allegations, thinly veiled racism, alternative facts, and dubious business practices was the Republican front-runner, they reversed position. Now they didn't seem to care so much about the moral practices of politicians. Jerry Falwell Jr., who had been an unabashed Trump supporter during the primaries, said, "We're not choosing a Pastor-in-Chief. We're choosing a President of the United States."[7]

After stories that Trump had an affair with porn star Stormy Daniels, Rev. Robert Jeffress, pastor of the First Baptist Dallas megachurch, went on Fox News to declare, "Evangelicals still believe in the commandment: Thou Shalt Not Have Sex with a Porn Star. However, whether or not this president violated that commandment is *totally irrelevant* to our support for him."[8]

When pressed by the host that this might make evangelicals hypocrites, he said this was "absolutely ludicrous," because "evangelicals knew they weren't voting for an altar boy when they voted for Donald Trump."[9]

Many Christians, including me, were not only heartbroken we had elected such a wounded, narcissistic man to the presidency, but dumbstruck by the enthusiastic support of conservative Christians. These were the same Christians who excoriated Bill Clinton for his moral failings, who railed against the "godless" Barack Obama, and who assailed Jimmy Carter. Now these same people called Trump the evangelical "dream president." One prominent evangelical leader said, "I like everything about him."[10]

Without question, this about-face among the evangelical community was the most head-spinning cultural development in my lifetime. Evangelicals not only elected a man who represented everything they said they stood against, but they did so with a passion we had not seen since the Reagan era. As comedian Bill Maher put it, "the world's least godly man has been so fully embraced by our most religious people, the evangelicals."[11]

The backlash within the church has been severe. In an opinion piece for *USA Today*, Billy Graham's granddaughter, Jerushah Duford, wrote, "I have spent my entire life in the church, with every big decision guided by my faith," then adds, "But now, I feel homeless. Like so many others, I feel disoriented as I watch the church I have always served turn their eyes away from everything it teaches."[12] As a therapist, I speak to young adults every week and I hear the same sentiment Jerushah expressed. Young people

7. Silk, "Of Pastors and Presidents."

8. Zhao, "Pro-Trump Pastor Says."

9. Brown, "Joy Behar, Mike Pence, Donald Trump."

10. Wehner, "There is no Christian case for Trump."

11. Maher, *Real Time with Bill Maher*.

12. Duford, "I'm Billy Graham's granddaughter."

who grew up in the church, whose faith was central to their lives, now feel "homeless." But it's not limited to young people. I also hear it from people my age. Their emotional reactions range from grief to anger to incredulity. Many of us have felt a great sense of loss related to faith in recent years. Many other Christians, however, don't understand this at all. For them, all is well. For them, the problem is godless liberals or weak-minded Christians worn down by anti-Christian messages or seduced by the world.

Passionate Christians can be liberal or conservative, Democrat or Republican. Most white evangelical Christians, though, have so commingled their faith with their conservative politics that they see these as synonymous. As one of my friends told me, "I'm sick of the message that being a good Christian means being a white, middle-class Republican."

I have a unique vantage point as a psychologist and as a Christ-follower who has been soaking in evangelicalism for over forty years. My training as a psychologist gives me the ability to synthesize social science research and clinical experience helps me understand the psychology of modern white Christians. My experience as a white Christian who has taught, led, spoken, and written about the faith allows me to portray the state of the church accurately and without caricature. And since I don't make my living or stake my professional identity on a Christian platform, I can step out more boldly than others.

This book is not for everyone. It's not even for all Christians. It's not for Christians who regard the white conservative Christian church as doing just fine. It's also not for the Christians who say "our way of life" is under attack by godless liberals. If you're in either group, I say this with sincerity: There are many other books for you. This book will only make you angry—or angrier. I have no interest in sticking my finger in your eye or provoking you. If you are a defender of the evangelical status quo or a culture warrior, nothing in here will change your mind, especially if you've dug into an intractable position. Please set the book down and step away.

Christians committed to the current paradigm will say this is just more liberalism or a lack of biblical literacy or poor discipleship. What those responses assume is that the status quo is not only good and right, but the true issue is with those who critique and expose faults. If you criticize, you are a weaker form of Christian. You should read your Bible, pray, get back in line, and shut your mouth. There is little self-reflection from the majority. The default assumption is they are right and others who oppose or critique them are wrong. As we'll see, that mindset is the central part of the problem.

It is not my goal to change the minds of the 81 percent of evangelicals who voted for Trump.[13] Those who see conservative politics and Christianity as unquestionably linked are unlikely to see the world through a different lens, no matter how well-reasoned or researched the counter-argument. I don't intend to change their minds, but to illuminate the psychology of most white Christians for others who want to understand, Christian or not.

My central premise is the worldview of white evangelicals is more bound up in their psychology than their theology. Each human sees the world through a unique lens, a lens shaped by both their biological makeup and their life experiences. It's unavoidable. Evangelicals, despite their claims of having a perspective shaped by a biblical worldview, are not immune to this. White evangelicals, like all humans, are products of their own psychology.

WHO ARE WE TALKING ABOUT?

Back in the early 2000s, social science researcher George Barna found 38 percent of the population would call themselves "evangelical," but when he applied a nine-point litmus test of core Christian beliefs, the number dropped to 8 percent who believe all the central tenets. When researchers required only four core beliefs, which some have done, the number increased.[14]

Today, about a quarter of Americans (24 percent) self-identify as evangelicals, but less than half of those who claim that title agree with core evangelical beliefs. In the reverse, of those who mostly agree with evangelical beliefs, a little over two-thirds (61 percent) identify with the label of "evangelical."[15] Either way, it's slippery to define evangelicals based on what they believe, often because what they believe changes and evolves. One thing is clear: defining evangelicals on endorsement of belief statements alone is problematic.

Another way to define an evangelical is to consider faith-oriented behavior. This would include actions like going to church, praying, tithing money, reading the Bible, and so on. This, too, can be problematic because people lie. They say they go to church more often than they do, for example. University of Michigan sociology professor Phillip Brenner's research concluded Christians "exaggerate their frequency of attendance" at church.[16]

13. Martínez and Smith, "How the faithful voted."
14. Barna, "Survey Explores Who Qualifies As an Evangelical."
15. Lifeway Research, "Evangelical Beliefs and Identity."
16. University of Michigan, "Pray tell."

The Public Religion Research Institute also found Americans weren't honest about how often they attended worship services.[17] Lying about religious practices isn't only an American phenomenon. In a survey of Christians in the UK, more people lied about having read the Bible than any other book.[18]

So we can't base whether one is in the tent on belief alone, nor should we judge whether someone is an evangelical based most on religious behavior. That leaves *belonging*. This seems like the weakest of the three, but it proves to be the most meaningful. A person rates high in belonging when being connected to the group matters to them, when it is important to have that kinship.

Here's an example: A guy named Mark is in his early thirties. He's a young commercial real estate broker who believes a few traditional Christian doctrines but not a lot of the other things. He lives with his girlfriend of two years and they may or may not get married. Mark never reads his Bible or prays, unless he is attending a worship service, which he does about twice a month. He may toss a few bucks in the offering bucket. However, he loves his church. He's got a close relationship with a pastor there and they meet about once a month for lunch. He went to a Bible study for a while and he goes to some men's retreats and special events.

Mark would rate low on belief, moderate on behavior, but high on belonging. From a conceptual standpoint, researchers like Barna would not consider Mark an evangelical. However, most pollsters would include him in that group based on his self-identification. This divide is one reason why surveys can be so divergent from each other. Researchers don't always agree on what an evangelical even is. Evangelicals themselves can't even agree on what an evangelical is.

CAUTIONS AND CLARIFICATIONS

I can't claim to have written this book as an impartial, dispassionate social scientist. My story is too bound up in this story to make that claim. However, I can say I followed the data and the evidence. I constructed the chapters around what I found, rather than starting with a preconceived idea and making the data fit. Sometimes the research confirmed what I might have suspected, but in other cases, it challenged my own assumptions or gave me a new framework to think about a topic that puzzled me. Most of the time, I picked a topic and posed a question ("Why are white Christians more likely than most to believe in the QAnon conspiracy theory?"). I read over eight

17. Cox, Navarro-Rivera, and Jones, "I Know What You Did Last Sunday."
18. Mbakwe, "Bible tops list."

hundred articles and three dozen books. I interviewed multiple experts. I spoke with unique people who had important stories to tell, like Patricia Turner, a woman now in her seventies who was an unwitting pioneer in the civil rights movement. I stitched qualitative information, like these interviews or clinical observations, together with empirical research. I wove it all together with my own life experience inside the church, to produce what I hope is a helpful picture of the psychology of white evangelicals.

I come neither to bury or praise white evangelicals, but to understand them. As with any group, all white evangelicals are not the same. They have distinct personalities, different values, different ways of seeing the world. Yet, there are some consistent themes and traits that emerge when we study them.

Before we dive in, let me hit you with a series of ten cautions and clarifications about what this book is—and is not—about.

1. It's worth repeating that my conclusions in this book are not true of every white evangelical. There are many white conservative Christians to whom much of this does not apply. Instead, the ideas here represent a broad understanding of this vast subculture.

2. Many people, myself included, do not identify as purely liberal or conservative. Political and social ideology are on a continuum. However, despite the entirety of all humans not falling neatly into one of two categories, the construct of liberal/conservative is often useful from a research and social science perspective.

3. I am not saying conservatism is bad and liberalism is good. In my view, either extreme can be problematic. For this book, though, I'm focused on understanding the psychology of the white—particularly the white *conservative*—faction of the church.

4. This book is not about Donald Trump. The fact that so many conservative white Christians voted for him, then continued to support him into the next election, was a big factor in my decision to study how white Christians think. However, you've read more about him in this introduction than you will in the rest of the book. To be clear, I find him tedious, morally bankrupt, small-minded, and uninteresting. I am interested, however, in understanding what drives the white evangelicals who support him.

5. I write in first person here, but sometimes I use "we" or "I" and sometimes I say "they" or "them" when I am referring to white Christians. Some of that depends on how well the discussion point describes me,

and some of it depends on how well it serves the flow of the writing. I'm not disavowing being a white Christian when I use "they" or "them."

6. Some in evangelical circles are hostile toward psychology, seeing it as an enemy of the church. As a psychologist, I don't share that view, of course, but I realize this book will not go far to change that perception, since it is critical of white Christians who, like most people, don't enjoy criticism. Psychology has much to offer us with understanding how human beings operate, including what motivates us, how we see the world, and why we behave as we do. As a field, it is not antithetical or antagonistic toward the church or matters of faith. A great deal of psychological research supports the benefits of church communities, prayer, and other spiritual beliefs and practices on individual, family, and societal well-being. Other research, however, uncovers unhealthy aspects of the church and certain expressions of faith.

7. The book is about the psychology of white Christians specifically. White evangelicals and African American evangelicals (or other Christians of color) see the world in vastly different ways. African American evangelicals, for example, did not turn out for Trump in droves. They do not see social issues the same way much of the time. While they share the same faith, their psychologies differ from each other in many important ways.

8. In psychology, we think about assessment first, then intervention second. When posed with a problem—Why is my kid struggling in school? Why do my thoughts get so irrational? How can I save my relationship?—we begin by assessing the problem clearly and accurately. If we don't understand a problem well, we have a much harder time improving it. Once we've assessed well, we can move into applying interventions or treatment strategies. Thinking from this framework, this book is only *assessment*. It is not intervention. It seeks to answer puzzling questions.

9. On the occasions when I tell a story about a client, I have changed all identifying details, sometimes combining individuals, and have taken great pains to protect each person's confidentiality. You may also notice most of my stories about clients involve young men. That's because my clinical practice consists of young adult guys. Boys and men usually choose male therapists and girls and women more often choose female therapists.

10. I have no interest in tearing down or destroying the conservative white church. Instead, I have great interest in understanding the psychology of white Christians, particularly evangelicals, and, if possible, being useful in some needed reform. Years ago, I was in Bermuda on vacation with friends. We had all gone to the beach for the day, and before we arrived, someone had built a massive sandcastle with the most intricate details—turrets and bridges and moats and courtyards. It was a thing of beauty. After a few minutes, three little Bermudian boys ran up and explored the abandoned castle. Without provocation, one kid kicked down a castle wall in the impulsive way boys do. His friend stopped him, saying, "Let's not tear down. Let's build." And with that, all three of the boys repaired the wall and then spent the next two hours enhancing the castle. They were still working on it when we left that afternoon. It's easy to tear down. It's hard to build. Both have their rewards, but building is more satisfying because it results in a creation. There are plenty of writers and speakers who have come to tear down, to destroy. I am not one of them. Though my conclusions may sting, I have come to build.

BLACK AND WHITE

You'll notice when talking about race, "white" is not capitalized in the book, except at the beginning of a sentence or in titles or headlines, while "Black" is always capitalized. There is some disagreement about this in both journalism and research scholarship, but I am using the standards adopted by organizations like the Associated Press, *The New York Times, Los Angeles Times, USA Today* (and their dozens of affiliates), *Chicago Tribune, Wall Street Journal, NBC News, Columbia Journalism Review*, and many others. The rationale is that Black refers to a shared identity in a way that white does not.

Not everyone agrees. The American Psychological Association, CNN, Fox News, the Center for the Study of Social Policy, and the National Association of Black Journalists, among others, advocate for capitalizing both terms, though none of them favor use of a color for describing any other racial or ethnic group.

There is no clear consensus on this. I made my choice based on the guidelines of an editor for a previous book chapter. By the time I wrote this book, the pattern was so strongly ingrained it was more a matter of habit than some deeper philosophical or ethical imperative.

THE ROAD AHEAD

I began this journey with honest questions: How can a group called to be other-centered be so self-centered? How can people so committed to the truth be so drawn in by conspiracy theories and lies? How can white Christians express such warmth toward Black people yet hold the most racist attitudes? How can those charged with being strong and courageous be so delicate and anxious?

I wanted to know the answers to these and other questions. I've been perplexed. I needed to know what has happened—and continues to happen—to white Christians particularly in the United States. That bewilderment set me on a years-long journey that resulted in this book.

I do not intend the book to be a bomb-thrower. I don't seek to poke my finger in anyone's eye. The message here is not anti-Christian. Instead, it is an honest exploration of the psychology of white Christians. I've tried to be fair, but also not pull any punches.

I assume my conclusions will make some white Christians angry. Those types of hostile responses I've seen from Christians toward others who challenge or criticize the faith are a big part of the reason I felt compelled to write this book. How could people charged with being vessels of love and grace be accurately characterized as hostile and angry? What has happened to us?

While I may have driven to the wrong Roanoke Rapids many years ago and ended up in the wrong state, I'm more confident now about the road ahead. My charge is to provide an accurate, grounded, research-based psychological assessment of white evangelicals. To do that, I start with a foundation of how human perception works. We perceive reality—what we take in with our senses and what meaning we make of it—differently than each other, yet we are all convinced we see things with absolute clarity and certainty. Why do we see the world in such contrary ways? I discuss the role of our senses, temperament, personality, and life experiences in shaping our perceptions. I explore the concept of mental "schemas" including what they are, how they form, and what this means for how we see ourselves, others, and the world (chapter 1).

Next, I share how narcissism is the central concept for understanding modern white Christians. Rates of narcissism in the US have climbed upward for the past fifty years and American Christianity is not immune to that trend. In fact, there is evidence that the present conservative Christian subculture attracts higher than average numbers of individuals with Narcissistic Personality Disorder and is rich in what we call "collective narcissism" (chapter 2).

Much research has documented how conservatives, including conservative Christians, are more fearful, more prone to perceive threats in their world, and more suspicious of the motives of others. I wrestle with the concepts of spiritual bypass, terror management theory, and the authoritarian tendencies that emerge during times of perceived threat. I also argue that conservative Christians are not just fearful people but have very specific fears (chapter 3).

As founder of the Public Religion Research Institute, Robert P. Jones was distressed to find that while white Christians rated themselves as having the most warmth toward African Americans, they also held the most racist attitudes of any group.[19] And while many evangelical churches have made great strides against racism, Jones's research found that more frequent church attendance correlated with more—not less—racist attitudes. Why the contradictions? I show how racism is not always conscious and crystallized, as in the form of white supremacist ideas, but is often unconscious. I discuss research from the Implicit Association Test (IAT), new research out of Yale on "broken patterns," and a phenomenon called the Dunning-Kruger effect where people misperceive themselves in important ways, including their degree of racism. I also explore why white Christians are so averse to acknowledging systemic racism (chapters 4 and 5).

Christian nationalism is a misunderstood but vitally important concept concerning white evangelicals. It's not just being a patriotic Christian. It's a belief that the US is a special country ordained by God for special historic purposes. Research by Andrew Whitehead and Samuel Perry shows how these beliefs are critical to understanding why many white Christians behave in ways that shock and puzzle (chapter 6).

White evangelicals seem obsessed with sex. One former pastor told me he left the ministry because "evangelicals have become the sex police." I explore how the powerful emotions of shame and disgust influence and bias Christians' sexual attitudes and theology. I also discuss the harm done to others and ourselves when we attach shame and disgust to sex (chapters 7 and 8).

Not only has the QAnon conspiracy theory grown in popularity, it has ensnared large numbers of conservative Christians, sometimes dividing families and even leading to violence. I examine who believes in conspiracy theories and why they do. The answers are complex, but they involve end-times theology, personal attachment style, and biased thinking styles that all create a vulnerability to believing implausible conspiracies (chapter 9).

19. Jones, *White Too Long.*

For decades, clinical psychologists only focused on what was wrong with people—their diagnosis, pathology, maladaptive patterns. During the past quarter century, however, there has been a shift toward focusing on positive aspects of human functioning, like what promotes well-being, how people and communities can thrive, and what makes some people more resilient. Our understanding of human resilience has uncovered a range of experiences, personality traits, and attitudes that make people more or less resilient. While we have seen some communities become more resilient over recent years, we have seen white evangelicals become less resilient. As an unfortunate effect of striving to create comfortable, self-satisfied lives, many conservative Christians in the US now find themselves more fragile and negatively affected by the cultural changes and new challenges they face (chapter 10).

In recent years, social scientists like Ryan Burge have contributed significant books on understanding white Christians and evangelicalism. Historians like Jemar Tisby, John Fea, J. Russell Hawkins, and Kristin Du Mez, and sociologists like Samuel Perry, Andrew Whitehead, and Josh Packard have all given us invaluable resources. What has been absent from that roster is psychology. While history and sociology have much to offer about this significant demographic of Americans, psychology brings a unique set of insights.

In graduate school, our joke was that psychology's answer to everything was "It depends." There was an aversion to giving easy, pithy answers to complicated questions. I wanted the answers here to be simple. *Why do white Christians deny systemic racism? Here's an uncomplicated answer. Why do evangelicals believe conspiracy theories? Here's your straightforward sound bite of an explanation.* What I found, though, was significant complexity. That doesn't mean the conclusions can't be presented in plainspoken and comprehensible ways, which is my goal. Hopefully, you'll find clear but not easy answers here.

Thanks for being on this journey with me. Let's start the ride.

CHAPTER 1

We See Them as We Are

Perception Shapes Reality

"We do not see things as they are, we see them as we are."
—THE TALMUD

BACK IN 2015, THE Internet erupted in a huge debate. It wasn't about politics or religion. It was about a dress. The Great Dress Debate of 2015 pitted brother against brother, co-worker against co-worker, and celebrity wife against celebrity husband. Kim Kardashian saw the dress as white and gold, while her husband, Kanye West, saw it as blue and black. Those who saw the dress as white and gold had no doubt what color it was, but the blue and black camp was equally convinced. Millions of views and retweets later, the case was settled by the manufacturer: the dress was blue and black. Kanye was right. Even still, those who saw it as white and gold didn't relent. They truly saw it differently. In an op-ed for *The Guardian*, neuroscientist Bevil Conway wrote, "The two camps will probably keep fighting to prove that they are right."[1]

The Great Dress Debate of 2015 teaches us a lot about ourselves. If we can disagree on colors, imagine how we see the rest of the world so differently. If we can see an objective reality like a color differently, imagine how easy it is for us to see more subjective realities in vastly disparate ways.

1. Conway, "Why Do We Care About the Color of the Dress?," lines 62–63.

To understand some of the deeper concepts that come later in the book, we have to start with a solid foundation: Why do we perceive reality differently? What causes those differences in perception?

OUR DUMB BRAINS

We used to have a little white fluffy dog named Chilli who was as cute as he was dumb. I've never met a cuter or dumber animal. He would stand guard at our front door every day. If there was any movement whatsoever—a lady pushing a baby stroller, a squirrel, a leaf falling from a tree—he would throw his head back and bark at the top of his lungs, spin around, bark some more, spin around, bark, then go into the dining room and pee on all the furniture.

In his mind, he was doing the Lord's work. He was protecting the house. He was the sentry, there to sound the alarm, keeping the family safe by marking the territory. And, of course, it worked. No lady tried to ram the house with the baby stroller. No squirrel breached the front door. No leaf attack was ever successful.

Chilli's perception was that he was playing a vital role in the safety of the family, that his vigilance was necessary, and that his actions were help-ful. None of that was true, of course, but try telling that to him.

One year during the Chilli era, Ellen bought me a gag Christmas gift: a flashlight and a pair of yellow sunglasses that were designed to locate where your dumb dog had marked furniture or the carpet. Turn off the lights, turn on the flashlight, put on the yellow glasses, and, like a miracle, the markings lit up like a *CSI* crime scene.

There are two lessons here: First, like Chilli, we all have our percep-tions of ourselves, others, and the nature of the world that we hold fast to, that we are convinced are true, that there could be almost no talking us out of. We could more easily convince Chilli a squirrel crossing the front yard meant us no harm than we could drop our own notions of how the world works.

Second, when we look through a new filter, we see new things—and perhaps miss other things. Our perception of reality is largely affected by the filters we use. Most of the time, we are unaware of our own filters, wrongly assuming we see the world as it is, not as we have come to see it. It's as if we have worn the colored sunglasses for so long that we are convinced the world truly is saturated yellow.

So the question is not whether or not we always see ourselves, others, and the world with perfect accuracy. We do not. Instead, the question is what are our mental filters and where did they come from?

The answer is complicated, but knowable. Understanding how and why we perceive things the way we do helps us understand ourselves and gives us more empathy for others. Unlike the chapters that follow, this chapter isn't just about white evangelicals. It's about how the human brain works and how we all come to perceive reality.

WHAT AFFECTS PERCEPTION?

Perception is the way you understand and interpret something, and there are at least five areas that affect your perception: your senses, your temperament, your personality, your life experiences, and your mental schemas. Nearly everything we will discuss builds on the foundation of perception. If you understand the complexity of perception, you go a long way in understanding how humans can be so different and why we are drawn to others who see the world as we do.

Come To Our Senses

Before we dig into the complexities of human perception, we have to take a step back and explain the idea of *sensation*. Sensation is easy to describe, even though the process is remarkably complex.

In essence, you take in information from each of your five senses. How does it look, sound, taste, smell, or feel? Your sensory organs—eyes, ears, tongue, nose, skin—take in data about the outside world. That's the purpose of sensation: to provide you with information you can interpret.

Sensation is not always as straightforward as it may seem. Some of our sensory organs are not as accurate as others or as sharp as they used to be. Sometimes they can be impaired by age, illness, injury, substances, or just the wear and tear of life. A friend who had lost his sense of taste and smell for months due to COVID told me, "Every meal was like eating cardboard." Another example: years ago I was interviewing an older man at his office and his wall thermostat suddenly emitted the most shrill, ear-piercing whistle. The man kept talking as if nothing were happening. His assistant, who was also in the room, looked over at me and mouthed, "He can't hear it."

Even when the acuity of what we sense isn't a problem, our brains are constantly screening out information, helping us focus on what it thinks is important, often to the neglect of other details. Notice the dancing dots in the image below.

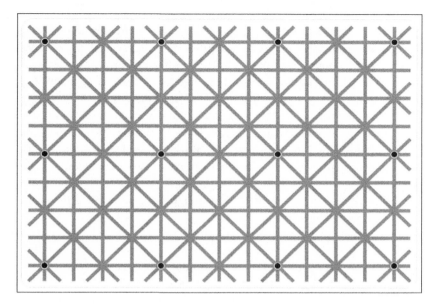

This image, called the Scintillating Grid Illusion, has twelve black dots in it, but you can't see all of them at the same time. Some dots appear, some disappear, depending on where you focus. This is your brain's way of helping you in most situations. Through a process called "lateral inhibition," when one neuron gets lit up, your brain dials back the nearby neural activity. This causes the area of focus to become sharper and pop out more.[2] It's kind of like a camera that focuses on one area of a picture with the foreground and background blurred. This doesn't just happen with things we see, it happens with sounds and textures, as well. Researchers have found this automatic process actually gives us more—and more accurate—sensory information rather than less.[3] It's just one of the many ways our brains control and manage our sensory input. Sometimes we sense reality not as it is, but the way our brains need it to be sensed.

We take our sensory information, gathered correctly or not, and our brains begin to make sense of it. This is where perception begins. Perception is an interpretation of your sensory information. *That tastes great! That tastes awful! That's beautiful looking! That's ugly looking! What a beautiful scent! What a gross smell!* And so on.

I hate the taste of brussels sprouts, but one of my friends says those little gross cabbages are his favorite veggies. Some people like perfume, while

2. Schrauf et al., "Scintillating Grid Illusion."
3. Cree and Weimer, "Sensory System, Overview."

others find the same scent noxious. It's the same sensation, but different perceptions. We each interpret these sensory experiences in unique ways. Even among humans, our senses are different from each other. In a study of nearly nine thousand adults, women outperformed men in all categories of smell accuracy. The researchers confirmed "female olfactory superiority," which means women have a better sense of smell than men.[4]

Often our senses mislead us, though. When my kids were younger, we took a weeklong family trip to Jackson Hole, Wyoming. We spent one day at the Grand Tetons and we attended a "Birds of Prey Demonstration." The facilitator brought out a huge owl that was about two feet tall and perched on his arm.

"How much do you think this owl weighs?" the man asked the kids.

"Ten pounds!" came the first reply.

"Good guess, but no," he said.

"Fifty pounds!" was the next guess.

"No, not fifty pounds," he said as a smile crept over his face.

"Five hundred pounds!" blurted out another kid.

"No, no, we're going in the wrong direction," he said, realizing the dialogue was getting ready to spiral out of control. "It's three pounds," he said, then repeated it for emphasis, "The owl weighs only three pounds."

The giant owl was basically just two feet of feathers. It looked heavier because of the limitations of our senses. We couldn't see beneath the feathers. One sense—vision—didn't have all the data it needed to perceive that reality accurately.

So we take in information from our senses and that information may or may not be accurate, but then we begin sorting out what we are seeing or hearing or smelling. We make interpretations and judgments about what we think we are perceiving. *Brussels sprouts are delicious. That lady with a baby stroller is a threat to family. The owl weighs as much as a vending machine.*

If perception gets wonky with basic sensory information, imagine what happens when we add the next few layers. It's a minor miracle we have any agreement on anything at all.

We're All Wired Weird

I was giving a presentation to a group of parents and I asked the room, "How many of you have more than one kid?" Most of the people in the crowd raised their hands. I asked them to keep their hands up, then I asked them, "How many of you would say your kids have been very different from

4. Sorokowski et al., "Sex Differences in Human Olfaction," 242.

each other, almost from the time they were born?" Nearly every hand remained in the air.

Why is that? How could siblings who are born to the same parents, who grew up in the same house, and had many of the same experiences, be so different from each other? One child is outgoing; the other is shy. One has a bright and sunny disposition; the other is a grump. One goes with the flow; the other gets upset if you change her routine. How can they be so different?

The answer is what we call "temperament." Our temperament is our biological predisposition. Researchers began studying the long-term effects of temperament back in the 1920s, but the field really took off when Alexander Thomas and Stella Chess began a longitudinal study of infants in the 1950s. They tracked children for many years and concluded there were nine dimensions of temperament.[5] Due to overlapping characteristics, later studies boiled them down to these six, each of them on a continuum from low to high:

- Activity—While some children seem always on the go, others are more sedentary. High-active kids get much more restless when they are required to be still.

- Attention—Some individuals have great attention spans and can focus on things, even when they are boring or require a lot of mental effort, but others have a hard time with this.

- Inhibition—This aspect of temperament is almost synonymous with shyness, but it's a little broader than that. It refers to holding back in front of unfamiliar people, in unfamiliar situations, or in performance situations. Some children hold back while others seem fearless in the face of strange people and situations.

- Irritability—Some kids are more easily annoyed and upset by minor discomforts than others. Some children get more easily frustrated than others. Those easily irritated or frustrated kids tend to turn into ill-tempered adults.

- Positivity—Happy little kids smile and laugh. They show more frequent and intense positive emotions than other kids. On the other side of the scale, you have kids who are mostly grumpy, mopey, not much fun to be around.

---

5. Thomas and Chess, "New York Longitudinal Study."

- Sensitivity—Loud noises, scratchy fabrics, weird tastes or smells, and other unpleasant sensory experiences really bother some people, while others hardly notice.[6]

Imagine these six dimensions of temperament are like little Wi-Fi signals, some of them low, some of them high, and some in the middle. For example, high activity would mean very active, while high irritability would mean extremely easily annoyed or frustrated.

A child we'll call Aaron is more active than most kids, maybe even hyperactive. He has trouble staying focused. He holds back socially, gets easily annoyed with others, rarely smiles, and is somewhat sensitive to unpleasant stimulation. Here's how his temperament profile might look visually:

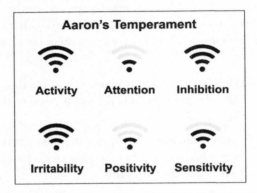

Now, let's use another child named Brittany as an example. Brittany has an average activity level and attention span. She is highly social, lets things roll off of her fairly easily, laughs and smiles with friends, and isn't overly sensitive. Her temperament profile looks like this:

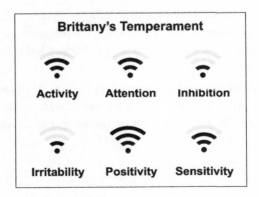

6. Zentner and Bates, "Child Temperament."

Imagine how Aaron and Brittany interact with the world as they grow. Imagine how a hardship, say being bullied or having a parent with a major illness, affects each of them and how they might react to that. Imagine if school is tough for them or they get rejected by peers. Their reactions are likely to be quite different.

In our example, Brittany is less likely to experience peer rejection, but if it were to happen, there's a better chance it would roll off her and she would put herself out there again and build a new social network. Aaron might have a harder time in school, experiencing more trouble sitting still and paying attention, having more struggle navigating the social realm, and being seen by peers as glum or unapproachable, more prone to negative emotions.

Our temperaments do not determine our lives, but they play a big role in how we behave and how we relate to the rest of the world. Kids with less sociable temperaments are going to struggle more in new social situations. That does not mean they can't do well socially, but it does mean social interactions will be harder for them. Kids who are more irritable are going to have a harder time managing frustration compared to less irritable kids. That doesn't mean they must fly off the handle, but they are more prone to it. Temperament is not destiny, but it does point each of us toward a certain trajectory.

If you drop two kids the same age into the same social situation, they are likely to react in different ways. One will be more outgoing and the other more reticent. One will be more able to flex and go with the flow and the other more rigid and inflexible. These reactions shape how others respond to them and how competent they feel.

Imagine how much impact temperament has on each kid's perception, including their perception of themselves and of others. How does a socially inhibited kid perceive the play date compared to the social butterfly? Both are making meaning of the experience, but in starkly differently ways. One of my own children was a "bumpy sock" kid, meaning every unusual clothing texture—shirt tags, pants fabrics, sock weavings—were like fingernails on the chalkboard. A kid with this type of temperamental sensitivity is going to perceive school picture day differently than another child. How we are wired neurologically and biologically radically affects how we see life.

Researchers observed 128 preschool children for seven months and assessed them with personality tests. Two decades later when the kids were twenty-four years old, they tracked down ninety-five of them and asked them a series of questions about political topics. They found traits evident at the age of three or four that accurately predicted both conservatism and liberalism in young adulthood. The kids who turned out to be liberals twenty years later were "expressive, energetic, and relatively under-controlled" as little ones. The researchers found them to be more curious and open in talking about negative feelings.[7]

The preschoolers who went on to be political conservatives were nearly the opposite. As younger children, they got more mentally rigid and inflexible under stress. They showed more discomfort with uncertainty and were more compliant and fearful.[8] Other studies involving both identical and fraternal twins, some raised together and others raised apart, consistently find political orientation has a huge genetic component. Our genes do not determine our political persuasions, but they have a major influence on them.[9]

Your brain structure, nervous system wiring, and biochemistry predispose you to certain ways of reacting and interacting with the world around you. How could they not? When these tendencies lead to long-term patterns, they become personality traits. Personality is your enduring and unique patterns of relating, shaped by both temperament and daily life. Like temperament, these personality traits, once established, influence perception across your life span.

Bursting with Personality

When I was in high school, my health teacher made our class take a personality test that divided people into four categories: sanguine, choleric, melancholic, and phlegmatic. I'm certain he had no idea the test was based on an ancient Greek medical theory proposed by Hippocrates that there were four main body fluids—blood, black bile, yellow bile, and phlegm. In this model, sanguine people are joyful, enthusiastic, and social, while choleric folks are decisive, goal-oriented, short-tempered, and domineering. The melancholics among us are introverted, deep thinkers, perfectionistic, and prone to anxiety or depression. The phlegmatics are more chill, easygoing, and empathetic. My test suggested I was phlegmatic, which made good sense to me, while my best high school friend scored high as a choleric, which seemed to position him well for his future career in law enforcement. For the remainder of the year, my friend explained all of my behavior through the lens of my phlegmatic personality.

My Christian high school's easy adoption of this personality test no doubt had to do with author Tim LaHaye's repurposing of the ancient

7. Block and Block, "Nursery School Personality and Political Orientation."
8. Block and Block, "Nursery School Personality and Political Orientation."
9. Hatemi et al., "Genetic Influences on Political Ideologies."

temperaments in his faith-based books. The research doesn't support that there are these four types of personalities, but the popularity of this and other dubious "personality" tests persists.

Lately in Christian circles, the Enneagram has risen in popularity. In this personality framework, you are one of nine personality types, each with a leaning, and all with variations that range from unhealthy to healthy. While there is some research to suggest the Enneagram types hold up to scrutiny, the framework is often treated in some conservative Christian circles as though it has been delivered from Mount Sinai. Its popularity among Christians was stirred three decades ago by Franciscan friar Richard Rohr, while Suzanne Stabile and Ian Morgan Cron co-authored the first Enneagram book published by an evangelical press, *The Road Back to You* (IVP, 2016).

The Enneagram has some usefulness and utility, but its grafting onto evangelicalism is a marriage of convenience more than evidence that the system aligns perfectly with Christian theology or that the nine types are the best ways to understand human personality. It's a good framework that can be helpful in some contexts, but not more than that.

The Enneagram also has a potential dark side observed in church and ministry contexts where people can justify all manner of selfish or abrasive behavior by ascribing it to their Enneagram type. ("I speak my mind. I'm a Type Eight.") The actions become difficult to challenge because they aren't just personal choices but expressions of a style that needs freedom to express itself. In the worst instances, self-centered behavior must not only be tolerated but celebrated as a necessary contribution to the well-being of others. This downside doesn't outweigh the potential positive benefits and utility of the Enneagram model, but it is a caution nonetheless.

As I've described, psychologists and others have developed hundreds of personality tests, some excellent and some worthy of no more than to be on the back page of a celebrity gossip magazine.

The most robust way of understanding human personality thus far emerged in the 1980s through a process called "factor analysis," a complex statistical procedure that finds underlying connections and groupings. This research found five consistent personality traits that could be rated from high to low. Those traits spelled out the acronym OCEAN, which stands for openness, conscientiousness, extraversion, agreeableness, and neuroticism. These five traits or "factors" are described on a continuum as:

- Openness—curious vs. cautious; open-minded vs. close-minded

- Conscientiousness—organized vs. disorganized; efficient vs. sloppy

- Extraversion—outgoing vs. reserved; talkative vs. quiet
- Agreeableness—harmonious vs. competitive; cooperative vs. uncooperative
- Neuroticism—sensitive vs. resilient; nervous vs. confident[10]

Hundreds of studies have found these five factors of personality hold up well in the research. We know much about these factors are influenced by our genetics. For example, on a pie chart, over half (57 percent) of the chart for the trait of openness would be accounted for by our genetic makeup. Similarly, the pie chart accounting for the amount of genetic influence would be 54 percent for extraversion, 49 percent for conscientiousness, 48 percent for neuroticism, and 42 percent for agreeableness. When considered together, right around 50 percent of our personality traits are accounted for by our genes.[11] In fact, we have pretty definitively settled the nature vs. nurture argument for personality. It's truly fifty-fifty.

These five factors affect how we perceive reality. For example, two different people might experience a bad breakup in completely different ways. People high in neuroticism perceive events like a breakup, a loss of a job, an illness, and so on, as more stressful than those who are low in neuroticism or even those who rate higher in extraversion, agreeableness, or conscientiousness.

Researchers at Johns Hopkins asked over five hundred people to think of their most stressful event over the past five years. Regardless of the nature of the event, folks high in neuroticism more often rated it as a "negative turning point," a moment where their quality of life declined and their world became worse. Those high in extraversion, by contrast, saw their most stressful event as a "lesson learned," an opportunity for growth or change. When people who were more neurotic perceived stress as catastrophic and a negative turning point in their life, they became even more neurotic in the long run, while the "lesson learned" folks became even more socially connected to others and used it as an opportunity for personal development.[12]

These five factors of personality also predict a person's political and social ideology. Conscientiousness, the tendency to be orderly and productive, is associated with conservatism, while openness, the quality of appreciating new experiences and curiosity, is connected to liberalism. Those who are high in openness perceive politically liberal messages more positively, while those high in conscientiousness experience politically conservative

---

10. Digman, "Emergence of the Five-Factor Model."

11. Bouchard and McGue, "Genetics and Environmental Influences."

12. Sutin et al., "Turning points and lessons learned."

messages more positively.[13] This isn't always true, of course. There are plenty of people high in openness who are fierce conservatives and plenty of conscientious liberals, but it does speak to a tendency, a predisposition, to perceive information in certain ways.

When it comes to faith, the evidence is a little less clear, but it seems to have more to do with the nature of an individual's faith. Those who experience more mature religious faith and spirituality, meaning they make room for more complexity and uncertainty, tend to rate higher on openness, while those drawn to fundamentalist and rule-governed faith are lower on openness. Those higher in neuroticism perceived God more negatively and had more anger toward him, while those rating higher in agreeableness and conscientiousness tend to report lower anger. Our perception of God, then, can be shaped by our personality. *God is angry. God is unconditionally accepting and loving. We must follow the rules that God has given us. We have freedom in Christ.* The degree to which these statements resonate with each individual will be largely shaped by how our personalities shape our perception of God.[14]

Whether it is with politics, social issues, religious views, perceived stress, or a whole roster of other differences, our personalities shape our perceptions. We see the world differently because each of us has a unique constellation of traits that cause us to interpret and relate to the world differently.

Sometimes Life Gives Us Lemons

Wes joined his brother and some older kids for an afternoon of paintball when he was nine years old. During the game, several of the bigger kids ganged up on him and shot him several times, then held him down on the ground, their guns pointing at his chest, taunting him. For those boys, this was all in good fun, no doubt. They laughed and joked the whole time. They probably didn't think about it much after that day, but Wes never forgot it. He played it over as he laid in bed each night, recalling it with a combination of terror and humiliation. The trauma of this seemingly innocuous event stayed with him for over a decade. As a college student, he took no chances socially, keeping mostly to himself, deeply mistrustful of others, drinking alone in his dorm room on weekends.

His parents didn't even know the paintball incident was traumatizing to him until many years later when he entered rehab after bombing out his

13. Gerber et al., "Big Five Traits in the Political Arena."
14. Hiebler-Ragger et al., "Primary Emotions and Religious/Spiritual Well-Being."

sophomore year of college. He kept it all to himself, thinking it was stupid that such a minor thing could have affected him so intensely. It's clear the event was not the only factor in charting the trajectory of his life, but it was a key moment. For someone else, that moment may have not warranted a second thought. They might have seen it as just part of the game, all in good fun, or a failed attempt by older kids to intimidate. For Wes, it was a turning point.

Temperament and life experiences conspire together to shape our perception. Wes had a combination of wiring and other life experiences that contributed to him experiencing that moment as profoundly wounding. By temperament, he felt uncomfortable and held back in new social situations (high inhibition), got upset by discomforts more readily (high irritability), and was a mostly dour kid (low positivity). The combination of this, along with his fairly sheltered early years, having a highly anxious mom, and being picked on by a kid at school had primed him for a much more intense reaction to the paintball incident than it might have been for other kids.

As we grow, we have life experiences, both good and bad, that shape us. These experiences can be within our families, at school, among peers, while playing sports, at our faith community, in the neighborhood, or in any other realm of life. At times, these are huge events, such as the death of a parent, the birth of a sibling, a family bankruptcy, a major achievement. In those instances, it's easy to look back on these times and see the impact they had on our lives. However, as was the case with Wes, sometimes even a negative but relatively normal life event can change someone's perceptions of oneself and others.

For all of us, our life experiences—big or little, good or bad—are seen and felt through the lens of our unique temperament. Over the years, I've had clients like Wes who were intensely affected by seemingly minor moments when they were kids. Being asked to do a presentation in front of the class, tripping in front of peers, or getting lost in a department store were all moments of profound horror. At the same time, I've known plenty of other people who had early major events—witnessing the violent death of a family member, suffering a life-threatening illness, experiencing abuse— that have not derailed them. The difference seems to be an interaction between the event itself, a person's temperament, and how the event was experienced at the time.

In psychology, there is a study of what has been called adverse childhood experiences, or ACEs, and the impact of these stressors on how kids develop. These include things like neglect, abuse in all its forms, witnessing violence, experiencing bullying, parental divorce or separation, parental alcohol or drug abuse, family mental illness or suicide, or parental incarceration. Numerous studies have looked at the long-term consequences of ACEs. In general, the more of these ACEs a person has experienced, the more negative impact they are likely to exert, causing emotional, academic, social, and even physical trouble.[15] But it's not as simple as that. Some kids are more adversely affected than others, often due to their specific temperament, their biochemistry, and their neurological wiring.

As one aspect of our life experiences, news and information consumption has even more impact on us now than it did in generations past. The types and sources of information we consume can dramatically influence our perception of reality. Specifically, we see the impact of social media on individual perception. There's a phenomenon called "The News Finds Me" among people who consume lots of social media, scrolling through Facebook or Twitter or other platforms in search of information and stories of interest. This phenomenon refers to the belief among many people that they don't have to get their news from traditional, vetted news sources because they will get all the news they need from their peers and social networks. These folks are less likely to get their information about the world from trusted media outlets and end up being far less informed about political and social issues over time. In turn, their views of the world are dramatically influenced.[16]

For example, one study found people who get their information primarily from social media, compared to traditional news sources, perceive much higher rates of political corruption. The authors concluded the lack of professional gatekeepers like editors and publishers allows the information to be presented in more sensational, negative, and extreme ways, which bias their readers' perceptions.[17]

Another study out of the University of Georgia concluded that even the comments below social media posts affect our perception. The researchers found people will repeat the opinions about politicians and journalists they read in the comments section, even when they are posted by anonymous strangers. Instead of creating a fake Twitter profile or a personal blog, the authors said someone would have much more impact simply by posting strong opinions in the comments of other people's posts. These comments shape our perception in significant ways, perhaps more than we realize.[18]

People who let news find them on their social media platforms of choice tend to be less informed, perceive more corruption, and are more

15. Felitti et al., "Adverse Childhood Experiences (ACE) Study."
16. Gil de Zúñiga et al., "Effects of the News-Finds-Me Perception."
17. Charron and Annoni, "Influence of News Media on Perception of Corruption."
18. Clementson, "Web Comments Affect Perceptions."

vulnerable to taking the same position of commenters, including ones unfamiliar to them. The social media posts populating their feeds shape their perception of the world.[19][20]

The culture in which we were raised is also part of the life experiences that shape our perception. Here's a simple example: Americans spend billions to smell good each year. We love perfume and cologne and body scents. We delight in our good smells. In other cultures, though, putting on fragrance is completely noxious. In those cultures, most men would never consider spraying a body scent on themselves. For them, that would be a crazy notion.

The same is true with other sensory experiences across cultures. What is considered visually beautiful? It varies by culture. What tastes good? That, too, is shaped by culture. What kind of touch is acceptable when greeting someone? Culture determines this. What is considered good music? There's a huge cultural factor there, as well. Culture shapes our perception. How things appear, taste or smell, feel, or sound all have a cultural component.

Life experiences, whether in the form of positive or negative events, the information we consume, and cultural differences all influence our perception. It's usually not one event, but the accumulation of these life moments and messages that powerfully shape how we see reality. Based on how powerful these experiences are, they can also merge with our temperament and personality traits to create mental frameworks that are called *schemas*. These schemas have deep-rooted impact on how we perceive ourselves, others, and the world around us.

In the Psychological Deep End

Even when nearly everything goes right in a person's formative years—no difficult temperament, no major traumas, no biological tendency toward mental illness, no destructive messages—our perceptions will still be faulty, at least on occasion. So what happens when something big does go wrong? For example, what happens when a person fails to meet a major core need, like acceptance or love or safety, when they are younger?[21] For some, these unmet needs cause them to form what psychologists call *maladaptive schemas*. These are negative patterns of relating to oneself and others. These schemas are like bundles of emotions, beliefs, and behaviors. They form over time, but once they are in place, they dig in.

19. Gil de Zúñiga et al. "Effects of the News-Finds-Me Perception."
20. Clementson, "Web Comments Affect Perceptions."
21. Martin and Young, "Schema Therapy."

These negative schemas are attempts to meet these basic, unmet needs. Most people who have taken an introductory psychology course have heard of Maslow's hierarchy of needs. His notion is that our human needs are like a pyramid, with each level building on the previous foundation of the one before. We start with basic physical needs, like food and water, warmth, and sleep. Without those, we can scarcely be concerned with anything else. If those basic needs are met, we can move on to safety needs. Here we focus on the security of our bodies, having enough resources, and being in good health. The middle level of need is about love and connection where we are concerned with friendship, intimacy, and a sense of belonging. In the fourth level, the needs are about esteem. This includes a sense of accomplishment, status, recognition, respect, and confidence. Finally, there is the need for self-actualization, which means we are focused on being all we can be, unlocking our full potential, and experiencing a sense of purpose.[22]

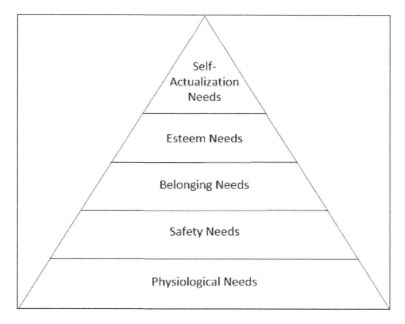

If Maslow was correct, we don't concern ourselves with self-actualization or even self-esteem until we have our basic physical or safety needs met. A few years back, I had a friend who told me he and his wife were having long dinner conversations about buying new art for their Nashville home. One week later, a massive flood left their downstairs with three feet of standing water. At that point, there was no longer any discussion of art. The

22. Maslow, "Theory of Human Motivation."

conversation was where they were going to live, whether their home was salvageable, and what priceless keepsakes, if any, they could save. When you are concerned with surviving, having shelter, and holding onto the essential things, you don't think about the finer things. There's no room for that.

Think of human development as a journey toward answering big questions. They are questions like, "Am I alone in the world?" and "Am I loved unconditionally?" and "Am I competent and capable?" Without fully realizing it, we are all answering questions about ourselves and others from the time we are very young. These questions emerge out of core needs, like these:

- Acceptance—Do people accept me unconditionally? What must I do to be accepted?

- Autonomy—Can I do life on my own? Am I capable of making good decisions?

- Empathy—Do people really understand me? Do they care about how I feel?

- Love—Am I truly loved? Do people really care for me?

- Nurturance—Will I get the physical and emotional care I need?

- Safety—Am I safe in the world? Will others keep me safe or must I try to keep myself safe?

- Significance—Do I feel like I am an important person? Is my life meaningful?

- Understanding—Do people really get me?

- Validation—Do others regard my opinion and experience?

In the struggle of life, it's unlikely any of us would get all our core needs consistently met in a healthy, positive way. There are too many ways for things to go wrong. Parents get too busy and don't pay enough attention to us. Peers gather in their cliques and leave us out. Teachers and coaches overlook us or berate us. We suffer big losses or a thousand little indignities. There are infinite possibilities of how we can get beaten up by life.

What happens when we don't get our core needs met? What happens when we don't feel accepted or understood or loved or kept safe? The short answer is something's gotta give. We'll either spend our life aggressively trying to fill that need or we'll capitulate and deny to ourselves the need could ever be met or that we even desire it to be met.

Let's use the need for acceptance as an example. What if you're a kid who felt constant peer rejection throughout school, starting in elementary school and going all the way through middle school? What kind of teenager or young adult might you be? One option is you might spend your life striving for acceptance. You might constantly seek approval, doing whatever you could to fit in. You might form connections with people who accept you, even if they are not good for you. You might always put your own needs below their needs in a desperate attempt to avoid further rejection.

There is another option, though. You might decide you don't want approval. You don't want to fit in, either, because you are too different or too damaged or the opposite, too good for all of them.

Whichever way you go, you'll find a way to deal with that unmet need. Years ago, I met a woman named Juliette, not as a client, but as a social acquaintance, who had carefully curated her life of singleness. I knew some of her story: a harsh, disapproving mother and an emotionally absent, passive father, along with some early bad dating relationships. By the time she was in middle age, she had not only resigned herself to being single, but had spiritualized it as a calling.

"I figured out a long time ago that God just wants me to be single so I can focus on him," she said. "And who am I to question God?" she asked rhetorically with a smile and a chuckle.

Now perhaps God did call her to be single, but you don't need to be a psychologist to see how the troubled family and dating history led her to guard her heart and not risk being hurt again. Not having unconditional love and acceptance or validation set her on a path of lifelong loneliness and disconnection, of distance from others, and a belief that she couldn't ever really be fully loved or understood by others.

When a person has core needs that go unmet, it can send them in several directions, but whichever way they go, they are pedaling hard either to meet that need or deny it.

Here are two guys the same age who responded to a tough childhood in completely opposite ways. The first, Alex, grew up in a chaotic, often dangerous home. There were fights, separations, the police were called. On one occasion, someone fired a gun. As a child, he was constantly worried about nearly everything. He worried that he had cancer, that he would be in a car accident, that he would be murdered in his apartment.

The second guy, Brandon, grew up in an equally crazy and unpredictable home. He became a thrill seeker as a young adult. He came to see me because he got a ticket for driving 140 mph on the beltway late one night. He jumped off a three-story balcony into a hotel pool on another occasion. He picked fights with guys bigger than him.

"Don't worry, doc. It's no big deal," Brandon told me.

Both guys had horrible and scary early home lives. One grew up with the expectation that calamity was always around the corner and he lived in fear of it. The other became a young adult who felt invulnerable, who felt no anxiety, not even normal fear. Both of them did not get the core need of safety met when they were young, so their lives became organized around trying to meet that need, either by being hypervigilant and expecting harm to come at any moment or by convincing himself that harm could never come his way. It was the same song, different verses.

No matter which way we go, the failure to meet a core need, if it is deep and abiding, either the result of mistreatment or negligence, sends us on a path toward developing a maladaptive schema. These are our mental filters, our yellow glasses if you will, for how we come to see the world.

When Steve was seven years old, his father deserted the family without saying goodbye. He left one Friday night with a backpack and never returned. Steve saw him only once over the next decade, but only by accident when he caught a glimpse of his dad at Walmart. Predictably, Steve didn't let anyone get close for fear they would abandon him. Over the years, as soon as someone would get close to him, he would push them away. This included girlfriends, best friends, even his own mother and sister. By the time he reached his twenties, he was isolated and angry, convinced the world was a horrible place.

He decided he would move out of town and go live with his grandparents in Florida and work at a surf shop there. When they heard about his plans, ten friends of his decided to throw him a going away party. He reluctantly attended the casual get-together. One of his friends had invited a girl, Katey, who was new in town. Steve and Katey began talking that night and hit it off.

"I wish you weren't leaving town," Katey said. "I think you're really interesting."

They exchanged numbers at the end of the night. His head was fizzy with infatuation.

He was leaving the following week, so he knew he had to act quickly. Later that night, he went to a twenty-four-hour drugstore and bought a piece of poster board and some flowers. He made a sign that said, "I like you a lot! I want to get to know you!" and left it on the hood of her car with the flowers, having tracked her down after a friend gave him the address of her apartment complex.

Not unexpectedly, Katey was completely freaked out by the shrine on her car. She texted him and said, "I saw the stuff on my car. You seem cool, but we just met and I heard you are leaving town, so I'm really not interested in anything. Sorry."

I saw him two days later, our last appointment before he moved. He plopped down in his chair and began to tell me the story, then after he shared the punch line of the girl's text, which he read aloud, he said, "See, this is what always happens. I get close to someone and then they leave me."

You won't be surprised to know he dismissed the possibility he had actually orchestrated the rejection, that he had created a scenario where that was the most likely outcome. But here's the point of this story: schemas fight for survival. Once schemas set up, they seem absolutely true. Once that happens, like Steve, we act in line with them, which further reinforces how true they are. Later in life, when they might get challenged by a loved one or a circumstance, the default is to dismiss the new evidence or behave in a way that proves the schema is still very much real.

On a logical level, this makes little sense. Why would anyone want to perpetuate a pattern that hurts them? The reason is simple but sad: we genuinely believe these schemas are true, so we can't take in contradictory reality. We have no slot for an alternative in our heads. If you believe you are inferior to others, then you will find lots of evidence to prove that. If you believe you must always meet impossibly high standards to be worthy or acceptable to yourself or others, you will live accordingly. There is no room for the possibility this isn't true.

We see the world through our schema filters that screen in certain information and screen out other facts. In essence, our reality gets curated. Once these filters are in place, we see the world in line with our schema. It shapes our politics. It shapes our biases. It shapes our theology.

Schemas are relatively invisible, yet they run nearly everything behind the scenes. I liken schemas to the operating system on your computer or phone. You might be more aware of the particular app you are using, but the operating system runs the show silently in the background. We make sense of our interactions and circumstances through this schema filter. However, since the filter usually began forming when we were younger and has been there so long, we no longer see it as a filter. We just experience it as reality. "Those people at the gym are judging me" isn't just a possibility. It is the truth. "I will inevitably fail" isn't one of several options. It is the only option.

Schemas start out as a reasonable way to meet some unmet need, but dig in and stay well past the time they served a good purpose. Jeffrey Young pioneered a therapy model designed to modify and dismantle these maladaptive, deeply entrenched schemas, but the process takes time and hard work. Over the course of his career, Young and his colleagues have identified eighteen maladaptive schemas.

This is not a complete list of all the maladaptive schemas, but I selected a dozen of them to give you a sense of what these deeply embedded patterns of thought and action are like. In each example, I've given a statement that gets at the essence of the schema. These statements might never be said out loud or even thought in these exact words, but this is the experience a person has when they hold this schema:

- Mistrust—"People will hurt me or take advantage of me if given the chance."

- Dependence—"I need the constant support of others in order to make it in life."

- Vulnerability—"Something bad is always right around the corner."

- Defectiveness—"Compared to other people, I am defective or inferior."

- Isolation—"I don't fit in anywhere and could never find people who would accept me."

- Approval-Seeking—"People have to always like me in order for me to be okay."

- Failure—"I have failed in life or will inevitably fail."

- Subjugation—"My needs and desires must be below the needs and desires of others."

- Unrelenting Standards—"I must meet very high internal standards in order to be okay."

- Negativity—"I always see what's wrong with situations and other people."

- Punitiveness—"I have to punish people who step out of line."

- Entitlement—"I'm a special person who deserves to be regarded as special."[23]

These schemas usually begin forming when we are young and get reinforced as we get older. For example, if we push ourselves hard to feel acceptable (Unrelenting Standards) when we are children, then we continue to be hard-charging and never let up as adults. When I was in fifth grade, a boy in my class, also named David, burst into tears when he got a ninety-five on a test. You won't be surprised to learn he was a wildly successful stockbroker as an adult. The high-achieving adult was just the older version of the high-strung kid.

Reality becomes retrofitted to our schemas. Some facts are emphasized, while others are ignored. We focus on some things, but overlook

23. Martin and Young, "Schema Therapy."

other important aspects that don't fit. Schemas influence how we see our-selves and others, how we relate to each other, what unwritten rules we live by, even our notions of God.

Take two people who grew up in the same church. One sees God as a loving father who is full of grace and mercy. She might know God can get angry or be displeased, but her dominant view is that God is kind and unconditionally loving. Another person in the same church may acknowledge the grace of God, but sees him as harsh and punitive, eager to catch her in some screwup. Same church and same God, but different views. Why? Because their schemas are different. They perceive information differently. They perceive life and God and human relationships in vastly different ways.

Not everyone has a maladaptive schema, but when they form, they are deeply entrenched and influence our perception in significant and per-vasive ways. Even later in life when they are challenged or no longer serve their purpose, they hang on for dear life, committed to their own survival, desperate to remain true. We bend reality around them, instead of the other way around. As a result, they always bias how we see ourselves and others.

OUR PERCEPTUAL ERRORS

With all these factors effecting how we view the world, there's no chance we will always have accurate perceptions. Regardless of our wiring or unique life experiences, we all make perceptual errors, at least some of the time. For example, we all have an uncanny knack for ascribing negative motives to others, while allowing ourselves the benefit of the doubt. This type of misperception where we misjudge the motivations of others is called the "fundamental attribution error." This is when we underestimate the role of external factors and overstate the role of internal factors when making judgments about the behavior of others. For example, when we see a person behaving badly in public, we think this has to do with his personality rather than his circumstances.[24]

Here's the fundamental attribution error in action: I was sitting at a stoplight and a guy with a sign announcing he was homeless and hungry came walking down the median when this thought came to my mind: *That guy panhandling probably wouldn't be homeless if he would just be willing to get a real job.* I had no idea of the circumstances of that guy's life, but it was so easy to come to that conclusion. The issue, as I had so rapidly diagnosed

24. Gawronski, "Fundamental Attribution Error."

it, had little to do with his life circumstances and everything to do with his work ethic.

That second type of erroneous perception where we give ourselves the benefit of the doubt is called the "self-serving bias." This is sort of the opposite of the fundamental attribution error. When we are successful, it is because of our talent and hard work, but when we fail, it's because of external factors, like an unfair boss or teacher, a rotten economy, or the deck stacked against us.[25]

Now here's the self-serving bias in action: I bombed a talk at a conference and these were my thoughts: *They really set me up to fail. They didn't have my projector ready. The sound was bad. The room was too hot and uncomfortable.* My misfire had everything to do with my circumstances and hardly anything to do with me. Again, it was so easy to reverse the source of the problem. It wasn't me; it was them!

We also make perceptual errors based on judging people too favorably because they are like us. This is called the "similar-to-me effect." We might have a higher regard for someone if she was in the same sorority or was from the same small hometown or worked for the same company.[26] The corollary of this is we are quick to negatively judge those who are different from us, whether different in race or culture, lifestyle or belief, or socio-economic status. Call this the "not-like-me effect."

We're all vulnerable to making these and many other types of thinking errors like stereotyping people or coming to conclusions based on the first information we get. The more aware we are of these cognitive flaws, the more likely we can avoid them. However, even with awareness, we can still find ourselves drawing erroneous conclusions, which can have a huge impact on how we see others who are different from us, the way we think about personal setbacks or hardships, and the way we view personal responsibility.

HOW WHITE EVANGELICALS PERCEIVE THE WORLD

Before we talk about the perceptual biases of white evangelicals, let's recap. We are all prisoners, for better or worse, of our own unique constellation of biology and life experiences. These come together to shape our perceptions. It all starts with *sensation*, the information we take in with our five senses. To interpret that information, our perception is first affected by our *temperament*, the unique wiring we each have, then *personality*, our long-standing

25. Boyes, "Self-Serving Bias," lines 1–3.
26. Decision Lab, "Similar-To-Me Effect," lines 4–6.

patterns of relating to ourselves and others. As we develop, our *life experiences* increasingly shape how we come to see the world. When we don't get certain core needs met, we find a way to meet those needs on our own terms or we deny the need itself. This process can cause us to develop *maladaptive schemas*, unhealthy or inaccurate ways of relating to ourselves and others. Once these schemas put down roots, they fight for survival, desperate to prove themselves to be true, and significantly influence and bias our perceptions in the process.

All of these variables, including our personal traits and life experiences and the filters they create, form a narrative in each of our lives. These are the stories we tell ourselves, the way we make meaning of the world and our place in it. These stories have good guys and bad guys, heroes and villains, challenges and successes.

White evangelicals have begun to tell themselves and each other a bad story, a narrative that is unhealthy, unwise, and unloving. It's a self-centered story, rife with fear and hostility. It's a story that runs counter to the good story they are called to inhabit.

Christian or not, our perceptions of the world—whether of the motives of others or the meaning of significant events—seem pure and unadulterated to us. Each of us is certain we interpret reality with something that approaches precision. As we've seen, though, there's no way this can be true. We have layers upon layers of our own psychology that has been shaped by our temperaments, our cultures, our life experiences, the kinds of information we consume, and the schemas these often form.

White evangelicals are not immune to this. Their perceptions are molded by how they are wired, what they have experienced, and the unique amalgam those ingredients form.

On the Saturday the presidential election was called for Joe Biden and Kamala Harris, I had one jubilant friend text me from a downtown celebration where the streets were filled with thousands of people, while another friend posted a meme likening the outcome to the horror of September 11, 2001. Both were professing Christians and good people, but they had vastly different perceptions of what the outcome meant. The first friend was politically liberal and passionate about the Black Lives Matter movement, while the other was politically conservative and active in the Republican Party. Both have perceptions influenced by all the factors we've discussed. Their temperaments and personalities interact with their life experiences to produce two different perceptions of the same event. For the first friend, it was a cause for celebration. For the other, it was a moment of disgust and horror.

There's plenty to discuss about the psychology of political liberals, but the focus here is on folks like my second friend, white conservative Christians. Many of them—perhaps most of them—are good, decent, and generous people. Yet, like everyone, all of them are products of their perceptions of the world. They are not simply Christians first who had no choice but to be political conservatives. To the contrary, most of the research suggests the opposite: they are political conservatives first.

Ryan Burge, author of *The Nones*, a professor of political science, and a pastor in the American Baptist Church, told me, "It's simply not true to think of white evangelicals as an 'uneasy' type of Republican," then added that "the overwhelming majority of white evangelicals are Republicans, through and through." He clarified that his and other social research finds conservative white Christians think like Republicans first and foremost. This is consistent with a large body of research that says our political leanings and worldview begin at an early age, then are often reinforced by the messages of family members and like-minded associates, as well as other life experiences.[27] Over time, there is no daylight between their Christian identity and their conservative political and social worldview. They perceive them as virtually synonymous.

White evangelicals in the United States perceive the world first through the grid of conservative and Republican politics, then through their racial identity, then through their identity as Christians. They may claim the reverse order, but the research tells us otherwise.

For most evangelicals, their view of the world is not influenced as much by their theology as they might claim or wish. Like all of us, it is mostly shaped by their psychology. It's inescapable. This notion is distasteful to evangelicals who want to claim a purity of influence. They frequently say their worldview is derived primarily from a "biblical perspective." After a presentation at a church, a man approached me and said, "You may say it's mostly about psychology, but my way of seeing things comes straight from the Bible."

I'm certain he believed what he was saying, but experience and social science research tells us differently. There is no pure reading of the Bible wholly separate from our psychology. That's why Christians of different backgrounds and temperaments come to vastly different conclusions about the full range of issues from parenting to politics. Consider how two Christians might give opposite answers to ten questions like these on social policy:

- Should we legalize marijuana?
- Should gay people be allowed to marry?

27. Young, "Why We're Liberal, Why We're Conservative."

- Is racial sensitivity training a positive development?
- Should a business be able to deny service to a customer when it conflicts with the owner's religious beliefs?
- Should gender identity be part of anti-discrimination laws?
- Is man-made climate change cause for alarm?
- Should the country take in more refugees escaping from violence and war?
- Is critical race theory a threat to our children?
- Should we have more stringent gun control?
- Is it the government's responsibility to take care of the poor?
- Should Confederate statues be taken down?
- Should we support the death penalty?

Even if you asked white evangelicals to decide these issues based on "biblical principles," most would still come to the conclusions that are almost perfectly aligned with Republican and conservative political views. After analyzing a dataset of over 3,200 individuals who were asked about a wide range of social issues, Burge found "there is essentially no difference between a Republican who is white and born-again and a Republican in general."[28]

The fact that conservative white Christians hew so closely to conservative and Republican positions on all these things is but one of many indications that conservative white Christians are, in the words of Burge, "Republicans first, white second, and evangelicals third." They perceive themselves and the world through a grid that sees Republicanism and Christian faith as almost fully aligned and congruent.

White evangelicals in the US have grown up in a subculture that says they are right and must be in charge to keep the country on the right track. At the same time, they have been largely isolated, ensconced in their churches and Christians schools and homeschools, cut off from those who are different, and told those outside the group are intent on destroying the country they love and are eager to persecute and harm them. It's up to them to save America, but they can only do it if they retain their power and their rightful place.

We could say they operate from an entitlement schema. We could also call it by another name: narcissism.

28. Burge, "'White Born-Again Christian' a Synonym?," lines 58–59.

CHAPTER 2

Voluntary Blindness

Narcissism in the Church

"Narcissism is . . . voluntary blindness, an agreement not to look beneath the surface."

—SAM KEEN, *THE PASSIONATE LIFE*

A CLIENT OF MINE in his early twenties, a college student named Martin, made local news for punching a girl in the face during a fraternity party. By most accounts, it was unprovoked. When the police arrived, he threatened to get them fired. His father was a prominent lawyer, he let them know. The officers were unimpressed and moved to handcuff him, prompting Martin to throw a drunken swing at one of them.

His university suspended Martin for at least a year. He lost his scholarships. His consequences didn't stop there, though. Police charged him with assault, communicating threats, and resisting arrest. His roommate later revealed Martin had stolen his personal medication and two pairs of his shoes, so they also charged Martin with theft and possession of a controlled substance.

In his first session with me following the assault, Martin went on about how everyone had done him wrong: the university ("unfair"), his friends ("threw me under the bus"), the girl ("kept running her mouth"), his roommate ("a liar"), the police ("morons"), the television news ("made up half of it"), and his parents ("didn't support me").

Martin gave me an unusual take for his troubles: "I'm just too nice to people and let them take advantage of me."

I was never sure how his extreme niceness led him to punch a young woman in the face, make threats, or steal shoes and drugs, but the meaning was clear: he was the victim, done in by his own awesomeness.

It's rare to find someone so malignantly narcissistic. They don't show up in therapy, unless they are under a court order or some other external pressure. Despite their personal reigns of terror, they go through life unchecked and undeterred, leaving a long trail of destruction. As the saying goes, "Damaged people damage people." Clinical neuropsychologist Rhonda Freeman writes, "A person with malignant narcissism has the potential to destroy families, communities, nations, and work environments."[1]

What we see more often in therapy and in our regular lives, though, is someone with less intense, but clear narcissistic traits. Most narcissistic folks aren't as aggressive or lawless as Martin. In fact, they can be alternately quite charming or quite pitiful. These people show up as co-workers and bosses, dating partners and spouses, college students and business professionals, ministry leaders and volunteers, and in many other key relationships.

Some researchers argue narcissism has been steadily rising in the US, leading to an increasingly narcissistic country, such that we rarely see these milder forms as a problem.[2] The impact has wormed its way into the church, particularly the white conservative church, and rather than pushing against it, we have embraced it and enabled it, to our own peril.

Narcissism is complex and shows up in complicated, sometimes contradictory ways. I'll explain the nature of narcissism and what causes it, then talk about the diagnosis of Narcissistic Personality Disorder. I'll close the chapter with a discussion of a vital concept called "collective narcissism" and show how the church has fallen into it. First, though, let's consider what has likely caused rates of narcissism in the US to increase over the past half-century, and the historical and cultural factors that have enabled it.

THE RISE OF NARCISSISM

Researchers have given incoming college freshman around the country the forty-item Narcissistic Personality Inventory (NPI) since the late 1970s. Over the decades, they've watched the ratings inch up, revealing a narcissistic

1. Freeman, "Dealing with a Malignant Narcissist," lines 121–22.
2. Twenge et al., "Meta-Analysis of the Narcissistic Personality Inventory."

nation. Based on these results, we are 30 percent more narcissistic than we were in the early 1980s.[3] Such an enormous increase in forty years is astounding.

It's easy to understand how this happened, though. We've had the perfect storm of factors that have made us more narcissistic. The founders forged America as a uniquely individualistic society. From the beginning, we wove individualism into the fabric of our culture in a way not seen in collectivistic civilizations. But individualistic doesn't mean narcissistic. Those are different notions. To understand the steady increase in narcissism over the past half-century, we must look at recent cultural trends.

Emerging from the 1960s with its social upheaval and challenges to tradition, American culture focused on adult well-being and fulfillment in the 1970s. The message was that adults should pursue their own careers and their own satisfaction. Divorce rates skyrocketed. We coined the term "latchkey kid," referring to children who let themselves into an empty home when they returned from school each day. Experts said kids were resilient, unharmed by family breakups or lack of attention or supervision.

By the mid-1980s, the culture came back to its senses. We realized we were neglecting our kids and needed to—pardon the phrase—focus on the family. Minivans became popular, often with "Baby on Board" stickers in the rear windows. Mountains of laws and ordinances passed at the federal, state, and local levels, including family leave acts, foster care and adoption reforms, education bills, curfews, and hundreds of other pieces of legislation and initiatives.

Most observers of American history notice a cyclical nature to our culture, regarding our view of children and teenagers. We prioritize their well-being, then become too restrictive and controlling, then ease up, then loosen up too much, then repeat the cycle. These cycles take around eighty years, with each quarter lasting a generation. What followed the 1980s re-emphasis on child well-being was the last part of that cycle: an intense overfocus on children beginning since the turn of the century, especially since September 11.

In this child-centric culture, parents have become so over-involved and micro-managing we had the "helicopter parent," followed by the "bull-dozer parent," referring to the adults who plow through whatever obstacles might be in their children's way to ensure they get what they want. It doesn't stop at childhood or even adolescence. These parents are unrelenting into the young adulthood of their kids. A major university's dean of students told me, "I've been in higher education for over thirty years and I've never

3. Twenge et al., "Meta-Analysis of the Narcissistic Personality Inventory."

seen anything like this. Parents will call and try to get a professor to let their son or daughter retake an exam or email the residence hall director, getting into the middle of a normal roommate dispute. A benefit of going off to college was becoming an adult and working problems out yourself. Now, the parents step in."

So, what happens to kids who are fawned over, overprotected, told they're so special, and pushed to compete with their peers? They are being primed for narcissism. Add to that a few decades of voyeuristic reality shows and social media where anyone can have their own platform with thousands—sometimes hundreds of thousands or even millions—of onlookers, even more if you're willing to be outrageous or semi-naked. Mix this together and voilà, a perfect potion. It's no surprise all this has led to years of climbing narcissism.

Many have argued the baby boomers—those born from the mid-forties to the mid-sixties—were America's most narcissistic generation. At one time, there was some evidence to support that, but we have seen narcissism creep upward since then, as if that egocentric generation begat another which begat another.

It's in that context of three generations of escalating narcissism that we find evangelicalism being molded and corrupted by the surrounding culture. Rather than standing in contrast to the culture, white conservative Christians have become more narcissistic. Instead of being the one group that doesn't behave selfishly and focus on its own self-interest, white conservative Christians have been among the most self-centered. The church's leadership, including public evangelical figures, often reflect this, and the attitude radiates downward to the rank and file.

One study found religious people score higher than nonreligious people on the Narcissistic Personality Inventory (NPI) scales that measure self-absorption and self-admiration, as well as superiority and arrogance.[4] Another study found Christians manifested higher levels of narcissism than nonbelievers.[5]

To better understand narcissism and its impact on the church, let's dive deeper into how narcissism develops, and the difference between narcissistic traits and Narcissistic Personality Disorder.

4. Hermann and Fuller, "Trait Narcissism and Religious Trends."
5. Gebauer et al., "Christian self-enhancement."

HOW NARCISSISM DEVELOPS

I once read the attraction rated highest by young kids during their trip to Disneyland was not Splash Mountain or the Haunted Mansion or Peter Pan's Flight or even It's a Small World. It was the hotel pool. You spend thousands of dollars for a Disney vacation and your kids love the pool most of all. We learned that lesson early, planning our family getaways around places with a kid-friendly pool.

When my two oldest were growing up, we were first members of the YMCA, then after we moved, we joined the Jewish Community Center within walking distance of our house. Access to pools meant our kids learned to swim at an early age. When they were both preschoolers, two years apart, we took a trip to Myrtle Beach and, as was our custom, stayed in a hotel with a nice pool.

One of my kids wanted to play a game: she jumped off the side of the pool and went underwater for a few seconds. I lifted her up out of the water into the air and deposited her back on terra firma. She did this approximately six thousand times. Exhausted, I gave her a final countdown. She could have ten more jumps. As the countdown got closer to the last jump, I could tell this would not end well. She was determined to keep going. After what I had said was the last jump, she begged me for another.

"One more, Dada! One more!" she pleaded.

"No, we're going to stop, but we can get back in the pool later," I said.

Instead of calmly accepting my parental limits, she . . . well, she lost her mind. She screamed and sobbed and then screamed louder until everyone in the pool area was staring at us with those "What have you done to that child?" sort of stares. I sat her on the deck chair and draped her in a blanket, but it did no good. She screamed and wailed at the top of her lungs, so much so it was impossible for anyone else to enjoy the sunny day at the pool.

I decided I had to make an escape plan, so I wrapped the towel snug around her, turned her sideways, and put her under my arm, like I was carrying a human burrito. I marched into the lobby—she screamed and cried—and into the elevator—with her still wailing—and down the hall and into the room. About a half hour later, there was a lull in the action and she sat in a stuffed chair, still panting, but not making any more noise.

"What was that all about, sweetie?" I asked her, trying to hide my annoyance.

"I wanted to do it again," she said between labored breaths.

Simple as that. I wanted to do it again.

While that may have been our most intense tantrum, such outbursts are normal for a person who has lived on the earth for less than three years.

Preschoolers want what they want when they want it. When they can't get it, they don't have the developmental skills or maturity to manage their intense feelings. When they accept not always getting their way is how the world works (for most people) and not always a bad thing, they learn to accept normal limits and manage their intense emotions.

Toddlers and preschoolers throw temper tantrums all the time. This is normal for that age. Before the toddler could toddle, he was an infant and everyone stared and smiled and peekabooed. The infant had no limits set on him because there was no need to set them. As far as he could tell, he was the king of the world, with adults holding him and poking his nose and delighting in him. Once he became ambulatory, though, we set limits all the time. *No, you can't grab that fork! No, you can't stick that paper clip in the electrical socket—and where'd you get that paper clip anyway?! No, you can't pull the dog's ears. No! No! No!*

He isn't used to "no," and it destroys him. I'm king of all I survey! I cry and people rush to feed me, hold me, comfort me. I call the shots around here! I do as I please!

But the next part is critical. The tantrum itself isn't a path to growth. For the toddler to make progress, he has to relinquish his sense of being omnipotent and the center of the universe without experiencing it as a shameful event. Parents who cave or who are too harsh or shaming can play a critical role in how this turns out.

So, when parents set the limits—they take the car keys out of his mouth, they sentence him to time-out, they don't let him get everything he sees in the grocery store—he flips out. In this sense, the tantrum is normal and expected among young children. In fact, we appreciate a little fire in the belly with toddler tantrums because they're developing like they should. This is what we will call "normal narcissism." Over time, he learns he is not the boss, that he must relinquish control, that life operates better when those wiser than he are in charge.

An adult narcissist is someone who never learned these developmental lessons. Perhaps he always got his way—or never got his way. Maybe he grew up either indulged or neglected, but limits were never set, boundaries never held. He may have been overindulged and given whatever he desired, growing up entitled and self-centered. However, he may have been so diminished and humiliated as a young person, he made his life a massive overcorrection.

Think about it like a pendulum you don't want to swing too far in either direction. If it drifts too far toward overindulgence and never having limits, made to feel omnipotent, you've got a kid bound to have trouble.

However, if we smash the child down, make him feel inadequate and small, you've got another problem. Both often end up becoming narcissistic.

That child grows up to be an adult who blows past limits with a sense of entitlement or won't accept limits for fear of being seen as small and inadequate. Either way, he wreaks havoc in business settings and in relationships. He must get what he wants and if he doesn't, there is hell to pay.

There's a concept called "narcissistic injury," dating all the way back to Freud, which refers to the experience a narcissist has when his true self, the part of him he has kept guarded and shielded from view, becomes exposed. He projects strength but reveals weakness. He asserts competence but displays ineptitude. He insists he is special but shows everyone he's ordinary. When this happens, he lashes out with "narcissistic rage." This kind of rage might include yelling and even physical assaults, but in most cases, it takes the form of passive-aggressive behavior, annoyance, aloofness, and punitive behavior. The basic message is, "You hurt me and now you are a bad person and you must pay." This rage also comes roaring out when someone sets a limit on the narcissist. We see it when he cannot do as he pleases, when he can't mistreat you or someone else. In this sense, a narcissistic rage is identical to my daughter's two-year-old tantrum.

The adult narcissist is the one who never stopped being the center of the universe or who experienced failures as moments of great shame and felt forced to compensate by making himself larger than life, better than everyone else. Most true narcissism has its roots in those early years, but growing up in a narcissistic culture, like the US, can also rub off on you, even as you get older. Think about the United States' narcissism-promoting features:

- Tremendous affluence
- A belief in being "exceptional" as a country
- A strong emphasis on individualism
- Overindulgent parenting
- Preoccupation with celebrity and fame
- Pathological obsession with self-promotional social media

The United States, with all its affluence, individualism, beliefs in exceptionality, overindulgences, and emphasis on fame and self-promotion, has become a breeding ground for narcissism. This narcissism seeps its way into all corners of our culture.

One study found the United States was the second most narcissistic country in the world, behind Russia, that wounded bully of a nation. Researchers came to this conclusion by comparing the average rating of each country's opinion of itself to how citizens of other countries viewed it. As a comparison, Japan came in fifteenth place globally, seeing itself only one point better than how most other countries viewed it. The United States had a twenty-three-point gap between how favorably its citizens viewed it and how others around the world perceive it. To the north, Canada (number twelve on the list) was off by five points, and to the south, Mexico (number seven) was off by 9.5 points.[6] Neither were anywhere close to the US, where we often view narcissism not as a pathology but an asset, not a bug but a feature.

One fascinating piece of research published in the journal *Psychological Science* asked thousands of residents across the US to rate how much their home state contributed to the history of the United States. There is no consensus answer for this, of course, but the researchers were more interested in how residents perceived their states' relative importance. Their responses were fascinating. Residents of tiny Delaware said, on average, their state created a full third of the nation's history. When the psychologists added the averages together for all fifty states, it added up to 907 percent.[7]

As these snippets illustrate, we Americans have a grandiose view of ourselves. We perceive our country as being much better than the rest of the world. Within our country, we view our specific state as having much more significant impact on our collective history than perhaps it deserves. As a people, we are so narcissistic we cannot see it and even regard it as an advantage.[8] Social psychologist Keith Campbell said of his own research on narcissism with over three thousand subjects across cultures, "It suggests to me that we [Americans] are moderately narcissistic people living in a highly narcissistic culture."

As with most things in psychology, narcissism is shaped by both genetics and life experiences, including one's culture. A person might have a biological predisposition toward certain personality traits, but typically (though not always) for narcissism to take root, there have to be certain life experiences. People made to feel small and diminished in their younger years are at risk for developing vulnerable narcissism, the wounded and overcompensating type. People who have been flattered and overindulged are at risk for becoming grandiose narcissists. In rare instances, both things happen and the child is both told they are special while simultaneously being diminished and humiliated. They are idiots who are so talented. They

---

6. Bolluyt, "Most Narcissistic Countries," lines 1–128.

7. Putnam et al., "Americans Exaggerate Role in U.S. History."

8. Campbell, "Narcissism and Romantic Attraction."

are so beautiful but will never amount to anything. These make for the most malignant narcissists.[9]

The vulnerable narcissist sulks and seeks attention. The grandiose narcissist dominates and controls. The mixed narcissist does it all.[10] We see all three types in the church. Often the grandiose narcissist is up front, perhaps seen as a charismatic leader. The vulnerable narcissist is fragile and constantly needs people to validate their wounded ego and minister to their needs. They idealize the charismatic pastor and are eager to follow him.

An obvious reason churches attract grandiose narcissists is because of the platform it offers. The grandiose narcissist can get in front of people—a small group, a class, a congregation, a streaming audience—and be the center of attention. Church platforms allow these narcissists to delude themselves: "I'm helping this city (or country or church or the kingdom of God), rather than just getting my ego stroked." Vulnerable narcissists, by contrast, are drawn to the church because they know good Christians should self-sacrifice for them and meet their needs. In either event, the church makes a delicious target for the narcissist, either as a platform where he can be in the spotlight or as a forum that assuages his needs and heals his wounds.

Not all Americans or all conservative white Christians are narcissistic, to be clear, but there is evidence our Christian subculture celebrates and nurtures these traits. For some individuals, these characteristics get so severe, they develop into a condition called Narcissistic Personality Disorder (NPD). One of my fellow therapists said, "These folks [with NPD] will stomp a mud puddle into everyone and everything they come in contact with." It's a folksy saying with horrifying implications. As you'll see, the church is not immune from this, and may even have higher rates of this diagnosable condition.

WHAT IS NARCISSISTIC PERSONALITY DISORDER?

Narcissism is annoying in some people and appealing in others, but not everyone with narcissistic traits has a true disorder. Allan Schwartz explains, "There are people who are narcissistic, but who do not have a mental illness. These are people who are experienced as obnoxious because they feel superior to others and see nothing wrong with that." He adds, "They have no awareness and no insight into what they do. As a result, they feel no shame or remorse." For it to cross over into NPD, it has to be so severe it interferes

9. Van Schie, "Narcissistic Traits in Young People."

10. Jauk et al., "Relationship between Grandiose and Vulnerable Narcissism."

with their normal functioning. Schwartz explains, "These are people who do not function well. They alienate friends and family and come to feel socially isolated and depressed."[11]

In the current diagnostic manual, a person has to meet certain conditions to meet the criteria for NPD. These conditions include things like:[12]

- Significant problems experiencing genuine empathy for others.

- Superficial relationships that meet the person's own selfish needs

- Strong sense of entitlement

- Excessive self-centeredness

- Belief that one is superior to others

- Frequently seeking admiration or excessive attention

Martin, the guy who punched the woman and then blamed her for it, had unmistakable Narcissistic Personality Disorder. His narcissistic traits were so severe they wrecked his life and caused him trouble with his school, with the law, and with all his relationships. Despite that, he had almost no ability to reflect on his role in all the dysfunction. He was the victim. Other people—the young woman, the university administration, the police, the media, his friends—were the problem.

It took months of work to get underneath the defensiveness, but once we were there, Martin revealed his malignantly narcissistic father berated him for being lazy and stupid, yet also screamed at Martin's teachers at parent conferences when they called out his bullying of other students. Martin was a depressed and empty soul, but you would never know it from his bluster and bravado.

Within the church, we not only see how the narcissism of the larger culture has pressed into it, but we find high rates of individuals with Narcissistic Personality Disorder, including many pastors and others in ministry.[13] A regular public platform and a chance to lead people eager for guidance makes sense of why the church draws those with this disorder. It provides them with a little kingdom to rule with many subjects who can adore them. It is the perfect context for a person with NPD to set up shop.

I know a therapist who specializes in seeing pastors with NPD. Contemplate that for a moment. While most therapists see a broad range of people with a wide variety of problems, this man sees only people in

---

11. Schwartz, "Narcissist Versus Narcissistic Personality Disorder," lines 17–22.

12. American Psychiatric Association, *Diagnostic and Statistical Manual*.

13. Ball and Puls, "Narcissistic Personality Disorder in Pastors."

full-time ministry with one particular disorder—and he's not the only one with such a specialty. He told me, "These men are among the most wounded and sometimes malignant narcissists I've ever worked with—and that's saying something!"

The research tells us that most people with NPD never seek treatment because they do not see themselves as being in the wrong or in need of help.[14] If that's true, imagine the implications for the church. It suggests leadership in the Christian ministries is rife with diagnosable narcissists.

Chuck DeGroat, author of *When Narcissism Comes to Church* and a gifted practicing therapist, says while we need more quantitative data, we have a "wealth of qualitative and experiential data" to suggest higher rates of NPD among ministry leaders.[15] He told me, "My own psychological assessment work with pastors and planters over the past fifteen years shows elevations almost exclusively in Cluster-B personality disorders (which includes narcissism and histrionic personality disorder). I think it's fair to assume that pastoral ministry attracts a particular kind of personality." Both of us would agree that not all pastors—certainly not most pastors or ministry leaders—have NPD or even pronounced narcissistic traits, but the church draws a disproportionate number of people who do.

Perhaps the church, with its emphasis on specialness and being the keepers of truth, produces narcissists. However, a more likely explanation is the church attracts narcissists because it provides a power base from which to operate. You have an entire community that provides validation of your views and beliefs. For narcissistic leaders, you also have a big platform that puts you in front of dozens, hundreds, even thousands of people.

Darrell Puls and Glenn Ball embedded a validated Narcissistic Personality Disorder test in a survey of pastors from one denomination. They found over 30 percent of pastors were in the diagnostic range for NPD. The rate of NPD in the general population is less than one percent and between 2–16 percent in those who seek mental health treatment, so the rate of this in pastors is up to fifteen times the rate of those who are in therapy.[16]

Another study found Christians scored higher on the grandiosity scale of the Narcissism Personality Inventory than nonreligious people.[17] Grandiosity isn't just garden variety arrogance or conceitedness. It refers to an unfounded sense of superiority. It could be moral or spiritual superiority, but it always means a belief that one is special and better than others.

14. Miller et al. "Controversies in Narcissism."

15. DeGroat, *When Narcissism Comes to Church.*

16. Ball and Puls, "Narcissistic Personality Disorder in Pastors."

17. Dubebdorff and Luchner, "Narcissistic Differences."

In a study of almost 650 individuals, researchers found those who scored high on narcissism also scored high on a need for power.[18] Grandiose narcissists want to be in charge. They can't stand being submissive to others. I cannot overstate the relationship between narcissism and desire for power in the church. Despite an explicit ethic of not seeking control, the church is full of people who seek to assert their power over others.

Likewise, the church attracts followers who resonate with its power-assertive message. It allows them to feel safe and morally superior. The position, in its essence, is, *We deserve to be in charge because we are God's chosen and have access to truth that others lack or reject, so we are right to assert our power over others because that is best.* This idea is appealing to narcissistic individuals who already believe they are right and that others should be deferential to them. Lest we forget, as a candidate, Trump secured his evangelical base of support with a January 2016 speech where he proclaimed, "If I'm there, you're going to have plenty of power. You don't need anybody else."[19] The promise to give Christians power was the key to his widespread appeal among them, especially white evangelicals.

C. S. Lewis, a patron saint of evangelicalism, warned of the harm that happens when "religion is confused with politics."[20] Jesus' own message was to give up power. It's impossible to read the Sermon on the Mount, for example, without concluding we should not seek power for ourselves, yet modern white evangelicalism sees gaining power and asserting it over others as a virtue and a goal, as if it were benevolent.

The larger American culture is full of narcissism, which has permeated the church, while the church and other Christian ministries make prominent targets for those with Narcissistic Personality Disorder to set up shop and consolidate power. I asked DeGroat what has astonished him the most in his work and study of narcissism in the church. He replied, "I continued to be surprised that in some contexts, narcissistic tendencies are renarrated as gifts for the church—that bullies are excused as 'confident,' that manipulators are excused as 'good strategists,' that a chameleon-like personality is seen as 'adaptable.'"

The church has proven to be a haven for narcissists. Once inside, they can behave as they wish with little fear of repercussion, especially if they are talented or charismatic individuals. They do as they please, often to the detriment of the community and to the church.

18. Hermann and Fuller, "Trait Narcissism and Religious Trends."
19. Dias, "'Christianity Will Have Power,'" lines 32–34.
20. Hooper, ed., *Collected Letters*, 358.

There is a final powerful concept that helps us make sense of narcissistic tendencies in the church. More than anything, it explains why the white conservative church has become so insular, self-centered, and hostile toward those outside of it. It's called "collective narcissism."

WHAT IS COLLECTIVE NARCISSISM?

Years ago, I was at a high school football game when a small group of rival fans of the home team offered a, shall we say, less than flattering assessment of the host school. It may have involved an expletive or two. Not to be outdone, the home team fans yelled their own evaluation back across the stands. This continued for a few minutes, tensions building, when the visiting team's fans ventured into enemy territory to mouth off. It didn't go well for anyone. Pushing and shoving. A couple of fists were thrown. Security was called. People were escorted out.

Since at least the 1800s, there have been thousands of documented incidents of fans of sports teams assaulting fans of the opposing team. International soccer is susceptible to what we term "hooliganism," where fans of opposing teams attack each other, resulting in beatings, stabbings, fires and property destruction, even full-scale riots. In many countries, being a fan of a local or national soccer team is an integral part of one's identity. Even in the US, where soccer has yet to stir the same level of fervor as other sports, there have been several documented brawls among fans of opposing teams. During an exhibition game in Columbus, Ohio, for example, fans of the local team fought rival fans of a visiting British team, injuring over one hundred people.

One study out of Liverpool, England, concluded, "Involvement in football [i.e., soccer] violence can be explained in relation to a number of factors, relating to interaction, identity, legitimacy and power. Football violence is also thought to reflect expressions of strong emotional ties to a football team, which may help to reinforce a supporter's sense of identity."[21] Other studies find when there are major differences represented by the opposing team, like religion, ethnicity, or social class, the chances of conflict among fans escalates.[22]

When you dig into the causes of hooliganism, you discover there are many contributing factors when violence breaks out: the time of day, the level of security, the design of the stadium, economic conditions, and more. However, there seems to be one consistent factor: it happens when a group

21. Gow and Rookwood, "Hooliganism in English football."
22. Dunning et al., "Spectator Violence at Football Matches."

believes they are part of an extraordinary group disrespected by those outside the group.

Something happens when someone becomes part of a group that believes it is special, but unappreciated. Group members create a narrative that they are part of something exceptional, but also believe those outside the group hate them. These are the two ingredients—a belief that you are part of a special group and a belief the group is unappreciated by outsiders—that create a phenomenon called "collective narcissism."[23]

Over the years, I've observed collective narcissism among fraternity members, members of certain professions, nationalists, and others. I've also heard it expressed many times from conservative white Christians. The sense of being exceptional, but unappreciated and disrespected by non-Christians, is a frequent theme. "The only people you can discriminate against these days and get away with it is toward white Christian men," a white Christian man told me. It's a sentiment I've heard more than once. As we would expect, collective narcissism is associated with greater sexism and tolerance of violence against women.

Conservative white Christians get angry at progressive Christians, whom they regard as not real Christians and worse than nonbelievers, like wolves in sheep's clothing. They believe these progressives seek to undermine the integrity of the Christian faith. That is also the nature of the collective narcissism where the in-group tightens the circle, drawing tighter lines for who is in bounds and who is not. Often the people just outside the interior bands of the concentric circle are seen as bigger threats, less pure, a risk for contaminating the group with their unorthodox ideas or practices.

I spoke with Agnieszka Golec de Zavala, the leading researcher in the world on collective narcissism, and she said her interest in the topic came out of her study of prejudice in the political realm, particularly nationalism. However, she has seen it apply to a wide range of groups. "If you hear your group is great, but it's not great enough or it's not as great as it used to be, then you begin to believe that," she said. "If you hear your group is not appreciated, then you begin to believe that it should be."

Golec de Zavala and her colleagues created the Collective Narcissism Scale, a short nine-item measure of how much a person perceives his or her group as being exceptional, yet not well-appreciated by others outside the group.[24] On the original scale, they used the phrase "my group," but allowed me to insert the word *Christian* in its place.

23. Golec de Zavala and Lantos, "Collective Narcissism and Its Social Consequences."

24. Golec de Zavala et al., "Collective Narcissism and Its Social Consequences."

1. I wish other groups would more quickly recognize the authority of Christians.

2. Christians deserve special treatment.

3. Not many people seem to fully understand the importance of Christians.

4. I insist upon Christians getting the respect that we are due.

5. It really makes me angry when others criticize Christians.

6. If Christians had a major say in the world, the world would be a much better place.

7. I get upset when people do not notice achievements of Christians.

8. The true worth of Christians is often misunderstood.

9. I will never be satisfied until Christians get the recognition we deserve.

In the original research, groups rated high on these items show more collective narcissism than those who rate lower. Now imagine how many white conservative Christians would endorse these items. Conservative Christians are the only group that believes Christians face more discrimination in the US than Muslims.[25] On the surface, just considering facts, this is an absurd claim, but it makes sense through the filter of collective narcissism. In a Pew Research survey, a near majority (46 percent) of white evangelicals said it has become harder to be an evangelical in recent years.[26] The belief among these Christians is they are an exceptional group, so exceptional, in fact, they should have the preeminent role in our culture, free of challenge. They see any criticism as an enormous affront. This is the essence of collective narcissism.

Collective narcissism involves beliefs that the group in question is extraordinary and important, should have power and influence, and deserves great respect, yet does not get the recognition it deserves. We see it across cultures, across countries, across groups. It is not unique to white evangelicals, but this has become a dominant conservative Christian narrative.

On an individual level, collective narcissism connects to the two seemingly opposite expressions of narcissism among group members: the vulnerable narcissist who is self-absorbed, prone to anxiety and depression, hypersensitive to criticism, and in need of constant reassurance, as well as the grandiose narcissist who boasts and brags, acts superior and entitled, manipulates and coerces.

25. Cox et al., "Religious Liberty Issues," lines 39–55.
26. Lipka, "Evangelicals say it's harder for them in America," lines 43–46.

The vulnerable narcissists are the clingy partners who are bottomless pits of need. These are the college roommates or adult co-workers who react with passive-aggressive anger or outright rage when others joke or challenge them. These are the needy, but self-absorbed friends or family members always in need of comfort, always making the relationship about themselves. On the surface, they seem nothing like the more overt narcissists, but don't be mistaken: they are just as self-centered and certain they are right and better and more deserving of attention than others.

The vulnerable narcissist craves positive attention and affirmation. As long as he is getting his "attaboys," he does well and keeps the shame-filled part of himself under wraps. But when he gets criticized or forced to look at the negative aspects of himself, the rage comes roaring out. For him, the reaction is on the level of survival and self-preservation. To be criticized is to be destroyed.

The grandiose narcissist is a lot easier to spot, though he can often be charming and magnetic, funny and intriguing, which makes it sometimes harder to avoid getting sucked in. Just like the vulnerable narcissist, though, you don't want to be on his nasty side. You avoid crossing him, lest he rip you to pieces.

So collective narcissism manifests in either flavor of narcissism, along with poor self-esteem, which seems contradictory until you realize narcissists always have a distorted sense of self. They either regard themselves as too much or too lacking, too big or too small, too perfect or too damaged. Never just right. Never healthy.

A few individuals can represent collective narcissism on behalf of the group, even if most of the members of the group are not narcissistic. More often, though, it shows up in the entire group where themes of both grandiosity and vulnerability dominate. *We are better than everyone else, worthy of power and special treatment, so don't you dare criticize us or ask us to share what is rightfully ours.*

In a study entitled "You Remind Me of Someone Awesome," researchers found narcissistic people tolerate and even enjoy narcissistic peers because of the perceived similarity. They concluded narcissists gravitate toward each other. When they see themselves as similar to the other narcissist, they view the other person's actions and traits more positively, which endears them more to them. Like attracts like. This helps explain why some groups are more narcissistic than others.[27]

Collective narcissism has a way of rubbing off on individuals who might not be that narcissistic. Their association with a group that seems

27. Adams et al., "You Remind Me of Someone Awesome."

extraordinary might cause them to feel the same. Over time, a selfless and humble person might gravitate toward believing her needs and perspectives are more important—or more right—than others."[28]

Those hooligans who brawl with the other team's fans might be an example of this. Perhaps some of them joined the group out of love and devotion to the team. Maybe some individuals were not high in narcissism from the start, but being in the bubble influences their thoughts and convinces them support for the team is important and they must punish disrespect of the team. That's what collective narcissism does. It draws people into a group that may be good and admirable, but then groupthink arises. People derive their sense of identity and well-being from being a part of the group. They come to see the group as essential and protecting it is imperative. *Disrespect us and we'll take you down.*

Groups with high collective narcissism often experience what researchers have termed the "Charismatic Leader-Follower Relationship." In this dynamic, the leader is front and center, in need of constant adulation and hero worship from his people. He projects an unshakable self-confidence and speaks with certainty. There is often a lot of "we-they" talk. *We are chosen and special. We are right. They are evil and dangerous. They want to destroy us and everything we've worked for.*[29]

These leaders are what in psychology we often call "mirror-hungry," desiring constant applause and approval, especially from crowds and important groups. They find themselves up front, on stage, in the spotlight.

This only works if you have followers, though, and these leaders have the talent and charisma to attract disciples and supporters. We call the people drawn to these leaders "ideal hungry." These folks yearn for a great, inspirational leader to follow, to idealize, to place their hopes upon. This man—or woman—they put their trust in will lead them to a better life, will keep them safe, will look out for them and their needs first and foremost.

Both the charismatic leader and his followers possess strong collective narcissistic traits, they are just the yin and yang, the two sides of the narcissistic dance. They both want to bolster the group because doing so makes them feel special and important and gives them a sense of safety and protection from external challenges.

Groups that rate high on narcissism are also much more likely to be wounded by criticism or limit-setting by those outside the group. Criticism is viewed as an attack. Challenges are existential threats. As a result, they are

---

28. Golec de Zavala and Lantos, "Collective Narcissism and Its Social Consequences."

29. Post, "Charismatic Leader-Follower Relationship."

also more likely to lash out and to see justification for being harsh, rejecting, even aggressive toward their perceived enemies and attackers.[30]

Based on the research of Golec de Zavala and her colleagues, collective narcissism seems to be a stew of low self-esteem, individual narcissism (of both the vulnerable and grandiose varieties), and perceived threat from outside of the group. When those three conditions occur, they lead to a siege mentality, conspiratorial thinking, a desire for revenge, and the perception that others intend to do them harm. As a result, the group members become more prejudiced toward those who are different, retaliate or lash out at their would-be attackers or enemies, and want to exclude those within the group who don't hold the party line. Golec de Zavala describes it to me in this succinct way: "Collective narcissism is 'in-group love' associated with 'out-group hate.'"[31]

We see collective narcissism's vindictive ugliness across countries and cultures. In Turkey, those rated high on collective narcissism took great pleasure in the European economic crisis because they felt rejected and humiliated by having to wait to join the European Union. In Portugal, they supported hostile actions toward Germans and reveled in Germany's economic struggles when they viewed Germany's position in the EU as being more important than that of their own country. In Poland, they endorsed hostile actions toward a filmmaker who had produced a film they considered offensive to their country, and they responded with overt hostility to an actor who offended them with jokes about the Polish government.[32] In the United States, when collective narcissists read a fictional interview with a foreign exchange student who criticized her experience in the US, they not only got mad at the student, but at all citizens of her country.[33] Again, collective narcissism is a belief that my group—in this case, my country—is exceptional, and I take great offense to actions or comments to the contrary.

American exceptionalism can be a form of collective narcissism. Not that America isn't an extraordinary country. At its best, the industry and diversity of its people, the natural beauty of its landscapes, and its contributions to the world are all marvelous things. Yet this notion that America is so special is a narcissistic notion. A big component of the collective narcissism of conservative white Christians is the hostility with which they react to any criticism of the country. To them, those outside their circles, the "godless progressives," want nothing more than to destroy this great country.

30. Golec de Zavala et al., "Collective Narcissism Predicts Hypersensitivity."
31. Golec de Zavala and Lantos, "Collective Narcissism and Its Social Consequences."
32. Golec de Zavala et al., "Collective Narcissism Predicts Hypersensitivity."
33. Golec de Zavala et al., "Collective Narcissism Predicts Hypersensitivity."

Collective narcissism leads to a demonizing of those seen as outside or "other," even when those people are in need. Consider the plight of refugees, who, by definition, are fleeing their home country because of persecution, war, or threat of violence. Two studies of almost fifteen hundred individuals found collective narcissism predicted hostility toward refugees by seeing them as a threat, whether a threat to national security or a threat to a way of life. Collective narcissism caused people to conclude that those trying to enter their country out of fear for their lives were coming to do violence in the host country or would destroy the fabric of the country's society. These beliefs were so strongly held that most citizens of some countries endorsed violence as an acceptable way of handling refugee crises.[34]

Membership in a significant group doesn't always lead to high collective narcissism. In fact, people can be satisfied with their group, yet not have attitudes related to collective narcissism. These folks with high group satisfaction, but low collective narcissism, see others outside the group as trustworthy and well-intentioned. They also had healthier self-esteem, more positive emotions, and a greater sense of personal control over their life. The opposite was true of those rating high in collective narcissism. These folks viewed those outside the group with hostility and suspicion. They experienced much more negative emotion, either over- or undervalued themselves, and didn't believe they had much control over their own lives. They also had less sense of connection to others.[35]

We find collective narcissism in Christian communities of all types, little churches and megachurches, rural congregations and urban fellowships, across denominations or no denominations, in either church or parachurch settings. DeGroat told me, "I've seen collective narcissism in a Midwest church that demonized other churches as unfaithful, believing that it was specially chosen by God," he explained. "And I've seen it in large, multi-campus churches and ministries where there was a sense that God has specially blessed and multiplied their ministry."

Collective narcissists perceive outside disagreement or criticism as hostility or threat and have a much harder time regulating themselves when they sense they are under attack. When this happens, they're more likely to endorse more aggressive ways of responding.[36] The white evangelical church is susceptible to adopting more narcissistic themes, drawing more narcissistic personalities, and having more collective narcissism than the normal population. By nature, narcissism involves high defensiveness, which makes

34. Dyduch-Hazer et al., "Collective Narcissism Predicts Attitudes Toward Refugees."
35. Golec de Zavala, "Collective Narcissism and In-Group Satisfaction."
36. Golec de Zavala et al., "Investing Self-Worth in the Ingroup's Image."

the church less responsive to constructive criticism, less able to change, and more willing to fight.

When a narcissist buys a lavish house, drives a rare luxury sports car, wears designer clothes, or dumps his wife and dates a model, his behavior is a product of his narcissism. He may have a thousand justifications—the kids needed more room, I like a reliable car, dressing well communicates confidence to potential investors—but they all trace right back to his own narcissistic needs for attention and a sense that he is indeed special.

When churches construct mammoth buildings on sprawling campuses or focus on the size of their membership and attendance or wrap their identities around rock star teaching pastors or favor those with wealth, fame, and status, their decisions are a product of their collective narcissism. They might spiritualize their actions—growth is just a sign of God's favor, the pastor has a unique calling, influencing this high-status person allows us to reach so many more people for Jesus—but their choices are expressions of both narcissism and their need to feel special. The evangelical culture of celebrity pastors, massive facilities, and megachurches is a highly public, highly visible expression of narcissism.

One study found members of large churches tolerate narcissism more than those in smaller churches.[37] When we see the downfall of megachurch pastors and leaders of large ministries, we attribute it to moral failings due to temptation or stress, but if we look at it through the lens of narcissism, we see it as an inevitability. Puls writes that churches that lose their way morally "did not become unethical intentionally but because of their self-obsession, sense of entitlement, self-aggrandizement, denial, and rationalizations."[38] In an interview, Golec de Zavala told me, "Collective narcissists use (religious) groups to participate in their borrowed greatness, to feel entitled, better than others, and to demand privileged treatment."

SET APART AS SPECIAL

Over a decade ago, I was visiting an evangelical megachurch on a weekend when a guest preacher had control of the pulpit. He was, according to his introduction, a preacher of international acclaim, the author of some books, and the host of a radio show.

He began his sermon with a story about Benjamin Franklin who he said had spent long hours in prayer during the constitutional convention. The preacher raised his voice to underscore his message.

37. Dunaetz et al., "Churches Tolerate Pastoral Narcissism?"
38. Puls, "Narcissistic Pastors and Churches."

"Since the beginning," he said, "this country has been a Christian nation, founded on Christian principles, a city on a hill. Others want to tell you otherwise. Don't believe that. You're a chosen people. *You're set apart as special.* God has you here to protect this God-ordained country and to fight back against the forces that seek to destroy it."

While fear may drive white evangelicals, they also inhabit a narcissistic subculture, one especially high in collective narcissism. They see themselves as special, deserving of power and control. They look out for their own selfish interests and view their group as being unappreciated and undervalued in our culture.

Saying they are part of a narcissistic subculture is not the same as saying each individual within it has Narcissistic Personality Disorder or even has narcissistic traits. Instead it means a self-focused group culture shapes them and gives them an inflated sense of their own importance, their own rightness, their own entitlement to special favor and status. Life within that narcissistic bubble distorts and corrupts their thinking, bending their minds away from values and actions in line with Christian belief and toward favoring values and actions antithetical to the core of the faith.

Within this subculture, it has become reflexive to have animosity toward others outside the group. It's easy to become angry and vengeful, as opposed to compassionate and selfless. Rather than be a counterweight or a healthy challenge to the dominant narcissistic culture, the church mirrors it, taking on the same attitudes.

One study involving 787 individuals by Whinda Yustisia concluded that religious fundamentalism is more likely to result in higher levels of collective narcissism, especially when members adhere more closely to the in-group norms. In its most extreme forms, the collective narcissism can result in more extreme behaviors, especially targeted toward those outside the group who deviate from their group's values and norms. She found collective narcissism results in greater hostility and unwillingness to forgive those outside the group.[39] Other research also finds that when people become defensive and insecure about their group's perception by other groups, it biases their moral judgments, making them more open to mistreating or disadvantaging the other groups.[40]

Collective narcissism among white conservative Christians doesn't invalidate the core tenets of the Christian faith, but it has distorted and complicated the faith in negative ways. The embrace of narcissistic attitudes and

---

39. Yustisia et al., "Religious Fundamentalism and Collective Narcissism."
40. Bocian et al., "Moral judgements depend on collective narcissism."

values has polluted the church, making it safe or even expected to embrace self-centeredness while looking down at others outside the faith.

To understand how white Christians think, you must reckon with this hard but essential point: the white evangelical church in America has become infected with narcissism, as if a cancer has ravaged its internal organs. The external appearance may still look good, but its insides are full of rot.

CHAPTER 3

Fear Cuts Deeper than Swords

Evangelicals and Fear

"Strong as a bear. Fierce as a wolverine. Fear cuts deeper than swords."
—ARYA STARK, *GAME OF THRONES* (GEORGE R. R. MARTIN)

AN EVANGELICAL FRIEND OF mine explained how her family was going to drive across the country during the summer, exploring different parts of the country they had never seen before. Her two kids had been looking forward to it all semester. Once they arrived in the Pacific Northwest, her husband and two children were going to fly back for a family event, but she was going to drive back alone, nearly two thousand miles. I thought it was because someone needed to drive their vehicle back and she drew the short straw.

"No," she said. "We're renting an RV that we could drop off in Oregon. I just don't want to fly because I've heard terrorists may have an EMP bomb that would knock planes out of the sky."

I had so many questions I wanted to ask: Where had she heard this? How would this even work? What were the odds that, even if it were true, it would happen at the exact moment and location her own plane was in the blast zone? Why was she okay with her husband and children flying without her when they might get attacked by an EMP bomb?

I wish I could say this was a rare interaction with an evangelical, but over the years, I've had countless conversations with conservative Christians who are afraid. They are afraid of terrorists and immigrants and Marxists. They are afraid the country is going to hell. They are afraid their children will be morally ruined. They are afraid they will be persecuted for being a Christian.

In my professional life, it's the evangelicals who seem more fearful than others. I see parents who are deathly afraid of threats to their children and teenagers. I see young adults flooded with anxiety. The irony is they are the ones who profess casting their worries on God. Are conservative Christians really more fearful than most people? As I dug into the research, I found the answer is more complicated than I realized.

Fear is our most adaptive and commanding emotion. It is a gift, a beautiful adaptation that has allowed us to survive for millennia. Our brains have alert systems that spring into action in an instant at the first whiff of danger, pumping a cascade of adrenaline into our bloodstreams, racing our hearts, dilating our pupils, tensing our muscles, quickening our breathing. All of this in service of either attacking our threat or running from it. Without this elegant fight-or-flight response, we would be too weak or too slow to fend off predators and enemies.

As our brains developed, the front of our brains became more logical, intentional, and deliberate. This part makes sense of the world, uses language, organizes and conceptualizes. The structures that stand guard for us remain tucked underneath, always scanning for threats. Like different business departments that don't always share information with each other, these parts of the brain don't always communicate well.

In his brilliant book *The Righteous Mind*, Jonathan Haidt likens the human mind to an elephant and a rider. Imagine a man needs to ride an elephant to a nearby village. The elephant is big, powerful, and necessary. However, it is also easily spooked and can rampage, trampling everything in its path. The man is tiny by comparison but much smarter. He steers the elephant through the narrow pathways, beside the village market, near children playing and people doing laundry in the river. He knows that one loud noise or a pesky mouse might cause the elephant to lose control, knocking down tents and putting people in danger. The man is there to guide, steer, direct. He needs the elephant for his strength and stamina. The elephant is bigger and stronger, but he needs the man to be in charge. They need each other. For the human brain, the emotional part of the brain is the elephant. The rational front part of the brain is the man. We'd love to think the man is always running the show, but the truth is the elephant often gets startled and freaks out.[1]

1. Haidt, *Righteous Mind.*

Buried deep in your brain is an almond-shaped cluster called the amygdala (pronounced uh-MIG-duh-luh) that manages your intense emotional responses, particularly related to scary things. It reacts in milliseconds and causes you to have a "fight-or-flight" reaction to a perceived threat.

Recently, I was walking my dog, a blind border collie, around the perimeter of a park. At the far side of the park, a boy who looked to be about twelve or thirteen was walking his pit bull. His dog saw my dog, broke free of the boy's grip on the leash, and began sprinting across the park, heading straight for us. My brain lit up as I watched the pit bull run furiously toward my defenseless pet. When the other dog was within a couple of feet, I lunged for him, grabbed his collar, and yanked him up, his back feet barely touching the ground. I yelled for the boy.

"Come get your dog!" I shouted. The boy stood in place, paralyzed into inaction. He looked like a statue.

"Come get your dog!" I yelled louder.

Still, he didn't move.

"Hey, kid! Come get your dog now!" I yelled even louder.

He walked toward us, slowly, as if he were in a trance. I handed his dog off to him and we exited the park. I was returning home down the sidewalk of the main road when I looked back and saw, once again, the pit bull had gotten away from the kid and was barreling straight toward me and my dog. Once again, my brain sprung into action. I stepped into the road to signal for the oncoming cars to stop, then grabbed the pit bull's collar as he flew across the street and lunged for my dog. I held the snarling dog aloft until another adult rushed over to hold the dog and let me get out of the area. As I left, I looked back and saw the kid frozen in place, unable to move.

The incident illustrates fight or flight. As the pit bull ran for my dog, my brain had a "fight" response—go toward the dog, subdue it, keep it away from my border collie. The kid had a classic "flight" response—avoid, lock up, stay away. Some people call this kind of flight response a "freeze" response, but it is the same idea. For both me and the kid, our brains lit up and we were both governed by our amygdala. Every other thought in my mind evaporated as I focused on the dog attack.

This was my amygdala responding properly. A legitimate threat unfolded. My amygdala sounded the alarm, my smart frontal lobe determined the threat was real, and my brain created a response to the threat. This differs from what Harvard professor Dan Goleman, author of *Emotional Intelligence*, coined "amygdala hijack," which is a sudden and disproportionate response to a real or perceived threat. An amygdala hijack happens when a perceived threat evokes an irrational response. The amygdala overpowers the entire brain and shuts down logical thinking in favor of a more intense, emotional response.[2]

We are witnessing what is essentially amygdala hijack on a grand scale within the white evangelical community. They won't get onto a commercial airliner with their family because of terrorists. They shriek at school board meetings and on cable news that teaching critical race theory will damage their kids for life and is the road to the death camps. They panic that "deep state" politicians, celebrities, and business executives are kidnapping children so they can drink their blood. They become hysterical that the "homosexual agenda" will seduce their children. They sound the alarm that godless liberals seek to destroy the country. They accost educators and health officials over mask mandates during a pandemic. Let's be clear: these are not normal fear responses. This is amygdala hijack writ large.

THE PANDEMIC OF FEAR

American evangelicals don't have a corner on the market with anxiety. If we look at the rates of anxiety disorders around the globe, we find high amounts across countries and cultures, with the US ranking at the top of the list.[3] One large epidemiological study found anxiety disorders were the most common mental health diagnosis in the world, affecting over 284 million people. The United States has the highest percentages of any country, with rates of anxiety disorder in the US more than double those found in several other countries.[4]

Comparing massive surveys in the US and Europe, Borwin Bandelow and Sophie Michaelis found the lifetime prevalence of any anxiety disorder was 14.5 percent throughout Europe, compared to 33.7 percent in the United States.[5] The National Institute of Mental Health found comparable rates of anxiety disorders in the US, suggesting the lifetime prevalence was around 31 percent, representing 102 million living Americans.[6]

These national and international studies tell us the US has unacceptable rates of anxiety problems, but we learn even more when we examine the specific conditions that fall under the umbrella of anxiety disorders. Specifically, rates of Generalized Anxiety Disorder, Social Anxiety Disorder, and Panic Disorder in the US are revealing.

2. Goleman, *Emotional Intelligence.*
3. Ritchie and Roser, "Mental Health."
4. Ritchie and Roser, "Mental Health."
5. Bandelow and Michaelis, "Epidemiology of Anxiety Disorders."
6. National Institute of Mental Health, "Any Anxiety Disorder."

Generalized Anxiety is persistent worry and negative overthinking that interferes with normal life. Taking a snapshot of just 2019, 16 percent of American adults met the criteria for Generalized Anxiety Disorder during the two weeks leading up to the study. (The lifetime rates were much higher, of course.) Based on this finding, an American adult has a one in six chance of having Generalized Anxiety Disorder at this moment.[7]

Social Anxiety Disorder involves intense, persistent, and irrational fear in social situations. People with this condition worry so much about being judged by others or not performing well in front of them that it interferes with their normal life. To explore the rates of social anxiety around the world, Canadian researchers Philip Jefferies and Michael Ungar surveyed nearly seven thousand people in seven countries[8] chosen for their economic and cultural diversity. They found the prevalence of Social Anxiety Disorder was much higher than expected or previously reported, with over one in three (36 percent) meeting the diagnostic criteria. Again, the US had by far the highest rates of the disorder, with 58 percent of the sample reporting elevated symptoms. Although the causes of Social Anxiety Disorder are complex, such high rates suggest America's "all eyes on me" culture leads to distress.[9]

Panic Disorder involves a sudden, intense feeling of anxiety that swamps a person. Their heart pounds, their breathing quickens, their chest tightens. They feel like they are having a heart attack or going crazy or dying. It's an awful experience. Again, the United States has sky-high rates. Compared to countries in Europe, the US has three times the rate of panic attacks.[10]

Differences in Rates of Anxiety Disorders among Groups

In general, the US has shockingly high rates of anxiety disorders. As with all countries, we find these conditions vary by age and gender and race. Here's an overview of the rates for various groups in the US:

- Young adults (ages eighteen to twenty-nine) in the US were more likely than other age groups to struggle with anxiety symptoms.[11] Younger people in our culture seem more susceptible to anxiety problems

7. Terlizzi and Villarroel, "Symptoms of Generalized Anxiety Disorder."
8. Brazil, China, Indonesia, Russia, Thailand, Vietnam, and the United States.
9. Jefferies and Ungar, "Social Anxiety Prevalence Study."
10. Somers et al., "Prevalence and Incidence Studies of Anxiety Disorders."
11. Terlizzi and Villarroel, "Symptoms of Generalized Anxiety Disorder."

compared to older generations and have more difficulty coping with stress and worry.

- Mental health disorders are the leading cause of disability for American college students and young adults, with anxiety disorders being their chief complaint.[12] Between 2011 and 2018, anxiety disorders among college students rose an alarming 24 percent.[13] In the decade between 2007 and 2017, college students have used mental health services at a growing rate. That may be because of greater awareness and openness toward treatment services, but it is unlikely the increase is simply due to greater access, as some might argue.[14] The demand for college counseling center services has increased four times faster than the growth of the general student body. Across only a five-year span, there was an average increase in need for on-campus mental health services of 30 percent across the country, with a range of 15 percent to a whopping 165 percent.[15]

- Over one in every fourteen US children have an anxiety disorder.[16] That's about two children per classroom. The rates skyrocket during the teen years. Nearly one in three US teens meet the full criteria for an anxiety disorder.[17]

- Women develop anxiety disorders more often than men. Data from the National Institute of Mental Health found 23 percent of women had an anxiety disorder within the past year, compared to 14 percent of men.[18]

- A Harvard study found white men and women had higher rates of anxiety disorders in any given twelve-month period, but they had lower rates of persistent disorders compared to Black, Asian, or Latino people. White people got anxiety disorders more often, but recovered from them more quickly, presumably because of greater access to mental health services.[19]

12. Xiao et al., "Treatment trends in college counseling centers."
13. Duffy et al., "Trends in Mood and Anxiety Symptoms."
14. Duffy et al., "Trends in Mood and Anxiety Symptoms."
15. Xiao et al., "Treatment trends in college counseling centers."
16. Ghandour et al., "Prevalence of Depression, Anxiety, and Conduct Problems."
17. National Institute of Mental Health, "Any Anxiety Disorder."
18. National Institute of Mental Health, "Any Anxiety Disorder."
19. Vilsaint et al., "Racial/Ethnic Differences in Prevalence and Persistence."

Are Anxiety Disorders Increasing in the US?

Nearly everyone agrees the rates of anxiety and full-blown anxiety disorders are far higher than they should be, but are the rates of anxiety disorders going up? Depending on the study, anxiety rates range widely. It depends on the questions asked, the time frame, the criteria used to evaluate the responses, and other factors. Despite that, we can sift through the data to find trustworthy trends. The consensus among most is that we have seen anxiety disorders increase in recent years, compared to previous decades.

One large national survey found anxiety increased in the United States from 5.1 percent in 2008 to 6.7 percent a decade later in 2018.[20] While that percent and a half increase may not seem like much, consider that this means over five million more people struggle with anxiety compared to a decade earlier. A 2017 survey of one thousand adults by the American Psychiatric Association found 36 percent reported their anxiety had increased over the past year. The most common source of extreme anxiety was "keeping myself or my family safe." A year later, using the same questions and methods, self-reported anxiety increased to 39 percent with safety concerns still topping the list.[21]

Jean Twenge, author of *iGen*, and her colleagues collected scores from a standardized test called the MMPI across seventy years. They found general symptoms of anxiety have been "on the rise" over the past several decades.[22] Two large national surveys also found rates of anxiety disorders increased among college students from the mid-2000s to 2018.[23]

Though the trend of increasing anxiety has been present for at least two decades, rates of anxiety skyrocketed even further during the pandemic year, with individuals who were experiencing severe anxiety symptoms going from 8 percent in 2019 to 21 percent in April 2020. By the end of 2020, the rates of anxiety were still more elevated than they had been the year before.[24]

In May 2020, I surveyed eighty-one clinicians in group practices in every region of the country and asked what mental health conditions had increased among their clients during the first two months of the pandemic.[25] The top three answers were all linked to anxiety. A full two-thirds (67 percent) of therapists said they had seen increases in adult anxiety, followed

20. Goodwin et al., "Trends in Anxiety in the United States."
21. American Psychiatric Association, "Public Opinion Poll—2017."
22. Twenge et al., "Increases in Psychopathology Among Young Americans."
23. Duffy et al., "Trends in Mood and Anxiety Symptoms."
24. Daly and Robinson, "Anxiety During the 2020 COVID-19 Pandemic."
25. Survey of twelve large group psychology practices on May 4, 2020.

by 65 percent who had more clients reporting greater stress, and 57 percent who had more clients reporting sleep disturbance.

Reasons for the Increase in Anxiety

We can speculate about the culprits for this increasing anxiety. During the pandemic year, the sources of anxiety were obvious: a highly contagious deadly disease, swelling political division, economic uncertainty, job loss, racial turmoil, protests, and riots. But what accounts for the increases in the years leading up to that? One likely suspect is increases in mainstream media exposure. The research supports this. Multiple studies find excessive media exposure produces higher levels of fear and anxiety.[26] This makes sense. Someone watching Fox News or MSNBC all day will have a skewed picture of the world. They'll see it as full of constant threats. This is especially true of people who consume far-right news and opinion.[27]

Social media also contributes to increases in anxiety. The more time someone spends on social media platforms and the more social media platforms they frequent, the more likely they are to struggle with anxiety.[28,29] The more visual social media platforms, like Instagram or Snapchat, were more often linked to worsening mental health.[30] It's not because you are seeing disturbing images or videos, but because you are seeing a barrage of perfect bodies on beautiful beaches or a group of friends at a downtown bar that say you'll never have what they have, never be what they are, never accomplish what they did. If that sounds adolescent, it is. That's why Instagram and Snapchat and similar platforms can be poison for teens and young adults who are striving to figure out their identity and their place in the world.

We might agree on the noxious effects of consuming too much traditional news and social media, but what if the reason for all this anxiety is the world is just getting more perilous? Is the world more dangerous than it used to be?

26. Sasaki et al., "Exposure to Media and Fear and Worry."

27. Isom et al., "Status Threat, Social Concerns, and Conservative Media," 72.

28. Vannucci et al., "Social Media Use and Anxiety."

29. Primack et al., "Use of Social Media Platforms and Symptoms of Anxiety."

30. Glazzard and Stones, "Social Media and Young People's Mental Health."

IS THE WORLD MORE DANGEROUS?

Since the turn of the century, one horrible event after another has unfolded in front of us: terrorist attacks, natural disasters, mass shootings, wars, riots. These awful moments sear into our memories, the details still fresh in our minds. Let's take a whirlwind tour of major events of the past twenty years. Imagine each of these events as they happened in real time:

In 2001, terrorists rammed commercial airliners into both World Trade Center towers and the Pentagon, killing nearly three thousand people and injuring over six thousand more. The following year, we were fighting the war in Afghanistan. The year after that, we declared war on Iraq. In 2004, one of the most devastating natural disasters in modern times occurred when a tsunami in the Indian Ocean killed 230,000 people in fourteen countries. The following year, the United States faced its own natural disaster when Hurricane Katrina devastated New Orleans, killing over eighteen hundred people and ruining entire communities.

In 2008, the subprime mortgage bubble burst, plunging the economy into the deepest recession since the Great Depression and sending many corporations and small businesses into bankruptcy. Two years later, the Gulf Water Horizon oil rig exploded, sending millions of gallons of oil into the Gulf of Mexico. Two years after that, a teenaged gunman opened fire at Sandy Hook Elementary School, killing twenty-six people, including twenty children, the worse massacre of children in our nation's history.

In 2014, Ferguson, Missouri exploded in violent protests as racial tensions erupted. Over the next several years, we saw a series of horrific terrorist attacks across Europe. In 2016, a gunman killed forty-nine people in a gay nightclub and wounded fifty-three more. Two hurricanes in 2017 submerged another major US city and Puerto Rico. The same year, a gunman rained down fire on a music festival in Las Vegas, killing sixty people and wounding over four hundred others, making it the worst mass shooting in US history. In 2018, the worst high school shooting in US history happened at Marjory Stoneman Douglas High School, killing seventeen students and faculty and injuring seventeen others. Multiple terrorist attacks in other countries marked 2019, while more mass shootings continued in the US. In 2020, a global pandemic killed millions, racial tensions boiled over leading to protests and riots in most major US cities, and wildfires burned over eight million acres in the American West.

I have just reminded you of terrorist attacks, institutional collapse, massive natural and man-made disasters, gun violence, war, racial tensions, deadly disease. They're all horrific and traumatizing. However, the question remains: Is the world more dangerous than it used to be?

The answer is no.

Consider these facts: You are 271 times more likely to die in a workplace accident than from an act of terrorism in the United States.[31] Bullying among children and teens is one-third of what it was twenty years ago.[32] The murder rate has dropped by half over the past twenty years, while the juvenile homicide rate in the US is the lowest since the 1960s.[33]

Like many people, these statistics may surprise you. There are scores of other facts that make the case the world is improving and getting safer, not deteriorating and getting worse. On Slate's *I Have to Ask* podcast, Harvard psychologist Steven Pinker said,

> Contrary to the impression that you might get from the newspapers—that we're living in a time of epidemics and war and crime—the curves show that humanity has been getting better, that we're living longer, we are fighting fewer wars, and fewer people are being killed in the wars. Our rate of homicide is down. Violence against women is down. More children are going to school, girls included. More of the world is literate. We have more leisure time than our ancestors did. Diseases are being decimated. Famines are becoming rarer, so virtually anything that you could measure that you'd want to call human well-being has improved over the last two centuries, but also over the last couple of decades.[34]

Pinker's book, *The Better Angels of Our Nature*, cites scores of references to bolster his claims.[35]

So why do we think the world is getting worse? Why is our perception of danger so wrong? If we look at the crime rate in the US over the past several decades and compare it to the public's perception of crime, we see a strong correlation between perception and reality until the turn of the century. At that point, crime kept going down, which it had since the mid-nineties, but public perception was crime was going up.[36] What caused this change in perception?

There is little question this shift corresponded with the advent of broadband Internet. As Internet speeds went from the snail's crawl of dial-up to the blazing speeds of broadband and fiber-optic, more and more people

31. Washington's Blog and Global Research, "Terrorism Statistics," lines 51–52.
32. National Center for Education Statistics, "Indicators of School Crime."
33. Gramlich, "Crime in the United States."
34. Chotiner, "Is the World Actually Getting . . . Better?," lines 15–23.
35. Pinker, *Better Angels of Our Nature*.
36. Gramlich, "Voters' Perceptions of Crime Conflict with Reality."

got their information online. We shared articles and videos with news and opinion, information and misinformation. For the first time, more people got their news from the Internet than from a television news program. The barrage of unvetted videos and screeching commentaries shaped our perception. Terrorism was getting worse. Teenagers were more violent. More kids were being abducted.

Though none of it was true, the perception shifted. As the chart illustrates, the two graph lines diverged around 2000, separated profoundly in 2002 (by thirty points), and have remained worlds apart since then.

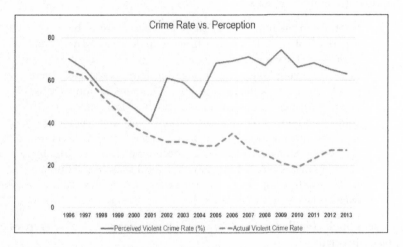

This misperception is no small issue. In *Prius or Pickup: How Answers to Four Simple Questions Explain America's Great Divide*, Jonathan Weiler and Marc Hetherington write, "Of the many factors that make up your worldview, one is more fundamental than any other in determining which side of the divide you gravitate toward: your perception of how dangerous the world is."[37]

While one study found both liberals and conservatives are prone to seeing the world as perilous,[38] other research has found those high in right-wing authoritarianism are especially likely to view the world as dangerous.[39] *The godless liberals hate the country and seek its destruction. A secret deep state cabal of blood-drinking pedophiles runs the country. Atheists have declared war on Christmas and on the entire lifestyle of all good, God-fearing*

37. Weiler and Hetherington, *Prius or Pickup?*

38. McAdams et al., "What if there were no God?"

39. Perry et al., "Dangerous and Competitive Worldviews."

Americans. Muslims at home and abroad plot our demise. Undocumented
immigrants bring violence and disease to the country.

Using an inventory called the *Belief in a Dangerous World* scale
(BDW), a series of experiments found people who saw the world as dangerous were more prone to fear and have negative attitudes towards groups
that were stereotypically associated with threats to safety, like Muslims or
undocumented immigrants.[40]

The world is not getting more dangerous, but those who perceive it
that way are prone to be more fearful. More often, they are political conservatives, of which evangelicals make up the largest segment now in the US.[41]

ARE CONSERVATIVES MORE FEARFUL?

For the duration of the pandemic, I was baffled about why more progressive people seemed so eaten up with fear, while the conservatives, especially
conservative Christians, seemed unconcerned. They flaunted their lack of
mask-wearing in public, were eager to gather in large worship services, and
refused to get vaccinated. If conservatives are more fearful than progressives, this was the opposite of what we would expect. Writing for *Vox* during
the height of the pandemic, Ezra Klein explained, "Perhaps, in laboratory
conditions, conservatives would be more afraid of the virus. But politics
doesn't play out in laboratory conditions."[42]

Prior research suggested conservatives were more anxiety-prone, but
more recent research has called that into question. There have been mixed
findings in recent years about whether conservatives are, in fact, more fearful than liberals. Later research gives us more clarity and reveals the complexity of the relationship between fear and political orientation.

In 2007, a team of social scientists called people off a random phone
list in Lincoln, Nebraska to identify individuals who held strong political
attitudes, both liberal and conservative. Forty-six people who qualified
agreed to come in to a lab at the University of Nebraska to take a survey
that gathered more specific political views. They also measured personality
traits and gathered personal demographic information. About two months
later, these same people returned to the lab to wear instruments measuring
"skin conductance," microscopic changes in sweat production that reveals

---

40. Cook et al., "Individual Differences in Belief in a Dangerous World."

41. Pew Research Center, "Religious Landscape Study."

42. Klein, "Why Are Liberals More Afraid of the Coronavirus?," lines 103–4.

a person's nervous system activation. This "electrodermal activity" (EDA) seemed to be a commonsense measure of anxiety and nervousness.[43]

In 2008, the team published their results in the prestigious journal *Science*. They found those who held more traditional conservative views had more electrodermal activity when they looked at threatening images, like an enormous spider on a frightened person's face, an open wound with maggots in it, or a dazed and bloodied individual. The researchers also exposed these participants to sudden, loud noises to see how their nervous systems responded. They found individuals who had lower physiological reactions "were more likely to support foreign aid, liberal immigration policies, pacifism, and gun control, whereas individuals displaying measurably higher physiological reactions to those same stimuli were more likely to favor defense spending, capital punishment, patriotism, and the Iraq War." The results were earthshaking. Here, for the first time, was physiological evidence of differences between conservatives and liberals. Conservatives, it seemed, were more clearly startled and responded more intensely to threats in their environment.[44]

Since that seminal study, social scientists have assumed conservatives are more fearful than liberals. Over time, though, the findings have not remained as clear-cut as the original study suggested. Newer research finds an individual's level of fear depends on what they fear, how their fear reaction is measured, and their reasons for fear.

Other EDA research followed the original study. Researchers in Europe and the US conducted replication studies with over seven times the number of participants as the original 2008 study. They also reanalyzed the data of all previously published studies. They found the original results held up in the US, but not in a European country, based on the skin conductance measure. However, when they added a self-report measure, once again, conservative individuals in both the US and in Europe reacted more negatively to threatening images. While cultural differences could have accounted for the differences in electrodermal activity, it could also be because of subtle differences in the measurement equipment, causing the researchers to say "that efforts to measure threat sensitivity specifically using EDA will be fraught with difficulty." They concluded conservatives react more to threats, but cast doubt on whether the skin conductance measures can measure this reliably.[45]

43. Oxley et al., "Political Attitudes Vary with Physiological Traits."
44. Oxley et al., "Political Attitudes Vary with Physiological Traits."
45. Osmundsen et al., "Psychophysiology of Political Ideology."

Reviewing a massive amount of data from over sixty thousand individuals who took part in the *World Values Survey*, Mark Brandt and his colleagues couldn't simply proclaim conservatives are fearful and liberals are not. Their research concluded, "the relationship is not simple" between fear and political orientation. They found liberals have more fear around economic concerns, whereas conservatives have more fear around violence, for example. Liberals also have more worries of police overreach and racist attitudes. The differences also varied by country.[46]

Other researchers in Germany used two games to come up with fascinating insights about political orientations and fear. The first game, called BeanFest, allowed participants to explore novel "beans" to determine which beans were good (which would add points) and which ones were bad (which would deduct points). They framed the game as a survival task where good beans gave them energy and bad beans drained them. If their points dropped below zero, they "died" in the game. Conservatives were more cautious, exploring fewer beans than the liberals, who were more open and adventurous. As a result, the conservatives gained more negative attitudes about the bad beans, while the liberals had more balanced attitudes. This would seem to support the notion that fear leads conservatives to be more cautious.[47]

However, the researchers added a twist. They created a variant of the game called StockFest, which was identical to the previous game, but with stocks instead of beans. They framed this game as being about wealth vs. bankruptcy, not as a willingness to explore novel or uncertain objects. Buying good stocks increased wealth points and buying bad stocks decreased wealth and eventually led to bankruptcy if their points dropped below zero. Here researchers found the exact opposite pattern. The conservatives were much more adventurous in exploring stocks and liberals were more cautious. They concluded, "The assumption that conservatives are more resistant to social change than liberals is true only with some political and societal issues but reverses with other issues."[48]

We have to be cautious about drawing too big of a conclusion about a game, but we shouldn't miss the point: subtle changes can evoke big differences in what people might fear. Changing a game from a survival task with unfamiliar beans to a wealth-accumulating task with familiar stocks resulted in big behavioral changes from both liberals and conservatives.

46. Brandt et al., "Association Between Threat and Politics."
47. Fiagbenu et al., "Political Ideology and Attitude Formation."
48. Fiagbenu et al., "Political Ideology and Attitude Formation."

Researchers at Northwestern University asked both liberals and conservatives who were active churchgoers to imagine what the world would be like if there was no God. They found conservatives envisioned a world without God as one in which governments fall apart, humans run wild with unrestrained violent and sexual urges, and chaos reigns. The liberals imagined a world without God as lifeless, barren, and meaningless. The researchers concluded Christian conservatives in the United States are more fearful of chaos and disorder, while Christian liberals are more fearful of emptiness and a loss of meaning.[49]

One of the study's co-authors, psychology professor Dan McAdams, told *Science Daily*, "Social scientists long have assumed that liberals are more rational and less fearful than conservatives, but we find both groups view the world as a dangerous place. It's just that their fears emerge differently."[50] Liberals, they concluded, saw their faith as something that fills them up and gives them meaning, whereas conservatives see their faith as something that brings order to the world.

The emphasis on order and hierarchy is an essential part of conservative Christians' experience and expression of faith. When asked why he believes wives should submit to their husbands, I heard one evangelical preacher say, "God is a God of order. He brings order and he has an order to things." Repeatedly, we hear talk of order, hierarchy, and control in evangelical churches. Psychologists have long known a need for order and control is usually a defense against anxiety and fear.[51] If you can order your environment, you can feel safer and in control. As with any issue, it becomes easy to find biblical support for requirements of submission, hierarchy, and obedience to authority. *Followers comply with leaders. Children obey parents. Wives submit to husbands. Slaves respect masters.*

Aspects of obedience and authority, order and control, are not always bad, of course, but they loom large in evangelical theology. This makes sense if their faith is used to meet an underlying need for order and control. This need for order and control and a resistance to change are part of the psychological makeup of conservatives.[52] Ezra Klein writes, "Conservatives are psychologically tuned to see threat, and so they fear change. Liberals are tuned to prize change, and so they downplay threat."[53]

49. McAdams et al., "What if there were no God?"

50. Northwestern University, "Conservatives Fear Chaos; Liberals Fear Emptiness," lines 3–6.

51. Gagné and Radomsky, "Manipulating beliefs about losing control."

52. Carlucci et al., "Does a Fundamentalist Mindset Predict a State or Trait Anxiety?"

53. Klein, "Why Are Liberals More Afraid of the Coronavirus?," lines 28–30.

There is reason to be cautious about the original 2008 electrodermal study that convinced many that conservatives are more fearful in the face of threats. Despite the caution, other methods of measuring differences in fearfulness have bolstered support for the notion that conservatives may be more prone to fear reactions and anxiety. Researchers at University College London Institute of Cognitive Neuroscience used structural MRI data to compare the brains of ninety liberal and conservative individuals. They found liberals had greater volume in the anterior cingulate cortex, a part of the brain that helps regulate intense emotion. They found conservatives had increased volume of the right amygdala, responsible for reacting to threats. The larger the amygdala, presumably the more reactive a person is likely to be.[54]   *scientific data*

There are fearful emotions, which can be automatic reactions, as well as fearful thoughts. As with fearful emotions, there are some key differences in how liberals and conservatives react to fearful thoughts. One series of three experiments found conservatives are better at a thinking process called "response inhibition," which refers to suppressing thoughts that conflict with existing information. Liberals are better at "response updating," which refers to constant revision of beliefs and knowledge based on new information. This process allows liberals to be more mentally flexible and open, allowing them to regulate their emotional reactions better in the face of uncertain or threatening information. This is not true for all liberal-minded people, of course, but it suggests there are some important differences in how liberals and conservatives process potential threats.[55]

In another excellent study, Daniel Fessler of UCLA asked nearly a thousand adults from across the political spectrum to rate how strongly they believed in sixteen statements. They were told "some" but not all the statements were accurate. They didn't know fourteen out of the sixteen statements were made up. Examples of the scary false statements included: terrorist incidents in the US have gone up since 9/11, a drunk passenger can open an airliner door mid-flight, criminals can read your personal information from a hotel keycard, and kale contains levels of toxic heavy metals. They also mixed in some positive but false statements, including people who own cats live longer than those who don't. Conservatives were more willing to believe the threatening but false statements, while liberals had a more balanced skepticism between the positive and the scary statements. Even within the group, though, there were differences. When Fessler and his colleagues grouped the traditionalists into social/cultural

54. Kanai et al., "Political Orientations Correlated with Brain Structure."

55. Buechner et al., "Political Ideology and Executive Functioning."

conservatives or fiscal conservatives, they found those aligned as social and cultural conservatives were more likely to believe the threatening comments, while the fiscal conservatives were not.[56]

Conservatives and liberals may have different-looking brains, different cognitive styles, and different internal biases, but external forces also play a major role in their level of fearfulness. A study by the *Columbia Journalism Review* found that political polarization is more common among conservatives than liberals and is fed by higher volumes of exaggeration and misinformation emanating from right-wing news outlets.[57] According to Andy Norman of Carnegie Mellon University, author of *Mental Immunity*, "fearmongering is now the defining feature of American conservatism. Socialists aim to destroy our way of life. The government is planning to seize your guns. Secularists will steal your freedom to worship. Gays will destroy the institution of marriage. BLM protesters will burn down your neighborhood. Cognitive scientists call what Republican strategists do 'amygdala hijacking,' after the brain module that responds to fear." He adds, "Brains manipulated in this way lose the capacity for reasoned reflection."[58]

EVANGELICALS AND FEAR

Neither conservatives nor liberals are immune to fear, but an abundance of evidence from psychological studies and brain scans finds conservatives are more prone to fearfulness and anxiety. Though there is not much daylight between white political conservatives and white evangelicals, they are not synonymous. However, we can assume what is true of most conservatives regarding fear is true of most (but not all) white evangelicals since there is so much overlap between the two groups.

We also know certain spiritual beliefs can foretell one's fear of danger and harm. For example, the Chapman University Survey of American Fears found a belief in the devil or demons increased a person's fear of crime.[59] Why? The research team concluded that people who believed evil was active in the world became more expectant and fearful of malevolent motives and actions from other humans. Someone who has absolute belief in the existence of demonic forces scores, on average, twenty-two points higher on measures of crime-related fears than someone who does not hold these

56. Fessler et al., "Political Orientation Predicts Credulity."

57. Benkler et al., "Right-Wing Media Ecosystem Altered Media Agenda."

58. Norman, "Cause of America's Post-Truth Predicament," lines 16–21.

59. Bader et al., *Fear Itself.*

beliefs. The active presence of evil and the idea of the world descending into chaos and horror go hand in hand.

Given their elevated fears about the condition of the world and the moral decline of the country, how do white evangelicals deal with fear? There are at least three ways: spiritual bypass, terror management, and authoritarianism.

Spiritual Bypass

The mom of a client came to the beginning of the session to explain why they had to cancel the next appointment.

"My mother died unexpectedly," she said, "so we're going to Michigan for the memorial service."

"I'm so sorry to hear that," I said.

"Well, God knows what he's doing," she said with a forced smile. "His plans are not my plans."

"Were you close with her?" I asked.

"Oh, yes, we'd talk on the phone at least twice a week. She was my best friend." Her face was still covered with a vague grin.

"That must be a big loss for you and for the grandchildren," I said.

"I'm just glad to know she's in heaven, dancing with Jesus," she replied.

You've had similar conversations with Christian friends or family members that leave you with a knot in your stomach. Something feels wrong. You might not even disagree with any statement or sentiment, but the emotional experience seems off. The person is using their faith as a defense, as a shield against unpleasant emotions. We call this process *spiritual bypass.*

Spiritual bypassing involves the use of spiritual explanations or strategies to avoid dealing with challenging emotional issues. First described by John Welwood in his book *Toward a Psychology of Awakening*, he showed how people can use spiritual and religious ideas and practices to sidestep difficult emotional struggles. This can happen when processing old losses and traumas or attempting to bolster shaky self-esteem, but gets expressed as minimizing one's own needs and feelings. Those who engage in spiritual bypassing might pretend all is well when it isn't and get angry or frustrated when faced with contrary facts.[60]

Craig Cashwell and his colleagues asked 339 students at two large public universities to rate themselves on a series of personality and spiritual measures. They found those who use spiritual bypass more often seem to be

---

60. Welwood, *Toward a Psychology of Awakening*.

high on general measures of spirituality, like Bible study or prayer. However, they also endorse higher levels of both narcissism and what psychologists term "alexithymia," a form of excessive emotional restrictiveness where people cannot describe what they are feeling. These are people who go to church, read their Bible, and pray, but they also find it hard or impossible to know what they are feeling. They also are more prone to think they are spiritually special and superior. The researchers write, "Spiritual bypass has been hypothesized to manifest in a number of ways, such as extreme external locus of control and abdication of personal responsibility, spiritual obsession, and the repression of emotions, as well as spiritual narcissism— an 'I'm enlightened and you're not' syndrome."[61]

Though the research on spiritual bypassing is sparse, consistent conclusions have emerged. People who rely on spiritual bypass to cope with anxiety are more emotionally repressed, detached, and blind to their own failures. They talk in "let go and let God" language. Spiritual bypass also leads to more controlling behavior, addictions, and failure to take personal responsibility. According to one author, "spiritual bypass compromises long-term spiritual well-being because it leaves the process of spiritual development incomplete."[62]

People who use spiritual bypass have less healthy, less engaged relationships. They have great difficulty being empathetic toward others who are struggling, which, in turn, promotes narcissistic traits. They suffer greater emotional problems, being more prone to chronic negative emotions and sometimes even obsessive-compulsive symptoms. It's not uncommon for those with a personal history of trauma or neglect to use spiritual bypassing as a way of protecting themselves against upsetting thoughts, feelings, or memories.

Spiritual bypass causes people to get stuck emotionally, resulting in less spiritual growth and greater emotional immaturity. They rely on magical thinking or over-spiritualized solutions to problems in their life.

Used in short-term, highly limited amounts, spiritual bypass can be an effective way of coping with stress and uncertainty during overwhelming times. However, when it is more ongoing and frequent, it becomes an unhealthy strategy. For white evangelicals who use spiritual bypass as a reflexive reaction to painful situations, it becomes an unsophisticated defensive strategy to avoid sadness, anger, or fear.

61. Cashwell et al., "Spiritual Bypass."
62. Picciotto and Fox, "Experts' Perspectives on Spiritual Bypass."

Terror Management

In 1973, anthropologist Ernest Becker won the Pulitzer Prize for his book *The Denial of Death*, in which he argued that most human behavior is ultimately a series of efforts to avoid or fend off the inevitability of death. The looming certainty of death, he suggested, is so strong we spend our whole lives trying to manage it. For Becker, creating culture, developing a worldview, exploring values, and practicing religion are all efforts to contend with the certainty of our death, even if we are not always fully aware of the connection. He wrote, "The idea of death, the fear of it, haunts the human animal like nothing else; it is a mainspring of human activity—activity designed largely to avoid the fatality of death, to overcome it by denying in some way that it is the final destiny for man."[63]

In Becker's framework, we all have a need to think of ourselves as beings of value who will live on forever. The real notion of death, though, strikes hard at that desire, so people spend their lives trying to delay it, avoid it, or create enduring monuments to their lives that will outlast them forever.

Becker's work was the foundation for what psychology calls "terror management theory." TMT says our biological imperative of staying alive collides with our realization that we will die. This awareness produces terror. In response, we believe certain things and do certain actions to manage these intense feelings.[64] This terror of death's inevitability might drive us to leave behind something important to symbolize that we were here, that we existed, that our lives mattered. It moves us to build skyscrapers and synagogues, it inspires us to create families and fraternities, it compels us to form universities and governments. What we choose to leave behind or invest ourselves in varies, but the drive is the same.

One of those actions is to align with a group that has a clear mission and purpose. If I am a good citizen, a vital member of a group, a contributing part of a team, then I feel like I am part of something bigger than myself, something that will outlast me. In doing so, I infuse my life with some meaning and leave a mark that will survive me. As a result, I'm not as likely to worry about my death or fixate on my mortality. The symbolic power of their group helps me ward off the terror associated with my inevitable death.

A fear of death drives people to see their group as special and likely to leave a lasting positive impression of the world. Research tells us when people are reminded of their own mortality, they also embrace their values and positions more vigorously. This can drive them to display more prejudice

63. Becker, *Denial of Death*, 17.
64. Jonas et al., "Normative Conduct and Terror-Management Theory."

and hostility toward those outside their group, as a way of justifying the uniqueness of their chosen group.[65]

Terror management theory says we are compelled to affiliate with an enduring and special group. We also feel driven to leave something of value behind. Years ago, someone visiting for dinner asked if they could see a copy of one of my books. I realized I didn't have one in the house. In fact, I wasn't even sure I had one at my office. Days later, I ordered copies of all my books and sealed each stack in plastic wrap. I placed all four collections in separate boxes, one for each of my children. Though I hoped my passing would be decades later, I wanted them to have something that represented a tangible legacy of mine after I was gone. I realize the impulse to write a book is, at least in part, about that. It's a way of leaving something behind that endures, almost as if it guarantees you live on in someone's memory. It's about the possibility of making a lasting mark in the world in some significant way.

Even having children is a way of living on. Most of these impulses are not conscious for most of us, but they are real and powerful. At some level, whether we are fully aware of it, each of us knows we are mortal, that our lives are temporary. The thought of ceasing to exist is terrifying.

The motives for a person's faith make a big difference in how they respond to the certainty of death. One study asked people to write a short essay about their own death or to imagine their own funeral. Afterwards, the participants were asked questions to see if writing the essay made them more or less committed to their own worldview. The researchers noticed differences between groups of people based on the reasons why they held their personal faith. People who had more of an intrinsic faith, where their faith is about a connection with God for its own sake and not as a way of meeting psychological or social needs, didn't respond defensively when reminded of their own inevitable death. By contrast, those who used their faith primarily for comfort from anxiety, or a need to have a bigger social network, reacted more defensively.[66] A healthier, more authentic faith helped a person manage the terror of death, while an unhealthy, self-centered faith made a person more rigid and defensive when contemplating their own passing.

In another study, the more fundamentalist a person was in their faith, the more they focused on end times and apocalyptic beliefs when asked to contemplate their own death.[67] For them, their inflexible faith required them to focus on their rapture and rescue, the vanquishing of enemies, and triumphalism as ways of coping with their inevitable death.

---

65. Jonas et al., "Normative Conduct and Terror-Management Theory."

66. Kashima, "Culture and Terror Management."

67. Routledge et al., "Death and End Times."

These and other studies tell us two things. First, people with healthy, intrinsic faith meet the terror of death with greater confidence and lower anxiety. Second, less healthy, extrinsic faith meets the terror of death with more defensiveness and fear.

Terror management says when faced with our own mortality, we all take action to manage the terror of inevitable death. Some of those actions might be good and noble, like creating something beautiful—art, organizations, programs—of enduring value or by investing in the lives of other people. Some of those actions might be unhealthy and uncharitable, like becoming more hostile toward those outside of their group or more fearful and entrenched in hostile worldviews. What the research suggests is white evangelicals are prone to either, depending on the motives for their faith.

Authoritarianism

Founded in 1868, First Baptist Dallas boasts over fourteen thousand members and operates broadcasting outlets, a Christian school, and a small college. The megachurch has a historic role in the history of evangelicalism. One of its senior pastors, W. A. Criswell, was a two-term president of the Southern Baptist Convention, author of fifty-four books, and an influential figure in evangelical culture. Billy Graham joined his church in 1958 during the week of one of his Dallas crusades and remained a member there for over fifty years. The church's current senior pastor, Robert Jeffress, is known for his regular appearances on Fox News and his early support for candidate Donald Trump.

In a March 2016 interview with Julie Lyons, Jeffress spoke of his affection for Trump, saying, "I couldn't care less about a leader's temperament or his tone or his vocabulary. Frankly, I want the meanest, toughest son-of-a-gun I can find. And I think that's the feeling of a lot of evangelicals. They don't want Caspar Milquetoast as the leader of the free world."[68]

When Jeffress was speaking for "a lot of evangelicals"—which he undoubtedly was—he was describing an affinity for authoritarianism, where a strongman, a savior of sorts, appears and crushes their enemies. We have not always described it with this term, but authoritarianism is as old as humankind, as ancient as the earliest civilizations. In more modern times, it has become more sophisticated, but its primitive heart remains intact.

We've established that both liberals and conservatives experience high levels of fear and anxiety, but research over the decades has confirmed this

---

68. Lyons, "Jeffress Wants a Mean 'Son of a Gun' for President," lines 39–44.

progression: when conservatives, including religious conservatives, perceive danger and feel afraid, they are more likely to adopt more increasingly conservative ideologies. Ultraconservative ideologies then cause people to embrace authoritarian policies and leaders in the face of persistent threats, real or imagined.[69] This happens cross-culturally. The specifics may be different, but the general process is the same.

Researchers Gary Leak and Brandy Randall assert, "being religious does not insulate one from authoritarianism, nor does it condemn one to those same tendencies."[70] Not all conservative Christians are authoritarians. However, it is common for conservative people to slide into authoritarianism when their fear increases.

Early experiences, personality traits, and adult life stressors and threats all play a role in who becomes authoritarian. Some researchers believe authoritarianism is the product of deep insecurity resulting from excessive parental control and restricted autonomy in childhood.[71] While there are clear links between attachment insecurity and authoritarianism, this is a far-too-simple explanation. Often childhood experiences pave the way for future authoritarian attitudes and behavior, but we know individuals and groups become authoritarian following painful and overwhelming events. While there may be vulnerabilities that take root in childhood, there are often circumstances later in life that can tip someone toward authoritarianism.

Defining and assessing authoritarianism has spurred much debate among psychologists and other social scientists. In furthering our understanding of his essential concept, we owe an enormous debt to two men who were, not coincidentally, personally affected by the rise of Nazism in Germany.

Born at the end of World War II, the culture of his homeland shredded for decades to come, German scholar Detlef Oesterrich published extensively on authoritarianism. The state of research on authoritarian personalities disappointed him. He wrote, "A stable relationship between the characteristics of an authoritarian personality and corresponding overt behavior has not been established." However, he eventually argued he had developed survey instruments that found "high correlations between authoritarianism and indicators for orientation toward and support for the extreme political right, denial of women's and immigrant's rights."[72] Since then, others have consistently assessed authoritarian traits and tendencies.

69. Jost et al., "Politics of Fear."
70. Leak and Randall, "Link Between Right-Wing Authoritarianism and Religiousness."
71. Sochos, "Authoritarianism, Trauma, and Insecure Bonds."
72. Oesterreich, "New Approach and Measure of the Authoritarian Personality," 280.

Theodor Adorno was fired from his position as a sociology professor at a German university in 1933 because he represented a double offense to the Nazis: he was Jewish and his academic work challenged authoritarianism. In 1944, a year before the end of World War II, an international group asked Adorno and a team of scholars to determine how an entire society could fall into the grip of authoritarianism so firmly it permitted the murder of millions.[73] Six years later, in 1950, they completed a five-volume set entitled *The Authoritarian Personality,* with Adorno serving as the lead researcher. Gathering mountains of data from previous research, structured interviews, self-report instruments, and psychological tests, they found nine traits that composed the authoritarian personality. I've changed some of the language because the older terms are no longer in use, but the meaning remains the same:

- Conventionalism—rigid conformity to traditional, majority-culture values

- Submission—obedient, unquestioning, uncritical adherence to authoritarian leaders

- Aggression—vigilance toward those who violate traditional values; quick to judge, condemn, and punish those outside the norm

- Anti-imaginative—disdain for the artistic, creative, imaginative, and tender-minded; resistance to new ideas

- Superstition—belief in mystical and overly spiritual determinants of one's fate

- Toughness—preoccupation with dominance vs. submissiveness, strong vs. weak, power vs. impotence

- Cynicism—a hostile view of others; belief that most people would lie or cheat if they could

- Projectivity—belief that dangerous and outlandish things are always happening in the world (thought to be a projection of their own impulses)

- Sexual Preoccupation—intense preoccupation with the sexual behavior of others, especially sexual minorities and those who engage in nontraditional sexual behavior[74]

Adorno's research led him to conclude authoritarians are often weak men disguised as strong men. They are full of fear, uncomfortable sexual

73. Wilcock, "Negative Identity."
74. Adorno et al., *Authoritarian Personality.*

impulses, violent desires, and weakness, yet they cannot acknowledge these in themselves, so they see others as hostile and threatening. They feel justified in lashing out, bullying, and mistreating those less powerful. I argue Adorno was describing a form of vulnerable narcissism.

Later, other researchers elaborated on the essence of authoritarianism. Psychologist Bob Altemeyer conducted dozens of studies on authoritarian personalities and boiled his conclusions down to three consistent themes. He found authoritarians are nearly always:

- Conventional—they fight to uphold traditional, conservative values.

- Submissive—they believe people must be obedient to proper (as they deem it) authority.

- Aggressive—they are hostile and advocate forcefulness to enforce adherence to these values.[75]

It is this hostility and promotion of violence to enforce compliance that most clearly separates right-wing authoritarians from nonauthoritarian conservatives.

In his book on the psychological treatment of authoritarian personalities, *Tough Guys and True Believers*, John M. Robertson describes the authoritarian as being high on needs for power, dominance over others, exploitation, and manipulation, but low on empathy and equal regard for others.[76]

As one of the country's most experienced living experts on the psychological treatment of authoritarian personalities, Robertson emphasizes both the similarities and important differences between authoritarian leaders and followers. Though we think of authoritarians as being strongmen leaders, most authoritarian personalities are followers who are submissive toward those strongmen or charismatic leaders and blindly follow them. We see this in politics and in churches.

Nothing illustrates this better than a series of three studies involving over twenty thousand subjects. Researchers asked participants to what extent they believed their future had been predetermined. Those who believed their futures had been predestined scored higher on authoritarianism. Why? Because they believe their futures are determined by the power of outside forces or the will of powerful leaders. They might have a role to play in the plan, but the direction comes from a higher authority or unstoppable forces.[77]

---

75. Sibley and Duckitt, "Personality and Prejudice Meta-Analysis."

76. Robertson, *Tough Guys and True Believers*.

77. Costello et al., "Authoritarianism-Related Traits and Belief in Determinism."

One study gave 332 people the OCEAN personality test and two other inventories of authoritarianism. They looked at not only the big five traits, but the secondary traits within each one. Here's some of what they found:

- Both authoritarian leaders and followers were very low on facets of openness and agreeableness (a finding supported by another meta-analysis of seventy-one studies, as well.)[78]

- Authoritarian leaders, but not the followers, were low on the warmth and straightforwardness, suggesting they were more prone to flatter, manipulate, and deceive.

- Authoritarian leaders were not at all altruistic, suggesting self-centeredness and a lack of generosity.

- Authoritarian leaders were not compliant, indicating they were more interpersonally competitive and aggressive.

- Authoritarian followers were low on openness to ideas. They were not willing to consider new thoughts or ideas. Even if they were highly intelligent, they preferred only to pay attention to specific sets and sources of information.[79]

Regarding this point, the unbending attitudes of authoritarians often have little to do with intelligence. A series of two fascinating studies found those high in Right-Wing Authoritarianism (RWA) didn't do as well on some critical thinking tasks, not because they couldn't do the task, but because they weren't motivated to perform well. With no incentive for their performance, those high in RWA performed more poorly on these tasks than others. Here's the twist: when they were offered money, their performance was significantly better. In short, they could do the task, but they just didn't care enough to try hard until researchers gave them a payoff. The researchers concluded the issue was not cognitive ability but their low motivation to reason through the tasks.[80] Why would that be?

They offered two explanations. First, right-wing individuals may view critical thinking negatively, seeing it as a challenge to the group's authority and in conflict with the message of group loyalty. The second reason is that low critical thinking might be a strategic advantage to limit their analytical and reasoning skills. This makes sense if their goal is to avoid information, ideas, and conclusions that might threaten their view of the world. In other

78. Sibley and Duckitt, "Personality and Prejudice Meta-Analysis."
79. Akrami and Ekehammar, "Right-Wing Authoritarianism Roots."
80. Burger et al., "Role of Motivation in Cognitive Performance."

words, they try not to think about anything that might challenge their al-ready established ideas.[81]

Some people have authoritarian personality structures that do not change, while others are less authoritarian in normal circumstances, but can become authoritarian followers under certain conditions. For them, the flight to authoritarianism is a desperate, fearful response to threat.

Authoritarians have some fight-or-flight responses to threat that may be tough to discern, however. When a conservative experiencing threat supports crackdowns and strongmen who will squash dissent, he is engaging in an authoritarian *fight* response. Likewise, when he supports or participates in right-wing extremism, he is also having a *fight* response. However, if he gets fearful and clings to the status quo, resists social change, or becomes more close-minded, he is having authoritarian *flight* responses.

In either instance, fight or flight, fear negatively affects his information processing. Fearfulness narrows his attention, causing him to laser-focus on the perceived threat. This takes up a tremendous amount of mental bandwidth, which makes the cognitive resources needed for memory and higher-order thinking less available. His brain's hyperfocus and state of alarm impairs his judgment and decision-making. A person in this state would be expected to be rigid in his views and willing to do things he might not ordinarily do.

Fear can keep us safe, but it can also cause us to act in dangerous or self-centered ways, including a descent into authoritarianism. Among evan-gelicals, we find a consistent progression that starts with fear, moves to more conservative, right-wing attitudes, then often ends in authoritarianism.

SOCIALIZED TO FEAR

While fear can be an automatic physiological response, it can also be a so-cialized response, which explains why different groups fear different things. Sociologist Andrew Whitehead, author of *Taking America Back for God*, told me, "Fear is such a powerful motivator for humans. What we fear is collectively defined and described. *The groups that they're a part of signal to them what to fear. What they fear is collectively decided upon* (italics mine)." Whitehead and other researchers conclude our fears are decided by our group. Those like-minded people with whom we affiliate, whether in person or online, socialize us to fear. If the group says we should fear the govern-ment will take our guns, we fear government intrusion. If our group says we

---

81. Burger et al., "Role of Motivation in Cognitive Performance."

should fear vaccines, then we find evidence to support that position. Our group tells us where to place our fears.

Both liberals and conservatives, Christians and atheists, have their fears, but, as Whitehead says, each individual is socialized by their group as to what they should fear. For many evangelicals, they were socialized not to fear COVID, but to be afraid of government overreach. They are not that afraid of climate change, but terrified of allowing their child to learn about institutional racism in public schools. They don't fear the inordinate amount of guns in the country, but fear Muslims and undocumented immigrants.

Evangelicals don't fear pandemics or mass shootings or irreversible climate change. They fear any group or social force that might displace them. Because they have long held power and control, threats from usurpers evoke the biggest fear. They have a core fear they will be pushed aside, no longer at the head of the table.

Evangelical anxiety about being displaced, though, is rarely presented as fear. It is packaged as action that comes from a theological or moral imperative. For example, we must oppose critical race theory, not because we fear our children being exposed to the reality of historic and systemic racism, not because it says the church has been complicit, and not because it implies power should be shifted, but because it is "Marxist," "anti-Christian," and a "destructive heresy." As a Christian, then, we have no other choice but to oppose it to preserve the integrity of the church and to fight for the gospel.

White Christians might deal with fear by spiritualizing it (spiritual bypass) or doubling down on their commitment to the church and its causes (terror management), but they also might become more authoritarian in their attitudes, willing to detour around democratic processes in favor of strong leaders who will protect them and keep them in control. Unfortunately, that is what we have seen with increasing frequency among white Christians who drape their desire to hold on to power with "biblical" justifications.

In *Hope Against Darkness*, Richard Rohr and John Feister write, "The best and most convincing disguise for fear is virtue itself, or godliness. Then it never looks like fear. For fear to survive, it must look like reason, prudence, common-sense, intelligence, the need for social order, morality, religion, obedience, justice or even spirituality. It always works. What better way to veil vengeance than to call it justice? . . . Only those practiced at letting go, see fear for the impostor that it is. To be trapped inside of your small ego is always to be afraid."[82]

---

82. Rohr and Feister, *Hope Against Darkness*, 150.

CHAPTER 4

Nothing Can Be Changed
Until It Is Faced

The Denial of Personal Racism in the Church

"Not everything that is faced can be changed, but nothing can be changed until it is faced."

—JAMES BALDWIN

NINE AND A HALF minutes.

The video is almost too horrible to watch. A white officer presses his knee into the neck of a Black man, George Floyd, in Minneapolis. He leaves it there for over eight minutes, despite Floyd's pleas, despite Floyd calling out for his momma, despite Floyd going limp and unresponsive. Floyd, a forty-six-year-old father of five, a big man who briefly played college basketball, a man who lived a complicated story, who had trouble throughout his life, but had volunteered for various ministries over the years, who had mentored young men who were at risk for trouble of their own, was dead.

Nine and a half minutes.

Imagine a sturdy man with his knee dug into your neck nine and a half minutes. Imagine the terror of beginning to lose consciousness, fearing you might die.

George Floyd was being charged with trying to pass off a counterfeit twenty dollar bill. He paid for it with his life.

Years prior to his murder, he had recorded an anti-gun violence video. "I've got my shortcomings and my flaws and I ain't better than nobody else," he says, then adds, "I love you and God loves you."[1] His friend Ronnie Lillard talked about George's early mistakes, saying, "When he got out of that (trouble), I think the Lord greatly impacted his heart."[2]

After the murder of George Floyd, protests spilled over into rioting and looting. News outlets showed terrifying footage of a burning police precinct in Minneapolis. Real-time footage of court buildings and broadcast centers and businesses being trashed in cities across the country shocked viewers. The world was on fire and rage was on vivid display.

Like many, the scenes of violence alarmed conservative white Christians, yet, in keeping with their troubled history with race, they focused on the riots and looting and minimized the catalytic event. In a survey by the Public Religion Research Institute, white Christians believed the police killings of Black citizens were merely "isolated events" and nothing more.[3] Their solution has been to say the US is "not a racist country" and change the subject. In a 2020 study, a full two-thirds of white evangelicals said they were unmotivated to address racial injustice in our society.[4] The white Christian antidote to racial injustice: decide racism is no longer a problem and move on.

The burden, in their view, wasn't on the country to address deeper racial issues or on the church to grapple with its legacy of racism, but on Black people to behave better. "Peacefully protest all you want, but don't resort to violence" was their refrain. They conveniently forgot how much they had dogged Colin Kaepernick for doing just that when he knelt before NFL games. Pastor of the megachurch First Baptist Dallas, Rev. Robert Jeffress, said, "These players ought to be thanking God that they live in a country where they're not only free to earn millions of dollars every year, but they're also free from the worry of being shot in the head for taking the knee like they would be in North Korea." He went on to say kneeling during the national anthem was "disrespecting our country."[5]

Since before the civil rights movement, white evangelicals have viewed peaceful protests about racial injustice with disdain. These demonstrations

1. Henao et al., "For George Floyd," lines 7–10.
2. Henao et al., "For George Floyd," lines 28–29.
3. Vandermaas-Peeler et al., "2018 American Values Survey."
4. Barna, "Black Practicing Christians Are Twice As Likely."
5. May, "Trump Pastor on 'Fox & Friends,'" lines 9–12.

rarely result in much self-reflection or talk of change among them. They are tired of all the talk about race and racial division. *We've dealt with our racism and it's time to move on*, they say. They reject claims that organizations and systems perpetuate racial inequality. They also seem blind to their own personal racism, even when it is on full display. Brief snapshots of four different Nashville-area Christian schools illustrate this well.

SAME CITY, FOUR EXAMPLES

Nashville is one of the great cities in the country, with a nearly unmatched vibrancy. I was at a concert where the performer told the crowd, "If you don't live here, don't move here. Feel free to come back and visit, but we don't need any more people living here." At the time, about eighty-two people a day were moving to the city, putting it on pace to add thirty thousand each year.[6] It's a town people love. Most of the city is progressive and welcoming, but, like many cities in the South and elsewhere, there remains a vein of racism that still runs deep throughout it. One place where this abides is in many of its Christian schools where the old guard holds on tightly.

One Christian school in Nashville hired a Black woman as a dean of diversity. Her job was to facilitate open discussions about racial inequality among its mostly white student body.[7] When she did, the roof caved in. Many parents, including a prominent country music star, reacted with shouts of outrage, forcing the woman to leave her position.[8]

White Christians are uneasy with discussions of racial injustice. They don't want their children to hear a narrative of how white people—especially white Christians—are complicit in the sins of racism. A white father told me he removed his son from another Nashville-area Christian school because a chapel speaker made the students sit in silence for the same amount of time George Floyd was under the knee.

"I've never heard of anything so ridiculous in my life," the man told me, his face red with anger. "Why would you put those kids through something like that?"

It was almost as if the kids at the predominantly white Christian school had suffered more than George Floyd. The man's son was an upperclassman who had been a student at the school for many years, found most of his friends there, played sports there. Yet the father's discomfort with his son having to contemplate racial injustice infuriated him enough to pull the

---

6. Ashton, "Moving to Nashville," lines 8–9.

7. Benkarski, "Nashville Star Outraged Over Teaching of White Privilege."

8. Ramirez, "John Rich Is Angry About Dean of Intercultural Development."

boy out of a school that was 94 percent white and averaged only one Black student per grade.

Christian school alumni at another school in the Nashville area recounted when one teacher held up a stick wrapped in black tape and asked students to guess what it was supposed to be. After a few wrong guesses, the teacher said, "No, it's an emaciated Black woman." The class sat stunned, except for a smattering of nervous laughter. The former student wrote, "This joke was made more than once that year." Another alumni of the school wrote about how this same teacher pressured a white student to read the n-word out loud from a passage in *To Kill a Mockingbird* while the only Black student in the class squirmed in their chair. The teacher took the book from the student and read the passage himself, saying the n-word out loud, the alumni wrote, "and pointed at the Black student in our class while doing so."

And at yet another Nashville-area Christian school, one student painted a Black Lives Matter picture for an art show. Another student painted a Blue Lives Matter piece for the same show. The student who painted the Black Lives Matter work was told they could not exhibit the piece because it was "too political," but the other student who had painted the Blue Lives Matter piece had theirs displayed at the show.

All four examples—ousting of the diversity dean, withdrawing the son from school, making racist jokes, and omitting the BLM painting from the art show—were from four different Christian schools in the city where I live. Nashville is no more racist than many other cities and towns in the country.[9] These are just local examples, so imagine this multiplied thousands of times across the country in Christian schools, churches, and other Christian organizations.

RECKONING WITH THE RACISM OF OUR PAST

Robert P. Jones, founder of the Public Religion Research Institute, was raised in the Southern Baptist tradition and attended both a Southern Baptist college and seminary. In my conversation with him, he said he didn't hear any significant conversation about the white supremacist connections of his spiritual lineage until young adulthood. In his American Book Award-winning work, *White Too Long*, he states, "It is time—indeed, well beyond time—for white Christians in the United States to reckon with the racism of our past and the willful amnesia of our present."[10]

9. *World Population Review*, "Most Racist Cities in America 2021."
10. Jones, *White Too Long*, 6.

He meticulously makes the case that "white Christian churches have not just been complacent; they have not only been complicit; rather, as the dominant cultural power in America, they have been responsible for constructing and sustaining a project to protect white supremacy and resist black equality. This project has framed the entire American story."[11]

Almost invariably, white Christians bristle at any suggestion they might be racist, even as they hold racist attitudes. The father who yanked his kid from school made a point of telling me he "ain't no racist." Why did he remove his seventeen-year-old son from a school community the boy had been part of his entire academic life, where all his friends attended, and where he had been successful in class and in sports? Because a chapel speaker led a discussion about the murder of George Floyd. Is it possible this man and other white Christians are racist without being fully aware of it? If so, how is that possible?

Jones said he reflected on how race had intersected his own story as he wrote his book. He encouraged me to do the same. The experience was eye-opening, sad, and profoundly affecting. Before we answer the central question of how white evangelicals can be so warm toward Black people, yet harbor racist attitudes, I'll share how race cuts through my personal history.

HOW RACE INTERSECTS MY STORY

My family story is deeply affected by race. I could go back further, but I'll start with my father, who was part of what some have called "The Lost Class of '59." A few years after the US Supreme Court decided *Brown v. Board of Education*, a federal mandate required the public schools to integrate. In Norfolk, Virginia, where my dad had just begun his senior year, seventeen African American students were slated to enroll in the public schools. The Governor of Virginia, J. Lindsay Almond, a professing Christian who led a men's Bible study, shut down six Norfolk public schools to keep out this handful of Black students. In doing so, he denied tens of thousands of white students an education for an entire year.

My dad was one of those students. He was told to either come back the following year to complete his diploma or go elsewhere and get a GED. He chose the latter, going to the Norfolk Naval Shipyard, where he learned to be an electrician's apprentice, which he later parlayed into a long and significant career in civil service.

I never heard a racist comment in my home, but neither did I know any Black or Hispanic people. I went to a private Christian school that had one

11. Jones, *White Too Long*, 6.

Black family with one kid in my class and another in my younger brother's class. My mom was a district manager for Avon Products and worked with a good number of Filipino women who were frequently at our house. The two Black kids in my school and the occasional Filipino Avon ladies were the full depth of our exposure to diversity.

We never discussed race in our family. The topic wasn't considered taboo, but our lives had been curated to keep us away from people who differed from us, particularly Black people. My family lived in a white bubble: a white neighborhood with white neighbors, venturing out to attend a white church and a white school, playing sports with all white teammates.

In the 1970s, my private Christian school wasn't officially white, but it was functionally white. There were no teachers of color nor any administrative staff members. In my fifth grade class, they kicked out the one Black kid in my grade for misbehavior, leaving us with exactly zero students who were not white in our entire middle school. It wasn't until my tenth-grade year that we had another Black student in our all-white class. He and his brother were the entirety of diversity in my high school during those years. My old yearbooks confirm this. By my math, our small Christian high school was 99.2 percent white.

In later years, I learned many private Christian schools in the South were founded as a way for white families to avoid integration during the fifties and sixties. My stomach knotted when I discovered the year my high school was founded: 1959—the same year the Norfolk Seventeen hoped to be the first Black students to attend the all-white Norfolk public schools. The lower school had been founded the year after *Brown v. Board of Education* was filed and the upper school was established the year the public schools were compelled to integrate. The timing of both schools was not a coincidence. It reveals an undeniable intent to shelter white kids from desegregation efforts.

I never heard racist comments in my high school from teachers or students. Nothing they taught smacked of overt white supremacy. What I now realize, however, was the school served as a vehicle to keep us "precious" white kids away from "scary" Black kids without ever having to say a word about it. We weren't exposed to racist rhetoric or white supremacist ideology or cruel theology. We were simply isolated from Black people. We attended a school that had not one Black teacher, administrator, assistant, or support staff and only one Black family in a city that was 42 percent Black. It wasn't a coincidence.

Every year, the school held World Missions Week, where we were all encouraged to go overseas to places that might not have heard the gospel, including—perhaps especially—African countries. At the same time, it was actively sheltering us from Black people in our own hometown. Upon reflection, the disconnect makes little sense and was one of the most baffling aspects of my conservative evangelical upbringing. Why would conservative Christians protect their kids from Black people in their cities, but willingly send them across the world to spread the gospel to Black people?

I couldn't understand how this made sense, so I reached out to Beverly Daniel Tatum, a former university president, fellow psychologist, and author of the masterful best-selling book *Why Are All the Black Kids Sitting Together in the Cafeteria?* Why would Christians who apparently started a school to keep their white kids away from Black kids support sending their own young people to African countries?

She replied, "In my view, both actions—segregated schools in the US and missionary outreach in Africa—are rooted in assumptions of white supremacy and Black inferiority. The Black Africans were being viewed as in need of white help through salvation of Christianity—*as practiced by white people.* Offering of such help, however well-intentioned, is still rooted in assumptions of Black inferiority."

This made sense. But why work so hard—to the point of opening an entire school—to keep away from Black folks if you desire to help them, even if it is rooted in a conscious (or unconscious) assumption of white supremacy?

She continued to explain that "because the people are so far away—on another continent—there is no perceived risk of 'contamination' of white communities, schools, neighborhoods. Wanting to keep Black American children out of historically white schools and their families out of white neighborhoods is also rooted in assumptions of Black inferiority. Proximity increases concern about 'race-mixing' and potential erosion of 'whiteness.' So while the behaviors are different in expression, they are both fueled by the same race-based ideological assumptions."

My unintentional arm's-length distance from people of color continued through college and graduate school, where I didn't have a single Black or Brown friend. As strange and disgraceful as that seems now, I can't think of a moment where I challenged myself on this. My white bubble seemed normal to me.

It was only when I entered the workforce as a twenty-eight-year-old psychologist after long years of education and training that I had genuine relationships with Black people. My first job out of graduate school was for a community mental health agency that served over 90 percent African American kids and had over 80 percent African American staff. I loved my clients and my co-workers and that experience opened my eyes to how much harassment and hardship Black people endure that I never experience.

My five years in community mental health was an incredibly rich, life-changing time for me that set the stage for further insight and growth. I never suspected a decade later, I would end up having two Black children and one Brown child of my own. Having a Black son, in particular, opened up the world in a completely new way.

We adopted Daniel and Maddie from an orphanage in Liberia, West Africa, just before he turned sixteen and she was fourteen. On the day we left Monrovia for the airport, Daniel said, "I want to come back to Liberia and show them my hair and muscles."

"That's great," I said, not understanding what he meant. Did he want to return to Liberia to live? Hair? Muscles? The day was a whirlwind so I didn't ask further questions.

Later, I asked him about it and finally understood. No, he didn't want to return to Liberia to live, just to visit. Yes, he wanted to show off his hair and muscles, which was odd because he had little of either. But this was the point. In the orphanage, they buzzed his hair down close to the scalp and food was rationed so much the kids were tiny little wisps, skinny as rails. Daniel's vision for himself was to grow out his hair and pack on muscle.

Within a year, it was mission accomplished. He had a big head of hair and solid muscles. He transformed himself into quite the athletic ideal. He stood nearly six feet—about six feet four inches if you counted the hair—and eventually 185 pounds of pure muscle. He ran track, played soccer and rugby, and worked out constantly. He ran Spartan races and mud runs and 5K's, often with no idea how long the races were or what obstacles were ahead. Many times he won races outright.

Once he asked me the evening before a race if I would sign him and his friend, William, up for a "battle frog." I looked it up online and it was about eight miles long and had dozens of obstacles. The only question he asked was, "Does it have water?," because he couldn't swim. When we found out he didn't have to get in the water, I signed him and William up for the competition and they arrived the next morning without a minute of training. Some people train for weeks and months for these kinds of races. Daniel just showed up. He posted the fastest time of the day and William was the second fastest—because Daniel had basically pulled him along the entire race. So not only did he run the fastest race of the competition, he did it while dragging another friend with him—and without a minute of training.

Daniel is incredibly kind and gentle and funny, but he is also big, strong, and dark-skinned. He evokes a fearful reaction from certain people. Some people get visibly uncomfortable around him. I've seen it many times. To be clear, though, you don't have to be big and strong and Black to be treated badly in our culture. Just being Black is sufficient. I've heard the stories of countless Black men—short, tall, thin, overweight, dark-skinned, light-skinned—who have similar tales of mistreatment. While I'd been told about these experiences, I'd never seen them up close until I became Daniel's dad.

I have observed this many times over the past decade because people don't know we are together. I saw him surveilled in a drug store immediately after he walked in the door. We had eaten dinner at a Chinese restaurant and he asked if he could go to the drug store to pick up a razor. I sent him ahead of me as I finished paying for dinner. I was probably twenty seconds behind him, but by the time I walked in the door, the assistant manager had darted out from behind the counter and was following him at a distance. I watched the man watch Daniel as he peeked over the adjacent aisle to observe him. When the man realized I was watching him, he got flustered and returned to his post.

On another occasion, we were standing on the sidewalk in front of an apartment complex when a man approached Daniel and said, "This is private property. You have to leave." There were between eight and ten white people standing there, including me, but he singled out Daniel. When the man realized I was with him, he stared me down in this defiant way, as if to say, *I know I just did something racist, but what are you going to say about it?*

One summer, Daniel accepted an offer from my brother to work for him during the summer. Daniel's only condition was that he be allowed to join a gym (of course!). We took him to a local fitness center and the person working the counter said I couldn't sign him up for a membership unless I could prove he was my son. We both showed IDs with the same last name (not a common name), but the woman rejected this as proof. Then I realized my brother, who was standing beside me, had signed his own son up for a membership at the same gym without "proving" he was his dad. Why couldn't I sign up my son?

"Let me see your policy that says I have to prove this," I said.

She took out the policy book from underneath the counter and started distractedly thumbing through the pages. Her expression changed, realizing she was getting in too deep. Obviously, she couldn't find the policy of proving paternity, but she still didn't budge. The manager showed up and quickly reversed course once he realized what was happening.

These few instances illustrate just how much nonsense Black people, particularly Black males, have to deal with in our culture. However, it's in dealing with the police where these cease being annoyances and become matters of life and death.

A few years ago, Daniel came to visit me and Ellen for spring break when he was a student at UNC-Greensboro. He brought a friend with him for the week, an African American college student. I told them to be careful on the seven-hour ride here.

I was getting concerned when they had not arrived by midnight. Suddenly, I saw blue lights flashing outside my window. I looked through the blinds and saw the police had pulled over Daniel and his friend right outside our place. We live in a predominantly white part of town and the only other time I had seen cops pull over someone on our street involved two young Black guys in a car on a weekend night. I threw on some shoes and marched outside. I asked Daniel what was going on and he said the police had followed him. Daniel and his friend had driven nearly five hundred miles with no problem and in the literal one mile since they had exited the interstate, the local police pulled them over.

The officer asked who I was. I told him I was this guy's dad, pointing at Daniel, who was still seated in the car. The cop looked shocked. A very white guy with a very Black son. I asked why they had been pulled over. The officer said because they had a rear light out. I looked at the car—stopped right in front of me—and there were no missing or burnt-out lights. The cop saw me notice this, then quickly changed his story.

"I started following them and he started slowing down, which is probable cause to pull someone over," he said.

I immediately got heated, a rarity for me.

"No, you pulled them over because they are two Black men driving around here after midnight," I said.

"No, I did not," he said.

"Yes, you did!" I replied, starting what sounded like a fight between two elementary school kids.

He told me to step back onto the sidewalk, which I did. He called his supervisor, who drove to the scene quickly, arriving in a large police vehicle. After they conferred for a few minutes, the supervisor approached me and basically said, "You're accusing us of racially profiling, which is illegal," to which I said, "I know. That's why I'm mad." I explained the reason for pulling them over made no sense and was highly suspect.

They conferred again and the first officer issued this warning: "Lights required—motor vehicles." Nothing was written on the warning to indicate the car was missing a light, just that lights are "required," as if the cops were driving around doing the community service of telling drivers their cars need lights.

Had Daniel not had this run-in right outside my window, what would have happened? If he's in the wrong place with the wrong cop in the future, then how will he be treated? We shouldn't have to worry that he'll be treated unfairly or harmed by the police, but I worry about that a lot, much more for him than for my other kids combined.

The problem is this: what happened in Minneapolis to George Floyd rarely happens to me or anyone who looks like me—and happens way too often to men who look like Daniel. It's not enough to say, "Most cops wouldn't put their knee on the back of a nonresisting person's neck for nine minutes or that most cops wouldn't pull over two Black college kids just for driving while Black in their white town." The problem is some do.

My life and my family have not just been touched by race, but deeply affected by it. And so has everyone who has lived in America. You would be wise to do what Robert Jones encouraged me to do and write your own racial biography.

Matters of race have shaped not only our individual stories, but our collective story as Americans. At our best, we are the great melting pot, the land that nurtures the tired and poor. At our worst, we are the land whose cardinal sin is our abiding racism, a deeply ingrained injustice present from our founding and continuing to this day.

The way white Christians think about race is complex. I grew up in the white evangelical subculture, and I can attest that white Christians can hold contradictory attitudes toward people of color. As the research suggests, they can express genuine warmth and acceptance, while holding racist attitudes. As this dichotomy has weighed on me, I want to answer this essential question: how can white Christians be so blind to their own racism?

BLIND TO RACISM

For years, Robert Jones has conducted studies on religion in American life. His Racism Index measures attitudes toward the Confederate flag and statues, the impact of slavery, police brutality toward Black people, and whether leagues should require professional athletes to stand during the national anthem.[12] He made a curious discovery: white evangelicals rate themselves as having the warmest feelings toward Black folks of any group, yet also have the highest scores on the Racism Index. They say they have warm feelings toward Black people, while holding the most racist opinions. They are more likely than any other group to endorse items like "If Blacks would only try harder, they could be just as well off as whites," while rejecting statements like "White people in the US have certain advantages because of the color of their skin."[13]

12. Jones, "Racism Among White Christians," lines 20–22.
13. Vandermaas-Peeler et al., "2018 American Values Survey."

Where does this come from? There are four psychological reasons why many white evangelicals express the most warmth but harbor the most racism toward Black people: subtle family messages, the unconscious impact of negative stereotypes, the Dunning-Kruger effect, and a strong dislike for changes in familiar patterns.

Subtle Family Messages

Sociologist Margaret Hagerman spent two years observing white families and their children who were growing up with privilege in a racially divided America. She found kids learn about race and racism not just from overt conversations with their parents but from the decisions their parents make about where they live, who gets invited to picnics, what schools they choose for their children, when they lock their doors, what media they consume, how they respond to racist comments and jokes, and other seemingly invisible choices.[14]

Even if the parents never express overtly racist attitudes—and even if they are outspoken in their support of racial minorities—these other small decisions have a big impact on their children's attitudes toward race and racism. These children often grow up to be adults who have internalized all the subtle but powerful racial messages of their youth, while believing they are free of racial biases.

This was true for me and I am certain true for most of my classmates and youth group members. Few of us were raised in overtly racist homes, but we lived in all-white neighborhoods, went to a nearly all-white school, attended an all-white youth group, played in nearly all-white sports leagues, and attended churches that were seas of mostly white faces. Nothing was ever said, but our families and schools and churches communicated volumes about race. Our lack of exposure to those of different races primed us for a lifetime of poor racial awareness and understanding.

Negative Stereotypes

When *The Hollywood Reporter* analyzed the types of roles that earned Black actors the most Oscars and accolades, they concluded they were "kingpins, addicts, slaves and maids."[15] Negative stereotypes of Black people from media portrayals and family messages seep into our unconscious over the

---

14. Hagerman, *White Kids.*
15. *Hollywood Reporter* Staff, "#OscarsSoWhite."

years. We see people of color as rude and lazy at best, or violent and scary at worst. These unconscious, automatic associations are a big reason white Christians claim warmth toward Black people while harboring negative and racist attitudes toward them.

In one study, researchers rapidly flashed two images to participants, telling them to ignore the first picture, which was the face of either a Black or white child. The second image showed either a gun or a baby toy. They asked the students to identify the object. Researchers found study participants more quickly identified the second picture correctly as a gun if they had also just seen a picture of a Black boy, even for a fraction of a second.[16]

And here's the kicker: they also *inaccurately* identified the picture of the toy as a gun if they had previously seen the picture of the Black boy. Two follow-up tests found participants associated Black faces with guns and white faces with nonthreatening objects, no matter the age of the person in the picture. For their fourth study, the researchers found participants were more likely to associate scary words, such as "violent," "hostile," and "dangerous," with Black boys than with white boys.[17]

The Dunning-Kruger Effect

One of the earliest lessons you learn as a psychologist is how good we all are at lying to ourselves. We are self-deceived, often rating ourselves as superior when we are measurably average—or even below average. It makes sense white Christians think they have the warmest attitudes toward Black people while holding the most racist opinions of them. Their life experiences have deceived them to think more highly of themselves than they ought.

We call this the Dunning-Kruger effect, which finds people who are the most incompetent in a particular area—teaching a class, financial knowledge, or test-taking ability, as a few examples—rate themselves as among the most competent.[18] If you remember the original *American Idol,* where the worst singers thought they were the best, you have seen this in action.

In the original studies in 1999, social psychologists David Dunning and Justin Kruger gave participants tests of logic, grammar, and humor. Those at the bottom of the distribution, at the twelfth percentile on average, rated themselves above average in all three areas. In one study, subjects took a twenty-item grammar test, then at the end, they rated how well they thought they performed. The people at the tenth percentile rated themselves at the

16. Todd et al., "Does Seeing Young Black Boys Facilitate Identification?"
17. Todd et al., "Does Seeing Young Black Boys Facilitate Identification?"
18. Kruger and Dunning, "Unskilled and Unaware of It."

sixty-seventh percentile on average. They did terribly, but thought they were better than average. They thought they were in the top third, but they were in the bottom 10 percent.[19] Other studies have found the same thing in everything from driving ability to work performance. The ones who think they are awesome are often terrible at the task, but lack the insight to know it.[20]

The same goes for attitudes and beliefs. For example, the people who strongly believe in the link between autism and vaccines are the most likely to believe they know as much or more than physicians about the causes of autism spectrum disorders.[21] Their "research" has given them expert status.

The Dunning-Kruger effect is evident in racist and sexist attitudes as well. Many people who hold the most prejudiced attitudes about racial minorities or women are unaware of their biases. Keon West, a professor at the University of London, asked over three hundred people to rate how much they supported equal rights and opportunities regarding race and gender. Then he asked them to take the Implicit Association Test (IAT), a computerized instrument that measures the attitudes and beliefs people are unable or unwilling to recognize in themselves. The test forces people to make decisions in milliseconds, revealing unconscious associations about different groups. This research-validated test identifies our automatic associations connected to gender, sexuality, religion, race, or other variables.[22]

West found individuals who were most prejudiced toward persons of color also most strongly overestimated their own commitment to equality. As a result, they were both prejudiced and clueless about their own prejudice.[23]

West explained his research to me like this: "Imagine you lined up everyone in the world from the worst—the most racist and sexist—to the best and least racist and sexist. You probably think that you'd be above average, meaning less racist and sexist than most. The problem is that everyone thinks that, both the people who are, in fact, above average and the absolute worst people in the group. So your assumption of being above average tells you very little. You could be above average, or you could be right at the bottom and unaware of how terrible you are."

He also made it clear his research was not just based on implicit tests. Direct questions often exposed racist attitudes just the same. In his research,

19. Kruger and Dunning, "Unskilled and Unaware of It."
20. West and Eaton, "Prejudiced and Unaware of It."
21. Motta et al., "Dunning-Kruger Effects and Anti-Vaccine Attitudes."
22. West and Eaton, "Prejudiced and Unaware of It."
23. West and Eaton, "Prejudiced and Unaware of It."

asking people how they felt about Black people at work also revealed their prejudice. "I don't want people to have the impression that this only emerges when you use the IAT," he told me. "You find this effect however you measure bias."

Does this help explain why white conservative Christians often claim to be so accepting and inclusive and egalitarian, yet are far from it most of the time?

"Yes," West said. White conservative Christians "are both among the most prejudiced and also the most inaccurate about how prejudiced they are. They strongly overestimate how fairly they treat other people relative to the rest of the population."

We know many factors influence our perception, but this is a strange psychological phenomenon. Why does the Dunning-Kruger effect even exist in humans? How can we see ourselves so imperfectly?

West explained, "According to the original Dunning-Kruger research on various facets of intelligence and ability, it's because the skills you need to do something well are, unfortunately, the same as the skills you need to know if you're doing it well. So if you're terrible at being a fair, egalitarian person, you probably also lack the knowledge and skills necessary to know that about yourself. You might have a simplistic or misinformed idea of what prejudice means or looks like. Or you may have no idea what other people think about issues of race and gender—or both."

Pattern Deviancy Aversion

Besides the subtle—or not-so-subtle—messages about race we received from our families, coupled with the negative portrayals of Black men in the media, there may also be another seemingly benign trait in humans that contributes to racist behavior and attitudes. To illustrate, let's do a very simple experiment. Look at this row of little pyramids and note how uncomfortable it makes you from 1 (not uncomfortable) to 10 (extremely uncomfortable).

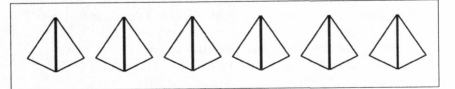

Now look at the next row of the same little pyramids and note how uncomfortable it makes you from 1 (no discomfort) to 10 (extremely uncomfortable):

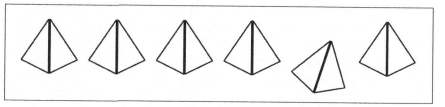

Was there any increase in your level of discomfort from the first row to the second row? For some people, there may not be the slightest increase, but for many others, there may be anywhere from a little more discomfort to a lot more discomfort. Why? And how does this relate to racism and prejudice?

One study conducted by Anton Gollwitzer and other researchers at Yale University provides a surprising insight: people crave patterns and they become uneasy when those patterns are broken. Our brains seek familiarity. From the time we are infants, we make sense of the world through patterns. Familiar patterns create safety and security. However, when the pattern is broken, it can create a sense of unease and insecurity.[24]

For their study, the researchers showed people a series of geometric shapes, like the first row of pyramids. Afterwards, they showed another series with one shape out of line, like the second set of pyramids. Researchers measured how much the disrupted pattern bothered the participants. They also asked them about their attitudes toward people who were different, including people of different races, physically handicapped people, and others. Those who scored high on discomfort for the broken patterns also had greater dislike of people who were different, including people of different races. So if someone looks or behaves differently than the norm, prejudice against that person takes root. The individual might not even be aware of his forming prejudice, nor might he hold overtly racist beliefs. This doesn't excuse racist actions, nor does it mitigate the harm done, but it partially helps us understand why people behave as they do.[25]

24. Gollwitzer et al., "Pattern deviancy aversion predicts prejudice."
25. Gollwitzer et al., "Pattern deviancy aversion predicts prejudice."

WHITE CHRISTIAN DEFENSIVENESS

Any of us can be blind to our own racism. Much of it is automatic and unconscious, not the product of racist or white supremacist attitudes. White Christians, though, often see racism as only willful, discriminatory attitudes and actions, so they scoff at notions they might harbor racist attitudes or take part in larger systems of racism. They acknowledge other people can be racist, while maintaining their own absolution from prejudiced attitudes. Their view is that when racism is present, it is always a willful attitude located in that individual's "heart." In essence, some people are racist and others are not. Since they love Black people, they cannot possibly be racist.

Throughout our lifetimes we all receive messages about race. These messages, whether seemingly benign or clearly negative, cause us to form assumptions, often at an unconscious level. These unconscious assumptions get expressed by having rapid negative associations about Black people.

Humans are also wired to seek patterns. Many people feel discomfort when their patterns are broken. A Black face in a predominantly white neighborhood evokes a strong subconscious response of unease, for example. As with many things, we also have an uncanny ability to overestimate ourselves, including our racial attitudes. We are blind to ourselves. Though the notion is mocked in conservative circles, it is possible to be racist and not know it. Not only is it possible but growing up in a country with such a complicated history with race, it is likely.

CHAPTER 5

This Country Does
Not Love Us Back

The Denial of Systemic Racism in the Church

"It's amazing we keep loving this country, and this country does not love us back."
—DOC RIVERS, COACH OF THE LOS ANGELES CLIPPERS

PATRICIA TURNER WAS THIRTEEN years old when they padlocked the school buildings.[1] As one of only seventeen Black children to integrate into the Norfolk, Virginia public school system in 1959, she was part of what would become known as the "Norfolk Seventeen."[2] Five years earlier, the Supreme Court decided *Brown v. Board of Education*, declaring "separate but equal" unconstitutional.[3] The time had come to integrate, but it would not be easy. In the last chapter, I shared the story from my dad's experience of being denied his senior year of high school, but this is the story from Patricia Turner's perspective.

Today, in her late seventies, she struggles with medical concerns. Because of her declining health, a struggle with lupus, and a stint in the ICU, it took me months to talk with her. When I did, she told me her illness had

1. History Makers, "Patricia Turner," lines 1–2.
2. Watson, "Norfolk 17 Face a Hostile Reception," lines 3–8.
3. History Makers, "Patricia Turner," lines 5–8.

taken a heavy toll. "I wouldn't give up," she told me of her hospital stay. "God was going to do one of two things. He was going to make me well or take me home—and I was okay with both of them. He chose to make me well, so I've got to believe in him. There's no other choice."

When I asked her about the year she was part of the first group of Black students to integrate into the public schools, she described it in one word: "Hell," she said. "It was pure hell." All she wanted to do was to be able to walk to her neighborhood school and not have to take two buses to a rundown school that had outdated textbooks with missing pages. She never expected to be treated like such a pariah. "You're in a place where nobody wants you," she said.

The mistreatment continued for years. When she was in the tenth grade, some teachers would not even read the papers she and other Black students had written. "They would write a zero on it without looking at it," she said, emotion crackling in her voice as she recounted it over sixty years later. "A judge had to get involved and make them regrade the papers."

She described one harrowing event after another. Her memory for the details of those years seemed incredibly sharp, I told her. "How do you forgot someone spitting in your face?" she asked. At first, I thought she meant it rhetorically, but then I realized she meant it literally. "I have forgiven it. The person who did it knows who they are."

She co-authored an illustrated children's book called *Today I Met a Rainbow,* which tells the story of her experience. In it, she writes, "Like the other black students, young Pat faced lots of challenges. The other students did not want to sit by her in class. Teachers and school leaders did little to protect her. People called her names and tried to discourage her from coming back to school."[4]

She told me of countless humiliations. "White parents told their kids that the Black kids had tails," she said. "They thought I had a tail. The white kids asked to see it."

She felt caught between worlds with few allies. "The white kids didn't like us. The Black kids didn't like us," she explained, then added, "I might as well have been alone." For her, it was "hell all day and double hell in the afternoon" when she returned to her neighborhood after school, only to be met with more hostility from Black peers who didn't like the trouble integration had stirred up.

She shared she "became another person" any time she told the story of what happened in 1959. I could feel what she meant. The traumatic experiences, the pain and woundedness, were still real for her.

4. Turner and Stockdale, *Today I Met a Rainbow,* 27.

She said she was still puzzled to this day about why the Governor would close the schools and put ten thousand white kids out of school "just to keep out seventeen Black kids."

Despite those challenges, she persevered and completed middle school, then graduated high school in 1963. She finished her bachelor's degree in mathematics from Norfolk State University in three years, followed by a master's degree in education from Old Dominion University.[5] In a bit of poetic justice, she worked as a math teacher at a school integrated by the Norfolk Seventeen.[6] A little over a decade later, a university awarded her an honorary doctorate for her contributions to the civil rights movement.[7]

Even now, her life's work is to ensure children get a quality education. Despite her challenged health in recent years, Turner continues to oversee a school in the Norfolk area. I asked her what sustained her during those years, how she withstood such mistreatment. She gave credit to both of her parents. Her father was a master chief in the Navy and her mother emphasized the value of education and not giving up. She also credited God with sustaining her and giving her strength. "I am a child of God," she said.

Since the days when Turner was spat at and the government padlocked the doors of her school, there has been major progress in the areas of racial justice. Barack Obama told podcaster Marc Maron, "It is incontrovertible that race relations have improved significantly during my lifetime and yours, and that opportunities have opened up, and that attitudes have changed. That is a fact."[8]

So apart from some remaining pockets of racism, a few bad apples, are we done with racism or is racism hardwired into the fabric of American institutions and power structures? Do you agree with former Vice President Mike Pence, a conservative evangelical, when he said, "It is past time for America to discard the left-wing myth of systemic racism. *America is not a racist country*"?[9] Or do you believe racism is deeply rooted in institutions and not just in individual persons' hearts? As Obama said in the same interview, "What is also true is that the legacy of slavery, Jim Crow, discrimination in almost every institution of our lives—you know, that casts a long shadow. And that's still part of our DNA that's passed on. *We're not cured of it*."[10]

5. History Makers, "Patricia Turner," lines 17–22.

6. History Makers, "Patricia Turner," lines 22–25.

7. History Makers, "Patricia Turner," lines 31–33.

8. Chappell, "Obama Discusses Racism," lines 24–26.

9. Cameron, "Pence Calls Systemic Racism a 'Left-Wing Myth,'" lines 21–25.

10. Chappell, "Obama Discusses Racism," lines 27–29.

A 2019 Pew Research Center Study found most Black adults have a negative perception of racial progress in the United States. Seven out of ten (71 percent) Black people surveyed said race relations in the US are bad, compared to 56 percent of whites. A full 84 percent of Blacks believe the legacy of slavery affects the position of Black people in American society a great deal or fair amount today, but only 58 percent of whites see it this way, a difference of 26 percent. The biggest perception gap, though, was on a question that said our country hasn't come far enough in giving Blacks equal treatment with whites, with 78 percent of Black respondents agreeing and 37 percent of whites endorsing this idea, representing a perception gap of 41 percent.[11]

We've long thought of racism as being individual prejudice, where a person views or treats others of different races in discriminatory and hateful ways. That was my only concept of racism growing up in the white evangelical subculture. Since I knew I didn't harbor ill feelings toward persons of color, I was off the hook. Those ugly white supremacists were few in number and their evil attitudes were between them and God, I reasoned.

Most white Americans held these or similar views until after the civil rights movements of the sixties. David Wellman's 1977 book *Portraits of White Racism* was among the first to focus on bias systemically, viewing racism as a condition where some get more advantages based on their race, even if prejudicial intent isn't deliberate. Using multiple examples, he argued white people can have warm attitudes toward Black people while supporting systems that benefit them and disadvantage people of color. The notion that institutions and organizations could embody racism, even without the presence of overtly racist individuals within them, was groundbreaking. Despite that, most white evangelicals have stubbornly held onto the notion that racism lives only in the individual human heart and is not cradled in human institutions of power.[12]

IS THERE SYSTEMIC RACISM?

I was enjoying lunch with a small group of friends, all white men and good-hearted people, talking about different news stories and cultural events. The discussion turned to Tamir Rice, the Black twelve-year-old holding a toy gun who was shot in under two seconds after police arrived on the scene. One of my friends grimaced and shifted uncomfortably in his seat. He stayed quiet for a while, listening to the others lament the pattern of police

11. Menasce Horowitz et al., "Race in America 2019."

12. Wellman, *Portraits of White Racism.*

killing young Black men. Finally he said, "There are definitely racist people, but there's no such thing as systemic racism. That's a myth."

No one said a word to challenge him, including me. It wasn't for lack of courage, but more out of a lack of knowledge. We all knew this statement didn't seem right, but we hadn't armed ourselves with evidence to refute it.

This set me on a path to equip myself more adequately. There were some questions I wanted to have answers to, such as: What is systemic racism? Does it exist? If so, what is the evidence of it? What is its impact?

My friend, and many folks like him, pride themselves on not being racist. "There's not a racist bone in my body," they'll say. What they mean is they don't hold racist attitudes, they don't subscribe to white supremacist ideologies, and they feel warm and kind toward people of different racial groups. What they are describing, though, is that they are, to the best of their ability, "non-racist."

I've learned there's a difference between being non-racist and anti-racist. To be non-racist means you don't hold any of those ugly racist views. In fact, you may find such attitudes disgusting. That's commendable, but it doesn't mean you are anti-racist. An anti-racist fights against racism in all its forms, from the individual to the systemic. By definition, to be anti-racist means you believe systemic racism exists and that it is a problem.

While I had considered myself "non-racist" before Daniel and his sister Maddie came into our lives, seeing the world through their experiences changed me in ways I had not expected. Awareness is the first step of a process toward becoming "anti-racist." I'm responsible not only for getting rid of racist assumptions and attitudes and behaviors, but for working against racism, swimming hard against the current.

In her book *Why Are All the Black Kids Sitting Together in the Cafeteria*, psychologist Beverly Daniel Tatum likens systemic racism to being on a people mover, like the ones at the airport, where people are being carried forward, some walking, some standing, but most moving forward by the larger systems that have been in place for a long time. It is only when someone walks hard in the opposite direction that they can become anti-racist. It's not enough just to stand still, allowing institutions and social order to carry you forward while disadvantaging people of other races.[13]

Systemic racism does not mean there is always racist intent or even knowledge of wrongdoing—or "mens rea," in the language of law. It refers to institutions, organizations, and larger social systems that perpetuate inequality and discrimination. Sometimes they do it willfully and other times unwittingly. Either way, the result is an imbalance that disadvantages racial

13. Tatum, *Why Are All The Black Kids Sitting Together in the Cafeteria?*

minorities. Because this notion of systemic racism is in dispute, I've prepared an appendix at the back of the book for you that provides details of these inequities. Unlike many appendices you choose to skip, I urge you to spend some time soaking up the information.

RACISM IN THE CHURCH

Ellen and I had just moved to a new town and we were looking for a church home. We visited several churches to narrow down the field and got invited to join a small group. Even though we had not yet committed to the church, we agreed to come. At the end of the first meeting, the leader, a real estate developer, had a prayer request.

"I'd like prayer for a hearing I have coming up. The city is considering allowing a low-income housing project to be built a few blocks from one of my developments and I'm worried if it passes, it will hurt my property values."

Thankfully, no one offered such a prayer, but Ellen and I cut our eyes at each other. We knew something was horribly amiss. Let me emphasize this was not some "baby Christian" who made this request. This was the leader of the small group.

Though he never mentioned Black people in his prayer request, everyone knew what he meant. His statement was contradictory to core tenets of the faith—an appeal for God to keep poor people away so it doesn't hurt one's property values—yet this type of attitude passes comfortably in many evangelical circles.

Robert Jones says his fifteen-item Racism Index is "designed to get beyond personal biases and include perceptions of structural injustice."[14] In his groundbreaking research, he found white evangelical Christians have the highest average score on the Racism Index of any group.[15] Even after controlling for many other characteristics like level of education, region of the country, and political partisanship, his data indicated "the connection between holding racist attitudes and white Christian identity remains stubbornly robust."[16]

It wasn't just Jones's research that found problematic attitudes about race among Christians, including denial of racial injustice. George Barna's

14. Jones, "Racism Among White Christians is Higher," lines 19–20.
15. Jones, "Racism Among White Christians is Higher," line 24.
16. Jones, "Racism Among White Christians is Higher," lines 36–37.

research during the summers of 2019 and 2020 produced similar findings.[17] Among the conclusions their surveys found:

- White Christians were less likely than any measured group to say the US had a problem with race.[18]

- One in five white Christians said race was "not at all" a problem in our country.[19]

- During both Barna surveys, white Christians were less likely than any other group to agree that the United States has historically oppressed minorities, with less than a majority agreeing with this (43 percent in 2019, 48 percent in 2020).[20]

- By their own admission, significantly more white Christians became more unmotivated to address racial injustice in our society during the summer of 2020, the months of protest and rioting following the George Floyd murder, compared to the year before (36 percent unmotivated in 2020 compared to 23 percent in 2019).[21]

- Previous research by the Barna Group found Black Christians far exceeded white Christians on measures of "spiritual vibrancy" on every metric, including the importance of faith to their daily lives, a strong commitment to love God, and adherence to specific Christian tenets.[22]

The roots of white Christian racism in America precede the country's founding. However, the notion that the church has evolved past its ugly history is demonstrably untrue. The white church has helped perpetuate racism and segregation in the United States, not only a hundred or two hundred years ago, but also in recent decades, leading up to the present day.

Less than three miles from my house in Nashville, a statue of Nathan Bedford Forrest riding a horse stood tall for everyone traveling down I-65 to see. Some in the South consider Forrest, a Confederate general during the Civil War, a hero. Shelby Foote called him a "military genius," referring to his prowess as a Confederate general during the Civil War.[23] He was also the first Grand Wizard of the Ku Klux Klan and responsible for a massacre of three hundred surrendering Black soldiers. In recent years, vandals

17. Barna Group, "White Christians Even Less Motivated."
18. Barna Group, "White Christians Even Less Motivated," lines 1–5.
19. Barna Group, "White Christians Even Less Motivated," line 31.
20. Barna Group, "White Christians Even Less Motivated," line 31.
21. Barna Group, "White Christians Even Less Motivated," lines 50–56.
22. Kinnaman, "Barna's Perspective on Race and the Church," lines 31–36.
23. Burns, Burns, and McCullough, *Civil War.*

painted the statue pink. Later, someone else spray-painted "Monster" on the monument. The statue stood until recently, a defiant tribute to the state's racist past.

One of Forrest's latter-day admirers is a young Alabama native named Will Dismukes. At twenty-eight, Dismukes became the youngest person elected to the Alabama House. He had attended a segregation academy founded by white parents to keep their children out of the desegregated public schools. Even within the past decade, the school prohibited a Black football player—who played for the school team named "The Confederate Generals"—from bringing his white girlfriend to the school's prom.[24]

Before being elected to the State House, the Southern Baptist Convention ordained Dismukes.[25] He'd also previously served as a youth pastor at another Southern Baptist church. Some regarded him as a rising star in both the denomination and in the state Republican party.

During the summer of 2020, when he was both a state representative and an ordained minister, Dismukes, surrounded by Confederate flags, gave the invocation at a birthday party in Selma, Alabama for General Forrest. It was the same weekend memorial services in the state were being held for Rep. John Lewis, the civil rights champion. Police officers had beaten Lewis bloody and cracked his skull during the march on Selma in 1965. Fifty-five years later, a horse-drawn carriage conveyed Lewis's body across the Edmund Pettus Bridge before he was laid in state at the Alabama State Capitol. On the same day, Dismukes posted a picture of himself at the birthday party of the KKK leader.[26]

An earlier invitation to the annual event read, "Our culture is a Christian culture and Christianity is the bullseye of their target." It implored people to join "the fight to save our noble Christian culture."[27] Dismukes and the others honored Forrest, the slave trader and owner, the man whose biographer, Jack Hurst, described as "an overbearing bully of homicidal wrath."[28] Dismukes, a minister of the gospel, prayed over the celebration of the racist icon on the same weekend John Lewis's body was carried across the bridge where he had been bloodied in the civil rights march.

Back in the 1980s, the founder of Liberty University and a mainstay on the national stage during the Reagan era culture wars, Jerry Falwell Sr., was undeniably racist. Like a lot of Christian leaders throughout US history,

24. Goodman, "How the Discrimination of Alabama Football Star."
25. Roney, "Legislator, businessman and now preacher."
26. Crawford, "Will Dismukes," lines 20–25.
27. Pulliam Bailey, "Alabama Politician Resigns."
28. Hurst, *Nathan Bedford Forrest*, 6.

he claimed the Bible and the Christian faith supported racist policies, including segregation of the races. Referring to the landmark *Brown v. Board of Education* that desegregated public schools in the 1950s, Falwell said, "If Chief Justice Warren and his associates had known God's Word and had desired to do the Lord's will, I am quite confident that the 1954 decision would never have been made."[29] Falwell's message was clear: God opposed desegregation. God was against the civil rights movement.

In *The Nation*, Max Blumenthal reports that the elder Falwell said, "The true Negro does not want integration . . . He realizes his potential is far better among his own race."[30] Blumenthal claims Falwell warned, "a pastor friend of mine tells me that a couple of opposite race live next door to his church as man and wife."[31] He meant it as a scandalous statement.

Dismukes and Falwell are public figures, but they are not outliers. We see conservative Christian leaders who—directly or in coded form—espouse racist attitudes and fight to protect the status quo where white men are in power.

In 2018, a group of evangelical pastors, led by John MacArthur, issued a statement decrying "critical race theory" and blasted social activism, saying it was not integral to the gospel or "primary to the mission of the church."[32] Emma Green writes, "White pastors aggressively enforce the boundaries of acceptable conversations on racism, weaponizing any position that bears even a whiff of progressive politics and slapping labels such as 'social justice' and 'cultural Marxism' on arguments about systemic injustice."[33]

Only a few months after George Floyd and Ahmaud Arbery were murdered and protests happened in every state, the presidents of all six Southern Baptist seminaries issued a statement denouncing critical race theory as "unbiblical" and "incompatible with the Baptist Faith & Message."[34] The announcement prompted Jemar Tisby, author of *The Color of Compromise*, to respond with an article entitled, "Southern Baptist seminary presidents reaffirm their commitment to whiteness."[35] Tisby chided the six older white men who claim they are "standing against the tide of theological compromise" with this parting statement: "There is no form of theological compromise that is more American than vigorously opposing those who

---

29. Blumenthal, "Agent of Intolerance," lines 43–49.

30. Blumenthal, "Agent of Intolerance," lines 52–53.

31. Blumenthal, "Agent of Intolerance," lines 54–56.

32. MacArthur et al., "Social Justice & the Gospel."

33. Green, "Unofficial Racism Consultants," lines 109–12.

34. Schroeder, "Seminary Presidents Reaffirm BFM," lines 7–9.

35. Tisby, "Southern Baptist Presidents Reaffirm Commitment."

advocate for racial injustice while remaining silent about the racism and whiteness running rampant in the church."[36]

Marshall Ausberry, president of the National African American Fellowship of the SBC, said, "The optics of six Anglo brothers meeting to discuss racism and other related issues without having ethnic representation in the room in 2020, at worst it looks like paternalism, at best insensitivity."[37] In lamenting the statement issued the day before the sixty-fifth anniversary of Rosa Parks's refusal to give up her seat on the segregated bus, Rev. Emory Berry, a member of the alumni board of Emory University's Candler School of Theology, said this "shows that we have really not made as much progress as we would have hoped."[38]

Following the statement, two large predominantly Black Southern Baptist churches severed ties with the denomination: Progressive Baptist Church, pastored by Charlie Dates in Chicago, and The Church Without Walls, pastored by Ralph D. West in Houston.[39] Rev. Dates called the statement "a final straw."[40] West said, "Their stand against racism rings hollow when in their next breath they reject theories that have been helpful in framing the problem of racism."[41] In a scathing editorial, Dates wrote, "When did the theological architects of American slavery develop the moral character to tell the church how it should discuss and discern racism? When did those who have yet to hire multiple Black or brown faculty at their seminaries assume ethical authority on the subject of systemic injustice? How did they, who in 2020 still don't have a single Black denominational entity head, reject once and for all a theory that helps to frame the real race problems we face?"[42] He added, "Conservatism is, and has always been, the God of the SBC."[43]

Conservative politics related to racial issues often gets wrapped in theological and biblical language in many pulpits. When the debate about immigration was heating up, I watched a prominent pastor of a Southern Baptist megachurch lay out what he said was the "biblical" model of immigration. It involved restrictions on immigrants and insistence on assimilation where those allowed to immigrate forsake their cultural

---

36. Tisby, "Southern Baptist Presidents Reaffirm Commitment," lines 113–17.

37. Banks, "Black Southern Baptists Weigh In," lines 33–5.

38. Banks, "Black Southern Baptists Weigh In," lines 41–5.

39. Shellnut, "Two Prominent Pastors Break With SBC," lines 1–9.

40. Shellnut, "Two Prominent Pastors Break With SBC," lines 35–6.

41. Shellnut, "Two Prominent Pastors Break With SBC," lines 49–50.

42. Dates, "Why His Church is Leaving the SBC," lines 36–41.

43. Dates, "Why His Church is Leaving the SBC," line 43.

traditions in favor of adopting the conventions of the dominant culture. The preacher peppered each point with biblical references from the Old Testament. Setting aside the mental gymnastics required of him to come to those conclusions, the clear message delivered to a predominantly white audience was that we had to protect our way of life against those who were racially and culturally different. It was not just okay to do this. It was God's imperative that we must.

In so many ways—messages from the pulpit, statements from seminary presidents, comments during Bible studies, editorials, support for racist historical figures, national surveys, and more—we see how both overt and subtle racism has permeated the white Christian church. In the US, it has always been there and has never left.

During his tenure, Russell Moore, the influential former president of the Southern Baptist Convention's Ethics and Religious Liberty Commission, had drawn heat from within the denomination for his denouncing of white supremacy and refusal to support Donald Trump during the 2016 election.[44] It wasn't until his 2021 resignation letter leaked that outside observers understood the level of opposition and animosity he had faced. "My family and I have faced constant threats from white nationalists and white supremacists, including within our convention," he wrote.[45] "Some of them have been involved in neo-Confederate activities going back for years. Some are involved with groups funded by white nationalist nativist organizations. Some of them have just expressed raw racist sentiment, behind closed doors. They want to deflect the issue to arcane discussions that people do not understand, such as 'critical race theory.'"[46] He described the criticism he had faced for advocating for an African American president for the SBC. He said one denominational leader "told a gathering that 'The Conservative Resurgence is like the Civil War, except this time unlike the last one, the right side won,'" which compelled Moore to walk out of the meeting.[47] At least three times in the letter, he describes deliberately inflicted "psychological terror" from within the denomination, mostly for his advocacy for repentance for racial injustice and his calls for racial reconciliation within the denomination.[48] He said some factions within the SBC "want me to live in psychological terror."[49]

44. Wehner, "Scandal Rocking the Evangelical World."
45. Religion News Service, "Russell Moore to ERLC Trustees," lines 117–18.
46. Religion News Service, "Russell Moore to ERLC Trustees," lines 118–21.
47. Religion News Service, "Russell Moore to ERLC Trustees," lines 126–30.
48. Religion News Service, "Russell Moore to ERLC Trustees."
49. Religion News Service, "Russell Moore to ERLC Trustees," lines 188–90.

THE PSYCHOLOGICAL IMPACT OF RACISM

One of my clients, a gifted artist, had an appointment with me about three days after the death of George Floyd. I asked him how he was doing with all of it.

"I'm not doing," he said.

"What do you mean?" I asked.

"I mean I'm not doing. I can't do anything. I feel paralyzed, like I'm being suffocated. I haven't talked to anybody. I haven't done anything. I don't even feel anything right now."

The research has found racism—both direct and vicarious—has a profound, often lifelong, adverse impact on people, dramatically affecting their emotional well-being, sense of safety and security, and self-worth. Those who are victims of racism often have negative, lingering effects, including:

- Increases in lifetime history of Major Depressive Disorder, Post-Traumatic Stress Disorder, substance abuse, and worse overall mental health.

- Adults who report direct experiences with racism also report higher levels of anxiety, guilt, shame, avoidance and numbing behavior, and hypervigilance, compared to those who do not.

- Young adults who experience racial discrimination are more prone to experience dissociative symptoms than those who have not. Dissociation involves the experience of feeling disconnected from one's self, including having gaps of memory or feeling detached or as if being outside of your own body.

- Those who have experienced racial discrimination or hostility are more likely to have a near-constant state of being on guard, feel more alienated from others, worry more about future negative events, and are more likely to view others as dangerous.

- Persons of color exposed to family, historical, or media accounts of discrimination or violence against racial minorities may also experience a form of vicarious trauma.

- Racism can have a negative impact on an individual's self-confidence and sense of identity.

- Some individuals may internalize the negative racial messages they have received, which may hinder them from achieving their academic or career potential, believing they are less capable than others or face insurmountable odds.[50]

50. Smedley et al., *Confronting Racial and Ethnic Disparities in Health Care.*

ɔn persons of color in our culture
.ave not walked in their shoes cannot
ɔ have family members, close friends,
/ho are Black cannot know what their
ɪe research tells us the emotional toll is

ΓE EVANGELICALS
ΓEMIC RACISM?

ɘ unwilling to see or acknowledge systemic
After the Ferguson, Missouri riots in 2015,
ed racial discrimination was a big problem,
accordɪng ᴗ ll. Five years later, over 75 percent said racial
discrimination was a bɪg ʀ ɔlem.[51] Online searches for the phrase "systemic
racism" had increased by one hundred times during the months of 2020
that followed the death of George Floyd.[52] Most Americans, it seems, are
becoming more open to the realities of systemic racism. This same trend
does not apply to white Christians.

The question is, why are white Christians so stubbornly committed to
their refusal to acknowledge systemic racism? Is it willful or out of ignorance?
The answer is a mixture of both. There are four interlocking reasons that
explain why white evangelicals deny systemic racism: suppressed history,
the just-world hypothesis, individualistic theology, and failure of empathy.

Suppressed History

In his song *Buffalo Soldier*, Bob Marley sings about how knowing your
own history helps you understand someone else's experience. "The Marley
Hypothesis," as researchers have labelled it, says knowledge of your
country's history can affect your perception of other individuals and groups,
particularly around issues of race.[53]

A study out of the University of Kansas and Texas A&M University
found African Americans had more accurate knowledge of historically documented racism compared to white Americans. This knowledge gap was a

51. Worland, "America's Awakening to Systemic Racism," lines 63–67.
52. Worland, "America's Awakening to Systemic Racism," lines 72–75.
53. Bonam et al., "Ignoring History, Denying Racism."

significant factor in how the two groups perceived both systemic and individual incidents of racism now.[54]

Another study by Courtney Bonam and colleagues also found less knowledge of past racism predicted more denial of systemic racism. As expected, white participants had less knowledge of specific incidents of historical racism than Black participants.[55] A follow-up study found participants exposed to a brief history of US housing policy acknowledged more systemic racism, suggesting exposure to accurate information can shift a person's openness to the reality of ongoing racism.[56] The problem, of course, is that much of our history of the country's racial past is often hidden, tucked away and out of sight.

I began writing this section on the day of the one hundredth anniversary of the 1921 Tulsa Race Massacre, May 31, 2021. I waited until then as a way of commemorating that sorrowful date. Historical accounts tell us a young Black shoe shiner named Dick Rowland bumped into a young white elevator operator. She screamed and police arrived on the scene, arresting Rowland.[57] The *Tulsa Tribune* ran a story the next morning saying Rowland had attacked the woman.[58]

Over two days, mobs of white people killed as many as three hundred Black people and hospitalized eight hundred more.[59] They burned thirty-five city blocks to the ground, including all of the Greenwood District, which had become a thriving center of Black business and culture, so successful it had been dubbed "The Black Wall Street."[60] Over twelve hundred homes were destroyed. Upwards of ten thousand people were left homeless.[61] Not a single person was ever charged with a crime. The local paper, the *Tulsa World*, printed this screaming banner headline the following morning: "TWO WHITES DEAD IN RACE RIOT."[62]

To be clear: *Hundreds* of Black people died and it was not a riot, it was a massacre.

What was the response of the local white church leaders at the time? Reverend Harold Cooke said, "There has been a great deal of loose-mouthed

54. Nelson et al., "Denial of Racism Reflects Ignorance of History."
55. Bonam et al., "Ignoring History, Denying Racism."
56. Bonam et al., "Ignoring History, Denying Racism."
57. Cho, "History Behind the 1921 Tulsa Race Massacre," lines 20–26.
58. Cho, "History Behind the 1921 Tulsa Race Massacre," lines 27–29.
59. Cho, "History Behind the 1921 Tulsa Race Massacre," lines 40–41.
60. Cho, "History Behind the 1921 Tulsa Race Massacre," lines 30–39.
61. Cho, "History Behind the 1921 Tulsa Race Massacre," lines 44–46.
62. Cho, "History Behind the 1921 Tulsa Race Massacre," lines 47–49.

and loose-minded talk about the white people of Tulsa being equally to blame with the Blacks."[63] Reverend C. W. Kerr of First Presbyterian Church agreed, saying, "The colored people must understand they started it. The fact of their arming and coming up through the city was an outrage to the citizenship of Tulsa."[64] Bishop E. D. Mouzon of Boston Avenue Methodist proclaimed, "If it is true that our wives, our children and the people of Tulsa were threatened with being at the mercy of armed negroes, then the white man who got his gun and went out in defense with it did the only thing a decent white man could have done."[65] First United Methodist's Reverend J. W. Abel warned against making a "martyr of the negro," then went on to extol white virtue and denigrate Blacks, saying, "What other nation in all human history has done as much . . . as the white race has done for the race which but a brief half-century ago emerged from slavery? A race which even in slavery was a thousand times better off than the Black princes who ruled their race in Africa. We tax ourselves to educate him; we help him to build churches, we are careful to keep him supplied with work at a good wage, and trust him with a ballot, and all we ask of him is to behave himself and prove himself worthy of our trust."[66]

As horrifying as the events were, most white people, myself included, had never heard of the Tulsa Race Massacre. I first became aware of it on October 20, 2019, the evening the first episode of HBO's *Watchmen* debuted. The opening sequence depicts the massacre, complete with white people dropping kerosene bombs from small airplanes. I looked over at my friend and asked, "Did that really happen?" Neither of us knew. After the show, some quick Internet searching found it was a historical event that was even worse than the masterfully produced show had depicted. "How come we never heard about this?" I asked.

Journalist Diane Cho gives an answer: "For years, the massacre that took place from May 31 to June 1, 1921, was left out of history books and school curriculums. It was underplayed, inaccurately reported or not reported on at all. It began to disappear from libraries and conversations about American history altogether."[67]

As a student, I never heard about the Tulsa Race Massacre. No one informed me of the Wilmington Insurrection of 1898, even though I lived in North Carolina for twenty-eight years. I never knew about Patricia Turner

63. Ross, "Tulsa Race Massacre Prayer Room," lines 99–101.
64. Ross, "Tulsa Race Massacre Prayer Room," lines 107–9.
65. Ross, "Tulsa Race Massacre Prayer Room," lines 110–13.
66. Ross, "Tulsa Race Massacre Prayer Room," lines 118–29.
67. Cho, "History Behind the 1921 Tulsa Race Massacre," lines 10–13.

and the other members of the Norfolk Seventeen, even though I lived in that city for over two decades. I never learned about John Lewis at the Nashville lunch counter sit-ins until well into my adulthood. No one educated me about Bloody Sunday in Selma. I hadn't heard the term "Juneteenth" or known its meaning until a couple of years ago. I'm not alone. When I talk to my peers, very few heard of these events in school, even when they lived in the states or cities where they happened.

The recent movement to forbid the teaching of critical race theory (CRT), which says racism is baked into key societal structures and institutions, seems like more of the same—an attempt to limit the exposure of the populace to our country's ugly history with race. Claims that the theory is Marxist may have threads of truth, but those were the same claims leveled at Martin Luther King Jr. and others during the civil rights struggles of the 1960s. The recent manufactured outrage against CRT is predictable. School boards around the country are voting on whether to ban it while tearful parents plead for their children to be spared. On the conservative news channel Newsmax, talk show host Michael Savage ranted that "children are being humiliated and hurt and damaged for life" by critical race theory.[68] "The same kind of thing started in Germany. The Jews were no good. The Jews did this. The Jews did that. The next thing you know they were being excluded from swimming pools. They didn't put them in concentration camps overnight," he said, adding later, "This is the road to the death camps."[69]

In every era of American culture, attempts to expose people to the country's sad history of racial mistreatment are met with hysteria and attempts to shut it down. Suppressing our country's history of race keeps many white evangelicals from being able to fully reckon with how systems perpetuate racism to this day.

Just-World Hypothesis

Whether or not we realize it, we all have assumptions or personal theories about how the world works. These assumptions emerge from our schemas that have been shaped by our personal experiences. The "just-world hypothesis" is one such personal theory. It is the belief that people get what they deserve. Those who work hard get rewarded, while those who are lazy don't prosper. Those who behave correctly do not get in trouble, but those who

---

68. Baragona, "Critical Race Theory Is 'Road to Death Camps,'" lines 28–29.
69. Baragona, "Critical Race Theory Is 'Road to Death Camps,'" lines 32–39.

misbehave are punished. Those who endorse the just-world hypothesis see an equal world, not one rife with discrimination and unfair suffering.[70]

The just-world hypothesis includes assumptions that rewards are fairly apportioned and punishments are impartially meted out. Underlying this way of thinking is a belief that some universal force—whether God or otherwise—restores moral balance to the created order. People get what they deserve. The world is just.[71]

Religious white people have greater belief in a just world than most others. African Americans and other racial minorities usually rate low on just-world beliefs. One researcher concluded, "belief in a just world reflects a 'white' experience of the world."[72]

Predictably, people who hold more just-world beliefs blame victims and underprivileged people for their hardships, including being more likely to see those who are bullied or sexually assaulted as being at least partially responsible for their attacks.[73] They see those in poverty as being in that condition because of their own laziness or poor decisions.[74] They also are more likely to deny racism and less likely to support programs that help racial minorities, like affirmative action hiring practices.[75]

Belief in a just world has its benefits. Those who hold these views often find more meaning in life, get less depressed, and have lower stress, but often at the cost of looking down upon poor people, racial minorities, and others in dire circumstances.[76] It also seems associated with more selfish behavior. In one surprising finding involving five hundred subjects, those who held just-world beliefs were more likely to cheat or be dishonest.[77] Perhaps cheating allows them to get the outcome they believe they deserve, their "just" and deserved reward.

White evangelicals often hold just-world beliefs, which shapes their understanding of the struggles of Black people. Their solution is simple: Black folks need to work harder and make the most of their opportunities. For white evangelicals, talk of systemic racism is just a smoke screen to excuse laziness and low motivation.

70. Wenzel et al., "Belief in a Just World Associated with Dishonest Behavior."
71. Hunt, "Status, Religion, and the Belief in a Just World."
72. Hunt, "Status, Religion, and the 'Belief in a Just World.'"
73. Strömwall et al., "Blame and the Just World Hypothesis."
74. Furnham and Gunter, "Just World Beliefs and Attitudes Towards the Poor."
75. De Cuyper, "Can Our Beliefs in a Just World Lead to Prejudice and Racism?"
76. Lipkusa et al., "Belief in a Just World Implications for Well-Being."
77. Wenzel et al., "Belief in a Just World Associated with Dishonest Behavior."

Individualistic Theology

In their book *Divided By Faith*, sociologists Michael Emerson and Christian Smith argue that white American evangelicals, including those who desire racial healing and reconciliation, have adopted a theology with three elements that either intentionally or unwittingly contribute to ongoing racial division in American churches. Those components are a focus on individualism, relationism, and anti-structuralism. In short, they focus on individual responsibility, place centrality on interpersonal relationships, and are unable or unwilling to see social structural influences.[78]

Why could this subvert racial progress within churches and lead to a denial of systemic racism? In *The Bible Told Them So*, historian J. Russell Hawkins writes, "Because of the significant influence of individualism, relationalism, and anti-structuralism, conservative white Christians often fail to even recognize the existence of structural and systemic racism, let alone conceive of ways to address such inequality."[79] With their overemphasis on individual heart and spiritual transformation, many well-intentioned white Christians miss the forest for the trees regarding the deeper requirements of racial repair. Hawkins adds, "White evangelicals who champion racial justice through individual heart changes, or reconciled relationships, or appeals to colorblindness are using the tools fashioned and utilized by their segregationist forebears precisely to avoid the racial justice their descendants now seek. It should not surprise us, therefore, that studies find these latter-day racial reconciliation efforts fall spectacularly short of their goals."[80]

There are many white evangelical churches with pastors and other leaders who desire racial reconciliation and healing, pushing hard for their congregations to become more multiethnic, seeking partnerships with Black and Hispanic churches, and challenging their members to serve needs with minority communities within their cities. These efforts are sincere, heartfelt, and infused with genuine passion. But if Emerson and Smith are correct, their limited theology of sin may trip them up, causing them to see racism as only situated in the individual human heart and not woven into larger institutions. They'll focus more on a Promise Keeper's style "hug a Black man" solutions than pushing hard to create lasting changes in the social centers of power.

only attitude change , not behavioral

---

78. Emerson and Smith, *Divided By Faith*.
79. Hawkins, *Bible Told Them So*, 166.
80. Hawkins, *Bible Told Them So*, 166–67.

Failure of Empathy

The research finds white Christians fail to see the struggles facing people of color as legitimate obstacles more than other groups. Public Religion Research Institute's *American Values Survey* found the overwhelming majority of white Christians rejected the notion that the legacy of slavery and ongoing discrimination make it harder for Black people to succeed.[81] According to these Christians, where racism exists, it is a problem of a few bad individuals and not something embedded in institutions or organizations.

In my study of 283 adult Americans from all ages, income levels, and geographic regions of the country, I found conservative white Christians were significantly more likely to agree with the statement: "The rights of minority groups do not need to be protected from the majority" than those who did not identify as Christian.[82] People of color, they seem to believe, have no big disadvantages.

Some argue the research is biased, that it is measuring those who are "Christian in name only" or cultural Christians uncommitted to their faith. These critics say those who claim to be Christian grow less racist as they become more serious about their faith, get plugged into a local church, and attend regularly. The research finds the opposite. I asked Robert Jones to name the most distressing fact he uncovered in his research. "The church attendance effect," he told me. "Church attendance doesn't make people less racist. It makes things worse." In his research, he found that people who attended church regularly were often more racist in their attitudes, rather than less, contrary to the prevailing opinions of many Christian thinkers.[83] There's no sadder statement in this book.

Most white Christians reject any suggestion they might be racist. Despite their denials, a deep and abiding vein of racism runs down the spine of white Christianity. Robert Jones writes, "While most white Christians think of themselves as people who hold warm feelings toward African Americans, holding racist views is nonetheless positively and independently associated with white Christian identity."[84] As we've seen, some of this discrimination is conscious, while some is not. Whether conscious or not, their partiality reveals a massive failure of empathy, something not lost on people of color when they observe the church today.

81. Vandermaas-Peeler, "2018 American Values Survey."

82. National survey of 283 US adults conducted on December 20, 2020.

83. Vandermaas-Peeler, "2018 American Values Survey."

84. Jones, "Racism Among White Christians is Higher," lines 41–42.

Take a simple example: the demonizing of the phrase and the movement "Black Lives Matter," a coalition borne out of injustice and legitimate suffering. At the height of the racial unrest of 2020, Vice President Mike Pence, a professing Christian, was given the chance on multiple occasions during an interview to affirm the statement "Black Lives Matter." Each time, he deliberately and conspicuously avoided saying the phrase, choosing instead to say, "All Lives Matter."[85] Beyond politics, the powerful pushback among white Christians to the phrase and the movement is painful to persons of color.

We were on vacation with friends of ours, an Indian family, and their van was covered in dust and dirt from the mountain roads we had traveled. Their teenage daughter wrote "Black Lives Matter" in the dusty rear window with her finger. We left to go tubing down a river and when we returned later that afternoon, someone had crossed out "Black" and had written "All."

From a distance, their daughter spotted the van and her face fell. She told her mother, "Momma, it's like if I was dying and you were at the hospital with me, but my brother said, "Momma, my life matters, too. Come home and play with me instead."

It's indisputable that all lives matter, but refusing to even say "Black Lives Matter" is a denial of the seriousness of the hardships that Black people face that white people do not have to contend with. Comedian Michael Che, known for *Saturday Night Live*'s "Weekend Update," said on his stand-up special *Michael Che Matters*, "As a country, we just can't agree. We just fight about everything. We can't even agree on black lives matter. That's a controversial statement? Not matters more than you. Just matters. Matters! Just matters."[86]

When I spoke with Daniel Jones, former multi-instrumentalist with For King and Country and other Christian acts, a Black man who has spent most of his life navigating predominately white Christian spaces in college, church, and in the Christian music industry, he expressed dismay about how his white spiritual brothers and sisters pushed back so hard on this issue. "Black Lives Matter was this rallying cry, but that became such a problematic phrase for so many white evangelical Christians. This mom lost her son who was a child and you're only defending George Zimmerman?" he asked, incredulously.

He then told me a story of Jesus' heartfelt reaction to loss as a contrast to the lack of empathy toward people of color among modern white Christians: "Lazarus died and Jesus wept. He had empathy. He had two to three

85. Shear, "Pence Won't Say the Words 'Black Lives Matter,'" lines 1–4.
86. Perry, "Michael Che's Fantastic Take on 'Black Lives Matter,'" lines 1–4.

days to process, then he gets there and still cries like a baby. Where's that from our leaders, the people leading the Christian community?" ✳

There is an absence of weeping, of sorrow, of bereavement over painful loss of Black lives and Black dignity among white Christians. In its place, there is defensiveness, anger, self-justification, resentment. On social media, we see racist vitriol and hostility from those who profess to be Christ follow-ers. Their teachers present political and theological arguments with dispas-sionate certainty designed to preserve the status quo, deny real inequalities, and assure white people remain in power. This is nothing new. It's always been part of the white church in America. It remains so today.

The racism among white Christians can be vile white supremacy and outright bigotry, but also be the subtle, more covert variants that make it easy for them to believe they are not racist. The latter is a more unconscious form of racism that is self-centered and lacking in true validation and genu-ine compassion for people who are different. They see their own struggles as more real, more difficult, while having a near-complete failure of empathy for the centuries-old hardships of Black and Brown people.

To drive the point home, when the US government was intentionally separating children from their parents who attempted to cross the Mexico-US border as a deterrent, a 2018 poll found white evangelicals were more likely than any other religious group surveyed to support the policy. Over half of these Christians also reported feeling "uncomfortable" when they heard people from different countries not speaking English, and they were the most likely to say they had little or nothing in common with immigrants.[87] White evangelicals are not only more likely to see immigrants as "other" and feel un-comfortable around them, but have been more willing to endorse a horrifying policy devoid of empathy and regard for the dignity of immigrants.

Almost right on cue, there has been a movement among some white evangelicals to deprecate the very concept of empathy. John Piper, one of the most influential pastors of the past half-century, led Bethlehem Baptist Church in Minneapolis for thirty-three years. His successor, Jason Meyer, resigned during the summer of 2021 after being accused by members of the church's leadership of "the sin of empathy." This notion first emerged on Piper's website, *Desiring God*, in a 2019 article by Joe Rigney where he adopts the convention of C. S. Lewis's *Screwtape Letters*, as correspondence between two demons trying to subvert the Christian faith. In the piece, he writes, among other things, "empathy shifts the focus from the sufferer's *good* to the sufferer's *feelings*, making them the measure of whether a per-son is truly 'loved.'" Later he writes, "Things that he would have regarded

87. Vandermaas-Peeler, "2018 American Values Survey."

as foolish, sinful, and ungodly under normal circumstances will sail right along under the banner of empathy."[88]

Here Rigney conflates empathy, which is the ability to understand and share the feelings of another person, with some mindless capitulation to the feelings of an aggrieved person. In doing so, he sets up a straw man argument that is patently false on its face. His conclusion is that empathy is not just sometimes misguided or misapplied, but an inherent sin.

The end result is that some Christian leaders claim empathy, which is a great force for good in the world, is wicked and bad. One of the hallmarks of narcissism is a lack of empathy. Here, these Christians are calling empathy an insidious form of evil. Only a narcissistic subculture would entertain this notion for a moment.

A hallmark of narcissists and cultures of collective narcissism is their glaring lack of empathy toward others. Again, we see the powerful collective narcissism of the white Christian church at work, having real-life consequences that affect others, particularly the oppressed and mistreated. The absence of genuine empathy in matters of race is further evidence of the troubling narcissism and self-centeredness among white Christians. There is no greater blind spot, no stronger self-delusion, no deeper sin among white Christians in the US than racism.

88. Rigney, "Enticing Sin of Empathy."

CHAPTER 6

America Ain't a Christian Nation

Christian Nationalism

"America ain't a Christian nation, a chosen nation, or an innocent nation."

—DANTÉ STEWART

ON JANUARY 6TH, 2021, I had just finished a teletherapy session and checked my phone when a deluge of breaking news popped up furiously on the lock screen. I turned on the TV just in time to see a mob bust out a window and push their way inside the Capitol building. Christian flags were sprinkled throughout the crowd, including one carried through the Capitol. There were signs reading, "Jesus Saves," "Jesus 2020," and "In God We Trust." Christian music blared. Rioters wore "God, Guns, Trump" T-shirts. People prayed beside a large wooden cross. A protestor carried a banner proclaiming "Proud American Christian." A huge flag read, "Jesus is my Savior. Trump is my President."

Footage from the rally before the attack shows Pastor Joshua Feuerstein screaming to the crowd, "We as the church of the living God are standing up saying we are not just mad at hell, but we're mad as hell." He yelled, "It is time for war. Let us stop the steal!"[1] he admonished the crowd, fanning the conspiracy theory that liberal Democrats had orchestrated a successful nationwide plan to steal the election from Donald Trump.

1. Right Wing Watch, Twitter, January 18, 2021.

At that time, nearly all Democrats (98 percent) said Joe Biden was the legitimate winner of the 2020 presidential election, but that number dropped to less than a third (32 percent) for Republicans. Among Republicans without a college degree, that number dropped to less than a quarter (23 percent), in a demographic made up largely of white evangelicals.[2]

The rally just prior to the attack whipped the crowd into a frenzy of clapping, cheering, and booing. Leading up to the attack on the Capitol building that followed, members of the crowd yelled, "Shout if you love Jesus!" A protestor clutched a book with giant letters on the cover: HOLY BIBLE. The Proud Boys, the far-right violent nationalists, prayed together before the attack.

Once the crowd (or mob) breached the Capitol, the rhetoric became even more explicit. A woman shouted she came "in the name of Jesus" as she stormed the building. Another woman prayed "for the evil of Congress to be brought to an end." The crowd chanted, "No Trump, No Peace," a play on the old Christian bumper sticker, "No Jesus, No Peace . . . Know Jesus, Know Peace."

Many video clips showed people praying individually and in groups. A man led a group in prayer as they took the Capitol building. Once inside, a group prayed in the rotunda, while another prayed in the Senate chamber.

One man whom the FBI said was the first to enter the Capitol building through a broken window wore a shirt with Ephesians 6:11, "Put on the full armor of God, so that you can take your stand against the devil's schemes." It was apparent within days—hours, really—that the insurrection had a strong white Christian odor to it.

Peter Manseau, the curator of American religious history at the Smithsonian, wrote in *The Washington Post* that "Christians made up the core of the mob that attacked the Capitol," adding, "their actions were a natural and perhaps inevitable outgrowth of the kind of rhetoric that [Franklin] Graham and other prominent faith leaders used for months to describe the election."[3]

Michael Sparks, one of the first to breach the Capitol through a broken window, wrote on Facebook, "Trump will be your president four more years in Jesus name."[4] Leo Kelly, charged with violent entry, said another rioter "consecrated [the overtaken Senate chamber] to Jesus."[5] Pastor Ran Schuffman prayed over another rioter, "Lord, protect this soldier for you."[6]

2. Cox, "After the Ballots Are Counted," figure 1.
3. Manseau, "Capitol rioters believed they answered God's call," lines 28–30.
4. Manseau, "Capitol rioters believed they answered God's call," lines 43–45.
5. Manseau, "Capitol rioters believed they answered God's call," lines 48–49.
6. Manseau, "Capitol rioters believed they answered God's call," lines 51–52.

Political scientist Paul Djupe wrote of that day, "It is not a stretch to call this a Christian Insurrection, though Christians of a particular sort."[7] Something horrifying happened at the Capitol that day, something with predominantly Christian overtones. There was anger and vitriol, cheers and laughter, all swirled together with Christian symbols and rhetoric. The Christian faith—or at least some perversion of it—had been at the forefront of our country's most substantial insurrection in the modern era.

In *The Righteous Mind* Jonathan Haidt says we are both "selfish" and "groupish," both competitively animalistic and, when needed, unified and bound together, like honeybees in a hive that function together as a single organism. Most of the time, we put our own individuals needs ahead of others, but under certain rare conditions, we flip on what he calls "the hive switch" that causes us to "transcend self-interest and lose ourselves (temporarily and ecstatically) in something larger than ourselves."[8]

I asked Haidt if he saw the Capitol riots as an example of the hive mind. He agreed it was on full display that day. "I think the attack on the Capitol on January 6 shows these dynamics well," he answered. "The event was celebratory, fun, joyous, and angry. Many people did things as a group that they would not have done on their own."

The hive switch activates when a group needs to come together and become more united in order to outcompete and dominate other groups. In its most benign forms, we see it happen in competitive games and sports. In its most malignant forms, we see it in riots and violent insurrections.

Judging from its participants and supporters, it appears the "hive" of January 6 was an extreme picture of what we call Christian nationalism. And white evangelicals held more explicitly Christian nationalistic views after the insurrection than before.

Lauren Kerby, who spent two years observing "Christian heritage" bus tours in Washington, DC, wrote in *The Atlantic*, "When Trump's insurrectionists stormed the Capitol, they were living the dream of countless frustrated white evangelical Christians . . . They lived out a fantasy of taking back the country, or at least its Capitol, for God."[9]

WHAT IS CHRISTIAN NATIONALISM?

In January 2016, Donald Trump stood in front of a massive three-story pipe organ in B. J. Haan Auditorium on the campus of Dordt University, a small

---

7. Djupe, "Christian Nationalist Democracy," lines 9–10.

8. Haidt, *Righteous Mind*, 283.

9. Kerby, "Christian Nationalists Want More Than Political Power," lines 31–40.

Christian college in the northwest corner of Iowa. He smiled and waved as the crowd cheered. His speech ran over an hour and one now-notorious line of him bragging of his followers' loyalty caught the media's attention: "I could stand in the middle of Fifth Avenue and shoot somebody and I wouldn't lose any voters."[10] But the line missed in the frenzied coverage is the most important: "Christianity will have power," he promised the elated crowed, adding, "If I'm there, you're going to have plenty of power."[11]

"That's Christian nationalism in a nutshell, advocating for Christian power rather than Christian principle," said Georgetown professor Paul D. Miller, author of *Christian Nationalism in the Age of Trump*.[12] Researchers found those who subscribed to Christian nationalist ideology were much more likely to vote for Trump, even after controlling for such factors as anti-Black, anti-Muslim, anti-immigrant, and sexist attitudes. It was an even more important predictor than economic dissatisfaction.[13] It was the key to his election success.

Beyond partisan politics, many see Christian nationalism increasingly aligned with white supremacy and militant movements. In a poll of nearly two thousand registered voters, about half (47 percent) found Christian nationalism to be a significant threat to the country.[14] By contrast, a nearly equal number (46 percent) of evangelicals said it wasn't a threat to the country at all. Many conservative Christians say Christian nationalism is not even real.[15]

Bill Donohue, president and CEO of the Catholic League for Religious and Civil Rights, calls Christian nationalism a "fiction" that others are using "as a weapon to assault our Judeo-Christian heritage."[16] Russ Vought, the former director of the Office of Management and Budget under Donald Trump, referred to "so-called" Christian nationalism in an opinion piece for *Newsweek* before making the case that the United States is "a historically Christian nation," which, as you'll see, is the essence of Christian nationalism.[17]

"Christian nationalism doesn't exist," Franklin Graham told *The New Yorker*, adding it was "just another name to throw at Christians. The left

---

10. Dias, "'Christianity Will Have Power,'" lines 1–23.
11. Dias, "'Christianity Will Have Power,'" lines 32–34.
12. Lee, "Christian Nationalism is Worse Than You Think," lines 186–7.
13. Federico and Golec de Zavala, "Collective Narcissism in the 2016 Election."
14. Piacenza, "Christian Nationalism as a Threat," figure 1.
15. Piacenza, "Christian Nationalism as a Threat," figure 2.
16. Donohue, "'Christian Nationalism' is an Invention," lines 68–70.
17. Vought, "Is There Anything Wrong With 'Christian Nationalism'?," lines 7–19.

is very good at calling people names."[18] He's incorrect about the existence of Christian nationalism, though he may be confused about the meaning and definition of it. Christian nationalism is not simply being a patriotic Christian. It is not pride in one's country or faith-based engagement in politics. Christian nationalism is an ideology that the United States is a Christian nation that Christians who follow biblically based laws should govern. For Christian nationalists, the success of the US is part of God's larger plan for the world and allowing it to be governed in a non-Christian manner will bring God's judgment upon us.

Television anchor Will Cain approached a group of men at a diner in Missouri for a segment on *Fox and Friends*, the Fox News morning show. He met Mitch, who sat in a booth with three other men, his Bible open on the table before him.[19]

"What are your biggest concerns with the state of the country right now?" Cain asked.[20]

The possibility of greater gun control and more illegal immigration worried Mitch, but his biggest concern was fewer people going to church. The decline of people "claiming Jesus Christ as their Lord and savior" dismayed him, he said as he gestured down at his Bible.[21]

"And I also am concerned that people my age and people younger than me, I feel like, have lost the knowledge of American exceptionalism," he said. "And the fact that I do believe that we are the greatest country on the history of the Earth."[22]

Mitch claimed the Bible says America is a special, chosen nation. "*Like it says in the Bible*—and like Ronald Reagan echoed in the eighties—I feel like *America is supposed to be the city on the hill* and we're supposed to be the example for the rest of the world as Christians and as patriots and I feel like we're starting to lose that."[23]

Many agree with Mitch. They believe God ordained the United States as "the city on the hill," a notion tracing back to the Puritan preacher John Winthrop in 1630, which he derived from Jesus' Sermon on the Mount in Matthew 5, though the passage is in no way a reference to any specific country. To Mitch and millions of others, God established the US and gave it special favor and a unique role and responsibility in the world. These twin

18. Griswold, "Pennsylvania Lawmaker and Christian Nationalism," lines 111–15.

19. Edwards, "America is supposed to be the city on the hill," lines 3–4.

20. Edwards, "America is supposed to be the city on the hill," line 5.

21. Edwards, "America is supposed to be the city on the hill," lines 6–8.

22. Edwards, "America is supposed to be the city on the hill," lines 9–11.

23. Edwards, "America is supposed to be the city on the hill," lines 12–15.

attributes of the country's specialness and obligation are the heart of Christian nationalism.

Sociologist Andrew Whitehead, co-author of the definitive text *Taking America Back for God*, told me, "Christian nationalism is this narrative that God has a plan for the US, that there's a covenantal relationship with the Christian God, that part of God's plan for the world includes the United States. And one that if we fulfill the terms of this covenant, then God will bless us and it will go well with us. But if we don't, then God will be angry with us as a nation."

Yale sociologist Philip Gorski asserts Christian nationalism has roots in a belief that God's Old Testament commands and promises to Israel now apply to the United States as the country ordained by God to occupy a special place and role in the world.[24]

Christian nationalism begins as a story that many people believe, then emerges as a creed that guides social and political engagement. Paul Miller told *Christianity Today*, "Christian nationalism is a political ideology about American identity."[25] He added, "It takes Christian symbols, rhetoric, and concepts and weaves [them] into a political ideology."[26]

Far from being a fringe notion, more Americans believe in Christian nationalism than reject it. The Baylor Religion Survey found most Americans (58 percent) believe the United States has been a Christian nation.[27] These beliefs are strongly correlated with self-identifying as "very religious."[28] Only 20 percent believe the US has never been a Christian nation.[29] Not surprisingly, more than any other religious group, white evangelicals were more likely to say that the US has always been and is still a Christian nation or that it was in the past, but is no longer.[30]

In *Taking America Back for God*, Whitehead and his research partner Samuel Perry define four main orientations toward Christian nationalism, which they see as different from civil religion or the practice of religious faith. "Christian nationalism really is a spectrum and people fall at different places," Whitehead told me. He cautions these are not rigid categories but

24. Gorski, *American Covenant*.

25. Lee, "Christian Nationalism is Worse Than You Think," line 31.

26. Lee, "Christian Nationalism is Worse Than You Think," lines 58–59.

27. Froese et al., "Baylor Religion Survey, Wave 5," figure 19.

28. Froese et al., "Baylor Religion Survey, Wave 5," figure 21.

29. Froese et al., "Baylor Religion Survey, Wave 5," figure 19.

30. Froese et al., "Baylor Religion Survey, Wave 5," figure 22.

guidelines for understanding. These are the four orientations that make up a continuum from low to high Christian nationalism:[31]

Rejectors—These people believe there should not be any link between Christianity and the politics and government of the United States. They emphasize the wall of separation between church and state, though a third of them identify as Christian. They are the more highly educated of all the groups. They represent 21.5 percent of the US population.

Resistors—These individuals are more indecisive regarding the role of religion in the public square. Representing 26.6 percent of the US population, they lean away from Christian nationalism, but with some inconsistencies. Compared to the Rejectors, they are more likely to be Black or Hispanic. Fewer are married. They engage in more religious practice than Rejectors.

Accommodators—These folks lean toward accepting Christian nationalism. They might be undecided about such things as wanting the federal government to declare the United States to be a Christian nation, but favor allowing religious symbols like the cross or the Ten Commandments to be displayed in public spaces. There are more women Accommodators than men. They are older and live in more rural areas. About a third are evangelical and another third are Catholic. They represent 32.1 percent of the total US population.

Ambassadors—These are the true believers, the ones who give full-throated support to Christian nationalism. For them, the US is without question a Christian nation. Representing one in five Americans (19.8 percent), they are the oldest of all four groups and majority female and white. They are more likely to live in rural areas and in the South than any other group.

"Maybe not a lot of Americans are at the far end of our scale, but you're looking at many who are at least friendly towards it. A lot of them are," Whitehead told me. The distribution of these four groups among the entire population looks like this:

---

31. Whitehead and Perry, *Taking America Back for God*, 24–53.

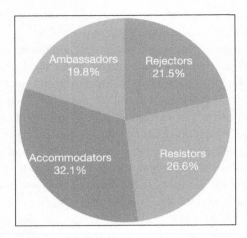

The numbers change radically when you consider conservative white Christians. Whitehead told me his research shows the strong majority of conservative white Christians are Christian nationalists. "When you look at white evangelicals, close to 80 percent are Accommodators or Ambassadors," he said. "And when you look at Catholics and the Mainline, over half are Accommodators or Ambassadors."

PREDICTORS OF CHRISTIAN NATIONALISM

Based on data from the 2007 Baylor Religion Survey analyzed by Whitehead and Perry, the top ten predictors of strong adherence to Christian nationalism, in order from strongest to weakest, are:[32]

- *They are politically conservative*—most Christian nationalists are aligned with Republican and/or conservative politics and are more politically engaged than average.

- *They identify as "Bible-believing"*—they endorse the Bible as the foremost authority for all of life, including matters related to personal moral life, civic engagement, and understanding of how the world operates.

- *They view the Bible as the literal word of God*—Christian nationalists see the Bible as directly inspired by God and consider all accounts of history to be literally true. Since the Bible says God created the world in six days, it means God created the world in six literal twenty-four-hour periods. Stories like the account of Job caught in a cosmic battle

32. Whitehead and Perry, *Taking America Back for God*, 12–15.

between God and Satan are matters of history, not parables or folktales with a lesson.

- *They see the Bible as perfectly true, though not literally interpreted*—Christians have held nuanced views of the Bible over the centuries. On a continuum, this belief would be just adjacent to the previous notion of the Bible requiring literal interpretation for all accounts. From this perspective, the Bible is still the Word of God, fully true, but with freedom to interpret some accounts as being nonliteral stories.

- *They are religiously affiliated*—Christian nationalists are affiliated with churches, parachurches, and other religious organizations at higher levels than the general population.

- *They engage in religious practices of church attendance, prayer, and Bible reading*—Based on their reports, going to church and engaging in the traditional faith practices of prayer and Scripture reading are important to Christian nationalists.

- *They believe the nation is on the brink of moral decay*—Most Christian nationalists believe the country is getting worse. They perceive increases in crime and violence, escalating rates of teen pregnancy and abortion, and full erosion of sexual values and boundaries.

- *They believe God requires the faithful to wage wars for good*—Christian nationalists endorse the notion of "just wars" that require the righteous to engage in warfare for moral purposes. This is in contrast to the pacifistic views of others within the Christian tradition.

- *They believe the rapture is coming*—For Christian nationalists, the end of the world is nigh and they play a role in ushering in the return of Jesus and the rapture of the faithful.

- *They have lower educational attainment*—Compared to others, Christian nationalists are more likely to have a high school diploma as their highest level of educational attainment and less likely to have a graduate or professional degree.

Most Christian nationalists are conservative, Bible-believing Christians with a pessimistic view of the state of the country and a conviction they are living in the end times. For them, God has chosen America as special, but in the hands of the godless, it has fallen into decay and must be restored. These nationalistic characteristics are tangled up with expressions of authentic faith, like engaging in regular religious practices and being part of a church. Alongside these practices are beliefs about the nation being on the brink of moral collapse, an accommodating view of war, and a belief in certain end times theology. All of this is mixed with conservative politics and lower-than-average levels of education.

Whitehead and Perry write, "Christian nationalism isn't localized primarily within particular religious traditions but is undergirded by a combination of conservative political ideology, belief in the Bible, apocalyptic visions of societal decline, and divine militarism."[33]

THE SURPRISINGLY ANTIDEMOCRATIC NATURE OF CHRISTIAN NATIONALISM

One surprising aspect of Christian nationalism is how antidemocratic it is. In a large national survey of over 2,500 Americans, researchers asked people about their sentiments toward different groups, then asked how much they would allow people of disliked groups to take part in various civic activities, like teaching in public schools, holding public office, or making speeches in the community.[34] Would white supremacists allow Muslims to teach in the local school system? Would atheists let Christian fundamentalists run for city council? Would Republicans let undocumented immigrants speak in a town hall forum?

Nearly two-thirds of atheists (65 percent) who regarded conservative Christians as their most disliked group would allow them to engage in three or more of the listed activities.[35] The white conservative Christians were not so charitable toward the atheists, however. When they selected atheists as their least-liked group, only 32 percent of the Christians would allow them to participate in three or more of the listed activities.[36]

In another study, 80 percent of Christian nationalists who believed the majority (i.e., white Christians) should rule the country saw the US as quite democratic.[37] These majoritarians believe those in control should exert their power on the less powerful. They have a much different conception of what democracy means than other citizens. Paul Djupe wrote, "Christian nationalism is a worldview in which the Christian majority is rightfully in power to protect the group and make the US into their vision."[38]

The emphasis on power, as well as the belief that power and authority should be in their hands is a defining feature of Christian nationalism.

33. Whitehead and Perry, *Taking America Back for God,* 13.

34. Djupe, "Are Atheists as Intolerant as Evangelicals Think?," lines 32–54.

35. Djupe, "Are Atheists as Intolerant as Evangelicals Think?," lines 56–58.

36. Djupe, "Are Atheists as Intolerant as Evangelicals Think?," lines 66–68.

37. Djupe, "What Does Christian Nationalist Democracy Look Like?," figure 2.

38. Djupe, "What Does Christian Nationalist Democracy Look Like?," lines 78–79.

"For white Christians who have been at the center essentially of American civic life from before the US was founded until now, Christian nationalism operates in a very particular way for them to want to defend what they see as their right to power and privilege," Whitehead explained.

The modern antidemocratic roots of Christian nationalism sunk down deep antidemocratic roots decades ago. In evangelical circles, it was normal—even expected—for parents and teens to attend the Institute for Basic Life Principles and the Institute for Basic Life Conflicts, founded by minister and author Bill Gothard. His ministry published a homeschool curriculum that was decidedly antidemocratic. These quotes come directly from their classroom materials:

- "Pure democracy did not work in Greece, or Rome, or France. Neither will it work in our country."[39]

- "Because a pure democracy makes the will of the majority the sovereign rule of the land, it violates the requirements for a Godly nation. A pure democracy fulfills the description of the broad way which leads many to destruction."[40]

- "In addition to advocating pure democracy, there is a strong emphasis in our country of separation of Church and State. However, those who advocate this idea are communicating their true intentions of separating God from government."[41]

The curriculum was also strongly authoritarian and emphasized hierarchy, control, and harsh punishment for those who transgress. Consider these direct quotes from the curriculum designed to educate school-age children:

- "The proper picture of authority in any relationship is established when that authority comes from above (God to government, parent to child, and husband to wife)."[42]

- "In a democracy, on the other hand, because of an overemphasis on fairness and rights, people begin to view all suffering, even justly deserved punishment, as something to be avoided."[43]

---

39. Gothard, *Wisdom Worksheet (Booklet 49)*, 2695.

40. Gothard, *Wisdom Worksheet (Booklet 49)*, 2645.

41. Gothard, *Wisdom Worksheet (Booklet 49)*, 2702.

42. Gothard, *Wisdom Worksheet (Booklet 49)*, 2691.

43. Gothard, *Wisdom Worksheet (Booklet 49)*, 2695.

- "Under this philosophy, democratic judges, as well as the general public, will misperceive the main purpose of punishment as the rehabilitation of the lawbreaker."[44]

- "In a sense, then, capital punishment (under God's direction) is the basis of all government."[45]

- "Without Biblical standards, such a society will eventually vote to abolish the death penalty."[46]

One hallmark of Christian nationalism is its harshness. Analyzing data from the Baylor Religion Survey, sociologist Joshua Davis found those who believe the federal government should declare the US a Christian nation were more likely to support harsher punishment for criminals and favor the death penalty.[47]

Davis also found those rating high in Christian nationalism were much more likely to support more severe penalties for criminals, favor the death penalty, and believe we needed to "crack down on troublemakers to save our moral standards."[48]

THE PSYCHOLOGICAL PORTRAIT
OF A CHRISTIAN NATIONALIST

Many years ago, my wife and I had just moved to a new town, and we were visiting different churches. One Sunday we attended a church with a guest speaker introduced as "an expert on the Founding Fathers," which seemed like an odd calling card. He was a bright, articulate man with a polished style. The motif of his sermon that day was "Coincidence or Providence." The premise was that God had moved the founders in various ways that allowed our country to form against great odds. The United States, he concluded, was not just a coincidence, but the result of God's hand at work. We were a special country, ordained by God, set apart to do great things for God.

I had no mental framework to understand what I was hearing. I knew it made me feel uneasy, but I didn't know why. There was nothing in his manner that made me recoil. He didn't use divisive or inflammatory language. Yet it seemed strange. Why had this man—and others—staked

---

44. Gothard, *Wisdom Worksheet (Booklet 49)*, 2695.

45. Gothard, *Wisdom Worksheet (Booklet 49)*, 2695.

46. Gothard, *Wisdom Worksheet (Booklet 49)*, 2695.

47. Davis, "Enforcing Christian Nationalism."

48. Davis, "Enforcing Christian Nationalism."

their professional identities on building a case for the specialness of the United States?

A few weeks later, we attended another church that had a "patriotic celebration of America" as we approached July 4. The choir sang "The Battle Hymn of the Republic" and "God Bless America." The preacher strode across the stage saying "America is the greatest country in the history of the world" because "we were and always have been a Christian nation." In this service, there was more emotionality, more applause, more "Amens." It was a pep rally for America.

Most Christian nationalists are not as clever and eloquent as the first speaker or as bombastic as the second, but they are committed to this worldview. For them, it is self-evident, indisputable, and a position to be guarded zealously. It took me many years to understand there was a deeper psychology at work that helped explain why so many who identify as being Christian are also passionate in claiming the US as a Christian nation.

A distinct picture is emerging of individuals who ascribe to this Christian nationalist perspective. To be clear, not all Christians are Christian nationalists. These are not synonymous. There is, depending on the definition, over 50 percent overlap, however. Among evangelicals, the number is closer to 80 percent.[49]

The psychological profile of Christian nationalists has emerged with four major themes: harshness and hostility, pessimism, inflexibility, and dominance.

Harshness and Hostility

One consistent quality of nationalists is their harsh interpersonal style. A survey of 1,800 scholars rated world leaders and concluded nationalists were more authoritarian with less agreeable personality traits. Significant amounts of research have found those who are low in agreeableness are more prone to anger and hostility toward others.[50]

Even Christian nationalists who are even-tempered and pleasant can show more harsh attitudes toward others, especially those who are different or not part of their group. They are especially intolerant of troublemakers and dissenters. As we've discussed, Ambassadors, the most ardent Christian nationalists, are more likely to approve of authoritarian crackdowns to keep people in line. Their approach to law and order is undemocratic, favoring

---

49. Lee, "Christian Nationalism is Worse Than You Think."
50. Nai and Toros, "Peculiar personality of strongmen."

policies like "stop and frisk" and the war on drugs. They are also hostile toward immigrants and even resentful of refugees.

Christian nationalists are mistrusting of other religious groups. In the US, that suspicion is usually directed at Muslims, including those who are American citizens. Nationalists are more likely than most to reject information about racial and ethnic inequality.[51]

Christian nationalists also have a negative and often hostile relationship with the scientific community. Christian nationalists are more anti-science than most. One study concluded that scientific findings that challenge—or seem to challenge—biblical authority are seen as a threat by Christian nationalists. This was on full display during the COVID-19 pandemic when Christian nationalists were more likely than other groups to resist mask and social distancing mandates, attack scientific authorities, and express little concern about the virus.[52] Often they couch anti-scientific attitudes in religious language and beliefs. In mid-2020, a survey of over one thousand Americans found that 67 percent of white evangelicals believed God would protect them from getting infected with the virus.[53] At the time, there had been about nine thousand documented deaths from the virus. A year later, that number had grown by 550,000, more US casualties than both world wars combined. Still, the hostility and rejection of scientific consensus among Christian nationalists remained high.

Contrary to popular opinion, Christian nationalism, not religious belief, was the strongest predictor an American would not follow recommended safety guidelines during the pandemic. These individuals would be more likely to eat at a restaurant or gather in larger groups or visit friends or family. They were among those least likely to wear a mask or sanitize their hands.[54]

Christian nationalists are not only harsh and critical toward others, but they see others as hostile toward them, even when the evidence does not suggest it. Christian nationalists appear to be prone to hostile attribution bias, which means they see others as having hostile intentions, even where none exist.[55] Their mental filter makes them see others as intending them harm and ready to pounce. Hostile attribution bias has profound implications for individuals and those in their orbit. Those with high levels of hostile attribution bias have much higher rates of marital and other partner

---

51. Froese et al., "Baylor Religion Survey, Wave 5," figures 9–18.
52. Baker et al., "Crusading for Moral Authority."
53. Earls, "Religious Americans See Pandemic as Sign From God."
54. Perry et al., "Culture Wars and COVID-19 Conduct."
55. Tuente et al., "Hostile Attribution Bias—Systematic Review."

relationship conflicts, and lower levels of relationship satisfaction. They are harsher with their children. They lash out at others and are more prone to aggression when provoked. They ruminate over perceived slights for six months or longer. Compared to others without this bias, they are also four times more likely to die by the age of fifty.[56]

Pessimism

Psychologists have long been fascinated with the study of optimism and pessimism. Both are relatively stable traits, fueled by our early temperaments. Optimists believe bad things come and go, just like good things. They see downturns as being contained and compartmentalized, not bleeding out into all areas of life. Optimists focus on their role in a problem and what they can control, not on the external forces over which they have no influence. They are usually psychologically healthier than pessimists. There are many well-documented physical and emotional benefits of optimism, ranging from longer life span, better stress coping, higher marital satisfaction, lower blood pressure, a stronger immune system, and greater well-being.[57]

Pessimists see bad things as all-encompassing, here to stay, and the result of outside factors that threaten to wreck them. Pessimists are more prone to anxiety and depression. They see conditions only worsening. Their pessimism increases their risk of heart disease and knocks about two years off their life, compared to more optimistic people.[58]

Christian nationalists are supreme pessimists, especially about the current state and direction of the nation. They believe our best days as a country are behind us. The massive cultural changes, especially the move toward pluralism and acceptance of diversity, are not positive developments in their eyes. They see the country on the brink of moral collapse, in need of radical intervention.

Christian nationalists believe we are living in the end times where civilization as we know it will come to a cataclysmic conclusion. The willingness of Christian nationalists to storm the Capitol building reveals the urgency they feel to turn the country around before all is lost. Elizabeth Neumann, a former high-ranking official with the Department of Homeland Security, told *Politico* that Christian nationalists "see it in cataclysmic terms: This is the moment and God's going to judge us. When you paint it in existential

56. Tuente et al., "Hostile Attribution Bias—Systematic Review."
57. Harvard Health, "Optimism and Your Health."
58. Pänkäläinen et al., "Pessimism and risk of death from coronary heart disease."

terms like that, a lot of people feel justified to carry out acts of violence in the name of their faith."[59]

For Christian nationalists, the country is headed toward ruin, which justifies any means necessary to correct the trajectory. If they fail, we face God's wrath and judgment. The stakes are high. The consequences for failure are unthinkable.

What often gets missed in this discussion is that by most indicators, the country is *not* devolving into a moral cesspool. Take abortion as a prominent example. You might imagine the rate of abortion has gone up over the past several decades, especially since the US Supreme Court legalized it. According to national data gathered by the CDC, the rate of abortion has gone down steadily since 1981. At that time, there were 29.3 abortion per one thousand women (ages fifteen to forty-four). By 2017, the rate had dropped to 13.5 per one thousand women, which is lower than in 1973 when *Roe v. Wade* was decided.[60]

Some also assume the rate of violent crime has gone up in recent years. Again, the opposite is true. According to data provided by the FBI, the rates of violent crime perpetrated by both adults and juveniles has dropped consistently since 1993.[61] The Bureau of Justice Statistics found an enormous 74 percent drop in violent crime and a 71 percent decline in property crime from 1993 to 2019. Crime is down and has been declining for nearly thirty years.[62]

In fact, there is evidence in a broad range of areas that the US and the world are getting better, not worse. The rate of poverty in the United States is declining.[63,64] We have cut the amount of air pollution almost in half over the past thirty years. Except during the COVID pandemic, life expectancy is way up.[65]

Around the globe, the trends are also good. There are half as many active wars as there were a quarter century ago.[66] Fewer people are living

59. Stanton, "Violent Christian Extremism," lines 36–39.

60. Kortsmit et al., "Abortion Surveillance—United States."

61. Federal Bureau of Investigation, "2017 Crime in the United States."

62. Gramlich, "Crime in the United States," lines 54–56.

63. Roser and Ortiz-Ospina, "Global Extreme Poverty."

64. Garfield, "Author of Bill Gates' Favorite Book"

65. Roser et al., "Life Expectancy."

66. Garfield, "Author of Bill Gates' Favorite Book."

in extreme poverty.[67] Rates of hunger have declined.[68] Child mortality is down.[69] Rates of literacy are up.[70]

Though we have many problems to solve, there is not strong evidence to support the notion of a country—or a world—falling into disarray. Christian nationalists, however, see the nation in moral free fall and are pessimistic about our future.

If there is any optimism to be found among them, most Christian nationalists believe the faithful will be raptured—taken up to heaven—hopefully before Armageddon begins. They get to escape while others endure the coming hell on Earth. Two-thirds of Ambassadors (65 percent) are convinced there will be a literal rapture, compared to only 38 percent of Accommodators, 11 percent of Resisters, and less than 2 percent of Rejectors.[71]

Inflexibility

By nature, some people are highly flexible thinkers, able to accommodate and synthesize new thoughts and ideas. They are skilled at problem-solving, proficient at generating options, adept at contemplating new paths forward.

Others who struggle with fluid thinking are inflexible. For them, problem-solving is a chore. Looking at situations through a new lens is nearly impossible. In therapy, a person's ability to make good progress is at least partially tied to their ability to think flexibly and contemplate new solutions to old problems. Flexible thinkers do better, while inflexible thinkers do worse.

Early in my career when I worked with aggressive teenagers, a group notorious for their mental rigidity, I would often have conversations that would go like this:

Me: You punched the principal in the face when he told you to stop disrupting your class.

Kid: Yeah. He made me mad.

Me: Now that you can think about it, what else could you have done?

Kid: Nothing.

Me: What other options besides hitting him are there?

Kid: That's the only thing I could have done.

---

67. Roser and Ortiz-Ospina, "Global Extreme Poverty."

68. Von Grember et al., "2017 Global Hunger Index."

69. UNICEF Data, "Under-Five Mortality."

70. Roser and Ortiz-Ospina, "Literacy."

71. Stark, "Findings From the Baylor Surveys of Religion."

This, in a nutshell, is mental inflexibility. It may be an extreme example, but it makes the point. Like these kids, inflexible people can't problem-solve well. They find it hard to generate options. They rarely consider new ways of seeing a situation. As a result, they often struggle with managing their emotions and have greater difficulty in the workplace and in their relationships. Psychologist Todd Kashdan writes, "Psychological flexibility makes a major contribution to daily well-being and lasting psychological health."[72] The opposite is true of psychological and cognitive inflexibility, which often leads to more struggles in life. Across several studies, psychological inflexibility was related to having more mental health problems, like anxiety and depression or behavioral problems.[73]

Mental inflexibility is not exclusive to violent adolescents. Many adults, including lots of high-functioning people, rate high in this kind of cognitive rigidity. We see it among people who gravitate toward fundamentalism where mental inflexibility is not just a hallmark but a badge of honor, not a bug but a feature. Accommodating new thoughts and allowing new ways of seeing the world is a weakness and failing among true fundamentalists.

We also see mental inflexibility among Christian nationalists. Researchers gave over three hundred people tests that measure mental flexibility. One test, called the Wisconsin Card Sorting Test, shows how well people change and adapt to new rules and rewards on a task. People who do well on the task are more cognitively flexible and those who do poorly are more inflexible. In this study, those who were more mentally inflexible were also more likely to endorse nationalistic positions. Before the study, the authors had hypothesized "that nationalistic thinking may be an instance of a general tendency to rigidly categorize information and to process information in an inflexible manner." Their educated guess proved accurate, leading them to conclude, "While upholding tight, impermeable mental boundaries between concepts can be beneficial for mechanistic thinking, it can also lead to challenges in adapting to change or uncertainty."[74]

Another study of over one thousand individuals in the US and the UK found cognitive inflexibility had significant, even life-altering, implications. People who were more cognitively rigid were more likely to endorse violence to protect their group and more willing to fight and even die for their group.[75] They can contemplate no other conclusion. If a rigid member of a fringe group is told his group is under attack and he must fight to the death

72. Kashdan, "Psychological Flexibility as a Fundamental Aspect of Health," 2.

73. Kashdan, "Psychological Flexibility as a Fundamental Aspect of Health."

74. Zmigrod et al., "Cognitive Underpinnings of Nationalist Ideology," E4533.

75. Zmigrod et al., "Cognitive Inflexibility Predicts Extremist Attitudes."

to protect it, he is more likely to do so. While Christian nationalists are not fringe, they are still prone to inflexible thinking. With that rigidity comes a certainty and an unyielding dogmatism. For the most rigid thinkers among them, debate and honest discussion of ideas is not a consideration.

Dominance

Perhaps the most prominent trait among Christian nationalists is their dominance orientation. They believe they should be in the seats of power. For them, they believe God has not only ordained the country to be a Christian nation, but, by definition, they and other Christians should rule it. They should be in positions of control in all significant areas of government and culture.

Christian nationalists rate high on Social Dominance Orientation (SDO), which involves vigorous support for social hierarchies and a resistance toward equality. Those who rate high in SDO believe culture should have structures with their group on top and others beneath them. The SDO scores of those who endorse Christian nationalism are 2.5 times more than those who reject this orientation.[76]

A person rating high in SDO likely perceives the world as competitive, dangerous, and cutthroat. He is less agreeable and less open to new ideas and experiences than most others, making him especially disdainful of the perspectives of those who come from different cultures, lifestyles, or backgrounds than his own.

All this contributes to him having less empathy for people. He has little regard for the plight of the refugee or the immigrant or the unprivileged person. He has a negative attitude toward women's rights. He places himself in an elevated position of power and others in their subordinate roles. This is the order of things. For him, seeing one group as better, more capable, and more deserving than others isn't wrong, but a necessary way to preserve the way the world should be. His SDO worldview leads him to exhibit more prejudice toward those outside his group, especially those who challenge his authority.

He's also more likely than most to be active in politics, advocating for laws and policies that favor his group. He favors any means necessary to keep his group in power and engaging in politics is often the most powerful, socially sanctioned means to achieve that. He votes in every election, but favors restrictions on the voting times and conditions of those outside his

76. Djupe, "Christian Nationalism is about Dominance," lines 41–44.

group. For him, politics is less about a democratic process and more of a vehicle to hold on to power to preserve the social hierarchy.

For Christian nationalists, SDO gets justified in an ideology called dominionism, which has been discussed on Christian radio and television shows and written about in books. Dominionists believe Christians should have dominion over the key realms of our society.[77]

Relevant magazine senior editor Tyler Huckabee explains, "At their most extreme, Christian Nationalists may describe themselves as "dominionists," who believe Christians ought to have dominion over what they consider to be the seven forces—or, in their parlance, "mountains"— that shape culture: business, government, media, arts and entertainment, education, family and religion."[78]

In his book, *Invading Babylon: The 7 Mountain Mandate*, Lance Wallnau wrote, "I sensed the Lord telling me, 'He who can take these mountains can take the harvest of nations.'"[79] Of this approach, conservative columnist David French wrote, "You'll note the extent to which the heart of this strategy (or mandate) isn't based on clear scriptural commands but on claimed special revelations from God. Second, you'll note how much it emphasizes placing people in positions of power and control."[80]

This emphasis on moving Christians into seats of influence and power flows from a Social Dominance Orientation. Researchers have found a clear link between SDO and greater levels of Christian nationalism, as well as fear and narcissism.

ONE LEVEL DEEPER

When faced with a challenging case, psychologists dig deeper, eager to understand more fully. When I was in training, one of my supervisors would often ask things like, "You say your client feels like a failure, but why does he feel like that? What in his life led to that feeling? Go another level deeper." With Christian nationalism, we see the harshness and hostility, pessimism, inflexibility, and domineering attitudes, but what lies beneath those traits? When we peel back the layers, our two dominant themes of fear and collective narcissism lurk underneath. These two propulsive forces take the form of Christian nationalism.

77. French, "Religious Movement Rationalizes."
78. Huckabee, "Under God," lines 73–77.
79. French, "Religious Movement Rationalizes," lines 52–53.
80. French, "Religious Movement Rationalizes," lines 95–98.

Fear

When the *New York Times* interviewed a drywall contractor from Robbins-ville, North Carolina named Adam Phillips, he made a claim that resonates with millions of Christian nationalists: "It has been obvious for a while that Christians are under suppression, they are under scrutiny by everyone. All of the things the country was founded on are under attack, they are trying to get the name of God out of everything, especially the name of Jesus."[81] For Mr. Phillips, the country is being purged of its Christian heritage and Christians and their faith are under attack.

Two and half months before the election of 2020, Franklin Graham appeared for an interview on the Christian Broadcast Network. He predicted dire consequences if Trump did not win the election. "I believe the storm is coming," he said. "You're going to see Christians attacked. You're going to see churches close. You're going to see real hatred expressed toward people of faith. That's coming."[82]

Reading this well over a year past the election of 2020, I suspect you have yet to see widespread attacks on Christians, churches forced to close, and true persecution of the faithful in the United States. Yet Graham, who proclaimed, "God was behind the last election," regularly stokes alarm.[83] He and others foment a particular type of fear—fear of the other, fear of persecution, fear of loss of power and influence.

I asked Andrew Whitehead what he believes to be the psychological driver behind Christian nationalism. Without hesitation, he said it was fear. Christian nationalists are afraid, afraid of change, of being displaced, of being pushed aside. "Political scientist Paul Djupe called it the inverse of the golden rule where you treat them the way you fear they're going to treat you. They're kind of on edge and trying to fight against the people they think are trying to strip away what is theirs."

On the surface, though, Christian nationalists appear angry, embittered, even rageful. The Capitol rioters, the Twitter quarrelers, public scene-makers all seem furious. Anger seems to be the dominant emotion. But, as in much of psychology, one emotion often obscures another, deeper emotion. This is often true of fear. We see this all the time: A man gets a poor performance evaluation at work and comes home and yells at his kids. A woman learns her child has a learning disability and blows up at her husband for his lack of support and involvement. A teenager whose girlfriend says she's thinking

81. Dias and Graham, "Evangelical Christians Fused," lines 95–100.

82. Brody, "Franklin Graham Thinks Democratic Party is 'Opposed to Faith,'" lines 58–60.

83. Body, "Franklin Graham Thinks Democratic Party is 'Opposed to Faith,'" line 57.

of breaking up with him loses his temper at his coach. In each case, a person faces uncertainty that leads to anxiety, yet comes out expressed as anger.

Christian nationalists worry they are getting pushed aside, losing their grip on the steering wheel. They are fearful, but it comes out as rage and indignation. I asked Whitehead if individuals interviewed for his research seemed more angry or fearful. He said, "Underlying anger was there, but I think a lot of it is fear of change and fear of what they perceived as what the United States used to be or should be, compared to their perception of what it is now. So fear of change or fear of the US not being what they had hoped it would be, I think that would be the big one. When we look at demographic cultural change around, I think that's a big part of it, too. There's just an underlying fear and then I think anger comes through for some."

Collective Narcissism

In their analysis of the research literature entitled "Nationalism as Collective Narcissism," Aleksandra Cichocka and Aleksandra Cislak found that, across countries and cultures, we can conceptualize nationalistic attitudes as a form of collective narcissism. The need for a nation—or a group within a nation—to be viewed as great and special "is captured by the concept of collective narcissism—a belief in in-group greatness contingent on external recognition."[84]

Their interpretation of the research finds collective narcissism increases as a person's way of coping with unmet needs. Collective narcissism escalates when people experience low self-worth and feel little control over their lives. It is a coping strategy for feeling badly about one's self. Cichocka and Cislak explain that collective narcissism "helps manage psychological needs of the individual" within the group, calling it a "group-based ego-enhancement strategy."[85] Translation: *My connection to the group helps me feel better about myself.*

A central premise of my psychological exploration of white Christians is, having experienced the sea change of culture over the past decades, they have become a subculture of collective narcissism, perceiving themselves as special and rightly privileged, yet unappreciated and under attack. As a result, they feel justified in demonizing their detractors and lashing out at them.

Christian nationalism is, in essence, an ideological weapon that flows from collective narcissism. It is the justification for engaging in culture wars and acting in harsh ways toward those outside the group. With its

84. Cichocka and Cislak, "Nationalism as Collective Narcissism," 69.
85. Cichocka and Cislak, "Nationalism as Collective Narcissism," 72.

justifications and organized worldview, it becomes a vehicle by which collective narcissism can exert power and control. Christian nationalism is the chief weapon of collective narcissism among white evangelicals.]

I surveyed 291 US adults from every region of the country and representing all socio-economic levels and found a very high correlation (.85) between Christian nationalism and collective narcissism. As collective narcissism increased, so did Christian nationalism. The two constructs are linked and embodied among white Christians at rates higher than what we'd expect to find in the general population. The two are intertwined, bound up together.

I asked Whitehead if he agreed that Christian nationalism might be an expression of collective narcissism as I described it. He said, "That would play into this idea that 'we are special and the defenders of this Christian nation are the ones that are truly trying to save it and we have some sort of special relationship with God.' This narrative that they're living according to what God surely wants and are really the true defenders of not only the faith, but this nation, I think would play into this idea of being special and set apart."

A necessary part of collective narcissism is not just the conviction that one's group is special and entitled, but the belief that others outside the group don't appreciate or respect the group. Often there is a belief the group is being unfairly attacked or persecuted by others. The perception of increasing discrimination against white Christians is higher in US states with larger Christian majorities. In states where Christians hold more seats of power and control, the perception is that they are more excluded and pushed aside. This is the nature of collective narcissism, where perception about the group does not always align with reality.

Author and sociology professor Phil Zuckerman explains that people turn to ideologies that make them feel safe and special during times of uncertainty and cultural turmoil. He writes, "It can be comforting to think that God is looking out for you and yours and that you are a member of the 'best' country. Hence, it makes sense that many Americans embrace Christian nationalism. It likely feels good to believe that you are a special favorite of a powerful deity and that your nation is Number One."[86]

SIGNS OF HOPE

You may feel both intrigued and discouraged by all this nationalism, narcissism, racism, fearfulness, and the rest. Yet hidden in the middle of all this

86. Zuckerman, "COVID-19 and Christian Nationalism," lines 80–84.

disheartening research are glimmers of hopefulness. This is especially true
in the realm of Christian nationalism. When skillful researchers like Andrew Whitehead, Sam Perry, and others attack the data, they find very heavy
and dispiriting results sitting alongside encouraging findings.

We must restate a simple but important distinction: Christian nationalism and Christian faith are not synonymous. There are significant points
of overlap, but there are also big differences. When asked what one should
do to be a good person in the Baylor Religion Survey, both Christian nationalists and non-nationalists who engaged in regular religious practice said it
was important to value faith in God, transmit good morals to others, and
convert others to their faith. The differences, though, were revealing. The
non-nationalists who engaged in religious practice advocated taking care
of the sick and needy and emphasized being less consumerist and mate-
rialistic as a measure of being a good person. However, these values were
not important to Christian nationalists. The non-nationalists who engaged
in religious practice said we should seek social and economic justice, but
Christian nationalists disagreed with this.[87]

Once you pull Christian nationalism out of the equation, Christians
look a lot more like Christians. How they think and what they value aligns
with traditional notions of the Christian faith. The non-nationalists who
practiced their faith through prayer, Scripture reading, and worship service
attendance looked much more like Christ followers. They not only placed
a high value on their relationship with God, upholding moral values, and
sharing their faith, but they also believed they should take care of the sick
and needy, eschew materialism, and advocate for justice for the oppressed
and marginalized.

Once Christian nationalism gets stirred into the mix, however, the
picture gets murky. These nationalists also believe in traditional faith and
values, but they have low regard for the poor. They have a much greater
embrace of wealth and materialism than non-nationalists. In all ways, these
dismissive attitudes toward the poor and aspirations of wealth are antithetical to the traditional Christian faith, yet they not only go unchallenged, but
have been embraced by wide swaths of white Christians, particularly evangelicals. It is as if Christian nationalists have snuck inside undetected and
contaminated the group.

Whitehead told me, "I want to distinguish between religiosity and
Christian nationalism. So while a lot of Americans who embrace Christian
nationalism are very religious, once we account for Christian nationalism,

87. Whitehead and Perry, *Taking America Back for God*, 14–15

religiosity operates differently. So it isn't just being religious that might push people certain directions politically. It's their cultural framework."

It isn't just the desire to take care of the needy and reject materialism that re-emerges when we pull Christian nationalism out of the equation. The same is true of punitiveness and the willingness to forgive. In a study by sociologist Joshua Davis, when Christian nationalism was statistically pulled out of the mix, people who rated high in religiosity—they prayed, read the Bible, went to church regularly—were more forgiving than punitive toward offenders. "So it really is the conflation of people's religious and national identities, not religion per se that predicts these punitive attitudes," Davis explained.[88]

During the pandemic year, those high in Christian nationalism prioritized the economy and their own personal freedoms and deprioritized the needs of vulnerable people with COVID restrictions.[89] However, those who rated themselves as higher in religiosity but not nationalism were the opposite. These people placed a priority in the needs of vulnerable people—older folks, those with chronic conditions, ethnic minorities—over economic considerations. The important takeaway here is that Christian nationalism and authentic expressions of Christian faith are not the same. There are significant differences in how they see the world and what they value.

Returning to the Capitol insurrection, of all the groups surveyed, white evangelicals were the least likely to hold President Trump accountable for escalating the violence that led to the Capitol riots on January 6, 2021 and the most likely to believe the storming and breach of the Capitol building was "overblown" compared to the riots associated with racial protests the previous summer. More than any other segment of the population, they held firm beliefs that Antifa or Black Lives Matter mixed into the crowd and started the violence.[90]

My survey of adults of all ages and from every region of the country confirmed that white Christians who rate high on Christian nationalism were by far the group most likely to blame other groups like Antifa for starting the Capitol building riots. Data from the *Public and Discourse Ethics Survey* found the higher those self-identified Christians rated in Christian nationalism, the more likely they were to hold these beliefs.[91]

Here's the twist: the opposite was also true. White evangelicals who rejected Christian nationalism were less likely than other groups to hold

88. Davis, "Enforcing Christian Nationalism," 300.

89. Perry et al., "Save the Economy, Liberty, and Yourself."

90. Grubbs et al., "Status Seeking and Public Discourse Ethics."

91. Grubbs et al., "Status Seeking and Public Discourse Ethics."

these beliefs[The research shows the issue was not whether someone was a self-described white evangelical, but whether they held Christian nationalist beliefs.]It appears Christian nationalism is a key variable in understanding what has happened to the evangelical church in America and why it has fallen so far from Christian tradition.[92]

Even regarding racism in the church, the deeper understanding of Christian nationalism gives us reason for hope. While other research, including the work of Robert Jones with the Public Religion Research Institute, has found more church attendance was associated with increases in racist attitudes, Whitehead and Perry find an important nuance.[93] Whitehead told me, "What Jones could be picking up on are the really religious people who strongly embrace Christian nationalism. If we were able to look at the relationship between high attendance and more racist attitudes while controlling for Christian nationalism, I think you would find the opposite effect, because in our models, if we don't account for Christian nationalism, we replicate Jones's finding: the more you attend church, the more racist your attitudes are." It appears Christian nationalism is the culprit for the increase in racist attitudes, not religiosity itself.

What is passing for zealous Christian faith is a forgery, an imitation called Christian nationalism. When removed from the equation, Christians look the way we would expect. They care about the poor. They love and accept, rather than hate and exclude. They are less self-centered and more selfless.

It's easy to assume Christian nationalists represent authentic Christianity. They are numerous, loud, confident, and preach the importance of the Bible, prayer, and devotion to God, yet they represent a counterfeit version of the faith. They are wounded and fearful narcissists who use nationalist ideology as a rationale to cling onto power and control.

92. Grubbs et al., "Status Seeking and Public Discourse Ethics."

93. Luo, "Christianity's White-Supremacy Problem," lines 37–45, 271–79.

CHAPTER 7

The Most Powerful
Master Emotion

Evangelicals and Sexual Shame

"Shame is the most powerful master emotion."
—BRENÉ BROWN

MOST KIDS INSIDE THE evangelical bubble of the late nineties and beyond knew about Josh Harris. The previously homeschooled twenty-one-year-old had written a book in 1997 titled *I Kissed Dating Goodbye*, which promoted the virtues of courtship over modern notions of dating and became a catalyst for the evangelical purity culture. Couples were not only to wait until marriage to have sex, they were not to kiss, hold hands, or even spend time alone. The book sold over a million copies and launched Josh into evangelical stardom, where he headlined conferences and wrote five more books. He married the woman he had been courting, Shannon, and they had three children together. A few years later, he became the lead pastor of Covenant Life Church, a large congregation in Maryland. He was among the most influential voices in the evangelical purity culture movement, which emphasized abstaining from sex until marriage.[1]

---

1. Sherwood, "Author of Christian Relationship Guide," lines 1–20.

Two decades after the book became a phenomenon, Josh burned it all to the ground. In 2018, he issued a statement renouncing his book, saying, "I no longer agree with its central idea that dating should be avoided. I now think dating can be a healthy part of a person developing relationally and learning the qualities that matter most in a partner."[2] He added, "To those who read my book and were misdirected or unhelpfully influenced by it, I am sincerely sorry."[3]

A year later, he announced he and his wife were separating. Less than two weeks after that, he posted a statement saying he had left the faith, writing, "By all the measurements that I have for defining a Christian, I am not a Christian."[4] He followed with a full-throated renunciation of his past writing and teaching. "I have lived in repentance for the past several years—repenting of my self-righteousness, my fear-based approach to life, the teaching of my books, my views of women in the church, and my approach to parenting, to name a few."[5]

Notably, he apologized to the LGBTQ community, saying, "I want to say that I am sorry for the views that I taught in my books and as a pastor regarding sexuality. I regret standing against marriage equality, for not affirming you and your place in the church, and for any ways that my writing and speaking contributed to a culture of exclusion and bigotry. I hope you can forgive me."[6]

The evangelical old guard was unmoved. Al Mohler, president of Southern Baptist Theological Seminary, responded with a statement asserting marriage should only be between a man and a woman and, referring to Josh, "We can place our trust in no sinful human being, but in Christ alone, the one who alone is worthy of our trust."[7]

Despite the damage control, purity culture had taken a gut punch. Those within evangelical culture and outside observers had taken note. What became clear in subsequent conversations was the good intentions of abstinence and purity messages were fraught with negative consequences.

The message of purity culture has been a colossal failure. In the 1970s during the so-called sexual revolution, 21 percent of women reported being virgins when they were married. By the 2010s, the number had dropped to just 5 percent. Worse, in the 1970s, only 6 percent of women claimed to have

2. Sherwood, "Author of Christian Relationship Guide," lines 21–23.
3. Sherwood, "Author of Christian Relationship Guide," lines 24–25.
4. Sherwood, "Author of Christian Relationship Guide," lines 32–33.
5. Sherwood, "Author of Christian Relationship Guide," lines 35–38.
6. Sherwood, "Author of Christian Relationship Guide," lines 39–44.
7. Mohler, "Tragedy of Joshua Harris," lines 188–90.

slept with six or more partners before getting married, but by the 2010s, the number was 32 percent.[8]

Based on interviews with thousands of teenagers over a seven-year period, sociologist Anthony Paik and his colleagues compared outcomes of those who had made purity pledges with those who had not. They concluded the vast majority of pledgers did not wait until they were married to have sex. Prior research found around two-thirds of pledgers had intercourse before marriage and over three-quarters had oral sex. Paik found 30 percent of women who had taken and broken a purity pledge got pregnant before they were married, compared to 18 percent of those who had never made a pledge.[9]

Teenage girls who had taken a purity pledge and had two or more sexual partners were more likely to have contracted HPV, a sexually transmitted disease that causes genital warts and has been linked to cancer.[10] Antoinette Landor and Leslie Simons found when religious commitment was strong, the chance of keeping the promise was higher, but when someone with low religious commitment signed a pledge, they actually increased their chances of engaging in risky sexual behavior.[11]

In her book *Pure: Inside the Evangelical Movement That Shamed a Generation of Young Women and How I Broke Free*, Linda Kay Klein writes, "The purity message is not about sex. Rather, it is about us: who we are, who we are expected to be, and who it is said we will become if we fail to meet those expectations. This is the language of shame."[12]

Over the decades, innumerable Christian leaders have preached sexual purity, but not lived it themselves. Even after the high-profile televangelist scandals of the late eighties, the list of conservative Christian leaders found to have committed sexual indiscretions or even abusive behavior has continued to swell. Several prominent ministry leaders have gotten entangled in their own sexual scandals, including:

- Ravi Zacharias, an evangelist and apologist who was among the most respected evangelical thinkers of the modern era. He authored over thirty books, including several bestsellers, and spoke at massive conferences around the world. Following his death in late 2020, his ministry's own investigation acknowledged Zacharias had engaged in sexual inappropriate behavior, molested and exposed himself to multiple

8. Wolfinger, "Premarital Sex and Marital Stability," table 1.

9. Paik et al., "Broken Promises."

10. Paik et al., "Broken Promises."

11. Landor and Simons, "Why Virginity Pledges Succeed or Fail."

12. Klein, *Pure*, 14.

massage therapists, and solicited nude photos from over two hundred women until just months before he died of cancer at age seventy-four.[13]

- Carl Lentz, who was pastor to stars like Justin Bieber, Selena Gomez, Kevin Durant, and many others at his NYC megachurch. He acknowledged being unfaithful to his wife and there were reports of multiple, "significant" affairs.[14]

- Jerry Falwell Jr., former president of the largest Christian university in the world, who posted a photo on Instagram taken aboard a yacht of him with his arm around a younger woman with his jeans unzipped. The woman also had her shorts unzipped. A hotel pool attendant reported he had sex with Falwell's wife while Falwell watched on multiple occasions. The man shared email, texts, and audio with a news organization as proof of his claim.[15]

- Bill Hybels, pastor of the famed Willow Creek Church and author of dozens of influential books, who allegedly engaged in multiple episodes of sexual misconduct with employees and members of his church over decades. A six-month independent investigation found the allegations to be credible.[16]

- Bill Gothard, founder of the *Institute of Basic Life Principles* and one of the most influential Christian leaders of the past several decades, who was alleged to have sexually harassed up to thirty-four female employees and volunteers.[17] They withdrew their lawsuit because of the statute of limitations, but the women issued a statement saying, "We are not recanting our experiences or dismissing the incalculable damage that we believe Gothard has done." An investigation found Gothard had acted in "an inappropriate manner."[18]

- Ted Haggard, the former president of the *National Association of Evangelicals* and pastor of New Life Church in Colorado Springs, who preached against gay marriage and put his weight behind Colorado's 2006 Amendment 43 that banned same-sex marriage in the state.[19] That same year, he was caught with a male prostitute who claimed

13. Silliman and Shellnutt, "Ravi Zacharias."
14. Graham, "Rise and Fall of Carl Lentz."
15. Stevens, "Purity culture enables predatory behavior."
16. Goodstein, "He's a Superstar Pastor."
17. Pulliam Bailey, "New Charges Allege Religious Leader."
18. Horst, "Bill Gothard."
19. Harris, "Haggard Admits Buying Meth."

Haggard had paid him for sexual acts for three years.[20] Haggard admitted some wrongdoing and resigned.[21] His former church later paid out $179,000 in a settlement based on another man's allegation that Haggard had engaged in a physical relationship with him when he was twenty-two years old.[22]

A Southern Baptist Convention investigation found 380 sexual abuse allegations against church leaders involving over seven hundred victims over two decades. Most of the accused were convicted or took plea bargains. The investigation's findings represent three victims every month for twenty years.[23]

I have little interest in exploring how people can be hypocrites. This isn't a mystery to anyone with a basic understanding of human nature. I am interested in why, despite abundant evidence it might be counterproductive, evangelicals remain laser-focused on sexual purity. Are they in denial about how sexually compulsive and unhealthy many fellow evangelicals are? Do they believe their purity message has made it better?

We can't understand the white Christian posture toward sex and sexuality without understanding the psychology of shame and disgust. These two powerful emotions dictate sexual attitudes and behaviors. Conservative Christians say the Bible shapes their attitudes toward sex and sexuality, but more often, their emotions shape these perspectives first. Shame is an emotion directed at one's self, while disgust is most often aimed at the other person. The next chapter explores disgust, but first we begin with sexual shame.

THE IMPACT OF SHAME

Josh Duggar is the eldest of Jim Bob and Michelle Duggar's nineteen children, appearing with them on TLC's *19 Kids and Counting* across seven seasons.[24] The conservative Christian parents eschewed birth control, homeschooled their children, and preached purity and modesty to their children. Josh and his siblings practiced chaperoned courtship in which a young couple is permitted to spend time together only around others.

The network canceled the reality show in 2015 after Josh admitted he had molested at least five girls, including four of his sisters, when he was a

20. Harris, "Haggard Admits Buying Meth," lines 30–32.

21. Harris, "Haggard Admits Buying Meth," lines 14–17.

22. Spellman and Marrapodi, "New Haggard Accuser," lines 23–27, 41–42.

23. Roach, "SBC Recalls 'Year of Waking Up,'" lines 31–36.

24. Ali, "Josh Duggar Will Be Released Pending Trial," lines 48–50.

teenager.[25] Josh resigned from his position at the Family Research Council, a conservative organization promoting family values in the public square.[26] Later that year, a data breach of the *Ashley Madison* website revealed Josh had paid for nearly a thousand dollars in subscriptions to the service marketed to married people seeking affairs.[27] He checked himself into an addiction treatment program afterwards.[28] He posted a statement that read, "I have been the biggest hypocrite ever. While espousing faith and family values, I have secretly over the last several years been viewing pornography on the Internet and this became a secret addiction and I became unfaithful to my wife."[29]

In November of that year, a porn actress named Danica Dillon filed a half-million dollar lawsuit against him, alleging physical and emotional assault during an occasion of consensual sex at a Philadelphia strip club. Months later, she agreed to dismiss her lawsuit.[30]

In 2021, US Marshals arrested Josh on charges of receiving and possessing child pornography. According to reports, some images depicted sexual abuse of children younger than twelve.[31] He pled not guilty to the charges that were disclosed the same week he and his wife shared the news on Instagram that she was pregnant with their seventh child.[32]

I debated whether to recount Josh's troubles with his sexual behavior. He has hurt people and is a man with deep sexual struggles, but my goal is not to shame him or to single him out for monstrous behavior. My goal is the opposite of shaming. It is to show how sexual shame affects people. This is a pattern I've seen repeatedly for the three decades of my career: sexual shame leading to unhealthy sexuality leading to even more sexual shame.

Shame is a powerful emotion. Researcher and speaker Brené Brown rightly calls it "the most powerful master emotion.[33]" Shame has the power to drive people to many unhealthy and self-destructive behaviors. An adult family member had sexually abused one of my clients when he was a child. The boy felt deep shame because of it. When he was in his early twenties, he drunkenly ran his car onto a sidewalk and struck two people, seriously

25. Ali, "Josh Duggar Will Be Released Pending Trial," lines 51–61

26. Hearon, "Josh Duggar's Controversies Over the Years," lines 49–50.

27. DenHoed, "Josh Duggar's Ashley Madison Problem," lines 44–52.

28. Hearon, "Josh Duggar's Controversies Over the Years," lines 83–4.

29. Mauch, "Josh Duggar Pleads Not Guilty," lines 43–5.

30. Hearon, "Josh Duggar's Controversies Over the Years," lines 90–6.

31. Ali, "Josh Duggar Will Be Released Pending Trial," lines 25–30.

32. Ali, "Josh Duggar Will Be Released Pending Trial," lines 39–45.

33. Brown, "Listening to Shame."

injuring both of them. Years later he saw the link between early shame and his trajectory toward wrecking the lives of other people.

Noël Clark asserts, "Sexual shame is a visceral feeling of humiliation and disgust toward one's own body and identity as a sexual being and a belief of being abnormal and inferior; this feeling can be internalized but also manifests in interpersonal relationships having a negative impact on trust, communication, and physical and emotional intimacy."[34]

A study that seems laughable at first holds a powerful finding relevant to Christians and their feelings of sexual shame. Researchers found US states with the highest per capita rates of evangelicals have a higher volume of Google searches for penis enlargement, male enhancement, and similar queries. The authors conclude that the "evangelical subculture explicitly or implicitly promotes equating masculinity with physical strength and size, leaving men influenced by that subculture (whether evangelical or not) to seek solutions for their privately felt failure to measure up."[35] The implication here is that evangelical men—and those influenced by proximity to hyper-masculine evangelical subculture—worry about being sexually inadequate, small, ineffectual. In other words, they feel shame.

RECIPE FOR SEXUAL SHAME

What is it about evangelical subculture that makes men and women experience such sexual shame? The answer lies in an undeniable reality: they are held to a standard of sexual behavior that most people cannot meet. When they fail—which is often—the failure is an offense against God met with disfavor by other Christians if revealed. What results is a pattern of striving and failing, followed by internalized shame.

While evangelicals want to believe their beliefs and convictions govern their sexual behavior, the research says they usually find it difficult to keep their sexual behavior within prescribed boundaries. According to the General Social Survey, 74 percent of evangelicals have had at least one sexual partner before getting married and 43 percent of evangelical women and 52 percent of evangelical men between the ages of eighteen to twenty-two have already had four or more sexual partners.[36] Even among those who attend church weekly and say their faith is "very important," a majority of never-married evangelicals have had sex.[37] Despite this, the purity culture

34. Clark, "Etiology and Phenomenology of Sexual Shame."
35. Perry and Whitehead, "Linking Evangelical Subculture."
36. Ayers, "Sex and the Single Evangelical," figures 2–3.
37. Ayers, "Sex and the Single Evangelical," figure 4.

standards remain, setting evangelicals up for secretive behavior and feelings of shame over their perceived moral and spiritual failures.

In my clinical practice, the vast majority of clients who enter therapy because of sexually compulsive behavior are evangelical Christians. More than any other group, feelings of deep shame often torment these young adults. The more shameful they feel, the more compulsive they become. When I reviewed fifty young adult clients who had sexual compulsivity or great shame related to their sexual behavior or sexuality, forty-five out of the fifty (90 percent) were raised in conservative Christian homes. This has been the experience of large numbers of my colleagues in different regions across the country. One study confirmed there were greater rates of sexual compulsivity among religious people compared to the nonreligious.[38]

The profile is nearly always the same: homeschooled or Christian-schooled kid, conservative Christian family, clear messages about the rules and boundaries regarding sex, strong warnings about the consequences for violating those rules, and an unmistakable and unquestioned understanding that sexual sin is much worse than other types of sin.

The result is a pressure cooker that produces sexually unhealthy young men and women, some of whom are taught they can't even masturbate without offending God. They must save themselves for marriage. If they don't, trouble will befall them, including God's judgment, the burden of having memories of previous sexual experiences intrude upon their times of marital sex, and the guilt of giving away "pieces of their soul" to other sexual partners. When they slip up—which for many of them is often—shame and anxiety and sometimes outright panic consumes them. Rather than keeping them from messing up again, these experiences make them more preoccupied, more likely to act out again, and more self-loathing. All the while, they have had to keep it all secret and hidden for fear of being shamed, of disappointing God and parents and partners. I've seen this hundreds of times.

All this takes root during a vulnerable time, those raw teenage years. Research confirms adolescents experience more shame than adults.[39] Shame strikes at the heart of one's sense of identity, of one's sense of self. Teenagers are on the launchpad for developing an adult notion of self. Whereas children often think about themselves in concrete terms—*I'm a fast runner; I'm good at math; I have a brother and a sister*—adolescents develop a deeper, more complex sense of themselves. Their brain poses questions: *Who am I? What do I like? What do I value? Where do I fit? Who are my people?* Around the middle school years, young teenagers embark on the often rocky journey

38. Hotchkiss, "Sexual Compulsivity of Religious Internet Pornography Users."

39. Ulrich et al., "Trajectory of Shame Across the Life Span."

of defining themselves. When temperament and life experiences conspire to cause them social or emotional trouble during this time, they can internalize shame. The answers to those questions become poisonous. *I am a bad person. I am not worthy of love.* Research confirms shame-proneness puts adolescents at greater risk for depression and anxiety-related problems.[40] Sexual shame also leads to more compulsive behavior.[41]

When these teenagers become young adults, they often see the prohibitions against sexual behavior have less to do with theological and biblical contemplation and more with behavioral control. Christians have used prohibitions against certain forms of sexual conduct to manage behavior for millennia. The rules and regulations can create protection against disease, unwanted pregnancy, assault, and abuse. However, the church has created a theology of sex and sexuality, associating prescribed sexual behavior with the very nature and character of God, while seeing other sexual expressions as an affront to God and a most grievous sin. Christians, especially conservative Christians, have grown up with the message that there is nothing worse than committing sexual sin. Having intercourse or other forms of sex before marriage is a chart-topping offense, while in many evangelical quarters, the message is that even having "lustful thoughts" or masturbating makes God upset.

Impossibly high standards—no sexual behavior, including masturbating, and no sexual thoughts allowed—set the stage for the shame cycle.

THE CYCLE OF SHAME

One young man named Mason explained how he was told by his parents, Christian school, and youth pastor that God required him to "save himself for marriage." For all of high school and the first year of college, he did his best to fulfill this directive. When the dam burst his sophomore year, he swung hard in the opposite direction, having sexual hookups with ten girls that year and many others in the years to follow. At the same time, he worked hard to be the best Christian guy he could be. He took a leadership role with a campus ministry. He went on a summer mission trip. He kept a nightly quiet time of personal Bible study and prayer. Each time he slipped up, though, he would suffer deep shame. He prayed that God would not let him be tempted again. Sadly, the opposite happened. He became more promiscuous, even sleeping with a woman in the group he was serving during

---

40. Mills, "Taking Stock of the Developmental Literature on Shame."
41. Bilevicius et al., "Vulnerable narcissism and addiction."

his missions trip. His conclusion, which he had never said out loud until he told me, was, "I am a monster."

Mason was neither an angel nor a monster, but his gut-level shame had wrecked his sense of himself. He felt evil and out of control. Over time, as his anguished prayers seemed to go answered, instead of drawing closer to God, he felt alienated from God. The quiet times stopped. He dropped out of his Christian organization. He created distance with his Christian friends. Such is the legacy of shame. It destroys relationships with God, others, and one's self.

Some processes in psychology are intuitive while others are "counterintuitive." They operate differently than we would expect. Shame is one of those counterintuitive psychological processes. Instead of helping someone correct their behavior, a shameful person is more likely to engage in the behavior that made them feel disgraceful.

Why would this be? If someone feels awful about something, why are they often more likely to engage in it? Why would a good guy like Mason go against his own moral and spiritual code? The shame cycle below helps shed some understanding.

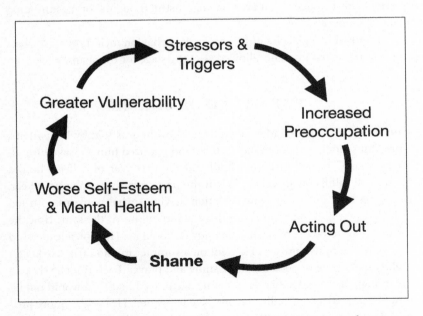

The shame cycle begins with life stressors and triggers. Perhaps a person experiences stress at work or school. Perhaps he endures social exclusion or rejection. Maybe he has financial struggles. He sees pictures or video of beautiful, barely dressed women on Instagram. These stressors lead to a buildup of negative emotion like loneliness, anger, sadness, or anxiety. This sets the stage for the next part of the cycle.

He searches for ways to reduce his stress and negative feelings. Maybe he overeats or drinks or gets high. Perhaps he spends too much or gambles. For our purposes, let's say he thinks about something sexual—a casual hookup, porn, sexting, or something else. At some point, his resistance and willpower fail and he acts out. He searches for porn. He sends a sexual message. He creates a hookup account. He sleeps with someone.

Now he has deep shame. At this stage of the cycle, several things happen. He often makes promises to himself, to God, and possibly to others (especially if he got caught) to stop the behavior. He feels shame, but he is also full of "high-minded resolution." *It won't happen again*, he says to himself and God.

Yet the experience of another random hookup or binging on porn or creating a Tinder or Grindr or Ashley Madison profile takes its toll. The shame is caustic, cutting into him, eroding his self-esteem, causing him even more anxiety or sadness. One study found a significant relationship between low self-esteem and sexual shame, as well as low sexual satisfaction in relationships.[42] This creates a state of greater vulnerability where he feels run down, demoralized, and defeated. So when the next stressor or trigger comes along, he is more—not less—likely to act out. Often the cycle becomes more rapid, and he acts out more quickly and more frequently than the previous times.

After several rounds of this cycle, shame digs in so deeply he no longer feels bad. He makes no resolutions to improve. He just assumes he is a bad or weak person who engages in his acting-out way of soothing himself.

Over time, the behavior can become more severe because, like a drug, he becomes tolerant of it. Now he needs something more intense to experience pleasure and momentary relief. He looks at women in bikinis on Instagram, then graduates to porn, then needs more hard-core porn, then begins video chatting with strangers online, then masturbates in front of them, then meets people for casual hookups, and so on. He looks back and is stunned by where he finds himself. Full of shame, he thinks, "I am a terrible person," or "I am a bad Christian," or, like Mason, "I am a monster." Because he sees himself this way, the cycle continues.

We act in line with how we see ourselves. Those who are more shame-prone see themselves as bad, incompetent, weak, unable. When the slings and arrows of life return, shame-filled people behave the way they view themselves. The cycle continues.

42. Day, "Adults That Experience Sexual Shame."

Worse yet, they not only feel awful about themselves, they are also more likely to lash out with hostility. An extensive study by June Tangney and colleagues involving children, teens, and adults found shame-proneness related to displaced aggression and hostility.[43] Another study found shame-proneness connected to anger and hostility, a tendency to blame others, and passive-aggressive responses.[44] Shame-filled people take out their internal mess on others.

SHAME VS. GUILT

The emotion that drives this pattern of compulsive, unhealthy sexual behavior is not guilt, but shame. Guilt and shame seem identical, but they are different in ways that matter. Guilt is an emotion that alerts you to misbehavior so you can correct it. Guilt says, "I have done something wrong and I feel a sense of responsibility and remorse to correct that in the future." This can be a constructive, if painful, emotional experience leading to a course correction.

Guilt can be useful, but shame is never helpful. In *Scientific American*, Annette Kämmerer writes, "Shame makes us direct our focus inward and view our entire self in a negative light. Feelings of guilt, in contrast, result from a concrete action for which we accept responsibility. Guilt causes us to focus our attention on the feelings of others."[45] Psychologist Noël Clark writes, "Shame is an experience in which the self, rather than the behavior, is viewed as flawed and/or morally deficient."[46]

Guilt can help someone grow and become a better person. Shame cannot. Whereas guilt is "I have done something wrong," shame is "I am bad." It conflates destructive behavior with being a bad person. Guilt can guide you to better decisions. Shame makes you see yourself as bad.

Often shame emanates from early messages a person internalizes. The socially rejected child may come to believe she is unlikable. The kid who knows she is a disappointment to her parents believes she is unlovable. A teenager who makes poor decisions sees herself as unworthy. The logic of a young brain concludes these experiences make her bad, unlovable, unworthy.

I had a client who recovered from an opiate addiction, which is no easy feat, but had tremendous shame over having stolen from his parents

43. Tangney et al., "Relation of Shame and Guilt to Responses to Anger."
44. Tangney, "Moral Affect."
45. Kämmerer, "Scientific Underpinnings of Shame," lines 5–8.
46. Clark, "Etiology and Phenomenology of Sexual Shame."

THE MOST POWERFUL MASTER EMOTION 167

to support his drug habit. Stealing from your parents is always bad, but the sense of shame made him feel worse about himself and, for awhile, made him more likely to continue in this behavior. If you experience guilt, you are likely to want to correct your behavior, but when you feel shame, you see your behavior as you. It is not "I did a bad thing," but "I am a bad person." Though similar, these are worlds apart in their impact on a person's sense of self.

One of the most dramatic ways shame affects someone is by making them more compulsive, particularly with sexual behavior. A person who feels shame after acting out sexually views himself as bad, then becomes more likely to do it again for two reasons. First, he uses the acting out to cover over and soothe negative feelings. Second, and more importantly, he sees himself as someone who is unfaithful, promiscuous, perverse. It becomes part of his identity. It is no longer, "I did this," but becomes "I am this." The behavior reinforces his sense of self, which makes him more likely to stay stuck in it. Some would say we do what we know. That's true, but it's more true that we do what we think we are.

The difference between shame and guilt might seem small to some, but the distinction has profound implications for a person's journey toward getting sexually healthy. One study of 177 adults seeking treatment for problems related to compulsive pornography use found people who were prone to shame became more hypersexual. By contrast, those more prone to guilt had great motivation to change and they were more likely to use preventive behaviors and coping strategies.[47] Shame focuses on past, unchangeable misbehavior now attributed to one's self, as if those actions make one's self unredeemable.

CHRISTIANS AND PORN

One sweltering summer day, I was at a church picnic with a dunking booth, a magician, and games for kids, when a mom came up to me, distressed.

"You don't know me," she said, "but I need to ask you an important question."

"Okay," I said, maneuvering away from the crowd to the shade of a tree. I could tell she was going to tell me something personal and heavy. (Such is the life of a psychologist, by the way.)

"This week we caught my oldest son looking at pornography," she said, wide-eyed with terror.

"How old is he?" I asked.

"Fifteen," she said, "but he's not very mature for his age."

47. Gilliland et al., "Shame and Guilt in Hypersexual Behavior."

"How did you handle it?" I asked.

"We sat and down and told him it was wrong," she said. "We told him how it was not part of God's plan."

"I understand," I said. "What is your question?"

"Is this going to mess him up for the rest of his life?" she asked, almost in tears.

"Because he looked at porn?" I asked.

"Yes, he told us it was the only time he'd ever done it."

I didn't have the heart to tell her it was very unlikely this was the only time he had ever viewed porn. There was a low chance the one time they caught him was the only time he'd looked at it.

"What do you mean you hope it has not messed him up for the rest of his life?"

"You know, will it make him a rapist or a pervert, a molester?"

"Just based on what you've told me, there's no reason to think that," I said.

A visible sense of relief passed over her.

"Are you sure?" she asked. "Because I've heard that boys who look at pornography end up having lots of problems with being sexually deviant."

"Well, most boys his age have looked at porn, at least some—"

"You're kidding!" she interrupted. "Is that because of the Internet?"

"No, teenage boys have always gotten hold of porn," I said. "The Internet makes it more accessible, for sure."

"So it won't make him a become a rapist?"

"I'm not saying porn is good—or good for him—but the chance of him becoming a rapist or a child molester because he looked at porn this time or a few times is very low."

I've had variations of this conversation countless times with Christian parents—usually moms—terrified their son will become sexually deviant because of exposure to porn. That's because the evangelical message is that porn leads to sexual assault and molestation. The research on exposure to pornography is mixed. Most adolescent boys have some exposure to pornography and the vast majority do not grow up to become rapists or child molesters. Early intentional viewing of certain types of pornography, such as depictions of sexual violence, does put someone at a higher risk for sexually acting out, but this is rare. Most researchers and clinicians agree repeated exposure to porn is not good for children or adolescents, but Christian parents often experience unwarranted panic.

Recent research found anxious and stressed parents overreact to the discovery of their child's porn viewing and use strategies that are more harsh and strict and lacking in warmth. A study involving over one thousand participants found parents' own emotional struggles may cause them to re-act in ways "which may actually increase the problematic behaviors parents are trying to avoid. Heightened anxiety may lead parents to channel their distress into an authoritarian parenting style that ultimately works against their goals."[48]

One client in his early twenties named Mitchell recounted how his father screamed at him, then loudly wept following the discovery that Mitchell had been looking at porn.

"We've failed as parents!" Mitchell remembers his father exclaiming, tears streaming down his face. The confrontation, which lasted for an hour, was horrifying for the boy.

"I just wanted to disappear," Mitchell told me. "Not just from that room, but from the whole world. I didn't want to exist. It was mortifying. My dad was so loud. I was sure my brother could hear the whole thing upstairs."

Mitchell became compulsive with his porn use in college when it became a daily habit. He was also promiscuous, having hooked up with at least one girl almost every weekend since he moved into his dorm. He hid all this from his parents. Had they found out, they would be convinced they were right, that the early exposure to porn had caused him to become sexually out of control. The early porn use didn't help, but the emotionally intense, shaming reaction of his parents likely created the larger problem. The shame leads to the compulsive behavior and the compulsive behavior leads back to shame, creating the shame cycle. It all starts with the shame.

Evangelicals—particularly evangelical men—have a complicated relationship with pornography. If you base it on their own reports, they have much higher rates of addiction to porn. But if you base it on actual numbers and frequencies, there is not clear evidence that evangelical boys and men are looking at porn more often than others. They just perceive it as a greater problem and bear much more shame about it.

One study of 3,370 US teens across the country found that growing up in a conservative religious environment increased the chances that an adolescent would view porn by 67 percent.[49] However, most studies show the actual frequency of porn use is *not* higher among evangelical teens and adults, but they think their own use is much more frequent and problematic.[50] A study conducted by psychologist Joshua Grubbs and colleagues involving 1,400 men found more highly religious men watched less porn,

48. Efrati and Boniel-Nissim, "Parents' Psychopathology."

49. Nie, "Adolescent Porn Viewing."

50. Perry, *Addicted to Lust.*

but were more likely to believe they had a porn addiction.[51] Evangelicals are not more likely to look at porn compared to other groups, but they are much more likely to say their porn use is an addiction. This belief causes them psychological distress, and results in more hiding and secretive behavior than others.

In a survey of nearly 2,300 individuals, men who attended church frequently and prayed often were more likely to say porn is "always morally wrong," yet still viewed it during the past year. Evangelicals were more likely than other groups to be caught in this dichotomy of holding anti-porn positions while viewing it.[52]

In his book *Addicted to Lust: Pornography in the Lives of Conservative Protestants*, Samuel Perry finds conservative Christian men are not looking at porn more often than others. However, he argues the alarm over pornography use within the church is so elevated, it is causing or magnifying emotional and relational problems. Because of the prohibitions against its use and the zero-tolerance attitudes within the church, Christian men may see themselves as being addicting to porn, even with less frequent viewing, as compared to other men.[53]

Research says those high in religiosity report relational problems associated with pornography use. The taboo against porn among Christians, more than the porn use itself, may be paradoxically destroying their marriages. There is not firm evidence porn use contributes to higher rates of divorce among the larger population, but the divorce rates of Christian wives distraught about their husbands' porn use is more than double that of other American women.[54] Men who were more engaged in religious practice reported less sexual satisfaction in their marriages because of their porn use.[55]

Their shame may also hurt them spiritually. Christian men who view porn are more likely to reduce their involvement in church or depart their faith altogether, according to Perry. He found Christian men who viewed porn frequently were less likely to serve as a lay leader in their church or serve on a committee.[56] Sometimes, their porn use causes them to drop out of church involvement and even depart their faith. Among teens, more frequent porn viewing reduces church attendance, frequency of prayer,

51. Grubbs et al., "Addiction or Transgression?"
52. Perry, "Not Practicing What You Preach."
53. Perry, *Addicted to Lust*.
54. Perry, *Addicted to Lust*.
55. Perry and Whitehead, "Only Bad for Believers?"
56. Perry, "Pornography Use Reduces Participation."

perceived closeness to God, and diminishes the importance of faith. It also increases doubts about their faith.[57] Perry uses the term "sexual exceptionalism" to describe Christians who believe sexual breaches, like viewing porn, are far worse than other, nonsexual transgressions. Their spiritual identity often rests on this one factor and when they don't meet the standard, their identity collapses.

When we consider Christian nationalism, those who embrace this ideology are much more likely than others to say they have a porn addiction, that viewing it makes them depressed afterwards, and that it has made their life worse. Researchers have found Christian nationalism to be the strongest predictor of belief that porn causes a breakdown of morals in society and leads to rape. Those who hold Christian nationalist beliefs drive anti-porn legislation most often. Nearly half of all evangelicals—most of whom are Christian nationalists—would support a total ban on porn, which is double the percentage of non-evangelicals.[58] Porn has the potential for negative impact on individuals, but given what we know about evangelical porn use, we can assume their desire to restrict it arises from their own feelings of powerlessness, inadequacy, and shame.

NARCISSISM AND SHAME

The overarching theme that the evangelical church has become a subculture infected with collective narcissism ripples across nearly every chapter of this book, including this one. Once again, we find there is a connection between narcissism and the topic at hand. Here, we link narcissism to shame.

There are two variants of narcissism: the shameless and the shameful. The shameless form is called "grandiose narcissism," the big, bombastic, arrogant version. According to the research, grandiose narcissists are immune to shame. They behave in ways that prompt people to ask, "Have they no shame?" The answer is simple: no.

We call the shameful variant "vulnerable narcissism," less easily detected upon first meeting. These are the wounded, defensive, self-focused narcissists. Those with higher rates of vulnerable narcissism experience more shame than others. Their hypersensitivity betrays their fragile sense of self. Like the men in the male enhancement study, they feel small and inadequate. When they feel attacked or believe they have fallen short, they are prone to deep feelings of shame. Research finds those with elevated levels

57. Perry and Hayward, "Viewing Pornography Shapes Religious Lives."
58. Perry and Whitehead, "Porn as a Threat to the Mythic Social Order."

of vulnerable narcissism have higher levels of shame, which leads to more compulsive and addictive behaviors.[59]

Researchers asked nearly two hundred people to complete a daily questionnaire for a month, examining life stressors and their emotional and behavioral reactions to them. They found vulnerable narcissism related to feelings of shame. They also found grandiose narcissism—the arrogant and interpersonally aggressive type—was *not* related to feelings of shame.[60] It is only shame and vulnerable narcissism that go together. Psychiatrist Willem Martens writes, "Narcissism is a continuous attempt to shout down pathological vulnerability and shame."[61]

Fear and shame combine to form a noxious stew. If a person perceives threats but feels powerless and inadequate, they are ripe for vulnerable narcissism, which, when combined with other like-minded people, yields collective narcissism. Golec de Zavala found collective narcissism connects to vulnerable individual narcissism with its sense of entitlement, mistrust, and angry interpersonal style. She wrote, "The belief that the in-group's exceptionality is not sufficiently recognized by others is associated with a similar belief about the self. Moreover, such a belief about the self seems to motivate collective narcissism."[62]

Collective narcissism forms a shame-based community that produces shame-based sexuality. *Sex is of paramount importance*, they are told. *You must hold high sexual standards to please the group and please God. If you don't, you are bad and this displeases us. God is furious. You must try harder. If you fail, you are in great danger of being shunned by the group and punished by God. The stakes could not be higher.*

Sexual purity, or in the words of Samuel Perry, "sexual exceptionalism," is a validation of one's specialness and the group's superiority. Despite the obvious failures, purity culture remains largely intact among conservative Christians and is a focal point in their culture wars. There remains little question why so many evangelicals are sexually obsessed. Sadly, their shame drives them to lie and to hide.

---

59. Bilevicius et al., "Vulnerable narcissism and addiction."

60. Di Sarno et al., "Shame Behind the Corner?"

61. Martens, "Shame and Narcissism."

62. Golec de Zavala, "Collective Narcissism and In-Group Satisfaction."

CHAPTER 8

Only Narrowly Separated

Evangelicals and Sexual Disgust

"The greatest pleasures are only narrowly separated from disgust."
—MARCUS TULLIUS CICERO

ON *THE LATE SHOW*, Stephen Colbert asked celebrities like Tom Hanks and Meryl Streep the same fifteen questions. One of them was, "What is the worst smell in the world?" Most of the celebrities paused to think, but I immediately had an answer. Without fear of contradiction, I can tell you the worst smell in the world is a dead snake. I know this because my blind border collie decided she'd roll in it one afternoon during a walk. She came trotting back to me and I smelled it while she was still ten feet away from me. It's unlike anything I'd ever smelled before. Just utterly, indescribably, horrifyingly disgusting.

I have a far less intense reaction to the smell of green peas, but I still think they smell disgusting. I also can't stand descriptions of injuries to fingers or eyes. My best friend stayed with me during his med school rotation one summer and would put medical journal pages of horrible skin infections under my pillow and sheets when I was out of the apartment. I'd pull back the covers and see them right before going to bed. He knew they would gross me out.

I have what psychologists call "high disgust sensitivity." Though un-fazed by emotional traumas, I get grossed out by certain smells or injuries—even verbal descriptions of injuries. Once I was in a van while my Uncle Ron described accidentally jabbing a screwdriver into his eye and I got so clammy and nauseous I had to lie down in the back for the rest of the trip.

As with most human traits, people range in their disgust sensitivity and find different things revolting. A paramedic may see severed limbs, puncture wounds, and other gruesome injuries without a twinge of disgust, but might get repulsed by spiders or weird bugs. A teenager might enjoy pimple and cyst popping videos on social media but get grossed out by the smell of goat cheese. The common categories that cause people disgust are bodily fluids and excretions, rotten things, ugly things, injuries and surgeries, some foods, and perverse behaviors. It's this last category that is most relevant here. Christians have become notorious for their disgust at certain sexual behaviors and orientations in others, particularly toward gay and transgender people. If Christianity is an open, accepting faith, then why is there so much disgust and vitriol directed at LGBTQ people from within the church?

THE PURPOSE OF DISGUST

Disgust in humans and animals developed as a way of protecting our bod-ies from ingesting or getting near things that might cause us to get sick or even die. One series of studies found disgust has its roots in the experience of nausea. Researchers conducted a series of experiments where they gave people ginger, which lowered their disgust reactions by calming their stom-achs. When they saw images of blood or vomit, they didn't react as intensely because they weren't having a nausea response.[1]

A study that followed was even more fascinating. Previous research had found individuals who are more disgust-sensitive condemn moral violations more severely. The researchers in this study, however, found ginger also reduced the severity of a disgust-sensitive person's judgments of moral violations. Keeping people from having a nauseous reaction not only made them feel less disgusted by physically gross experiences, but also by what they saw as morally wrong. When controlled for the physical reaction of disgust, people had different moral appraisals of someone's moral behavior. What they viewed as morally bad ("That's disgusting!") was no longer judged as harshly.[2]

1. Tracy et al., "Physiological Basis of Disgust and Moral Judgements."
2. Tracy et al., "Physiological Basis of Disgust and Moral Judgements."

While disgust originated in humans to keep them from contact with toxic or contaminated substances, it later generalized to personal behaviors that might be detrimental to the individual or group. Finally, it transferred to social experiences, keeping us away from others who might harm or "contaminate" us. One significant study found those with high disgust sensitivity found people in their own group more attractive and held more negative attitudes toward those outside of their group.[3] For these people, those within their group seem safe, while outsiders were dangerous, perhaps full of disease. In his article "Mystery of Disgust" Erik D'Amato writes, "We are socialized by our disgust and, in turn, use it to socialize others; what better way is there to stop people from doing something socially undesirable than to make that something . . . disgusting?"[4]

THE LINK BETWEEN DISGUST AND SHAME

In the previous chapter, I showed how feelings of shame lead to more sexually compulsive and unhealthy behavior and how evangelicals' shame-based view of sexuality makes them especially vulnerable. Researchers consider shame and disgust to be separate emotions, but they are linked in key ways.

To understand this, travel back in time for a moment to an era when the human brain was more primitive and the world was full of constant threats from animals and warring tribes, where disease and infection could kill you more easily. In this world, you needed both disgust and shame to survive. Disgust kept you away from things that were toxic or contaminated, which would make you sick or even kill you. Disgust kept you from touching or eating something that smelled bad or tasted weird. Shame kept your behavior in line, stopping you from doing things that would cause exclusion from the group, which would put you at mortal risk from exposure and hostile outsiders.

These two intense emotions of disgust and shame served important functions and were not just designed to make us feel bad. They were there to help us. Our brains still give tremendous weight to these emotions. Regarding shame, psychiatrist Willem Martens writes, "We worry about losing social status in the eyes of others and . . . our every social act is influenced by even the slight chance of public shame or loss of 'face.' The external danger from the experience of shame is abandonment or rejection."[5]

3. Terrizzi, "On the Origin of Shame."

4. D'Amato, "Mystery of Disgust," lines 323–26.

5. Martens, "Multicomponential Model of Shame," 399.

Following a series of experiments, psychologist John Terrizzi concluded, "Across all four studies, shame and disgust were positively correlated
(i.e., those who were sensitive to disgust were sensitive to shame and vice
versa). In all the studies, disgust sensitivity was a significant predictor of
shame even after controlling for guilt and negative affect, emphasizing that
the relation between disgust and shame is unique." He added, "the same pattern was not seen with shame's sibling emotion, guilt."[6] In a follow-up study
that primed people with words meant to evoke disgust (diarrhea, vomit,
urine, etc.), Terrizzi and Natalie Shook confirmed disgust links to shame,
but not to guilt. They found, "a disgust induction increased shame, but not
guilt, for individuals who were sensitive to disgust." They suggest "shame
may stem from the primary emotion of disgust being reflected on the self."[7]

With sex and sexuality, shame is what we feel about ourselves; disgust
is what we feel about others, yet these two emotions entangle each other.
Sexual shame yields disgust that can be both be internalized ("I am disgusted with myself") and externalized ("I am disgusted by them"). Now,
according to research, it appears self-disgust causes shame.

CONSERVATIVES AND DISGUST

As with fear, conservative and liberal brains are different for disgust, with
conservatives being more disgust-sensitive. Researchers showed participants in a study disgusting pictures—skin sores, dead animals, disgusting
bugs, gross toilets—mixed with neutral pictures while their brains were being scanned by an MRI machine. Liberals and conservatives reacted to the
disgusting images, but in different ways. The researchers could predict the
political ideology of their subjects with 95 percent accuracy just by looking
at their scans.[8] One of the researchers, John Hibbing, told *The Atlantic*, "We
almost always get clearer results with stimuli that are disgusting than with
those that suggest a threat from humans, animals, or violent events." Conservatives were consistently more reactive to the disgusting images.[9]

Another meta-analysis of twenty-four studies found disgust sensitivity
correlated with a constellation of traits termed "conservative ethos," defined
by such qualities as religiosity, traditionalism, support of hierarchies, and
sexual conservatism.[10] A recent series of five studies, however, concluded

6. Terrizzi, "On the Origin of Shame."
7. Terrizzi and Shook, "Does Shame Emerge From Disease-Avoidance?," 19.
8. Ahn et al., "Nonpolitical Images Evoke Neural Predictors of Political Ideology."
9. McAuliffe, "Liberals and Conservatives React in Different Ways," lines 58–60.
10. McAuliffe, "Liberals and Conservatives React in Different Ways," lines 69–76.

"that the differences between conservatives and liberals in disgust sensitivity are context-dependent rather than a stable personality difference," meaning it had to do with the specific type of disgusting image. In particular, conservatives reacted with disgust to descriptions of gay people and drug abuse, but did not have disgust responses to descriptions of pollution or animal mistreatment.[11]

One study found "disgust-sensitive people extend their preference for order in the physical environment (e.g. tidying up one's room) to the sociopolitical environment (e.g. strengthening traditional norms)."[12] Conservative people who have higher disgust sensitivity feel compelled to clean things up in the larger culture.

Several studies have also found a strong and consistent link between conservative sexual attitudes and disgust. While this extends to all sexual behavior considered outside the norm, it is most directed toward LGBTQ people and behavior. One study found disgust sensitivity among conservative individuals is a significant predictor of negative attitudes toward contact with gay people, moral judgments of LGBTQ people, and stereotypes of the gay community. When made to feel more disgusted by exposing them to gross images or descriptions, socially conservative people increased in their prejudice toward gay people while nonconservative people reduced their prejudice toward gay folks.[13]

CHRISTIANS AND DISGUST

Conservatives are more prone to disgust, but Christians in particular may be more vulnerable to disgust reactions. I asked Bunmi Olatunji, a professor at Vanderbilt University and one of the world's leading researchers on the psychology of disgust, if more religious people show greater disgust responses. "We do tend to see significant correlations between religiosity and measures of disgust. This is because disgust has been adapted culturally as a moral emotion that can be deployed to convey that something is wrong or bad," he explained.

One fascinating series of experiments asked Christians to copy down passages from some text espousing beliefs they rejected. Some copied from the Qur'an, others copied from a book on atheism, while still others copied from a neutral text. The participants who copied from the first two books had an increased disgust reaction, but not those who copied from the neutral

11. Elad-Strenger et al., "Is Disgust a 'Conservative' Emotion?"

12. Xiaowen et al., "Orderly Personality."

13. Terrizzi et al., "Predictor of Social Conservatism and Prejudicial Attitudes."

passage. However, when people could wash their hands after copying from the books with opposing spiritual beliefs, their disgust reaction disappeared. The authors concluded that "contact with rejected religious beliefs elicits disgust by symbolically violating spiritual purity."[14]

One study conducted by Patrick A. Stewart, a political scientist at the University of Arkansas–Fayetteville, and his colleagues using a survey of over five hundred participants found many associated sexual disgust with fear of sin. People who said they were more likely to be disgusted by thoughts of casual hookups, for example, were also more likely to agree with statements like, "I am afraid of having immoral thoughts." The researchers write, "heightened disgust sensitivity affects behavior to such a degree that the efforts to keep oneself 'pure' may actually play a role in the formation of a variety of sexual disorders."[15]

SEXUAL DISGUST

According to 2020 survey data collected by Pew Research Center, nearly half (48 percent) of young adults (eighteen- to twenty-nine-year-olds) have used a dating or hookup app or website like Tinder, Bumble, or Hinge.[16] While some are looking for relationships, many are just looking for sex. Many (obviously) feel comfortable having sex with strangers, which seems to violate the protective function of disgust. One pastor told me, "I don't see how these young people have these casual online hookups and don't seem to think anything of it. I'm not trying to be judgmental. I just don't understand it." The answer seems to be found in the degree of one's disgust sensitivity. One study of 271 adults found Tinder users have lower disgust sensitivity than nonusers.[17] People with high disgust sensitivity aren't looking for sex with a stranger, while those with low disgust sensitivity are much more open to these experiences. Sexual decision-making is often more governed by emotion—in this case, disgust—than by steadfast moral standards.

If disgust drives sexual behavior more than coherent boundaries, we would expect most Christians to be more accepting of premarital heterosexual intercourse than any other form of premarital sex, even though both are seen as outside of church doctrine. That's precisely what we find. While they may disapprove of premarital sex at rates higher than nonreligious people, a majority of Christians (57 percent) say sex between an unmarried

14. Ritter and Preston, "Gross Gods and Icky Atheism."

15. Stewart et al., "Effect of Trait and State Disgust."

16. Vogels, "10 Facts About Online Dating," figure 1.

17. Sevi, "Tinder Users Have Low Sexual Disgust Sensitivity."

couple in a committed relationship is always or at least sometimes acceptable. Only a third of Christians say it is never acceptable. Even concerning
casual sex, 36 percent of evangelicals say casual sex is always or sometimes
acceptable, according to a national study.[18] However, a majority (59 percent) of white evangelicals believe homosexual behavior should always be
discouraged and nearly three-quarters (74 percent) found it incompatible
with the Christian faith.[19]

Those with rigid ideas of sexuality have greater sexual disgust.[20] For
these folks, sexual expressions in others that fall outside the lines of what is
considered culturally normal, like homosexual behavior or males who present in more effeminate ways, will be met with a reaction of disgust. This disgust reaction causes avoidance at best and aggression and hostility at worst.

It is not just Christians who have negative reactions to various forms
and expressions of sexuality, of course. People of other faiths or no faith
can have disgust reactions toward anything they regard as out of the norm.
While sexual disgust is common among those with high disgust sensitivity,
it is especially strong toward LGBTQ people. In a meta-analysis of seventeen studies involving 7,322 subjects, researchers found heterosexuals who
hold negative and prejudicial views toward gay men had greater disgust
sensitivity.[21] One study of 452 undergraduates found disgust sensitivity was
positivity correlated with hostile attitudes toward both homosexuality and
moral concerns regarding impurity.[22]

Earlier, I showed how the Implicit Association Test (IAT) revealed
unconscious, automatic, and rapid negative associations related to African
Americans. The same is true for LGBTQ individuals. Using the IAT, researchers found that as disgust sensitivity increased, so did a person's negative associations with homosexuality.[23] Negative attitudes toward gay people
often originate from unconscious, emotional reactions linked to disgust.

A series of two studies found disgust sensitivity connects with intuitive disapproval of gay people.[24] This is especially true of gay men and their
sexual behavior. Participants of one study who had disgust induced with
a noxious odor reported less emotional warmth toward gay men. It had
very minimal effect on their view of lesbians or other groups, like African

18. Diamant, "Half of U.S. Christians Say," figure 1.
19. Pew Research Center, "Beliefs and Views of Homosexuality," figures 3–4.
20. Ray and Parkhill, "Heteronormativity, Disgust Sensitivity."
21. Kiss et al., "Meta-Analytic Review of Disgust and Prejudice Toward Gay Men."
22. Wang et al., "Disgust Sensitivity and Negative Attitudes."
23. Inbar et al., "Disgust Sensitivity Predicts Intuitive Disapproval of Gays."
24. Inbar et al., "Disgust Sensitivity Predicts Intuitive Disapproval of Gays."

Americans or the elderly.[25] Another study found men had greater ratings of disgust for homosexual behavior between men—but not women—even compared to their disgust ratings for promiscuity and BDSM.[26] The disgust effect is most clearly seen directed at gay men.

One study of over four hundred heterosexual men found it was not worries about disease or moral offenses that elicited disgust responses toward gay men, but descriptions and thoughts of their sexual behavior.[27] Here we see how disgust has evolved from a way of keeping people physically safe to a means to keep someone socially safe. The sexual behavior of gay men is seen as disgusting because it is socially disdained. Engaging in it puts someone at risk for social judgment and rejection.

CHRISTIANS AND GAY DISGUST

More than a year before Bruce came out as Caitlyn Jenner, a boy named Blake Brockington had been named the homecoming king of East Mecklenburg High School in Charlotte, where my two Liberian children, Maddie and Daniel, attended. There are thousands of homecoming kings crowned each year, but this one made international news. Blake was the first transgender person in the history of North Carolina to win the title.

His story captivated me. I already knew of him because he had played on Daniel's rugby team, but it wasn't until he became homecoming king that I learned of his story. His family was so rejecting of his transition from female to male that he ended up leaving their home and living in foster care. Despite that hardship, he became involved in charitable work and social action. He helped set up a museum exhibit showing the history of the gay civil rights movement and he was the subject of a short documentary film entitled *BroKINGton* about his life experiences. He embraced his faith community and joined the Transgender Faith and Action Network Conference. After high school, he attended the University of North Carolina at Charlotte and planned to be a band director and composer.

But the responses to his coming out deeply troubled Blake. Most of the people at his high school were gracious and supportive, as were thousands in his local community, but online he got trashed. He told the *Charlotte Observer*, "That was single-handedly the hardest part of my trans journey.

25. Inbar et al., "Disgusting Smells Cause Decreased Liking of Gay Men."
26. Crosby et al., "Six Dimensions of Sexual Disgust."
27. Ray and Parkhill, "Heteronormativity, Disgust Sensitivity."

Really hateful things were said on the Internet. It was hard. I saw how narrow-minded the world really is."[28]

I saw this for myself. When I read the articles about him, I also saw the comments. And while there were many positive and encouraging words, there were also plenty of horrible and hateful comments, many spouting religious objections, others just plain mocking. The posts (many of which have since been removed) upset me so much that I reached out to him on Facebook and wrote him some words of encouragement, saying I was proud of him and advising him to tune out or avoid the Internet trolls.

He wrote back, "Thanks for this. I needed it." He continued, "Yeah, the negativity is so loud. It really sucks that I can't avoid it always. I just really hope that this is all worth it in the end. Thanks for being one of the positive people."

We never corresponded again, but I later learned he began to despair. A picture on his Facebook page showed him holding a handmade sign that read, "I am not a criminal," and another that said, "I have the right to be alive." In February 2015, he posted on his Tumblr page, "I'm waiting on the moment when me and my darkness split from my body." In March, he wrote, "I am so exhausted."

The day after that post, he walked into oncoming traffic on Interstate 485 and was struck by multiple cars. He died on the scene. County authorities ruled his death a suicide.[29]

I was sick to my stomach for days.

A few months later many high-profile Christians piled onto Caitlyn Jenner. Despite revealing herself to be a person of Christian faith (and a conservative Republican!), prominent evangelicals were nothing short of horrible. Most notably, prominent conservative Christian blogger Matt Walsh wrote an opinion piece with a headline that screamed, "Bruce Jenner Is Not a Woman. He Is a Sick and Delusional Man."[30] Franklin Graham wrote on Facebook, "I have news for them—changing the outside doesn't change the inside. No man-made modification can fix what's wrong with the heart."[31] Republican presidential candidate and former Southern Baptist minister Mike Huckabee dripped with sarcasm when he said, "Now I wish that someone told me that when I was in high school that I could have felt like a woman when it came time to take showers in PE. I'm pretty sure that I would have found my feminine side and said, 'Coach, I think I'd rather

28. Kellaway, "Trans Teen Activist Dies," lines 14–17.
29. Garloch, "Charlotte-Area Transgender Teens' Suicides Rock Community."
30. Walsh, "Bruce Jenner Is Not A Woman."
31. Chapman, "Rev. Graham to Bruce Jenner."

shower with the girls today."[32] Other Christian writers and pastors, as well as countless Facebook posts, echoed similar sentiments of derision, mockery, and end-of-Western-civilization hysteria.

It brought to mind the days of the Moral Majority when Jerry Falwell called Ellen DeGeneres "Ellen Degenerate" and accused the Teletubby named Tinky Winky of being gay. Less amusingly, he accused gays and lesbians of being responsible for the September 11 attacks and also said years earlier, "AIDS is not just God's punishment for homosexuals, it is God's punishment for the society that tolerates homosexuals."[33] Pat Robertson was quick to pile on gay people, too, once saying, "Many of those involved in Adolf Hitler were Satanists. Many were homosexuals. The two things seem to go together."[34]

Research has found evangelical Christians are more likely to rate the value of transgender individuals lower than nonreligious people.[35] The people who identify as strongly pro-life attribute less value to people because of their sexuality or gender status. Not only that, some evangelicals have called for the death of gay people. For years, I had rolled my eyes when I heard some Christian leaders rail against LGBTQ people, saying they should all be rounded up and dumped on an island or blaming them for causing hurricanes. It wasn't until the "Sodomite Suppression Act" was filed in California that I realized this attitude was more than feckless ranting. The proposed legislation, filed in 2015 by lawyer Matt McLaughlin, begins with this sentence: "The abominable crime against nature known as buggery, called also sodomy, is a monstrous evil that Almighty God, giver of freedom and liberty, commands us to suppress on pain of our utter destruction even as he overthrew Sodom and Gomorrah."[36]

The proposed piece of legislation said gay people or those who engage in any homosexual activity should "be put to death by bullets to the head or by any other convenient method."[37] And those who distributed any material (or "sodomistic propaganda") aimed at creating acceptance of homosexuality would "be fined $1 million per occurrence, and/or imprisoned up to ten years, and/or expelled from the boundaries of the state of California for up to life."[38]

32. Campbell, "Mike Huckabee," lines 13–17.

33. Kohler, "Gay History—Founder of the Moral Majority," lines 1–3.

34. Bentz, "Top 10," lines 48–9.

35. Kanamori et al., "Christian Attitudes Toward Human Value."

36. McLaughlin, "Sodomite Suppression Act," lines 2–6.

37. McLaughlin, "Sodomite Suppression Act," lines 11–12.

38. McLaughlin, "Sodomite Suppression Act," lines 13–19.

McLaughlin said the law "shall be prominently posted in every public school classroom."[39] I thought this was a joke, much like the "gays killed the dinosaurs" story, but with a little digging, I realized this guy was dead serious, with emphasis on "dead." He wanted to put a bullet in the head of all the gay people in California. The bill had zero chance of becoming a law, but that was almost beside the point. A professing Christian could say not only outrageous and hateful things about gay people, but downright murderous and evil things without a peep from the church community. It wasn't harmless ignorance anymore.

A few years later, Grayson Fritts, a detective with the sheriff's department and pastor of All Scripture Baptist Church in Knoxville, Tennessee, preached in a widely viewed YouTube video that gay people should be arrested and executed. He called them "animals" and "freaks."[40] Though widely condemned, it was another in a long series of hateful sermons and comments by Christians condemning gays. Several other documented examples of Christian pastors or platformed individuals calling for the mass round-up or execution of gays have occurred in the years since then, like Steven Anderson, pastor of Faithful Word Baptist Church in Arizona, who praised the massacre at a gay nightclub in Orlando, saying, "The good news is there are fifty less pedophiles in this world," adding, "because these homosexuals are a bunch of disgusting perverts and pedophiles."[41]

Some might argue hateful people like McLaughlin and Fritts are outliers who caught media attention and don't reflect most Christians. While that may be true in terms of the vitriol and rhetoric, there is much evidence of strong anti-gay bias among many white Christians. Consider The Nashville Statement, a widely viewed declaration issued by the Council on Biblical Manhood and Womanhood, which includes proclamations like, "We deny that adopting a homosexual or transgender self-conception is consistent with God's holy purposes in creation and redemption," and "We deny that the approval of homosexual immorality or transgenderism is a matter of moral indifference about which otherwise faithful Christians should agree to disagree."[42]

A survey conducted by the Associated Press and NORC Center for Public Affairs Research found that while two-thirds of Americans supported banning discrimination against LGBTQ people regarding jobs, housing,

39. McLaughlin, "Sodomite Suppression Act," lines 34–38.

40. Garcia, "Tennessee Pastor Calls for L.G.B.T. People to Be Executed," lines 3–8.

41. Lemons, "Tempe Pastor Hails Orlando Massacre," lines 14–18.

42. Council on Biblical Manhood and Womanhood, "Nashville Statement," articles 7 and 10.

and education, only one-third of evangelicals supported this.[43] Clearly, most evangelicals do not have a kind disposition toward the LGBTQ community.

They are not even kind toward their own who soften their attitudes toward LGBTQ people and their civil rights. Following Barack Obama's election, Richard Cizik, spokesperson for the National Association of Evangelicals, went on NPR's *Fresh Air* to talk about the evolving political decisions of many evangelicals, including himself. *Time* magazine had named Cizik one of the "100 Most Influential People" earlier that year. When host Terry Gross asked Cizik about his position on gay marriage, he responded, "I would willingly say I believe in civil unions. I don't officially support redefining marriage from its traditional definition." His statement seemed considerate and measured, but it was met with outrage. Within a week, he had lost his job.[44]

Cizik's departure from conservative orthodoxy was unacceptable. Chuck Colson, former Nixon lawyer turned Prison Fellowship founder, said "[Cizik] was gradually, over a period of time, separating himself from the mainstream of evangelical belief and conviction. So I'm not surprised. I'm sorry for him, but I'm not disappointed for the evangelical movement."[45]

While attitudes are softening, especially among younger conservative Christians, negative attitudes toward the gay community predominate in the evangelical community. This includes opposition to gay marriage, talk of a "gay agenda," resistance to civil rights protections for LGBTQ people, and vigorous support for a harmful practice called conversion therapy.

THE MYTH OF GAY CONVERSION

Years ago, a prospective client named Ryan asked for a fifteen-minute meet-and-greet appointment with me to ask me a simple question: "What is your opinion of conversion therapy?"

Without knowing what answer he wanted, I replied, "I think it's harmful and I would never consider offering it."

He booked an appointment with me the following week and told me his story of being forced into conversion therapy as a teenager and the negative effect it had on him. "Looking back, it was like a form of abuse," Ryan said, "and they forced me to do it until I turned eighteen."

For at least fifty years, the concept of conversion therapy has been a feature of evangelical subculture, though its roots go back over 125 years. The

43. Associated Press, "Divide Over LGBT Rights," lines 19–28.

44. NPR, "Ousted Evangelical Reflects on Faith, Future," lines 45–47.

45. Pulliam, "Richard Cizik Resigns," lines 13–16.

premise is that individuals with "same-sex attraction" undergo a rigorous process of therapy, often combined with spiritual disciplines like prayer and Bible study, to change one's orientation from gay to straight. The Williams Institute at the UCLA School of Law estimates that as of 2019, "698,000 LGBT adults in the US have received conversion therapy."[46] The practice continues despite stories like Ryan's, public failures of many high-profile "ex-gays," denunciation by those formerly involved in the practice, and research that reveals it not only doesn't work but can actually harm people.

Many in the evangelical community have been influenced by the work and advocacy of psychologist Joseph Nicolosi, founder of the National Association for Research and Therapy of Homosexuality and author of *A Parent's Guide to Preventing Homosexuality, I Want to Stop Being Gay, Healing Homosexuality: Case Studies of Reparative Therapy*, and other similar books. However, when Nicolosi appeared on a television documentary hosted by British performer Stephen Fry, he could not produce even one "ex-gay" individual to verify claims of successful conversion or reparative therapy. Fry later spoke with a former client who renounced Nicolosi's work, claiming it did not help him change his sexual orientation.[47]

Nicolosi based most of his work on self-reported change, so a professor at Northwestern University extended an offer for any of Nicolosi's clients who had completed reparative therapy to be tested for their automatic reactions to various erotic images. The automatic reactions, like pupils dilating, heartbeat increasing, and evidence of sexual arousal would provide much more compelling evidence than self-reports, they reasoned. Nicolosi never responded to the offer, nor did he provide any similar findings that would bolster his claims. Nicolosi could never produce more than anecdotal evidence for his claims that reparative therapy works.[48]

Basing claims of sexual orientation change on little more than self-report, as Nicolosi did, is problematic because individuals have incentives to lie or exaggerate. They want to please Christian parents, they hope to avoid stigma associated with being gay, they are self-loathing, as well as many other reasons which contribute to problems with self-reports. Repeatedly, we have seen those from the "ex-gay" movement who—once caught in a lie—then denied having changed sexual orientation or renounced the practice of conversion therapy altogether.

In 1973, Reverend Kent Philpott and two other men founded the country's first ministry to those who described themselves as "ex-gay," people

46. Mallory et al., "Conversion Therapy and LGBT Youth."
47. Fry, "Stephen Fry Meets an Ex-Gay Therapist."
48. Throckmorton, "New Sexual Reorientation Study," lines 60–67.

who had allegedly ceased being gay through some combination of prayer and therapy. He wrote a book called *The Third Sex?* that chronicled the story of six people who he said had become heterosexual through a devotion to prayer.[49] Inspired by the book, more than a dozen "ex-gay" ministries sprung up around the country. Michael Bussee and Gary Cooper, two "ex-gay" counselors at Melodyland Christian Center, organized a conference in 1976 for members of the nascent "ex-gay" movement to meet and network. Out of that conference, Exodus International, an umbrella association for "ex-gay" organizations, was birthed.

In 1979, just three years later, Bussee and Cooper announced they were in love with each other, had never stopped having homosexual thoughts and feelings, and were leaving their wives to move in with each other. They lived as a couple until 1991, when Cooper died of AIDS.[50]

In more recent years, Bussee, along with many others involved in the "ex-gay" ministry movement, issued an apology for his role and said, "In the almost 40 years since I started Exodus International, I can honestly say that I have never met a gay person who became heterosexual through conversion therapy or ex-gay programs."[51]

Researchers later found none of the people profiled in Rev. Philpott's book had ever changed from gay to straight.[52] One of Philpott's ministry co-founders, John Evans, denounced the organization after his best friend died by suicide over an inability to change his sexual orientation.[53]

Colin Cook, the co-founder of another "ex-gay" ministry called Homosexuals Anonymous, had sex with twelve out of fourteen of his male clients who were interviewed as part of an investigation. He also gave his clients massages while they were naked.[54]

Michael Johnston, founder of National Coming Out of Homosexuality Day, was featured in ads claiming to be an "ex-gay," saying, "A decade ago, I walked away from homosexuality through the power of Jesus Christ." Five years later, he was found to have transmitted AIDS to multiple male partners after having unprotected sex and failing to disclose his HIV status.[55]

John Paulk founded and led the ministry Love Won Out, an "ex-gay" ministry sponsored by Focus on the Family in 1998, the same year he

49. Philpott, *Third Sex?*
50. Throckmorton, "First study to refer to ex-gays discredited."
51. Bussee, "Michael Bussee."
52. Philpott, *Third Sex?*
53. Philpott, *Third Sex?*
54. Lawson, "Troubled Career of an 'Ex-Gay' Healer."
55. Merritt, "How Christians Turned Against Gay Conversion Therapy."

published his autobiography, *Not Afraid to Change: The Remarkable Story of How One Man Overcame Homosexuality*, in which he claimed to have changed his sexual orientation from gay to straight through counseling and prayer. He married his wife, Anne, who also identified herself as "ex-gay." He later became board chairman of Exodus International–North America. While Paulk was on a speaking tour as an employee of Focus on the Family, someone photographed him in a gay bar. Eyewitnesses said he flirted with other men and told others he was gay. Years later, he apologized for the harm he caused with his involvement in "ex-gay" ministry, writing, "I no longer support or promote the movement. Please allow me to be clear: I do not believe that reparative therapy changes sexual orientation; in fact, it does great harm to many people."[56]

In 2012, the president of Exodus International, Alan Chambers, acknowledged that gay conversion—or "reparative"—therapy was worse than ineffective, saying it was harmful, and he apologized for the hurt caused by their program. The *New York Times* reported on an interview with Chambers: "He said that virtually every 'ex-gay' he has ever met still harbors homosexual cravings, himself included." A year later, Exodus International was closed.[57]

For two decades, McKrae Game was a fervent supporter of the "ex-gay" ministry movement. He founded an organization called The Hope for Wholeness Network, a Christian gay conversion therapy program. Married to a woman with two children, in 2019 he admitted he was still gay and renounced reparative therapies of any kind that proposed to change gay people into straight people. "I was a religious zealot that hurt people," he wrote.[58]

In an open letter, nine leaders, founders, and promoters of the "ex-gay" therapy movement decried "the ineffectiveness and harm of conversion therapy." Calling for a ban on the practice, they wrote, "We know first-hand the terrible emotional and spiritual damage it can cause, especially for LGBT youth."[59]

The American Psychological Association, the American Psychiatric Association, the American Counseling Association, and many other organizations representing nearly a half-million mental health professionals have all denounced gay conversion therapy or other efforts to change someone's sexual orientation.

56. McDonough, "Conversion therapy advocate."
57. Eckholm, "Rift Forms in Movement as Gay 'Cure' is Renounced," lines 20–21.
58. Iati, "Conversion Therapy Founder Says He's Gay," line 33.
59. Merevick, "9 Former Ex-Gay Leaders Join Movement," lines 12–15.

A research review by Cornell University found twelve studies that concluded gay conversion therapy is ineffective and/or harmful, often resulting
in depression, anxiety, suicidal thoughts, social isolation, and diminished
capacity for intimacy.[60] One small study concluded that efforts to change
sexual orientation could be successful, but only among a minority of
its subjects.[61] The Cornell researchers concluded that study had many
limitations, however, including its selection bias with only "religious"
subjects and basing the conclusions solely on self-report.[62]

How could we know if someone's sexual attraction was truly different,
if not for self-reports? Is there any other way to measure this? Actually, there
is. Researchers have used a device called a plethysmograph that measures
blood flow during sexual arousal. Researchers in at least two studies found
men who had undergone gay conversion therapy were still aroused by imag-
ery of men. The therapy, they concluded, had not been effective in reducing
same-sex attraction.[63]

A recent systematic review of the research literature concluded sexual
orientation change efforts "are not efficacious in altering sexual orientation" and "many studies report negative outcomes," including depression
and relationship problems.[64] Psychologist Warren Throckmorton at the
conservative evangelical Grove City College interviewed 239 men married
to women but attracted to other men. Half of the men had undergone conversion therapy. Throckmorton found the men's attraction to the same sex
increased and "attractions to their spouse decreased."[65] Mark Yarhouse at Pat
Robertson's Regent University conducted his own research and came to the
same conclusion.[66]

Despite this, support for conversion therapy among evangelicals
remains higher than for any other group. The rhetoric hasn't cooled either.
In an interview with NPR, seminary professor Robert Gagnon offered
support for conversion therapy, acknowledged "it might not even work for
most people,"[67] then stated, "Homosexual practice is regarded by the writers
of Scripture as a particularly severe sexual offense that's on the order of say,

60. What We Know, "Scholarly Research About Conversion Therapy," lines 5–7.

61. Nicolosi et al., "Changes in Homosexual Orientation."

62. What We Know, "Scholarly Research About Conversion Therapy," lines 7–10.

63. Bailey et al., "Sexual Orientation, Controversy, and Science."

64. Przeworski et al., "Systematic Review."

65. Hagerty, "Evangelicals Fight Over Therapy To 'Cure' Gays," lines 23–28.

66. Hagerty, "Evangelicals Fight Over Therapy To 'Cure' Gays," lines 29–30.

67. Hagerty, "Evangelicals Fight Over Therapy To 'Cure' Gays," line 46.

incest with one's parents."[68] He added, "The problem is, you can't assure people that are engaged in serial, unrepentant sin of an egregious sort that they're going to be in heaven."[69]

The message of disgust (comparison to incest), shame ("egregious"), and judgment (threat of hell) is unmistakable. Gay people have heard these messages—and worse—from Christians their whole lives.

IMPACT ON LGBTQ PEOPLE

Sociologist Bernadette Barton interviewed dozens of individuals in the LGBTQ community who had lived in the South. She writes, "Of the 46 lesbians and gay men interviewed for this study (age 18–74 years), most describe living through spirit-crushing experiences of isolation, abuse, and self-loathing." Their experiences caused many of them to get depressed, grow up afraid of going to hell, and have low self-esteem, she reports.[70]

In my practice I have heard these stories countless times. They are stories of young men who are full of self-hatred and deep woundedness. The wounds come from parents and family members, from peers and church members, from strangers. The stories are heartbreaking. More often than not, they involve gay kids raised in conservative Christian homes and raised in the church who feel rejected and unacceptable. They sense the disgust directed at them from the Christian community.

Compared to LGBTQ youth accepted by their parents, youth rejected by their parents were 8.4 times more likely to have attempted suicide, nearly six times more likely to experience depression, and over three times more likely to have used illegal drugs.[71] Rejection by loved ones—a horrific form of shaming—is not only tolerated in evangelical circles, it is sometimes actively encouraged.

While evangelicals couch their opposition to LGBTQ rights and their rejection of gay people in biblical terms and frameworks, their own sexual behavior and willingness to equivocate on sexual matters that affect them personally reveal the truth: their hostility to gays is more rooted in their primitive emotion of disgust than in their theology.

Desmond Tutu, the South African bishop and Nobel Peace Prize laureate, said, "I would refuse to go to a homophobic heaven. No, I would say sorry, I mean I would much rather go to the other place." He added, "I

68. Hagerty, "Evangelicals Fight Over Therapy To 'Cure' Gays," lines 56–57.

69. Hagerty, "Evangelicals Fight Over Therapy To 'Cure' Gays," line 67–68.

70. Barton, "'Abomination'—Life as a Bible Belt Gay."

71. Ryan et al., "Family Acceptance in Adolescence."

would not worship a God who was homophobic and that is how deeply I feel about this."[72] Tutu, who dedicated his life and work to the Christian faith since childhood, was not disrespecting God. Instead, he was saying his view of God left no room for hatred and rejection of LGBTQ people. It's an attitude some younger conservative Christians are taking hold of, but that has yet to prevail in the larger evangelical community. For now, they are still reacting out of disgust and calling it righteousness.

72. BBC News, "Archbishop Tutu," lines 15–19.

CHAPTER 9

A Devil behind Every Door

Christians and Conspiracy-Mindedness

"If one looks hard enough, one can find a devil behind every door and a conspiracy behind every corner."

—ANGELA MULLINS, *WORKING FOR UNCLE HENRY*

MADDISON WELCH LIVED IN Salisbury, North Carolina, a quaint town an hour outside of Charlotte. His friends called Maddison "a devout Christian" and he had gone on a mission trip with a Baptist Men's Association to help rebuild earthquake-damaged Haiti. He was a local volunteer fireman. A devoted father of two young girls, he was a man who helped others during times of need. He had tattooed on his back the verses in Isaiah about those who hope in the Lord soaring on wings like eagles, running and not growing weary, walking and not fainting.[1]

On Sunday morning, December 4, 2016, Maddison armed himself with an AR-15 assault rifle, a shotgun, and a revolver, and drove six hours to Washington, DC to enter a popular family pizzeria called Comet Ping Pong.[2] He swept into the restaurant, pointed his gun at an employee, shot several rounds into a lock, and forced the door open.[3] He expected to find

1. Alexander and Svrluga, "'I am sure he is sorry for any heartache he has caused.'"
2. Hermann et al., "Comet Pizza Gunman," lines 83–86.
3. Herman et al., "Comet Pizza Gunman," lines 23–28.

191

a basement where child sex slaves were being held. Instead, he found only a small computer server closet.[4]

When he realized there were no child sex slaves, that the restaurant was, in fact, just a pizza parlor, he laid down his guns and surrendered to the police. For weeks, he had been watching online videos about a conspiracy theory that would come to be known as Pizzagate. He texted some friends to help him fight "a corrupt system that kidnaps, tortures, and rapes babies and children in our own backyard."[5] He set off, heavily armed, to stop what he thought was a horrible atrocity. And yet there was no truth to it. None at all. It had all been a fable, spun by conspiracy theorists online.

Welcome to QAnon, a web of overlapping, impossible-to-disprove theories about the underground battles raging in the world. The Q conspiracy is replete with ideas so ridiculous and cartoonish they'd be laughed out of any Hollywood pitch meeting, yet wide swaths of white evangelicals have thoroughly embraced them, sometimes dividing families.

A March 2021 study of 5,625 Americans anchored by the Public Religion Research Institute found white evangelicals were the most likely of any group to endorse QAnon conspiracy beliefs and the least likely to reject those beliefs.[6] Those who indicated their most trusted news came from "far-right sources" were much more likely than others to believe the QAnon conspiracies, including 40 percent who agreed that "the government, media, and financial worlds in the US are controlled by a group of Satan-worshipping pedophiles who run a global child sex trafficking operation." Even more (42 percent) of this group believe "true American patriots may have to resort to violence in order to save our country."[7]

A recent college graduate named Harrison booked an appointment to see me to discuss his relationship with his parents. They had always been "very religious," he told me, and had reacted with sadness and rage when he told them the previous year he was an atheist. When he found it difficult to find a job because of the pandemic, he moved back home after graduation. Now he was experiencing something he could not believe. His parents, who used to watch YouTube videos of sermons every day, were now watching conspiracy theory videos, scribbling into notebooks, and having lengthy and intense discussions about their new insights at the dinner table.

"The things they say are so unbelievable," he told me, "that at first I thought they might have been joking, but then I realized they were serious.

4. Herman et al., "Comet Pizza Gunman," lines 97–100.

5. Herman et al., "Comet Pizza Gunman," lines 14–17.

6. Public Religion Research Institute, "Understanding QAnon's Connection," figure 3.

7. Public Religion Research Institute, "Understanding QAnon's Connection," figure 2.

They believe the Democrats are part of a worldwide conspiracy to abduct children, abuse them, and even drink their blood. They really believe that. I've got to get out of there."

I pressed him to explain the shift he had seen in his folks. His mother used to lead Bible studies at church. His dad had been a deacon. All they talked about before was the church and Jesus, but now QAnon theories consumed them. They believed God had chosen Donald Trump to save America.

"In the past, they were focused on Jesus, their savior who was coming back to save them," he explained, "but now Donald Trump has taken his place. He is the embodiment of Jesus to them. He is their new savior."

Harrison's story would have sounded ludicrous and unthinkable only five years earlier, yet variations of it were being experienced all around the country and all around the world during the Trump presidency.

Harrison's story and those like it have puzzled me. Why would the earnest Bible study leader and the serious-minded deacon find it so easy to fall prey to an absurd conspiracy theory? Why do some people seem so vulnerable to the QAnon hoax? Why are Christians especially susceptible to it? The past few years of psychological research can help us understand.

WHAT IS QANON?

QAnon began in 2017 when a shadowy figure nicknamed Q posted anonymous (thus, QAnon) online first-person accounts of a supposed secret high-level conspiracy.[8] Q claimed to have confidential insider information about his claims, which he sometimes shared in coded language that needed to be interpreted by other followers. The many details of the plot are far-reaching and sometimes contradictory. They become more outlandish and bizarre the more it continues and the further it sprawls. If you haven't heard the claims before now, buckle up:

Throughout his presidency, there was a secret plot against Donald Trump and his adherents, led by members of the "deep state," the hidden government within the legitimately elected government. Trump was pitted against an international cabal of Satan-worshiping, baby-blood-drinking pedophiles who control the major institutions in the world, including all of Hollywood and the media. Bill and Hillary Clinton are part of this shadowy group, as are many famous actors. Some Q adherents believe the Clintons and others seek a chemical compound called adrenochrome, which they say

8. An investigation found Q may have started as one person, but became three, if not more, in subsequent years.

produces mystical and psychedelic sensations and extends their life span, but is only harvested from torturing and killing children.

"The Storm" was supposed to be an uprising where faithful members of the armed forces would arrest thousands of this evil syndicate of politicians, business leaders, and Hollywood elites and send them to Guantanamo Bay. The US military would assume control of the country, leading us to a utopian state where evil is vanquished and good prevails.

Had it not been for the unforeseen 2016 election of Trump, this dangerous web would have continued to rule the world and abuse children. With his help and direction, the evil syndicate would be vanquished and the world would be saved.[9]

When the Storm did not materialize during Trump's first term, Q followers understood this meant the uprising would happen in the second term. Trump's loss to Biden by seven million popular votes and seventy-four electoral college votes could only mean one thing: the evildoers, who will stop at nothing to remain in power, stole the election.

For many Q followers, the Capitol building attack marked the beginning of the promised Storm. For others, the Storm was still going to happen on Inauguration Day, January 20, 2021. When none of that materialized, Q followers recalibrated and predict dates in March or August or later, while never acknowledging Trump had lost the election. He could not have lost, they reasoned, because Q told them Trump would have a second term and justice would be served. The only explanation was widespread coordinated voter fraud, which fit with their "deep state" beliefs.

Q, who claims to have the highest security clearance and full insider information about the highest levels of government, saw his influence increase exponentially in the run-up to the 2020 election. One researcher found a 651 percent increase in QAnon content on Facebook between March and July of that year.[10] Most worrisome, though, was how pervasive belief in the QAnon narrative had become among white Christians.

One woman shared that twenty-five women in her homeschool circle, all evangelicals, were now adherents to QAnon. Others have written about losing friends and family over their loved one's devotion to QAnon.

The Week wrote, "Q's apocalyptic writings increasingly echo evangelical Christian beliefs about the end times, with Trump described as a messiah-like figure."[11] They quoted Laurie Shock, a fifty-seven-year-old woman from Ohio who was then spending up to six hours a day researching

9. Carter, "What Christians Should Know About QAnon."

10. Argentino, "QAnon Conspiracy Followers," lines 39–42.

11. *The Week* Staff, "QAnon Goes Mainstream," lines 51–53.

QAnon-related theories and claims. She told them, "I feel like God led me to Q."[12] They added, "For those who view Q as a religion, their beliefs by definition can't be falsified, while their deity continues to send signs to reinforce their faith."[13] *Vanity Fair* quoted a Q supporter named Diane at a Florida Trump rally who said, "It's all about God! All about spiritual warfare. Trump will tell you that. Over and over."[14]

Joe Carter, author and editor for The Gospel Coalition, wrote of the QAnon movement, "It is likely that someone in your church or social media circles has either already bought into the conspiracy or thinks it's plausible and worth exploring."[15]

During the miserable summer of 2020, Rock Urban Church, a megachurch down the road from Grand Rapids, Michigan, used its July 4th weekend service to show a twelve-minute video called "COVID 911" that promoted many QAnon theories, including the deranged notions that Democrats staged the death of George Floyd, planned to inflame racial unrest, and promoted the hoax of COVID-19 as a way of reclaiming power.[16] Afterwards, the pastor, Gary Peterson, took the stage and lamented the condition of the country, saying, "This has gotten ridiculously out of control. It is time to speak up."[17] The event showed how easy the marriage between evangelicalism and right-wing conspiracy theories has become.

In Indiana, a conservative church hosted a two-hour Sunday service that linked Q's messages with Bible prophecies.[18] In one service, they explained how the US government had developed time travel technology. The leader, Russ Wagner, claimed biblical passages supported time travel.[19] A week later, the church explained how godless liberals planned the COVID pandemic.[20]

Some call QAnon a "big tent conspiracy theory," an evolving, hermetically sealed belief system that had become impossible to prove or disprove. While it was the largest and most far-reaching conspiracy theory due to social media and anonymous message boards, it was not the first.

12. *The Week* Staff, "QAnon Goes Mainstream," lines 53–55.

13. *The Week* Staff, "QAnon Goes Mainstream," lines 73–75.

14. *The Week* Staff, "QAnon Goes Mainstream," lines 76–78.

15. Carter, "What Christians Should Know About QAnon," lines 282–84.

16. *Relevant* Staff, "This Megachurch Spread QAnon Conspiracy Theories," lines 1–8.

17. *Relevant* Staff, "This Megachurch Spread QAnon Conspiracy Theories," lines 28–31.

18. Argentino, "Church of QAnon," lines 25–37.

19. Argentino, "Church of QAnon," lines 38–40.

20. Argentino, "Church of QAnon," lines 41–45.

CONSPIRACY THEORIES THROUGHOUT AMERICAN HISTORY

Conspiracy theories are not new on the American landscape. They've been woven through the culture for hundreds of years. QAnon isn't even the first conspiracy theory to attract large numbers of Christians.

In the early 1800s, a conspiracy theory about the Masons took hold, alleging some of their members had formed a secret cabal called the Illuminati, a group plotting to undermine all religions and subvert government authority.[21] This alarmed Christians.

When a former Mason, William Morgan, threatened to publish a book exposing ritual secrets, police arrested him for a three-dollar debt. Upon his release from jail, he vanished and was never seen again. Many suspected the Masons had murdered him.[22]

Anger at the Masons rose and eventually led to the Anti-Masonic Party.[23] The party won dozens of congressional seats in the 1830s thanks to prominent supporters, rich patrons, Christian leaders, and extensive media coverage. At least thirty-five party backers were newspaper publishers around the country.[24] The party did especially well in areas influenced by evangelical revivals. The party's anti-vice platform attracted conservative Christians. Its anti-elitist positions drew other groups.[25]

Since then, we've had one conspiracy after another:[26]

- The CIA or the mob or the Russians or the Cubans or others killed JFK.

- The FBI conspired to kill Martin Luther King Jr.

- NASA faked the moon landing.

- Area 51 contains alien bodies and spacecraft.

- There is an Illuminati headquarters in an underground bunker beneath the Denver International Airport.

- The military created a massive tornado that leveled Joplin, Missouri.

---

21. Bjork-James, "Two centuries ago, a QAnon-like conspiracy," lines 39–43.

22. Bjork-James, "Two centuries ago, a QAnon-like conspiracy," lines 44–52

23. Bjork-James, "Two centuries ago, a QAnon-like conspiracy," lines 53–55.

24. Bjork-James, "Two centuries ago, a QAnon-like conspiracy," lines 56–61.

25. Bjork-James, "Two centuries ago, a QAnon-like conspiracy," lines 62–66.

26. And overseas, Princess Di either faked her own death or was murdered by the Royal Family or the British government. Another European conspiracy is a belief that large numbers of Muslim immigrants were sent by "Zionist Supremacists" to Europe in order to outbreed white people.

- The contrails of commercial airliners are mind-control chemicals meant to keep the population docile.

- Anti-gun groups stage school shootings.

- The US government orchestrated the 9/11 terrorist attacks.

- A Jewish-funded organization developed space lasers to clear areas for a high-speed rail project, but accidentally ignited the California wildfires.

- Liberal factions planned the coronavirus pandemic.

- Bill Gates placed a microchip in COVID-19 vaccines to track our movements.

QAnon is a more sophisticated, complex version of the conspiracies that have long been part of our culture. It often weaves old and even contradictory conspiracies together. While it has the benefit of social media and websites to spread it, it remains only the latest iteration of a centuries-old phenomenon. A high number of Christians have embraced this web of conspiracies. QAnon has infiltrated the church more deeply than any other in history, so we need to understand what draws people into these fringe beliefs.

PERVASIVENESS OF CONSPIRACY-MINDEDNESS

Be honest: Do you think the government is concealing what they know about the North Dakota Crash? In a survey of American citizens, one-third of the respondents (32 percent) agreed this was likely. Over 7 percent strongly agreed the government was covering it up. In fact, in this survey, more people believed this than other possible cover-ups, like the idea the moon landing was a hoax or that Justice Scalia was murdered.[27]

The problem is the researchers made it up. There was no North Dakota Crash—or South Dakota Crash in a follow-up study that found roughly the same percentage agreed there had been a cover-up. A third of respondents agreed the government concealed an event that was completely fabricated.[28]

I asked Joseph O. Baker, one of the study's authors, about the origin of the idea. He said, "The South Dakota Crash was the brilliant idea of Chris Bader, who runs the Chapman University Survey of American Fears. He

27. Chapman University, "Survey on American Fears."
28. Chapman University, "Survey on American Fears."

thought it would be interesting to come up with a way to gauge baseline willingness to believe in a governmental conspiracy. We were honestly shocked at how high the affirmative response was."

The researchers found the higher the level of fear, the more likely a person believed in the made-up conspiracy—as well as other conspiracies. They asked people to rate how afraid they were from one (not afraid) to four (very afraid) of the following things: blood, needles, spiders, bees, snakes, dogs, deep water, flying, sharks, clowns, ghosts, heights, public speaking, enclosed spaces, zombies, strangers, and walking alone at night. Of those who believed in the fabricated cover-up, 57 percent had "very high" levels of self-reported phobias, double the amount of those who reported no phobias. The higher the level of fear, the more prone to conspiracy thinking.[29]

Another one of the biggest predictors of conspiracy thinking was being "a biblical literalist," meaning those who hold a literal interpretation of the Bible were more likely than others to believe the federal government had covered up the South Dakota Crash. This includes those who believe that God created the Earth in six twenty-four-hour days, that Noah kept two kinds of every animal in an ark to repopulate the planet after a worldwide flood, and that there is an ongoing, unseen battle between supernatural forces, i.e., God and Satan, angels and demons. Not all biblical literalists are drawn into conspiracy theories or primed to endorse a phony cover-up, but it is one of the biggest predictors.[30]

I asked Baker what conclusions he drew when a full third of those surveyed believed a fabricated conspiracy. "My main takeaway from this is that there are very high levels of pre-existing willingness to distrust the government among the American public," he said. "Given this high general propensity, we might say that some level of conspiratorial thinking will necessarily occur, and that conspiracies have a very welcome environment in which to spread. It also means the American public is ripe area for exploitation by public figures and hucksters who are willing to do so."

I asked him what shocked him in his research findings on conspiracy beliefs. "The biggest surprise was how prevalent they were," he said. "I had no idea of how widespread those beliefs were. For example, the idea that the government is hiding what it knows about mass shootings is shocking."

29. Bader et al., *Fear Itself*.
30. Bader et al., *Fear Itself*.

WHAT MAKES SOMETHING A CONSPIRACY THEORY?

What constitutes a conspiracy theory? Is it just an odd belief about an event or a group? Social psychologist Jan-Willem van Prooijen proposes five essential components that are true of all conspiracy theories. First, they explain events by showing *patterns of intentional actions that all connect to each other.*[31] This notion of connection between events or people is essential to the definition of conspiracy theories, as well as to understanding who is most susceptible to them.

Second, conspiracy theories always propose the events were *done on purpose.*[32] As an example, we know that plane crash was not an accident. Deep state operatives blew it up to silence a professor onboard who has proof the virus was intentionally spread by the CIA.

Third, conspiracy theories always involve *multiple people or organizations working together.*[33] They have to involve people conspiring together. A lone wolf acting alone is not a true conspiracy. Many others have to be in on the plan.

Fourth, they did these events *for some evil or selfish reasons.*[34] Cover-ups! Greed! Power! Intimidation! The more nefarious, the more credible the theory becomes. The government doesn't put fluoride in the water to prevent tooth decay. No, in the words of General Jack D. Ripper in the film *Dr. Strangelove*, "Do you realize that fluoridation is the most monstrously conceived and dangerous communist plot we have ever had to face?"

And fifth, *ongoing secrecy obscures the truth of the event.*[35] The lack of full exposure keeps it in the realm of theory rather than fact. It has not been exposed—until now! And the man who has cracked this wide open is a dentist from Omaha or a Navy veteran from San Diego, who has pieced together secret knowledge and now shares it all with you—often at great personal risk.

Said altogether, conspiracy theories speculate about a series of interconnected evil acts done on purpose by multiple individuals who have yet to be verifiably exposed to the public. The job of the conspiracy theorist is to establish this connection and bring the evil deeds into the light for people to see.

31. van Prooijen and van Vugt, "Evolved Functions."
32. van Prooijen and van Vugt, "Evolved Functions."
33. van Prooijen and van Vugt, "Evolved Functions."
34. van Prooijen and van Vugt, "Evolved Functions."
35. van Prooijen and van Vugt, "Evolved Functions."

Belief in conspiracy theories is more widespread than you might imagine. Five years after the terrorist attacks of 9/11, a nationwide survey found over a third of Americans (36 percent) believed US officials were responsible for the acts or knew about them in advance and did nothing to stop them.[36] Over fifty years after Kennedy was assassinated, about 60 percent of Americans believe Oswald was part of a conspiracy and didn't act alone.[37] In one 2017 study, more than a quarter of Americans believe there are conspiracies "behind many things in the world." Conspiracy belief is shockingly common.[38]

A big predictor of whether someone will believe a particular conspiracy theory is whether they believe other conspiracy theories. A person who believes one is much more likely to believe more than one.[39] This holds true even if the conspiracy theories contradict themselves. It is less about the content of a particular conspiracy theory and more about the unique psychology of those who believe them. It's not because a specific conspiracy theory is especially believable, it is because conspiracy theories appeal to certain types of people or people in certain conditions.

STATES VS. TRAITS

There is ample evidence ordinary people can be nudged toward a greater openness to conspiracy-mindedness. One study randomly assigned college students into three groups. In the first group, researchers asked them to recall and write about a time when they felt powerless. They asked the second group to write about a time when they felt completely in control. They asked the third group to write about something neutral, like what they had for dinner the night before.[40]

The researchers then asked the groups to describe their beliefs about a new subway construction project that had been overrun with delays and other problems. The first group was more likely to support conspiracy ideas about the subway line.[41] Perhaps the city council was intentionally putting citizens in danger. Maybe they were stealing money earmarked for the project. The participants who felt powerless, even momentarily, found the city officials to be more underhanded and untrustworthy.

36. Torchia, "9/11 Conspiracy Theories Rife in the Muslim World."
37. Swift, "Majority in U.S. Still Believe JFK Killed in Conspiracy."
38. Wenner Moyer, "People Drawn to Conspiracy Theories."
39. Goreis and Voracek, "Systematic Review and Meta-Analysis."
40. Stojanov et al., "Does Perceived Lack of Control Lead to Conspiracy Beliefs?"
41. Stojanov et al., "Does Perceived Lack of Control Lead to Conspiracy Beliefs?"

In psychology, we make distinctions between "state" and "trait." For example, a person can have state anger or trait anger. Those with state anger are not normally mad or hotheaded, but could be induced to that state under the right conditions. A person high in trait anger, however, feels more anger and rage most of the time and is more prone to erupting in situations where other people might normally keep their cool. The same can be true of anxiety, perfectionism, optimism, and other qualities.

For conspiracy theories, the states that seem to make ordinarily normal people more likely to endorse these beliefs include feeling stressed, anxious, uncertain, unwanted, or alienated. In research studies, when people felt these unsettling emotions, even for short periods of time, they rated conspiracy ideas as more likely. The unpleasant emotions of fear and rejection nudged them toward being open to ideas they previously would never have considered. If researchers can create this experience, even for a brief time in a lab setting, imagine what can happen when these experiences occur for a sustained period in real life.

A person might be more anxious or socially disconnected by nature (*trait*), but others who are not as prone to anxiety or social disconnection can be made to have those experiences for a period of time (*state*). When they do, they are more vulnerable to conspiracy thinking.

In their book *American Conspiracy Theories*, Joseph Uscinski and Joseph Parent claim conspiracy theories "tend to resonate when groups are suffering from loss, weakness or disunity."[42] Certain states coax people toward conspiracy belief. People believe in conspiracy theories much more often when they face uncertainty in their personal life, like not knowing if they will have enough money to pay the bills, or when the social order feels less stable, such as times of political upheaval, protests and rioting, or national tragedy. During these times, people turn to conspiracy theories for answers and a sense of security. However, the research says this pursuit often leads them deeper down the rabbit hole, further unsettling them, which leads to even more conspiracy thinking.

A *Washington Post* study of 125 rioters who breached the Capitol building on January 6, 2021, many of whom believed they were part of the Storm, found the majority (nearly 60 percent) had significant financial problems, including bankruptcies, tax problems, evictions, foreclosures, or bad debts. Their bankruptcy rate was twice as high as the general public. Around one in five had faced losing their home in the past. A quarter of them had been sued for money owed to a creditor.[43] News accounts showed

42. Uscinski and Parent, *American Conspiracy Theories*, 131.
43. Frankel, "People Arrested for Capitol Riot," lines 13–21.

many of the rioters espousing QAnon beliefs the day of the attack and on their social media accounts. Financial insecurity may have contributed to their openness to the conspiracy theory that led to violence on that day.

The higher the life stress a person is under, the more she is vulnerable to conspiracy theories. Even "perceived life stress," where the objective amount of stress is not that high, but the person subjectively believes she is facing a tremendous amount of stress, puts her at risk. Much of modern stress is subjective. One person who has to present at work might not sleep the night before. Another person might not give it a thought until he gets up in front of his colleagues. One parent with a special-needs child may feel a low amount of stress while another may see it as catastrophic. The research says it isn't the objective amount of stress that makes someone more vulnerable, but it's the subjective "perceived life stress" that matters most.[44]

A former QAnon believer on Reddit, nicknamed "diceblue," writes, "There is a perverse comfort in Con Ts [conspiracy theories] because of the false sense of order and purpose it brings to the world. Either the world is a board game/chess match between Good and Evil forces working behind the scenes, and you might be a pawn but at least you are on The Right Side or you admit that the world is a mess, nobody is in charge, there is no grand battle of good and evil behind the scenes and your life has less purpose and order than you hoped."[45]

Those under stress may be drawn to conspiracy theories "because of the false sense of order and purpose it brings to the world," in the words of the former QAnon follower. White Christians perceive more stress now than in the past, especially as their preferred positions of influence and privilege are threatened. This understanding has profound implications for how we understand why many seemingly normal white Christians go down the rabbit hole of conspiracy theories in ways that seem baffling to those who know them.

While certain stressful conditions and states of mind can predispose someone to believe in conspiracy theories, there is much more research on what individual traits make a person more vulnerable to these strongly held but wrongheaded, often dangerous, convictions. Some of these traits are predictable, while others are surprising.

44. Swami et al., "Putting the Stress on Conspiracy Theories."
45. Reneau, "Former QAnon believer," lines 55–62.

TRAITS OF CONSPIRACY THEORY BELIEVERS

On the morning of October 19, 2020, former Houston police captain Mark Aguirre ran his SUV into an air conditioner repairman's truck, then pointed a handgun at him, ordered him to the ground, and pressed his knee into the man's back.[46] The repairman thought he was being robbed and feared for his life, he later said. But Aguirre was not there to rob him.[47] The activist group Liberty Center for God and Country had hired him for over a quarter of a million dollars to investigate allegations of voter fraud, following claims the election was stolen from Donald Trump.[48]

Aguirre had been surveilling the repairman's home for several days and became convinced the man had 750,000 fraudulent mail-in ballots signed by Hispanic children whose fingerprints authorities would not find in government databases.[49] After the incident, the repairman gave permission for law enforcement officers to search his house, truck, and even a storage shed. They found no evidence of fake ballots or other voter fraud.[50] Aguirre was arrested and charged with aggravated assault with a deadly weapon.[51]

Nearly two decades earlier in 2002, the *Houston Press* ran a story about Aguirre following a botched raid that got him suspended from the department, calling him a "no-nonsense kind of tough guy."[52] After his more recent assault on the repairman, he faced twenty years in prison on several felony charges.[53]

The local district attorney, Kim Ogg, said, "His alleged investigation was backward from the start—first alleging a crime had occurred and then trying to prove it happened."[54] This tendency to reverse engineer reality seems to be a consistent feature of conspiracy theorists. What is it about someone like Mark Aguirre that makes him so vulnerable to believing in grand conspiracies, even when the evidence is lacking, manufactured, or not credible? Intelligent, capable people fall prey to some of the most far-fetched conspiracy theories. Why does this happen? Research has given us many strong, sometimes surprising insights.

46. Fortin, "Houston Officer Investigating 'Fraudulent' Ballots," lines 1–11.
47. Fortin, "Houston Officer Investigating 'Fraudulent' Ballots," lines 41–42.
48. Fortin, "Houston Officer Investigating 'Fraudulent' Ballots," lines 12–26.
49. Fortin, "Houston Officer Investigating 'Fraudulent' Ballots," lines 43–48.
50. Fortin, "Houston Officer Investigating 'Fraudulent' Ballots," lines 57–58.
51. Fortin, "Houston Officer Investigating 'Fraudulent' Ballots," lines 5–6.
52. Downing, "Myths and Legends," lines 11–13.
53. Douglas, "Former Houston Police Captain Accused," lines 77–78.
54. Fortin, "Houston Officer Investigating 'Fraudulent' Ballots," lines 13–17.

A Multi-Determined Phenomenon

Early in my career, I worked for a community mental health agency that served extremely violent juveniles. These kids were so violent officials had expelled them from schools and treatment programs. They were often incarcerated for brutal crimes. To be included in our program, you had to be certified by a state panel who judged you to be so violent you qualified for the most intensive services possible. One teenager had originally been turned down for the program because he had committed only one murder and didn't have any other history of violence.

During my time there, Randy Borum, one of the world's leading authorities on violence risk, approached me. Splitting his time between his tenured position at the University of South Florida and the US Secret Service, he was instrumental in some of the major research into the mind of assassins and terrorists. He asked if I would be open to writing a book with him on violence risk for juveniles. He had done all the research and put it in a ninety-page outline. My job would be to put this in book form with compelling real-life stories and clear explanations.

Writing the book proved much more arduous than I had expected. The research was complex and nuanced. The exact language was important. For example, in the research on violence, there is a difference between "aggression" and "violence." Aggression is rough behavior—pushing, shoving, attacking language, and so on. Violence is an attack with a weapon or any intentional action that causes bodily damage.

Why is this important? Because it makes a difference with what you are studying. If you were interested in the effects of violent video games, for instance, you'd be right to say exposure to these games can produce short-term aggression in children, say for an hour after playing. You'd be wrong to say they produce violence in children. There's no support for that, despite misinterpretations of studies by some news outlets and blogs.

A central finding from Borum's research was that violence is always *multi-determined*. There is not just one solitary reason for it. After every school shooting, people—including mental health professionals—begin popping off their favorite theories. The most common is to place blame on the parents of the shooter. They were either too lax or too strict. Variations of these theories always emerge.

There are other proposed reasons for the horrific event: *He played violent video games. He listened to rap or heavy metal music. He looked at pornography. He wasn't involved in sports. He took antidepressants. He was bullied. He was mentally ill. He was probably abused.* These all reflect each individual's own biases more than an accurate analysis of what drove the behavior.

The research says there is rarely just one reason someone commits an act of violence—and it is often not the proposed explanations. It's a convergence of several factors at once. Borum's research found twenty-four risk factors that raised one's likelihood of violence. Some of them were historical factors, like early abuse or neglect, witnessing violence in the home, or losing caregivers. Some were social factors, like peer rejection or a lack of a support system. Another set of variables were clinical risk factors, like anger management problems or low empathy. There was no single factor that alone predicted risk for violence, but the combination of variables painted an accurate picture of a person's probability of trouble.[55]

There is not just one reason people embrace conspiracy theories, in the same way there is no single reason someone might be violent or become obese or get cancer or enjoy folk music. Simplistic, one-dimensional notions of why someone behaves in a certain way are not only unhelpful, but they can often obscure factors we need to know. The more we understand why something occurred, the better we are at managing it.

Twelve Traits That Predict Conspiracy Belief

When I first tackled this subject, I expected to find one or two main reasons that best explained what drew people to conspiracy theories. I was wrong. The considerable body of research comes to a variety of conclusions about this complex phenomenon. Rather than being contradictory, though, I liken it to the old metaphor of the blind men and the elephant, each having one part of the beast to touch and interpret. What is clear is there is no one explanation for conspiracy-mindedness. There are several factors that predispose someone toward this tendency.

Based on my review of the research, I found individuals who are more prone to believing in conspiracy theories like QAnon often share two or more of at least twelve personality traits or attitudes. Some of these traits are overlapping or adjacent to each other. Most people who subscribe to conspiracy theories don't have all of these traits, but it's likely they hold a combination of some of them. These traits and attitudes that put people at greater risk for conspiracy-mindedness include:

55. Borum et al., *Structured Assessment of Violence Risk in Youth.*

- Paranoia—people who believe in conspiracy theories are more suspicious of people and believe others might intend them harm. They are on guard against potential threats most of the time.

- "Dangerous World" Beliefs—while some view the world as safe and under control, others see it as a dangerous place. Those who are more on that side of the scale are more likely to endorse conspiracy theories.

- Alienation—those who believe in conspiracy theories are more cut off, isolated, and detached from others, compared to most people. Sometimes their alienation is not by their choice, while other times it is. Either way, the lack of healthy attachments makes these individuals more likely to see others as underhanded and untrustworthy.

- Collective Narcissism—conspiracy theory thinking and collective narcissism go together, which makes sense given that those who are in a group high in collective narcissism feel like others have it in for them, so they feel compelled to gather information to protect themselves. They find information that confirms others despise them and want to destroy them and their way of life. Individuals who endorsed statements like "The United States deserves special treatment" were more likely to endorse conspiracy-related statements like "Much of our lives are being controlled by plots hatched in secret places."[56]

- Need for Uniqueness—this aspect of narcissism—a deep desire to be seen as special—is commonplace among those who are more conspiracy-minded. Conspiracy theories appeal to those who think they have knowledge others don't have. Narcissism involves a sense of being special, which makes it easier for a person to believe he has access to secret information that others are too ignorant to see.

- High Anxiety—people who believe conspiracies have more trait and state anxiety. They have personality traits that are more geared to anxiety, as well as more anxiety and apprehension in certain situations.

- Need for Control—related to anxiety is this need to be in control of one's environment. People with a high need for control also have a need for certainty and understanding, as well as the drive to predict what will happen.

- Authoritarianism—related to the need to control is authoritarianism that values status quo, order, and control over personal freedoms. Authoritarians gravitate toward conspiracy theories because they explain difficult and uncertain things.

56. Golec de Zavala and Federico, "Collective Narcissism."

- Extreme Political Views—those with political views that are on either extreme, either right or left, are much more prone to conspiracy
  thinking.

- Schizotypal Personality Disorder—a mental illness akin to schizophrenia, this personality disorder involves odd thinking, lack of close
  friends, and peculiar interpersonal style.

- Insecure Attachment Style—people who are insecure and fretful in
  their close relationships may have an attachment style that also makes
  them more open to conspiracy notions.

- Cognitive Biases—research has uncovered at least three thinking errors those who embrace conspiracy theories are prone to make: teleological thinking, illusory pattern perception, and agency detection.

These risk factors are not true of all people who are conspiracy-prone,
but together, they reveal who is more vulnerable. While each of these risk
factors is important, the final three—Schizotypal Personality Disorder, insecure attachment style, and cognitive biases—require elaboration. I'll explore
each of these in more detail. The first explanation, mental illness, helps explain why some people may be more conspiracy prone, but it does not tell
us why Christians are more likely to endorse these improbable beliefs. The
second one, insecure attachment, sheds more light on conspiracy thinking,
but also does not explain why white Christians are more prone to believe
conspiracy theories. The final explanation, cognitive biases, however, is our
biggest key to understanding why white Christians are especially vulnerable
to embracing conspiracy theories, including outlandish ones like QAnon.

SCHIZOTYPAL PERSONALITY DISORDER
AND CONSPIRACY BELIEF

One psychologist linked belief in conspiracy theories to "attenuated psycho-
sis," which is a syndrome that involves some mild hallucinations, delusions,
or disorganized speech, but without a psychotic disorder diagnosis. The
term *psychotic* means a loss of contact with reality.[57]

The claim that conspiracy theories are the product of mild psychotic
symptoms seems to forget that nearly half the population has a belief in at
least one conspiracy theory. Half of the population is not psychotic (though
some days you might be tempted to believe otherwise). There are, however,

---

57. Marino, "Psychology of Conspiracy Theories."

a small group of people whose mental illness produces odd beliefs and leads them to seize on conspiracy theories.

On Christmas Day of 2020 at 1:22 AM, Anthony Warner, a sixty-three-year-old computer consultant, parked his large Thor Motor Coach Chateau RV along Second Avenue in downtown Nashville. Beautiful historic buildings that house restaurants and specialty shops and several residential units line the street, which sits just beside Lower Broadway, the famed strip of country music honky-tonks and restaurants, the beating heart of Nashville.[58]

Shortly after 5 AM, the sound of over twenty gunshots rang through the street, prompting residents to call 911. When police arrived, the RV was playing a recording over a loudspeaker: "The vehicle will explode in fifteen minutes," then counted down, minute by minute. At the end of the countdown, the sound of the optimistic Petula Clark song, "Downtown," filled the early morning air.[59]

The RV exploded with such force it could be heard miles away, ripping the brick facings off the historic buildings, shooting fiery debris several blocks, wounding a communications hub that knocked out Internet and cell phone service across a four-state region, and leaving the area looking like a war zone.

Two days before his suicide bombing, Anthony Warner had mailed letters and flash drives with Internet videos to acquaintances, claiming, "I now understand everything, and I mean everything from who/what we really are, to what the known universe really is." He espoused conspiracy theories about the moon landing, 9/11 cover-ups, and lizard people, which he claimed "put a switch into the human brain so they could walk among us and appear human." He added, "There is no such thing as death."[60]

We know he didn't have a sudden psychotic break. There is sound evidence his unusual thinking had been present for a long period and he had planned his hideous act well in advance. Over a year earlier, his girlfriend called the police on Warner, claiming he was building a bomb in his RV. They came to his door and when they got no answer, they left and the investigation ended soon afterward.

Based on his letters, it's likely Warner had either schizophrenia or a condition called Schizotypal Personality Disorder, most likely the latter. To my knowledge, Anthony Warner was never formally diagnosed with Schizotypal Personality Disorder, but he exhibited many, if not most, of the traits. People with this personality structure don't have schizophrenia, which is a

58. Allison and Tamburin, "Retracing the Christmas Morning Bombing."
59. Allison and Tamburin, "Retracing the Christmas Morning Bombing."
60. Hall and Sisniewski, "Nashville Bomber's Bizarre Writings," lines 14–39.

disease of the brain, but they have similar characteristics. They are odd and eccentric, have few close friends, and are mistrustful.

Personality disorders are forms of mental illness that differ from diseases of the brain, like schizophrenia or bipolar disorder. They occur when an individual's personality forms in a maladaptive way. In the old days of psychiatry and psychology, researchers believed personality disorders were always the result of negative early life experiences—parents who were too harsh or too cold, trauma, rejection or neglect, overindulgence, and so on. However, more recent research finds personality disorders can be the product of a dynamic interplay between a person's biochemistry and life experiences, with one or both tipping the scale toward difficulty.

For the person with the schizotypal personality, their way of seeing the world in a delusional way is more similar to someone with a major mental illness. These are emotionally flat loners who misinterpret benign events as threatening or offensive, have peculiar thinking, and are paranoid and suspicious. Sometimes they believe they have special powers, like mind reading, or they have unusual perceptions. They may appear very unkempt or dress in eccentric ways and have an odd style of speech. They may ramble and mumble when they talk. For the schizotypal person, belief in conspiracy theories are part of his disordered thinking, which is full of paranoia and delusional beliefs.

People with schizotypy don't do well in large groups and social settings, such as a church congregation. While they may be full of religious thoughts, that doesn't translate to church involvement. Many churches have a few people who have these types of personalities. They usually represent less than 1 percent of their church attendance. There are far higher percentages of narcissists in most churches.

While Schizotypal Personality Disorder or other mental illness can predispose individuals to conspiracy-mindedness, there is no evidence this explains why so many white Christians believe QAnon or other conspiracies. A somewhat more likely explanation has to do with attachment style.

INSECURE ATTACHMENT AND CONSPIRACY BELIEF

Erik was a physical therapist in his mid-twenties, dating a school teacher named Leah, who was only a month younger than him. They'd been dating for six months and things looked good, but fear gripped him.

"This is the best relationship I've ever been in," he told me, "and I'm freaked out."

"Tell me why," I replied.

"Because she's awesome and I keep worrying that she is going to wake up one day and realize she's made a terrible mistake and break up with me."

"What would make her do that?" I asked.

"Because I'm so needy and weak sometimes," he began, "or because I get jealous or act weird when she talks to other guys when we're out."

"What do you do?"

"This weekend she caught me looking through her phone when she left the room for a minute. She got mad. I apologized, but I could tell it bothered her."

"What were you looking for?"

"Her texts. To see if she was texting other guys."

"Did you have reason to think she was?"

"Not really. No. I just . . . I just always worry about that kind of thing."

Although you might not know what to call it, you sense something is wrong here. You can tell Erik is not a relationally healthy person. He has what we call an insecure attachment style. There is accumulating evidence that those drawn to conspiracy theories have significant problems with forming healthy human attachments. In particular, those with insecure attachment are more prone to conspiracy thinking.[61]

All humans are wired to attach to other humans. It's a biological imperative. When you were an infant, you had to draw close to a caregiver to get food, remain safe and warm, and feel secure. If you didn't do this, you'd likely die. In the early years, what starts as biological drives extends to emotional needs. We all need to be close to at least one other person in order to make sense of the world and feel special and validated when we are very young. The collision of your unique wiring—what we referred to as your "temperament" in the first chapter—and your life experiences shape a certain style of attachment, the way you connect and relate to others. Since the 1950s, researchers beginning with Mary Ainsworth and John Bowlby have found almost all of us have one of three attachment styles. (A fourth style is rare and found in only about 1 to 5 percent of the population.)[62]

We call the three styles secure, avoidant, and anxious. About half of the population (50–56 percent) are securely attached.[63] These folks feel confident and calm when they are in a relationship and unworried and unhurried if they are not. They find it easy to get close with others and they don't play games or manipulate in their relationships. Their view of

61. Green and Douglas, "Anxious Attachment and Conspiracy Theories."

62. Wallin, *Attachment in Psychotherapy*.

63. Levine and Heller, *Attached*.

themselves and others is positive and they expect their close relationships to be satisfying and balanced, with both partners getting their needs met by the other.

About a quarter of all adults have an avoidant attachment style.[64] These people are content without being in close relationships. They keep others, especially romantic partners, at arm's length, preferring more independence over being tied down. These folks suppress displays of emotion so others don't know how they are feeling, and they deal with rejection—or potential rejection—by distancing themselves from people who might rebuff them.

That leaves people who have an anxious attachment, like Erik, the young man who worried his girlfriend would leave him. About one in five people have this style of attachment, which is characterized by a strong desire to be in close relationships, but lots of worry when they find those relationships. This is a person who doesn't like to be alone, wants a committed relationship, but then when she is in it, becomes consumed with worry, jealousy, and insecurity. Sometimes these feelings get the best of them and the relationship blows up and the entire cycle starts again. Unlike the avoidant folks, anxiously attached people often show lots of emotion, much of it negative, and have a lot of trouble reining in their feelings.

This study of attachment styles helps us understand a lot about relationships, including the level of satisfaction, stability, and feelings of intimacy that people with different styles experience. They also tell us about who buys into conspiracy theories like QAnon.

In a groundbreaking series of studies, researchers Ricky Green and Karen Douglas found a strong relationship between anxious attachment and belief in conspiracy theories. They began with the hypothesis that people use conspiracy theories as a defense mechanism to manage deep psychological needs, like the need for security, safety, and control. We already knew from previous research that those with an anxious attachment style are focused on their safety and security, are more sensitive to perceived threats, and are more negative and suspicious of those who differ from them. We also knew anxiously attached people don't trust people as much as securely attached people and they see the world as scary and dangerous. At least one other study found those with anxious attachment are also more likely to agree with extreme right-wing attitudes. When you roll this all up together, it makes sense that they would line up with conspiracy theories, especially ones like QAnon.[65]

64. Levine and Heller, *Attached*.

65. Green and Douglas, "Anxious Attachment and Conspiracy Theories."

In their first study, Green and Douglas found those who rated higher in anxious attachment style revealed a greater likelihood of believing conspiracy theories, even when they accounted for other factors that predict conspiracy-mindedness. In their second study, they found anxious attachment not only predicted a general tendency to believe in conspiracy theories, but made those so attached more likely to believe that various groups were conspiring against them. They exaggerate the threats they may be facing.[66]

There is a strong possibility that it is not just anxious attachment that is associated with conspiracy belief, but any significant problems with attachment and human connection. Researchers at Princeton asked 119 individuals to rate how much they felt excluded, then later asked them how much they agreed with conspiracy statements like, "Governments use messages below the level of awareness to influence people's decisions." They found people who felt excluded were more likely to endorse conspiracy beliefs. They repeated the study, with some twists, with 120 college students and came to the same conclusion. Once again, they found those who felt excluded were much more likely to believe conspiracies. The researchers concluded that "the feelings of despair brought on by social exclusion" lead people to embrace fantastical stories that help them explain their struggles and challenges.[67]

The Princeton study provides more insight into how poor attachment adversely affects a person's view of the world. Excluded people who lack meaningful attachments come to see the world differently. They become drawn to narratives that tell them other people have malevolent intent. And without the secure base that comes from healthy attachments, they find it easy to see others as scheming, manipulative, and untrustworthy. Research suggests that about half the population has some attachment difficulties,[68] so this may be a more plausible explanation for why many white Christians favor conspiracies, though it doesn't tell us why they might be *more* likely to endorse them than others. However, there is one last explanation that explains why: white Christians are trained to have certain thinking biases that make them more vulnerable to these conspiracy beliefs.

BIASED THINKING STYLES

Adrian Hon makes video games for a living. He founded a company, Six to Start, that develops games called ARGs, which stands for Alternate Reality

---

66. Green and Douglas, "Anxious Attachment and Conspiracy Theories."

67. Graeupner and Coman, "Dark side of meaning-making."

68. Levine and Heller, *Attached*.

Games. Players use clues to uncover secrets that unlock payoffs. Often companies use them to launch products or promote new movies or television shows.[69]

Hon noticed the similarities between these games and adherents to conspiracy theories like QAnon. He told *Wired* QAnon adherents are "looking for signals in the noise."[70] They are trying to find patterns where none exist. That insight comes up repeatedly in understanding conspiracy-mindedness. There's an attraction to patterns, to finding order in chaos. A giant conspiracy theory "offers convenient explanations for things that feel inexplicable or wrong about the world," Hon told the *New York Times*.[71]

I asked him what caused him to connect conspiracy belief and gaming. He said, "It's really the whole phenomenon of QAnon followers saying, 'I've done my research.' It struck me that the research they were doing was typing phrases into Google and just watching or reading whatever came up, uncritically. ARG players do the same, but obviously they're playing a game!"

People who strongly believe in conspiracy theories often have biased thinking styles. Research suggests there are at least three cognitive styles associated with conspiracy thinking, all with some similarities. Each of them has to do with making connections between unrelated people, things, or experiences.

Despite lots of speculation, there is not much support that conspiracy theories draw people because they need to simplify and make sense of a complex world. It is the opposite. Conspiracy thinking seems to be an attempt to connect the dots on lots of information—including speculative or false information—to see hidden patterns. It is the rush of leaning into the complexity that gives these conspiracy theories their power.

Here are three related patterns of cognitive bias that make someone more likely to be conspiracy-minded.

Teleological Thinking

You've heard many people say, "Everything happens for a reason." Perhaps you've said it yourself. This cognitive pattern called *teleological thinking* is a belief that "everything *exists* for a reason." People who have more teleological thinking understand things in terms of the purpose or function they serve, not what they are.[72] The sun rises so that it can give us light, bees exist

69. Warzel, "QAnon Creates Alternate Reality," lines 11–16.
70. Thompson, "QAnon Is Like a Game," lines 59–60.
71. Warzel, "QAnon Creates Alternate Reality," lines 31–34.
72. Wagner-Egger et al., "Creationism and Conspiracism."

to ensure pollination, flowers populate the earth to bring us beauty, and so on. The sun and bees and flowers and everything else exists because of a given, designated purpose.

Those with a teleological thinking bias are more prone to believing in conspiracy theories. One study found that creationists were more likely than most people to believe conspiracy theories.[73] This doesn't mean all creationists are conspiracy theorists. There is a consistent underlying cognitive process in both belief systems, however. Those raised to believe that God created the heavens and the earth are conditioned to believe all things exist and happen for a reason. There's an intelligent mind that built the machine. Belief in conspiracy theories requires a belief that things are not the product of chance. They are planned, intended, and desired by an intelligent mind—in the case of QAnon, a cabal of intelligent minds who have strategized and conspired together. Christians are primed to see the world in a way that leaves them vulnerable to conspiracy thinking.

Illusory Pattern Perception

Conspiracy theorists are also high in "illusory pattern perception." This cognitive bias happens when someone perceives a pattern where none exists. They "connect the dots" and see connections between people or events, even when there are none.[74]

In one study, people who saw a pattern in random coin flips were more likely to believe in conspiracy theories.[75] In another, people who saw patterns in the random paint splashes of a Jackson Pollock painting were also more likely to believe in conspiracy theories.[76]

Here's an important connection: The same people who were prone to seeing patterns in chaos or randomness were also more likely to believe in supernatural phenomena. It makes sense that the same psychological traits that draw Christians toward a greater openness to spiritual realities—angels, demons, miracles, and so on—also make them vulnerable to conspiracy theories. Both belief systems involve uncovering hidden or unseen phenomena that most people don't know or understand, being open to the transrational, and attributing connections and causes to unseen forces.

73. Wagner-Egger et al., "Creationism and Conspiracism."

74. van Prooijen, "Connecting the Dots."

75. van Prooijen, "Connecting the Dots."

76. van Prooijen, "Connecting the Dots."

Agency Detection

Believers in conspiracy theories say certain terrible events are not the result of coincidence, but the product of willful decisions by a group of evildoers. Like illusory perception, this involves a sense that events happen for a reason, but in this cognitive bias, people detect nefarious motives at work, even when there is no evidence.

The psychological trait that relates to belief in conspiracy theory is what researchers call "agency detection." Here, the word *agency* means intentional action. If someone has agency, it means they act of their own free will. Just as with illusory pattern perception, people make errors in their agency detection. Certain people see agency where none exists.

One study used old footage of a big triangle, a little triangle, and a circle moving randomly around a screen. Researchers asked participants to describe what they were seeing. Those who anthropomorphized the objects—gave them human attributes and motives—would come up with stories, like the little triangle is chasing the big triangle or the circle is visiting the triangle's house. Those who rated the shapes as moving with human intentions were more likely than others to endorse conspiracy theories.[77] These people saw agency where none existed.

One key ingredient of conspiracy theories is that, by definition, a conspiracy exists. Bad actors are doing bad things on purpose. They intend to act in a selfish or malevolent way. The bad outcomes are not the result of coincidence, but the product of willful decisions to do evil.

A fourth thinking error, called the *conjunction fallacy*, is a type of faulty logic. Some research has shown this cognitive bias is associated with conspiracy thinking.[78] I conducted a study with over two hundred subjects that measured both conjunction fallacy and endorsement of conspiracy beliefs. I found no relationship between these two variables. As a result, I omitted the conjunction fallacy from this discussion. However, there remains a strong research support for the connection between conspiracy belief and teleological thinking, illusory pattern perception, and agency detection.

It's not important you remember the names of these thinking errors, so long as you understand these three cognitive biases cause a person to see connection, meaning, or intention in circumstances, even if none is present. This is a search for the signal in the noise. It is a quest for meaning.

People prone to these cognitive biases come to erroneous conclusions about the likelihood and meaning of events. They assume all things exist for

---

77. Hart and Graether, "Something's Going on Here."
78. Brotherton and French, "Susceptibility to the Conjunction Fallacy."

a purpose (to make honey, to bring warmth and light, and so forth), which primes them to believe things happen because of intentional but unseen forces at work. They see connections where there are none and see intention where it is absent. These same people are more open to spiritual and supernatural beliefs.

More than any other explanation, these cognitive biases explain the attraction of conspiracy theories for evangelicals. Most Christians are conditioned for years, often since childhood, to understand hidden patterns and see forces and motives—whether good or bad—at work in all situations. An openness to invisible realities is a prerequisite for a robust faith, but creates a vulnerability to beliefs in grand good vs. evil conspiracies.

WHITE CHRISTIANS ARE PRIMED FOR CONSPIRACY THINKING

A survey by the American Enterprise Institute found more than a quarter (27 percent) of white evangelicals believed the QAnon conspiracy theory was completely or mostly accurate. This was nearly double the rate of white mainline Christians and over four times higher than Black Christians.[79] Daniel Cox, the director of the Institute's Survey Center on American Life, argued that white evangelicals are not disconnected from others, but are surrounded by other like-minded people who reinforce their beliefs. "You're seeing people embrace this sort of conspiratorial thinking, and everyone in their social circle is like, 'Yeah, that sounds right to me,' versus someone saying, 'You know, we should look at this credulously,'" he told Religion News Service.[80]

According to a national survey of over a thousand pastors by LifeWay Research, about half of them (49 percent) have heard members of their congregation repeating conspiracy theories.[81] White pastors heard this more often than pastors of Black churches.[82] Pastors of large congregations heard these theories circulating among their congregants more than those of smaller churches.[83] LifeWay Research's Executive Director Scott McConnell said, "At this time, it appears more of the theories are traveling in politically

79. Cox, "After the Ballots Are Counted."
80. Jenkins, "More Than a Quarter of White Evangelicals," lines 47–51.
81. Earls, "U.S. Pastors Hear Conspiracy Theories," lines 4–7.
82. Earls, "U.S. Pastors Hear Conspiracy Theories," lines 20–22.
83. Earls, "U.S. Pastors Hear Conspiracy Theories," lines 21–22.

conservative circles which corresponds to the higher percentages in the churches led by white Protestant pastors."[84]

In my own research, I asked over two hundred people of different ages and socio-economic backgrounds across the country how likely this statement was: "There is an underground network of highly placed politicians, Hollywood elites, and wealthy business leaders who secretly abuse children." Consistent with other research, white conservative evangelicals were the most likely to say this was very or somewhat likely, with nearly half of them (48 percent) agreeing with this statement.

My research also found white Christians endorsed other current conspiracy theories as more likely at rates higher than white non-Christians and those who were neither white nor Christian. These included beliefs the 2020 election was stolen by voter fraud and the Capitol building was stormed by Antifa and not Trump supporters. White Christians who considered themselves very conservative politically were the most likely to endorse these conspiracy theories as likely or very likely.

The Chapman University Survey of American Fears found belief in the statement "Satan causes the most evil in the world" to be one of the top predictors of belief in conspiracy theories.[85] They found church attendance and religious participation alone were not big factors for believing in conspiracy theories, but belief the devil and his demons were at work doing evil in the world was a big predictor. QAnon is a direct expression of a belief that evil people work covertly to harm the innocent while an army of the righteous is being marshaled to stop those ungodly forces.

The pervasiveness of conspiracy theory belief among these churchgoers shows how eagerly white conservative Christians accept these ideas. Christians have been conditioned to seek truth, but the irony is their self-protective desire to circle the wagons has led them to be more likely to reject objective, scientific, and vetted ways of knowing in favor of speculative information that favors their own biases.

QAnon and similar conspiracy theories also provide a convenient narrative that appeals to groups high in collective narcissism: we are under threat and treated horribly by outsiders, but our enemies will soon be vanquished and we will emerge victorious. In some ways, this is not dissimilar to the meta-narrative of the Christian faith, though it is also antithetical to more central aspect of that story, including the desire for redemption for

84. Earls, "U.S. Pastors Hear Conspiracy Theories," lines 27–29.

85. Bader et al., *Fear Itself*, 33–43.

all. One study found collective narcissism results in greater endorsement of conspiracy theories.[86]

Stoked by conspiracy theories, white evangelicals were also more likely than other groups to support the use of violence to "protect America" if they perceived elected officials were not doing enough. An alarming 41 percent agreed with this sentiment.[87] In its most extreme form, conspiracy thinking opens the door to violence. For those who come to believe that their country—or their families or defenseless babies—are in mortal danger based on horrifying but untrue information, it makes sense they might stop at nothing, including violence, to prevent their enemies from destroying vulnerable people. In this way, QAnon and similar conspiracies are not just amusing curiosities, but grave threats to the integrity of democracy, the church, families, and individual lives.

Christians have been conditioned from the time they were young to trust an invisible hand is at work, to believe spiritual unseen things are real and active. Some of the spiritual beliefs they hold may be true, but these thinking biases open them to conspiracy thinking.

Psychologist Steve Taylor, author of *Spiritual Science*, says the desire for connection and interconnection among religious and spiritually minded people makes them susceptible to conspiracy-mindedness. People are drawn to spirituality, he says, because they desire connection—connection with God, with our deeper selves, and with others. Conspiracy theories are also about connection.[88] *Everything is connected. There are no coincidences. There are secret networks of powerful people, unseen by most people, pulling the strings. Those with eyes to see can find the hidden connections if they look deeply enough.* Taylor says, "Spiritually-minded people become vulnerable to conspiracy theories when their impulse for connection is misdirected into their intellectual outlook."[89]

This doesn't mean what Christians believe must be untrue. It means their thinking is more susceptible to seeing invisible connections and assuming powerful but unseen forces at work. One study of over eight hundred people found that people who believed God created the Earth less than ten thousand years ago were also much more likely to believe officials faked the moon landing or that the 9/11 attacks were an inside job.[90] A massive narrative like QAnon fits well into the worldview of Christians primed to

86. Cichocka et al., "'They Will Not Control Us.'"
87. Cox, "After the Ballots Are Counted."
88. Taylor, "Spiritual Conspiracists," lines 112–46.
89. Taylor, "Spiritual Conspiracists," lines 127–28.
90. Wagner-Egger et al., "Creationism and Conspiracism."

look for hidden realities, especially those involving covert good vs. evil warfare.

QAnon has had deep and far-reaching implications for the church. The QAnon conspiracy was incubating and spreading at the same time a deadly global pandemic gripped the world. The parallels could not be more striking. QAnon became a social virus, infecting many who came into contact with it, who then passed it on to others. The effects, for our society and the church, have been ruinous. The COVID virus killed hundreds of thousands, but even among the infected people it didn't kill, it often wrecked their lungs, caused long-term neurological problems, produced unshakable lethargy and fatigue, created months of body aches, and damaged their hearts. QAnon has had similarly pernicious effects on the church. Not only did it contribute to misguided and even dangerous behavior among Christians, including the January 6 assault on the Capitol, it led to an even more hostile and insular tone within the church.

Just as younger and healthier people could still get COVID and suffer the ill effects of it, there are plenty of people who don't match many of the usual traits who still became infected by the QAnon virus. They may find themselves around many passionate QAnon adherents or in a time of financial and political uncertainty, making them more susceptible.

You are more likely to catch coronavirus at a concert or being in a nursing home or prison. In the same way, you are also more likely to fall prey to QAnon or similar conspiracy theories under certain conditions. Unfortunately, the white conservative church has become a place where it is easier to become more infected by these elaborate untruths.

When we pair these stressful realities with many Christians' longstanding view of end times, we see a period in history that provides fertile ground for conspiracy belief within the church.

End Times and Conspiracy Theories

In Grafton, Wisconsin, a pharmacist named Steve Brandenburg removed a box of vials of the newly received COVID vaccine from the freezer, intentionally attempting to destroy them. According to the police, he was "an admitted conspiracy theorist" who believed the vaccines would cause people to "change their DNA."[91] His wife reported he believed "the government is planning cyberattacks and plans to shut down the power grid." She told the

---

91. Dewan and Nolan, "Pharmacist Accused," lines 1–9.

court she was so alarmed for her own safety and the safety of her children that she "left town for a period of time."[92]

Investigators discovered Brandenburg said the vaccines would implant microchips into people, believed the Earth was flat, and the sky was a "shield put up by the government to prevent individuals from seeing God." Law enforcement officials report Brandenburg told a co-worker that "Judgment day is coming."

This notion of a rapidly approaching judgment day—Armageddon, doomsday, end of times—is a frequent motif among those who subscribe to conspiracy theories. Evangelicals believe all the world is headed toward Armageddon and final judgment. Conspiracy theories like QAnon fit neatly into that narrative.

My mother-in-law lives in a rural mountain community in the South. One morning after running errands during the height of the pandemic, she wrote me an email:

> I went to Walmart at 6:00 this morning. Had an unsettling mo-
> ment with a clerk. She very pleasantly asked how I was doing.
> And I told her, "Fine, it is just a scary time for everyone." She
> launched into a tirade—"That's just what the politicians want—
> for you to be afraid and make us wear these masks (hers was
> down below her nose) and take away our freedoms. The Rapture
> is coming! We don't have to be afraid of anything! It is all made
> up by the politicians. The Rapture is coming!"

The belief we are living in the end times when the Rapture is close at hand connects to conspiracy belief among Christians, particularly regarding QAnon. Champions of good will do battle against massive forces of evil. Hidden and undetected by most, the conflict will break into the open soon. Good will win, evil will be vanquished, and innocents saved. The narratives of end times theology and the QAnon conspiracy are essentially the same.

The Reddit user nicknamed "diceblue" took part in an AMA ("Ask Me Anything") on the platform where others could pepper him with questions about his past adherence to QAnon. He acknowledged he had been deeply into the conspiracy before realizing it was all a ruse that had duped him and many others.[93]

"It was massively humbling to realize I'd been a sucker," he said.[94]

He explained how Christian teaching set him up to fall for the expansive conspiracy theory: "I think a huge part of the problem was growing up

92. Dewan and Nolan, "Pharmacist Accused," lines 32–8.

93. Reneau, "Former QAnon believer," lines 17–22.

94. Reneau, "Former QAnon believer," lines 114–15.

fundamentalist Christian. Theories about evil evolution, science denial and The End of The World, rapture, return of Christ stuff is all pretty crazy, too. There's a strong link between the two."[95]

Tyler Huckabee, *Relevant* magazine's executive editor, told me he agrees Christians are especially vulnerable to conspiracy theories because of their theology of the end times. "Where Christians—particularly evangelicals—are vulnerable to conspiracies, in my view, is an apocalyptic view of the world," he explained. "With this lens, pretty much any significant cultural figure is ripe to be drafted into a war for the fate of the world, and any perceived shift in the accepted status quo can be interpreted as part of a prophesied moral decline."

For many white Christians, conspiracy theories fit their narrative of a world falling apart only to be saved by a powerful figure in the last days. Huckabee told me what he sees as the deeper issue with the white Christian embrace of conspiracy theories:

> Americans are engaged in a civil epistemological war to determine what *reality* is. White evangelicals in America have always taken it upon themselves to be the gatekeepers on this front, but they sense their hold slipping. The appeal of QAnon is that it assures believers that their vision of reality has always been correct—Democrats are evil, Republicans are good guys, American Christians are superheroes—and are about to be vindicated on the world stage. In that respect, the whole QAnon [thing] is not a political conflict between the Right and the Left. It's a fight between the truth and lies.

Too many Christians have found themselves on the side of the lies.

95. Reneau, "Former QAnon believer," lines 57–65.

CHAPTER 10

A Life That Leaves Its Mess

The Low Resilience of White Evangelicals

"So what should be said of a life that leaves its mess? For once your life was sold, it could never be possessed."

—SUFJAN STEVENS, *THE ASCENSION*

MY FATHER-IN-LAW, LEE, WAS, as we say, "a different breed of cat." Raised in the rural South, he grew up poor and enlisted in the military when he was seventeen years old. During the height of the Korean War, he was in the belly of a tank when it ran over a land mine, earning him his first Purple Heart. In the Vietnam War, a mortar round hit him, lacerating his leg so badly he nearly bled out and spent over two months in a military hospital. He didn't bother to pick up that second Purple Heart because he already had one. He thought, *What's the point?* He also earned two Bronze Stars for heroic achievement during battle.

After more than two decades in the Army, Major Lee retired and moved his family to the mountains of North Carolina, where he started a Christmas tree farm. He had ten acres of rolling hills, all teeming with Fraser firs and spruce. People would drive from hours away to get one of Lee's Trees, as he called his business. They'd pick out their best tree and signal for a worker to come up in the four-wheeler, chainsaw it down, run it through the bailer, and tie it to the roof of the car—all for cheaper than what a week-old tree would cost in a city lot. Families would take their holiday pictures and sip cider and warm themselves by the fireplace. It was a special experience, well worth the drive.

Lee had the misfortune of having me as a son-in-law. I was worthless with helping out on the farm, so when customers came up, I was always upstairs in the big house playing video games, while Lee and his hired help were outside driving four-wheelers, working chain saws, cranking up tree bailers, tying trees to car roofs, and the rest. I'd go out on the deck and watch the operation in action, but I was useless to my father-in-law.

One year, I was in the house playing a game when I heard the chain saw whirring, then come to an abrupt stop. A few moments later, the screen door swung open and there stood Lee with his right pants leg ripped from thigh to knee and his leg soaked in blood. My eyes widened.

"What happened?" I asked, already knowing the answer.

"I just cut myself with the dang chain saw," came his reply as he marched down the hall toward his bedroom.

Ten minutes later, he emerged wearing a fresh pair of pants, shot out the door, and fired up the chain saw once again.

If I cut my leg open with a chain saw, I'd never get over it. I'd constantly think about it, bring it up in every conversation, demonstrate how it happened. I'd do this for years on end. For Lee, I doubt he thought about it much again. When you are born during the Great Depression, grow up poor, get blown up in a tank in one war, and hit by shrapnel in another, cutting your leg open with a chain saw doesn't seem like such a big deal.

That's the nature of resilience. You experience hardship and struggle in life, push through them, and come out stronger and an even better version of yourself. In the most intense versions, it is what psychologists Richard Tedeschi and Lawrence Calhoun call "post-traumatic growth."[1]

You build resilience the same way you build muscle. Recently, my brother told me he had just bench-pressed 235 pounds earlier that evening, which is an impressive amount, especially at our age. He didn't get there overnight. Many weeks of hard work and feeling the burn went into that accomplishment. Emotionally, it's the same process. If I face no hardship— never lift that emotional weight—I'll crumple at the first sign of trouble; I'll collapse under the stress.

We are witness to decreasing resilience in the US over many decades. As a nation, we have been tough-minded in the face of adversity, but there is evidence we have lost that edge. During the COVID pandemic, for example, researchers with the Commonwealth Fund conducted an international

---

1. Tedeschi and Calhoun, *Trauma and Transformation*.

study and found stress, anxiety, and depression hit Americans the hardest of any country. A full third of Americans surveyed (33 percent) were struggling with mental health problems during the pandemic.[2] As a practitioner on the front lines of this, I can attest that I saw about a 25 percent increase in demand for services during the first COVID year. As one point of comparison, only 10 percent of Norway's population reported significant emotional problems during the same timeframe.[3] Another way to say this is Americans have become less resilient than other countries. When the big stressors came—a pandemic, financial collapse, racial protests, political division—they blew us up. We were ill-equipped to contend with them.

Granted, 2020 was a bit of a hellscape, but that's why resilience is important. Resilience is for times of hardship, not the easy times. We require emotional muscle to bear up under challenging circumstances. Otherwise, we fold like we did the year life hit us hard. You've heard that adversity reveals character. Well, adversity can also reveal a *lack* of character and a *lack* of strength, which is what happened.

The same has happened to white evangelicals in the US over the past few decades. Since our founding, white Christians have been in charge, able to create easy, self-satisfied lives for themselves. Now that this is being challenged, they feel aggrieved and wounded, persecuted and mistreated. They protest and become rageful. The lives of most white Christians have been easier than the lives of most other groups in our country. Now that they must share power or face challenge, they cry foul. Worse than that, they are falling apart.

Christianity was designed to be an underdog faith. It championed the poor and oppressed and marginalized, but it also eschewed power and status and control. Over time, though, white Christians have amassed power and still have most of the control in our culture. Within this paradigm, Christians have been running the show. However, now as the country is changing and their presumed rightful place is being challenged, fear and anger fuel them. They claim victimhood, spouting off grievances, appearing desperate for a return to a time when they ran the show.

"The only people it's okay to discriminate against these days are white Christians," one friend told me, a variation of a line I've heard or read dozens of times in recent years. This sense that white Christians are now the biggest targets of discrimination is rampant among white evangelicals. It is a prevailing source of both fear and anger among them, powerful enough to drive them to authoritarianism and antidemocratic gambits.

---

2. Thomas, "Coronavirus stresses Americans more than others, study finds."
3. Thomas, "Coronavirus stresses Americans more than others, study finds."

It's laughable that white Christians allege worse discrimination than people of color, gays, Muslims, and many other groups. The fact that white conservative Christians are so undone by this perception, though, speaks to their low resilience. Having never faced significant hardships and challenges makes them vulnerable to being hit hard when life becomes more difficult and more complicated. They react with fight-or-flight reactions: withdraw into the evangelical fortress only to emerge to jab at perceived enemies. Their low resilience leaves them defenseless in the changing culture where their grip on power is slipping.

Years ago, a client of mine, a junior in college, a Christian kid from a Christian family, began seeing me following a nasty breakup. He and his girl-friend had been together for over two years, but as she neared her graduation, she reevaluated her relationship and ended it. This guy, Brad, was so broken by this that he began to contemplate suicide. I asked him to reflect on why the breakup had hit him so hard it caused him to consider ending his own life.

"I've never had anything bad happen to me," he said.

Having lived twenty-one years and experiencing nothing bad did not set Brad up to be resilient. Quite the opposite. It set him up to crumble in the face of stress and heartache. A life of no struggle leads to a lack of resilience. There are large swaths of white evangelicals whose easy, self-satisfied lives make them less resilient than in the past. Not only have their comfortable lives undermined them, but the evangelical subculture has also conditioned them to adopt certain mindsets that make them less resilient.

RESILIENT MINDSETS

Robert Brooks, a psychologist and author on the faculty of Harvard Medical School, has built his career studying resilience. Most of his eighteen books revolve around the theme of how to help people become sturdier in the face of challenges. He's studied how the most resilient people think and he's found they have different mindsets than others.

"Resilient mindsets help people become more hopeful and optimistic," he told me. "They tend to have better relationships and they cope better with difficult circumstances."

He described the aspects of a resilient mindset, including seeing mistakes as moments of growth rather than moments of shame, taking responsibility for one's own actions, and being open to help and support. Conservative Christians feel shame when they screw up, they blame others or outside forces for their own problems (persecution, temptation, spiritual warfare), and they often associate seeking support with weakness. Their mindsets do not set them up for being more resilient. Instead, they are far less resilient than others.

Stanford psychologist Carol Dweck has changed the world with her research on mindsets, as well. Her work has pioneered a concept so simple yet so powerful it has revolutionized education, sports, business, and other fields.[4] Three schools asked me to speak in one month recently. Two schools had posters with Dweck's concepts on them in the hallways. Another school's principal included her ideas in my introduction. I've heard her premise discussed on television and on podcasts. I've seen YouTube videos and read magazine articles that discuss her work. Her impact has been widespread and profound.

Her research has uncovered two types of mindsets, fixed and growth. People with a *fixed mindset* believe they have a fixed amount of ability or skill. They believe they have a certain level of academic ability or athletic prowess or any other talent. Those with a *growth mindset* believe their abilities can improve through consistent effort and hard work.[5]

Multiple studies have shown how growth mindsets make students more likely to do better in challenging courses, even when controlling for aptitude and intelligence. A fixed mindset, on the other hand, makes it harder for students to recover from early lower grades. As Dweck noted, "Students who have a fixed mindset but who are well prepared and do not encounter difficulty can do just fine. However, when they encounter challenges or obstacles, they may then be at a disadvantage."[6]

This isn't just true in school. It's also true in many other areas like work performance, relationships, and sports. A few years back, I saw a heavily scouted high school basketball player named Pete after his game fell apart his junior year. He hit a growth spurt in seventh grade that caused him to tower over his classmates. He was not only the tallest kid in his middle school, he was also the most talented athlete. Coaches told him even then he could play Division 1 college basketball, perhaps even have a shot at the pros.

For the rest of middle school and the first two years of high school, he was the dominant player not only on his team, but in the entire conference. The city's largest newspaper named him Player of the Year two years in a row. His sophomore year, he led his team to a state championship.

Then the bottom fell out. His senior year, his shots were not falling. Smaller players denied his shots. His confidence plummeted. His team didn't even make it to the postseason.

4. Dweck, *Mindset*.

5. Dweck, *Mindset*.

6. Dweck, "Mindsets and Math/Science Achievement."

What happened?

Simply said, he had a fixed mindset. He was told he was the best, special, destined for greatness, and for many years, he was. But as the other players got older and taller, they were also working much harder than he was, putting in more time in both the gym and on the practice court. As a result, they surpassed him. Some had grown just as tall but had put the effort into strengthening their bodies and getting good at their game. On the court, they were now his equals. He was no longer the dominant force in the conference.

When that happened, he fell apart. This happens with a fixed mindset. It works in either direction. If someone believes they are just bad at something—say math or public speaking or free throws—and they have a fixed mindset, they will just draw the assumption life has dealt them a bad hand and they can't improve much, if at all. But, if they are like Pete and they believe they are good or superior at something and they also have a fixed mindset, they collapse when that sense of being exceptional gets challenged.

"I thought I was the best," he said, "and then, all of a sudden, it was like I was just a regular basketball player."

Pete had seen himself as possessing natural skill, which was true, but his fixed mindset led him to believe this was sufficient. Yes, he attended practices and worked out like his teammates, but, in his mind, he was good at basketball because of the talent he possessed, not because of his hard work and determination. The other players who possessed less natural abilities lapped him because they just worked harder.

When you study the lives of great players in any sport—Michael Jordan, LeBron James, Tiger Woods, Serena Williams, Cristiano Renaldo, Michael Phelps, Tom Brady—you see a combination of rare talent coupled with an unsurpassed work ethic. It is neither one nor the other, but both. The same is true in other realms of life: the outstanding scientists, extraordinary business people, brilliant military leaders, prodigious musicians, incredible entrepreneurs, successful actors. Grammy award winner Ed Sheeran said his plan was "basically hard work and persistence until it works out, so just not to have a backup plan. The only option is to succeed.[7]

Even those not possessed of tremendous talent benefit from a growth mindset. In research with students of all ages, those with a growth mindset outperform their peers who have fixed mindsets, even when matched for intelligence.

Those with a growth mindset rebound after setbacks. They know the key is perseverance and hard work. They push harder when faced with

7. Scott, "Ed Sheeran."

adversity. Setbacks devastate those with a fixed mindset. They shut down, like Pete, and lack the grit to push into their hardships or challenges. They have pinned their hopes on their natural superior skills and failed to cultivate the willingness to work hard and persevere.

THE FIXED MINDSET OF WHITE CHRISTIANS

Most everyone who grows up in the white Christian church knows how salvation works. You pray the "sinner's prayer"—*I'm a sinner and I accept God's gift of salvation offered by Jesus' sacrifice on the cross*—and that's it. You are now in the club, blessed with eternal salvation, spared eternal torment, heirs to the riches of the God of the universe. It doesn't matter whether you prayed this when you were five and scarcely knew what the words meant, or when you were on your deathbed having led a life of hostility toward God. Either way, you're good! Better yet, it doesn't matter what you do or don't do in your life, you can never have your membership revoked. You're set for all eternity.

Salvation by grace alone is an amazing and beautiful concept, one that distinguishes Christianity from all other religions. It's a lovely and attractive aspect of the Christian faith, but there is a striking downside to this limited conception of faith, at least as embodied in American Christianity.

It is possible that simple intellectual assent—you believe or agree with certain statements—is sufficient for salvation (though even that is arguable), but it does not build character or strength. Those things only come from hard work and perseverance. "Saved by grace" does not make a person more entitled, more deserving, more correct, or more special. None of that is true. Not only is this fertile ground for narcissism, it also promotes a fixed mindset. Greatness and specialness are already assumed. There is no need to work to build character, or to develop oneself. Consequently, when hard times come, there is a great chance of collapse.

We build growth mindsets through a willingness to work hard to improve. The Americanized version of Christianity strives to make everything easy and painless: Pray this simple prayer. Attend this church that caters to your every need. Hear this sermon on three simple steps to improving your quality of life. None of it favors a growth mindset.

The theology of most white evangelicals lends itself to a fixed mindset: I am already special, set apart, blessed, chosen—and I didn't have to lift a finger to get here.

CONCLUSIONS

Unfortunately, there is little doubt the white evangelical church will continue to see itself as overly special with no need to change or reform. They will value size over depth, power over humility, and self-centeredness over selflessness for the foreseeable future. They will still fight the culture wars, demonize their enemies, and battle for dominance. They will do this, as they have in recent years, to their detriment.

This book represents my assessment of how white evangelicals think; it's the synthesis of hundreds of articles and dozens of books. My task was to offer analysis and not prescriptions, but one thing is clear: the evangelical church needs a new reformation. Paradoxically, it's when the church lays down power and has more accountability that we see true transformation and change.

One significant study found that neither pluralism nor persecution ultimately harmed the church. Indeed, in other countries the Christian faith has flourished under these conditions. In pluralistic cultures, hardship compelled Christians to step up and take their beliefs more seriously. When faced with persecution, Christians increased their reliance on faith and healthy fellowship. In both situations, faith grew and deepened.

Therefore, if Christian faith becomes more vibrant in pluralistic and persecutory cultures, where does it decline in growth and vitality? In cultures where it is *privileged*. For example, in societies where the state supports Christianity, where religion is politicized, and where Christians are too comfortable, the Christian faith suffers. The researchers write that privileged cultures "encourage apathy" and the result is "a less dynamic faith and the overall decline of Christian populations."[8]

White evangelicals have proven to be all too human in their striving for power and influence, stemming from their entitlement and desire for control. They are self-centered and fearful, even though they were formed to be an other-centered community that serves the oppressed and needy, a people who cast out fear in favor of love. They have corrupted something that should be irresistible and engaging, and they have made it ugly and unappealing. However, if they humble themselves, stop clinging to power, and cease their self-serving culture wars, they may find their lives more challenging, but their faith richer, deeper, and far more beautiful.

8. Saiya and Manchanda, "Paradoxes of Pluralism, Privilege, and Persecution."

Appendix 1

Evidence of Systemic Racism

SYSTEMIC RACISM MEANS RACISM is baked into the very fabric of our society and our institutions. But is that even true? A fair look at the evidence convinced me systemic racism exists, but since it is vigorously disputed among many white Christians, I am sharing some evidence. These facts don't mean some evil mastermind or cabal is socially engineering inequality, but that the indisputable disparities and injustices are racist nonetheless. Here's what we know about systemic racism based on hard data, not speculation or opinion, not spin or propaganda.

WEALTH AND EMPLOYMENT

The median white family has a net worth ten times that of the median Black family.[1] According to one study, for every $100 white families make in income, Black families make only $57.[2] Put another way, if the average white family makes $66,000 per year, the average Black family makes $38,000.

Since the civil rights era of the 1960s, Black unemployment has been consistently double that of white unemployment.[3] One study found that when Black and white applicants had identical resumés, job applicants with "white-sounding names" got called back for interviews 50 percent more often than applicants with "Black-sounding names."[4]

---

1. Williams, "Closing the Racial Wealth Gap."
2. Badger, "Whites Have Huge Wealth Edge Over Blacks."
3. DeSilver, "Black Unemployment Rate is Consistently Twice That of Whites."
4. Bertrand and Mullainathan, "Are Emily and Greg More Employable?"

We tell our kids to go to college to better their chances of a higher-paying job, but the median wealth for black households where a parent has a college degree equaled about 70 percent of the median wealth for white households *without* a college degree.[5]

A shocking study by the *New York Times* found that even among children who were raised in wealthy families, whether Black or white, a person's race predicts who will remain rich as adults. Nearly two-thirds (63 percent) of white boys raised in rich families will be rich or upper-middle class as adults, but slightly over a third (36 percent) of Black boys will remain in those upper rungs of income.[6] On the other side of the scale, only 10 percent of rich white boys will be poor as adults, but more than double that number of Black boys will be in the lowest income bracket.

For poor children, the life span pattern reverses. White boys born to poor families have a 26 percent chance of becoming rich or upper-middle class, compared to Black boys born in poor families who have an 8 percent chance. If you track a random group of boys across their life span, nearly half (48 percent) of white boys end up rich or upper-middle class, compared to 15 percent of Black boys. On the other side, 17 percent of those white boys will end up poor, compared to 40 percent of Black boys.[7]

We often hear that education is the great equalizer, but the median wealth for Black families with college degree-earners at the head of the household was $84,000, compared to over $293,000 for white families with the same level of education, according to psychologist Michael Kraus,[8] an associate professor at the Yale School of Management. He told the *APA Monitor* that Black families often start off with less wealth and end up with more debt, compared to white families, when pursuing education. He said that a big barrier to racial income equality comes from the misperception most Americans have about it.[9] Americans consistently overestimate Black wealth. They also underestimate the income gap between Black and white families. In 1963, the income gap was perceived to be 40 percent smaller than it was. By 2016, a survey of over one thousand Americans judged it to be 80 percent smaller on average than it actually was.[10]

5. Hanks et al., "Systemic Inequality."
6. Badger et al., "Extensive Data Shows Punishing Reach of Racism for Black Boys."
7. Badger et al., "Extensive Data Shows Punishing Reach of Racism for Black Boys."
8. Stringer, "5 Questions for Michael Kraus."
9. Stringer, "5 Questions for Michael Kraus."
10. Travers, "Five Charts."

CRIMINAL JUSTICE AND
INSTITUTIONAL PUNISHMENT

Let's imagine you were faced with an impossible choice. A violent, horrific murder has been committed and you are on the jury. The person who will be convicted of it will likely spend the rest of his life in prison. Perhaps due to misinformation and not bad intent, you make one of two errors. You either wrongly convict an innocent person or wrongly free the guilty person. Admittedly, both are horrible choices, but as a juror, you are forced to make a choice: send the innocent to prison or release the guilty back into society. Which do you choose? Would it make a difference if it were a lesser crime, like robbery, where the penalty was not as severe, but still involved incarceration?

Sociologists Samuel Perry and Andrew Whitehead analyzed data from 3,785 respondents who were given a choice between these two bad options: they must either convict an innocent person or free a guilty person. They found the single biggest predictor of favoring convicting the innocent was being a white person who holds a literal view of the Bible.[11] The authors write, "Given that white Americans often have racial minorities in mind when queried about the criminal justice system, this finding furthers our understanding of white Americans' bent toward unjust punitiveness toward minorities."[12]

While Black folks make up 13 percent of the general population, they make up 40 percent of the prison population in the United States, which already has an outrageously high number of people in prison—over two million souls—more Black people behind bars than the entire population of Jacksonville, Florida or Fort Worth, Texas or Columbus, Ohio or Charlotte, North Carolina or many other large US cities.[13] We currently incarcerate more Black people than the total populations of four entire states.

When Black people are convicted of a crime, they are 20 percent more likely to be sentenced to jail for the same offense as white people[14] and have sentences that are approximately 20 percent lengthier.[15]

Even as children, they face harsher consequences. Black children make up 18 percent of the preschool population but represent about 50 percent of all school suspensions. From elementary to high school, Black kids are three

11. Perry and Whitehead, "Racialized Religion and Judicial Injustice."
12. Perry and Whitehead, "Racialized Religion and Judicial Injustice," 25.
13. Sakala, "Breaking Down Mass Incarceration."
14. Pryor et al., "Demographic Differences in Sentencing."
15. Ingraham, "Black Men Sentenced to More Time."

times more likely to be suspended than white students with the same infrac-
tions. Even though they make up 16 percent of the total school age population, Black students comprise 27 percent of the school referrals to police—and
once Black children are in the criminal justice system, they are eighteen times
more likely than white kids to be tried as adults.[16]

After Congress passed the Anti-Drug Abuse Act of 1986, which
jacked up the penalties for crack cocaine possession and required manda-
tory minimum sentences, the number of federal prisoners incarcerated for
drug-related offenses quintupled.[17] Prison populations soared, leading to
overcrowded and unsafe conditions, filled largely with low-level offenders.
A disproportionate number of those prisoners were people of color.[18]

Here's an even more infuriating fact: that law required a *minimum* federal sentence of five years for possession of five hundred grams of cocaine—
a drug used primarily by white people in the US—but required the same
sentence for possessing only five grams of crack cocaine, the much cheaper
version that was more in widespread use in poor Black communities.[19] That's
a one hundred to one ratio, favoring white offenders over Black offenders.
To put this in perspective, five hundred grams is over a pound, whereas five
grams is roughly the equivalent of a Sweet'n Low packet.

When the media hyped the notion of a crack cocaine "epidemic" in the
1980s, the social and legislative response was to increase criminal penalties,
but in more recent years when we have faced a similar opioid epidemic,
which affects more white people, the conversation has been more about increasing treatment options. The message is clear: Black drug users are scary
and dangerous; white drug users are sad and ill. We send more poor Black
people to prison for low-level drug possessions, but we send white people to
rehab and twelve-step meetings.

The government's ability to take your life as punishment for a crime is
also rife with bias. Consider this: those who kill white people are four times
more likely to be sentenced to death than those who kill Black people. The
Government Accountability Office reviewed multiple studies on the subject
and found eighty-two of them concluded the victim's race affected the chances of receiving the death penalty. And while most death penalty convictions
are never carried out, of those that are, a person is seventeen times more

---

16. NPR, "Black Preschoolers Far More Likely to Be Suspended."
17. The Sentencing Project, "Criminal Justice Facts."
18. The Sentencing Project, "Criminal Justice Facts."
19. Kurtzleben, "Data Shows Racial Disparity in Crack Sentencing."

likely to be executed if he kills a white person than if he were to kill a person of color.[20]

POLICE KILLINGS AND BRUTALITY

In the summer of 2020, a widely touted study by researchers at Michigan State University and the University of Maryland concluded, "We did not find any evidence for anti-Black or anti-Hispanic disparity in police use of force across all shootings, and, if anything, found anti-White disparities."[21] Significant statistical and analytical errors caused the authors to retract the article, but not before it became fodder in the culture wars, being quoted in articles and on cable news opinion shows and in books like *Fault Lines*. In their retraction, the authors wrote, "We take full responsibility for not being careful enough with the inferences made in our original article."[22] The publishing journal issued a statement saying, "The authors poorly framed the article (and) the data examined were poorly matched." That's a stuffy academic way of saying it was a bad article. Over eight hundred researchers in fields as diverse as criminal justice, statistics, and political science called it out for its "scientific malpractice."[23]

Research on police killings and brutality is difficult because many states and localities are reluctant to collect systematic data and because the definitions of what constitutes brutality—and whose account is considered—vary. Despite that, there is a consensus that Black people, particularly Black males, are killed by police at a much higher rate than other groups, even when they are unarmed.

A study out of Columbia Law School analyzed 3,933 police killings and found Black individuals are more than twice as likely to be killed by police compared to those of any other ethnic or racial group, saying this was true "even when there are no other obvious circumstances during the encounter that would make the use of deadly force reasonable."[24]

A study from Yale and the University of Pennsylvania analyzed 4,653 fatal police shootings over a five-year period and found Black people were shot and killed at a rate 2.6 times higher than white people. In incidents where the victim was unarmed, Black people were killed at three times

20. Liptak, "Vast Racial Gap in Death Penalty Cases."
21. Johnson et al., "Officer Characteristics and Racial Disparities."
22. Johnson et al., "Retraction for Johnson et al."
23. Knox and Mummolo, "Widely Touted Study."
24. Fagan and Campbell, "Race and Reasonableness in Police Killings."

the rate of white people.[25] Another study from Harvard's School of Public Health found Black Americans were 3.23 times more likely to be killed by police, as compared to white Americans.[26] An analysis in the journal *Proceedings of the National Academy of Sciences* concluded, "For young men of color, police use of force is among the leading causes of death."[27]

Beyond just shootings, a review of the data from New York's infamous "stop and frisk" program concluded, "blacks and Hispanics are more than fifty percent more likely to have an interaction with police which involves any use of force."[28]

HEALTHCARE

Susan Moore, a Black physician, shared a video online as she lay in a hospital bed in Indiana with COVID-19. She said her doctor ignored her complaints, minimized her pain, and declined her requests for medicine, even though she was a physician herself. She claimed her doctor told her, "You're not even short of breath." Despite her complaints, she was discharged from the hospital with no pain medicine. "This is how Black people get killed," she said. Twelve hours later, she was back in the hospital. "I put forth and maintain if I was white, I wouldn't have to go through that," she said. Two weeks later, she was dead. She left behind a son and two elderly parents, both of whom have dementia.[29]

Moore's case is not an isolated event. Mounds of research have documented the disparities between white people and persons of color in availability, access, and quality of medical care. The built-in inequities in healthcare are astounding. Besides receiving worse treatment on average, Black people have more chronic health conditions and a shorter life expectancy of any racial group in the United States.[30] Consider these facts:

- African Americans have the highest mortality rate for all cancers compared to any other racial or ethnic group.[31]

25. Lett et al., "Racial inequity in fatal US police shootings."
26. Schwartz and Jahn, "Mapping Fatal Police Violence."
27. Edwards et al., "Risk of being killed by police."
28. Fryer, *Empirical Analysis*, 1.
29. Eligon, "Black Doctor Dies of COVID-19."
30. Friedman, "This Chart Showing the Gap Between White and Black."
31. American Cancer Society, *Cancer Facts & Figures for African Americans.*

- Infant mortality is twice the rate for Black people compared to the national average.[32]

- Twenty-seven percent of Black men have hypertension, compared to 17 percent of white men.[33]

- A Black woman is 77 percent more likely to die of cervical cancer and 22 percent more likely to die from heart disease than white women.[34]

- Black women die at a rate of 243 percent greater than white women of pregnancy or childbirth-related complications.[35]

- Black women have the highest rate of breast cancer deaths of any racial group.[36]

- Nearly 13 percent of Black children have asthma, which is nearly double the rate for white children (7.7 percent).[37]

- Nearly 11 percent of Black people were uninsured, compared to 6 percent of whites.[38]

- Less than 9 percent of Black adults receive mental health services, compared to nearly 19 percent of white adults.[39]

- Six percent of Black adults have medicine prescriptions for mental health concerns, compared to 15 percent of white adults.[40]

The pandemic of 2020 brought the racial disparities in wellness and healthcare to the forefront. Black people were nearly four times as likely to die if they contracted COVID-19.[41] Black children were infected at five to eight times that of white children.[42] Black people had higher rates of all COVID deaths than all other racial groups.[43]

The National Medical Association, which represents fifty thousand African American physicians, examined six social factors that influence

32. Centers for Disease Control and Prevention, *Infant Mortality.*
33. Centers for Disease Control and Prevention, *Closer Look.*
34. Martin et al., "Nothing Protects Black Women From Dying in Pregnancy."
35. Martin et al., "Nothing Protects Black Women From Dying in Pregnancy."
36. American Cancer Society, *Breast Cancer Facts & Figures.*
37. Carratala and Maxwell, "Health Disparities by Race and Ethnicity."
38. Carratala and Maxwell, "Health Disparities by Race and Ethnicity."
39. Carratala and Maxwell, "Health Disparities by Race and Ethnicity."
40. Carratala and Maxwell, "Health Disparities by Race and Ethnicity."
41. Kaur, "These Variables."
42. Rabin, "Why the Coronavirus More Often Strikes Children of Color."
43. Ford et al., "Race Gaps in COVID-19 Deaths."

physical health and well-being, including healthcare access, food access, physical environment, economic stability, social content, and education, and shared its finding of huge deficits and disparities in African American healthcare with this statement: "These statistics are just an amplification of the 'Slave Health Deficit' which has been an aftermath of years of discrimination, unequal treatment and injustices in healthcare, criminal justice and employment."[44]

HOUSING

Paul and Tenisha Tate, a Black couple in Marin City, California, spent $400,000 renovating their home, adding an entire floor and over one thousand square feet of space. They installed new floors, added a fireplace and new appliances. When they got their home appraised, it was valued at just $100,000 more than its appraisal prior to the extensive renovations.[45]

Convinced race was a factor, they pushed back until their lender approved a second appraisal a month later. On the day of the inspection, they asked a white friend to greet the inspector at their home, saying she was Tenisha. The woman arrived early with pictures of her family, making it look like it was her home. The home was appraised for $500,000 higher than it had been just four weeks earlier.

One of the most insidious forms of systemic racism is in housing inequality. In the US, only 44 percent of Black American adults own their home, compared to 74 percent of white Americans. Black applicants are rejected for mortgage loans three times more often than white applicants, as well.[46]

A study by Housing and Urban Development conducted over eight thousand tests in twenty-eight large cities around the country. In each test, a white person and a person of color of the same gender and approximately the same age each contacted an apartment complex or a realtor about available homes. The punch line was that the Black, Hispanic, or Asian people were shown or told about far fewer housing options than the white people. Sometimes, it was nearly 20 percent fewer homes.[47] In 2021, the gap between Black and white home ownership reached an all-time high, with 72

44. Milloy, "Cure for Racial Disparities."
45. Glover, "Black CA Couple Lowballed"
46. Marksjarvis, "Why Black Homeownership Rates Lag."
47. Cha, "New HUD Report Shows Continued Discrimination."

percent of white people owning homes compared to only 42 percent of Black people.[48]

Because less than half of Black adults own homes, they lack a major source of income and wealth creation. When people buy homes, they build equity that permits them to do things like start businesses, buy other real estate, and send their kids to private schools and more competitive colleges. The homes are also passed down to future generations, which gives younger family members a head start.

In the 1930s, the Home Owner's Loan Corporation drew up maps of communities to decide which ones were good risks for mortgage lending. The neighborhoods that were lowly ranked were outlined in red, showing they were poor investments. These were often predominantly Black neighborhoods. Banks followed suit, marking off undesirable neighborhoods with red lines.[49] This process of "redlining" meant certain communities were locked out of capital that they would need to grow, improve, and thrive.

The practice was outlawed by the Fair Housing Act in 1968, nearly four decades later, but close observers argue that it still continues in different forms. The Department of Housing and Urban Development's analysis of loan applications in 2015 found that banks denied loans disproportionately to applicants in predominantly Black and Hispanic communities in several large cities around the country.[50]

The barriers to home ownership for persons of color may have their roots in the past, but the impact continues to this day. Editorializing for the *Washington Post*, Emily Badger writes, "If your family was denied a mortgage in the 1930s, or the 1950s, or the 1970s, then you may not have the family wealth or down payment help to become a homeowner today. In that way, the consequences of past redlining transcend time, even as new forms of it continue."[51]

We see bias not only with home ownership. We see the same obstacles even in renting an apartment. Consider an investigative report conducted by the Suffolk University Law School in 2020, which found that Black people posing as tenants were shown fewer apartments than whites in the Boston area and were offered less incentives to rent. Realtors cut off contact altogether more quickly when the supposed renters gave "Black-sounding" names like Lakisha or Kareem.[52] By contrast, the white folks posing as rent-

48. Marksjarvis, "Why Black Homeownership Rates Lag."
49. Hillier, "Redlining."
50. Chiwaya and Ross, "American Dream While Black."
51. Badger, "Redlining."
52. Irons, "Researchers Expected 'Outrageously High' Discrimination."

ers were offered the opportunity to view additional units much more often and were offered discounts to coax them to sign the lease. They also found it much easier to get tours of the property than their Black counterparts.

For example, one Black member of the study left three voicemails to a property introducing himself as "Tremayne" and never got a call back, but when a white male left a message as "Brad," he got a follow-up call and was offered a tour. Based on the analysis, Black renters experienced some measurable discrimination 71 percent of the time. Whites who were paying market rate for the apartments could view apartments 80 percent of the time, but for the Black renters, it was less than half the time (48 percent).[53]

EDUCATION

The importance of educational attainment as a means to unlock opportunities and secure livable wages cannot be overstated. Despite years of progress, Black students continue to struggle, compared to white students. Nowhere is this more apparent than in the area of literacy. In 2019, eighth graders around the country were tested for the National Assessment of Educational Progress (NAEP, which is also referred to as the "Nation's Report Card") in reading and other subjects. Reading progress was reported as advanced, proficient, basic, or below basic. In report card terms, they were graded as A, B, C, or D. The average student of any race had a 33 percent chance of being advanced or proficient in reading, compared to the average Black student who had a 15 percent chance of reading above average. About 19 percent of all white students were reading below average, while nearly half (47 percent) of Black students were scraping bottom, far larger than any other group.[54]

	Advanced	Proficient	Basic	Below
All	4	29	39	28
White	5	36	39	19
Black	1	14	39	47
Hispanic	1	20	40	38
Asian	12	42	31	15

53. Irons, "Researchers Expected 'Outrageously High' Discrimination."
54. Strauss, "No Systemic Racism?"

Author and educational consultant Michael Holzman writes, "Half of our Black students at the crucial eighth-grade level are having their life opportunities cut short because they have not been taught to read well." Black educational attainment is far below expectations in all areas.[55]

Business Ownership

When we talk about the American Dream, we think about home ownership and starting your own business, but Black businesses are denied loans at twice the rate of white-owned businesses.[56] In doing so, lenders limit the opportunity for these businesses to get off the ground or grow financially. Businesses require capital and without it, many find it nearly impossible to remain viable.

One study found African American-owned business were less likely to make a profit and the most likely to incur business losses. African Americans and Latinos are much less likely to own businesses, and when they do, those businesses are less likely to be successful. White-owned businesses have annual sales six times that of the average Black-owned business.[57]

The National Poverty Center identified several factors that accounted for these gaps, including greater difficulty gaining financial capital, having less family business background and experience, and lower educational attainment among both owners and workers.[58]

In Charlotte, North Carolina, the disparity in the sales and total receipts between white-owned businesses with employees and Black-owned business was striking. A UNC-Charlotte study found white-owned businesses had thirty-five times the total value of the Black-owned businesses in that county.[59]

Around the country, businesses owned by African Americans are more vulnerable than white-owned companies.[60] Given the challenges arrayed against them, they find it more difficult to weather economic hardships and fail more frequently. When the pandemic hit in 2020, the first round of the Paycheck Protection Program, designed to keep vulnerable businesses afloat, was given out across the country. During the first round of funding, loans for residents living in the 20 percent of zip codes with the

55. Strauss, "No Systemic Racism?"
56. Marks, "Black-owned Firms"
57. Fairlie and Robb, "Race and Entrepreneurial Success."
58. Fairlie and Robb, "Race and Entrepreneurial Success."
59. University of North Carolina Charlotte, "Racial Wealth Gap."
60. Fairlie and Robb, "Race and Entrepreneurial Success."

highest proportion of white residents were approved at nearly twice the rate of those for residents living in the 20 percent of zip codes with the highest proportion of Black residents. Black-owned businesses failed at nearly twice the rates of other businesses during the COVID crisis.[61]

VOTING

Voting is vitally important for a fair and just democratic society. During the pandemic, mail-in ballots became a political hot potato. Even before then, though, there was strong evidence that Black and Hispanic voters were more likely to have their mail-in ballots rejected than white voters. Political scientist Daniel Smith of the University of Florida examined mail-in voting during the 2018 general election. He found voters of color had their mailed ballots rejected more than twice as often as white voters.[62]

A study out of the Brennan Center for Justice at New York University Law School analyzing a sixty thousand-person post-2018 election survey found Black and Latino voters waited 45 percent longer to vote (on average) compared to white voters.[63] They also found counties that became more ethnically diverse had fewer electoral resources (voting stations, poll workers, etc.) than counties that grew whiter. For instance, where the population became whiter, there were 390 voters per polling location, compared to counties where the population became less white and there were 550 voters per polling place, with fewer poll workers, as well.

Another clever study looked at anonymous smartphone location data of over ten million voters in 93,000 polling locations. The researchers found voters in predominantly black neighborhoods waited an average of 29 percent longer to vote than those in white neighborhoods. The 2014 Presidential Commission on Election Administration set the standard as, "No citizen should have to wait more than 30 minutes to vote," yet this study found voters in Black neighborhoods were 74 percent more likely than voters in white neighborhoods to exceed that wait time.[64]

A study cosponsored by Harvard, the Robert Wood Johnson Foundation, and NPR found only 4 percent of white voters experienced racial discrimination when trying to vote or take part in the political process, compared to 19 percent of Black voters and 15 percent of Latino voters.[65]

61. Rosenberg and Myers, "Minority-owned Companies Waited Months."
62. Timm, "White person and a Black person vote by mail in the same state."
63. Klain et al., "Waiting to Vote."
64. Garisto, "Smartphone Data."
65. NPR et al., "Discrimination in America."

About 9.5 million Americans are denied voting rights in federal elections because of either felony convictions or their residency in Washington, DC or a US territory, like Guam or Puerto Rico. In both instances, these individuals are disproportionately persons of color.[66] To put this in perspective, this represents more people than twelve predominantly white states combined, with forty-one electoral college votes, twenty-four senators, and seventeen representatives.

In addition, there has been a flood of legislation across the country to gerrymander districts and add voter ID laws, both of which historically have disenfranchised voters of color. For example, Georgia's Exact Match system required the spelling of one's name on an ID to match the spelling they registered with.[67] If I registered as Dave Verhaagen, but my ID says David Verhaagen, I would be disqualified. It seems like a minor issue until you consider it kept 51,000 people from voting in Georgia in 2018, of whom 80 percent were African American.[68] After Georgia still swung for Donald Trump and elected two Democratic US Senators, one of whom was an African American preacher, the state legislature enacted new guidelines that seemed designed to create even greater barriers to Black voters, with what one appeals court said about similar efforts in North Carolina, "almost surgical precision."[69]

Whether it is making it harder for Black families to own homes or singling out Black children for harsher discipline in schools or sentencing Black people to lengthier sentences or denying more Black applicants jobs, all this is what we mean by systemic racism. It is baked into the core of the most fundamental institutions like schools and the court system and banks and corporations. It affects education and housing and healthcare and justice and employment. That's the essence of systemic racism. It does not mean individuals who are part of these institutions or processes harbor any overtly racist attitudes. It means the vital systems that support better quality of life for all people are unquestionably biased against people of color.

The effects of both individual racist acts and enduring, systemic racism are profound. People of color are psychologically harmed much more by overt and covert racism than most white folks can understand.

66. Balko, "There's overwhelming evidence."

67. Schaffer, "Georgia's Exact Match Voter-ID Law Tossed by Federal Judge."

68. Schaffer, "Georgia's Exact Match Voter-ID Law Tossed by Federal Judge."

69. Solomon et al., "Systematic Inequality and American Democracy."

Appendix 2

Glossary of Terms

Accommodator—a person who leans toward accepting the principles of Christian nationalism, but not in a full embrace like an Ambassador; see also, Christian Nationalism.

Agency Detection—a cognitive bias where an individual perceives intentional action where none exists; see also, Cognitive Bias.

Alexithymia—the inability to recognize or use words to describe one's own emotions.

Ambassador—a person who fully and passionately embraces the principles of Christian nationalism; see also, Christian Nationalism.

Amygdala Hijack—a sudden and disproportionate response to a threat; the amygdala is a tiny almond-shaped structure in the temporal lobe of the brain responsible for processing emotions like fear and anger.

Attachment—in human terms, this refers to an emotional bond or connection with another person; people can have different styles of attachment.

Authoritarianism—enforcing strict obedience to authority at the expense of personal expression and freedom.

Christian Nationalism—a belief that the United States is a special country ordained by God that holds a unique role in the history of the world and should be governed with rules and laws derived from biblical principles.

Cognitive Bias—a type of thinking error where someone's partiality influences how something is perceived.

Collective Narcissism—a belief that one's group is special and should be regarded as such by others, followed by a hostility toward those on the outside who criticize or challenge the group.

Conservative—a person who holds traditional values and resists progressive changes in society; see also, Fiscal Conservative, Social Conservative.

Conspiracy Theory—a belief in a series of interconnected evil acts done on purpose by multiple individuals who have yet to be verifiably exposed to the public.

Conversion Therapy—a discredited and unethical practice of attempting to change someone's sexual orientation from gay to straight, usually involving aversive strategies that pair homosexual attraction with pain or disgust; see also, Reparative Therapy.

Critical Race Theory—a controversial intellectual framework that argues the concept of race is socially constructed and used to oppress groups of people; it views racism as not exclusively an individual attitude of prejudice but as woven into organizations, systems, laws, and policies.

Democrat—a person affiliated with the Democratic Party in the US, usually more left-leaning or liberal politically; see also, Liberal.

Disgust—an emotional reaction related to revulsion or strong disapproval of something unpleasant or offensive.

Dones—a term coined by sociologists Josh Packard and Ashleigh Hope for people who have left the institutional church but have still held on to their faith.

Dunning-Kruger Effect—a type of cognitive bias where people who are incompetent see themselves as skilled or highly competent; see also, Cognitive Bias.

Evangelical—historically, a tradition within the Protestant church that emphasized the authority of the Bible, salvation through a "born again" experience of personal repentance and relationship with Jesus, the centrality of Jesus' death on the cross as a sacrifice to pay the penalty for personal sin, the exclusivity of faith in Jesus as the only path to salvation, and the command to spread the gospel ("good news") message to nonbelievers. In recent decades, it has transformed mostly into a conservative political faction.

Fiscal Conservative—a type of conservative who advocates for lower taxes, reduced government spending, free trade, deregulation, and low government debt.

Fixed Mindset—a belief that talents and abilities are predetermined and preset. Failure results from a lack of certain innate skills. See also, Growth Mindset.

Fundamentalism—a rigid and strict adherence to certain religious beliefs. In Christianity, it nearly always involves a literal interpretation of the Bible and a firm code of conduct. There is significant overlap between fundamentalists and evangelicals, with fundamentalists tending toward a more dogmatic view of the faith. See also, Evangelical.

Generalized Anxiety Disorder (GAD)—an anxiety disorder that involves persistent and excessive worry that is severe enough to interfere with daily functioning.

Growth Mindset—a belief that one can develop skills and abilities through effort, practice, and hard work. It stands in contrast to a fixed mindset. See also, Fixed Mindset.

Guilt—an unpleasant emotion that results from doing something wrong or something that violates one's moral code. In contrast to shame, guilt is focused on behavior and not one's sense of self or identity. See also, Shame.

Illusory Pattern Perception—a misperception that random patterns or events are meaningful or intentional.

Implicit Association Test (IAT)—a computerized or online test that measures split-second responses to certain words and determines what unconscious assumptions a person has about a particular topic or group of people.

Just-World Hypothesis—a belief that the world is fair, that people get what they deserve, that hardworking and good people are rewarded and lazy or bad people are punished. It usually implies the existence of cosmic justice and order.

Liberal—a person who values individual rights, civil liberties, social justice, and societal changes that favor the disadvantaged and underrepresented. See also, Progressive.

Mainline Christian—at present, Christians who tend to be more liberal in their theology, more open to different expressions of faith, and more concerned with social justice issues than evangelicals. Mainline denominations include Methodists, Presbyterians (PCUSA), Lutheran, and Episcopalians. See also, Evangelical.

Meta-Analysis—a form of statistical analysis that combines the results of several different studies that all address the same question.

Narcissism—a personality trait that involves excessive self-centeredness, a sense of entitlement, low empathy, and arrogance.

Nones—a term referring to Americans who do not claim or affiliate with any religious tradition.

Progressive—a person who advocates for social reform through government policy and action. In Christianity, it involves a believer who is willing to challenge the status quo and champion social justice issues. See also, Liberal.

Prospect Theory—a theory that says people give more weight to losses than gains. They focus more on what they have lost than what they have gained.

QAnon—a sprawling, complex conspiracy theory that says politicians, celebrities, and business leaders are secretly Satan-worshipping pedophiles who run the world.

Rejector—a person who rejects the main tenets and assumptions of Christian nationalism; see also, Christian nationalism

Reparative Therapy—a discredited and unethical practice of attempting to "repair" someone's nonheterosexual orientation that tends to mix prayer and counseling strategies; see also, Conversion Therapy.

Republican—a person affiliated with the Republican Party in the US; usually more right-leaning or conservative; see also, Liberal.

Resistor—a person who leans away from the main tenets and assumptions of Christian nationalism, but with some inconsistencies; see also, Christian Nationalism.

Right-Wing Authoritarianism (RWA)—an ideological attitude that includes political conservatism, submission and obedience to authority, a hostile and aggressive posture, and strong adherence to traditional social norms and standards; see also, Authoritarianism, Conservative.

Schema—a mental model or framework for understanding oneself, others, and relationships; they can often be maladaptive and the product of one's temperament and life experiences.

Schizotypal Personality Disorder—a long-standing pattern of odd thinking, unusual beliefs, lack of close friends, and paranoia; it is not schizophrenia, but shares some common symptoms.

Shame—a negative emotion that results from a negative evaluation of one's self, often involving a belief that one is unworthy of unconditional love or regard; see also, Guilt.

Social Anxiety Disorder (SAD)—an anxiety disorder that involves intense anxiety in social or performance situations.

Social Conservative—a political ideology that places high value on the preservation of traditional values and beliefs.

Social Dominance Orientation (SDO)—a personality trait that involves strong support for hierarchies in society where one's group is in a role of superiority or dominance over other groups.

Spiritual Bypass—a psychological strategy for using spiritual talk to avoid dealing directly with unpleasant emotions or circumstances.

Sunk Cost Fallacy—the error of believing you should persist with a losing course of action because of the amount of time, money, or emotional investment you have put into the venture.

Systemic Racism—the form of racism that is embedded in institutions and organizations through traditions, laws, regulations, or practices; it does not imply that all people in those institutions act with deliberate racist intent.

Teleological Thinking—a belief that everything *exists* for a reason; people who have more teleological thinking understand things in terms of the purpose or function they serve, not what they are.

Temperament—your inborn, innate predispositions and traits; these include your activity and attention level.

Terror Management Theory (TMT)—a theory that most of human behavior is the product of having an instinct to survive in the face of death's inevitability.

Bibliography

Abalakina-Paap, Marina, et al. "Beliefs in Conspiracies." *Political Psychology* 20 (1999) 637–47. https://doi.org/10.1111/0162-895X.00160.

Adams, Jennifer. "23 Percent of Republicans Agree 'Satan-Worshipping Pedophiles' Run Government: Poll." https://www.thedailybeast.com/23-percent-of-republicans-agree-satan-worshipping-pedophiles-run-government-poll-says.

Adams, John M., et al. "You Remind Me of Someone Awesome: Narcissistic Tolerance is Driven by Perceived Similarity." *Personality and Individual Differences* 104 (2017) 499–503. https://www.researchgate.net/publication/308183257.

Adorno, Theodor, et al. *The Authoritarian Personality.* New York: Harper, 1950.

Ahn, Woo-Young, et al. "Nonpolitical Images Evoke Neural Predictors of Political Ideology." *Current Biology* 24 (2014) 2693–99. https://doi.org/10.1016/j.cub.2014.09.050.

Akrami, Nazar, and Bo Ekehammar. "Right-Wing Authoritarianism and Social Dominance Orientation: Their Roots in Big-Five Personality Factors and Facets." *Journal of Individual Differences* 27 (2006) 117–26. https://doi.org/10.1027/1614-0001.27.3.117.

Alexander, Keith L., and Susan Svrluga. "'I am sure he is sorry for any heartaches he has caused' Mother of Alleged 'Pizzagate' Gunman Says." https://www.washingtonpost.com/local/public-safety/i-am-sure-he-is-sorry-for-any-heartaches-he-has-caused-mother-of-alleged-pizzagate-gunman-says/2016/12/12/ac6f9068-c083-11e6-afd9-f038f753dc29_story.html.

Alexander, Megan B., et al. "How Need for Power Explains Why Narcissists Are Antisocial." *Psychological Reports* 124 (2021) 1335–52. https://journals.sagepub.com/doi/10.1177/0033294120926668.

Ali, Rasha. "Josh Duggar Will Be Released Pending Trial: Everything We Know About His Child Pornography Charges." https://www.usatoday.com/story/entertainment/celebrities/2021/05/03/josh-duggar-child-pornography-charges-what-we-know/4923762001/.

Aliprantis, Dionissi, and Daniel R. Carroll. "What Is Behind the Persistence of the Racial Wealth Gap?" *Economic Commentary* (2009) 1–6. https://doi.org/10.26509/frbc-ec-201903.

Allen, Karma, and Dominick Proto. "White Yale Student Calls Police on Napping Black Schoolmate, College Vows to Become 'Truly Inclusive.'" https://abcnews.go.com/US/yale-responds-white-student-calls-police-napping-black/story?id=55060171.

Allen, Mike. "QAnon Infects Churches." https://www.axios.com/qanon-churches-popular-religion-conspiracy-theory-c5bcce08-8f6e-4501-8cb2-9e38a2346c2f.html.

Allison, Natalie, and Adam Tamburin. "Retracing the Key Moments After the Christmas Morning Bombing in Nashville." https://www.tennessean.com/in-depth/news/local/2021/01/10/timeline-christmas-morning-bombing-nashville/6578915002/.

Allport, Gordon W., and J. Michael Ross. "Personal religious orientation and prejudice." *Journal of Personality and Social Psychology* 5 (1967) 432–43. https://psycnet.apa.org/doi/10.1037/h0021212.

Alter, Charlotte. "How Conspiracy Theories are Shaping the 2020 Election—and the Foundation of American Democracy." https://time.com/5887437/conspiracy-theories-2020-election/.

American Cancer Society. *Breast Cancer Facts & Figures 2019–2020.* Atlanta: American Cancer Society, 2019.

———. *Cancer Facts & Figures for African Americans 2019–2021.* Atlanta: American Cancer Society, 2021.

American Psychiatric Association. *Diagnostic and Statistical Manual of Mental Disorders.* 5th ed. Arlington, VA: American Psychiatric Association, 2013.

———. "APA Public Opinion Poll—Annual Meeting 2017." https://www.psychiatry.org/newsroom/apa-public-opinion-poll-annual-meeting-2017.

———. "APA Public Opinion Poll—Annual Meeting 2018." https://www.psychiatry.org/newsroom/apa-public-opinion-poll-annual-meeting-2018.

American Psychological Association, Task Force on Appropriate Therapeutic Responses to Sexual Orientation. *Report of the American Psychological Association Task Force on Appropriate Therapeutic Responses to Sexual Orientation.* https://www.apa.org/pi/lgbt/resources/therapeutic-response.pdf.

Ames, Daniel R., et al. "The NPI-16 as a Short Measure of Narcissism." *Journal of Research in Personality* 40 (2006) 440–50. https://www0.gsb.columbia.edu/mygsb/faculty/research/pubfiles/1005/npi16_jrp.pdf.

Anderson, Monica, et al. "The Virtues and Downsides of Online Dating." https://www.pewresearch.org/internet/2020/02/06/the-virtues-and-downsides-of-online-dating/.

Ardi, Rahkman, and Diah Budiarti. "The Role of Religious Beliefs and Collective Narcissism in Interreligious Contact on University Students." *Heliyon* 6 (2020) 1–8. https://doi.org/10.1016/j.heliyon.2020.e04939.

Argentino, Marc-André. "The Church of QAnon: Will Conspiracy Theories Form the Basis of a New Religious Movement?" *The Conversation,* May 18, 2020.

———. "QAnon Conspiracy Theory Followers Step Out of the Shadows and May be Headed to Congress." https://theconversation.com/qanon-conspiracy-theory-followers-step-out-of-the-shadows-and-may-be-headed-to-congress-141581.

Arizona Christian University Cultural Research Center. "American Worldview Inventory 2020—At a Glance; AVWI 2020 Results—Release #8: Perceptions of Sin and Salvation." https://www.arizonachristian.edu/wp-content/uploads/2020/08/AWVI-2020-Release-08-Perceptions-of-Sin-and-Salvation.pdf.

Artiga, Samantha, et al. "Racial Disparities in COVID-19: Key Findings from Available Data and Analysis." https://www.kff.org/racial-equity-and-health-policy/issue-brief/racial-disparities-covid-19-key-findings-available-data-analysis/.

Ashton, Gary. "Moving to Nashville: 12 Things to Know (2021 Guide)." https://www.nashvillesmls.com/blog/did-you-know82-people-move-to-nashville-every-day.html#cost_of_living_in_nashville.

Associated Press. "High Court Decision Spotlights GOP Divide Over LGBT Rights." https://www.voanews.com/usa/high-court-decision-spotlights-gop-divide-over-lgbt-rights.

Ayers, David J. "Current Sexual Practices of Evangelical Teens and Young Adults." https://ifstudies.org/blog/sex-and-the-single-evangelical.

———. "Sex and the Single Evangelical." August 14, 2019. https://ifstudies.or/blog/sex-and-the-single-evangelical.

Bach, Brittany N. "The Impact of Parental Narcissistic Traits on Self-esteem in Adulthood." Masters thesis, Smith College, 2014.

Bader, Christopher D., et al. Fear Itself: The Causes and Consequences of Fear in America. New York: New York University Press, 2020.

Badger, Emily. "Redlining: Still a Thing." https://www.washingtonpost.com/news/wonk/wp/2015/05/28/evidence-that-banks-still-deny-black-borrowers-just-as-they-did-50-years-ago/.

———. "Whites Have Huge Wealth Edge Over Blacks (but Don't Know It)." https://www.nytimes.com/interactive/2017/09/18/upshot/black-white-wealth-gap-perceptions.html.

Badger, Emily, et al. "Extensive Data Shows Punishing Reach of Racism for Black Boys." https://www.nytimes.com/interactive/2018/03/19/upshot/race-class-white-and-black-men.html.

Baer, Stephanie K. "The Cop Who Said The Spa Shooter Had A "Bad Day" Previously Posted A Racist Shirt Blaming China For The Pandemic." https://www.buzzfeednews.com/article/skbaer/spa-shooter-bad-day-racist-facebook.

Bailey, J. Michael, et al. "Sexual Orientation, Controversy, and Science." Psychological Science in the Public Interest 17 (2016) 45–101. https://doi.org/10.1177/1529100616637616.

Bakan, David. The Duality of Human Existence: Isolation and Communion in Western Man. Chicago: Beacon, 1996.

Baker, Joseph O., et al. "Crusading for Moral Authority: Christian Nationalism and Opposition to Science." Sociological Forum 35 (2020) 587–607. https://doi.org/10.1111/socf.12619.

Bakker, Bert N., et al. "Conservatives and Liberals Have Similar Physiological Responses to Threats." Natural Human Behavior 4 (2020) 613–21. https://doi.org/10.1038/s41562-020-0823-z.

Baldwin, James. "As Much Truth as One Can Bear." New York Times, January 14, 1962.

Balko, Radley. "There's overwhelming evidence that the criminal justice system is racist. Here's the proof." https://www.washingtonpost.com/graphics/2020/opinions/systemic-racism-police-evidence-criminal-justice-system/.

Ball, Glenn R., and Darrell Puls. "Frequency of Narcissistic Personality Disorder in Pastors: A Preliminary Study." http://www.darrellpuls.com/images/AACC_2015_Paper_NPD_in_Pastors.pdf.

Bandelow, Borwin, and Sophie Michaelis. "Epidemiology of Anxiety Disorders in the 21st Century." *Dialogues in Clinical Neuroscience* 17 (2015) 327–35. https://dx.doi.org/10.31887%2FDCNS.2015.17.3%2Fbbandelow.

Banks, Adelle M. "Black Southern Baptists Weigh in on Critical Race Theory Critique by Officials." https://religionnews.com/2020/12/11/black-southern-baptists-weigh-in-on-critical-race-theory-critique-by-officials/.

———. "No Race Problem Here: Despite Summer of Protests, Many Practicing Christians Remain Ambivalent." https://religionnews.com/2020/09/15/despite-black-lives-matter-protests-practicing-christians-remain-ambivalent-barna/.

Banks, Antoine J., and Heather M. Hicks. "Fear and Implicit Racism: Whites' Support for Voter ID Laws." *Political Psychology* 37 (2016) 641–58. https://doi.org/10.1111/pops.12292.

Baragona, Justin. "Newsmax Goes There: Critical Race Theory Is 'Road to Death Camps' for White People." https://www.yahoo.com/now/newsmax-goes-critical-race-theory-153306224.html.

Barna, George. "Black Practicing Christians Are Twice As Likely As Their White Peers to See a Race Problem." https://www.barna.com/research/problems-solutions-racism/.

Barna Group. "Survey Explores Who Qualifies As an Evangelical." https://www.barna.com/research/survey-explores-who-qualifies-as-an-evangelical/.

———. "White Christians Have Become Even Less Motivated to Address Racial Injustice." https://www.barna.com/research/american-christians-race-problem/.

Barron, David, et al. "Associations Between Schizotypy and Belief in Conspiracist Ideation." *Personality and Individual Differences* 70 (2014) 156–9. https://doi.org/10.1016/j.paid.2014.06.040.

Barron, David, et al. "The Relationship Between Schizotypal Facets and Conspiracist Beliefs via Cognitive Processes." *Psychiatry Research* 259 (2018) 15–20. https://doi.org/10.1016/j.psychres.2017.10.001.

Bartlett, Bruce. "The Christian Devotion to a White America." https://newrepublic.com/article/158845/tom-cotton-slavery-christianity-white-supremacy.

Barton, Bernadette. "'Abomination'—Life as a Bible Belt Gay." *Journal of Homosexuality* 57 (2010) 465–84. https://doi.org/10.1080/00918361003608558.

Batson, C. Daniel, et al. *Religion and the Individual: A Social-psychological Perspective.* New York: Oxford University Press, 1993.

BBC News. "Archbishop Tutu 'Would Not Worship a Homophobic God.'" https://www.bbc.com/news/world-africa-23464694.

Becker, Ernest. *The Denial of Death.* New York: Simon & Schuster, 1973.

Bègue, Laurent. "Beliefs in Justice and Faith in People: Just World, Religiosity and Interpersonal Trust." *Personality and Individual Differences* 32 (2002) 375–82. https://doi.org/10.1016/S0191-8869(00)00224-5.

Bell, W. Kamau. "What Every American Needs to Know About White Supremacy." https://www.cnn.com/2020/07/19/opinions/united-shades-white-supremacy-kamau-bell/index.html.

Bell, Rob. *Everything Is Spiritual.* New York: St. Martin's Essentials, 2020.

———. *Love Wins: A Book About Heaven, Hell, and the Fate of Every Person Who Ever Lived.* San Francisco: HarperOne, 2011.

———. *What is the Bible? How an Ancient Library of Poems, Letters, and Stories Can Transform the Way You Think and Feel About Everything.* New York: HarperOne, 2017.

Belli, Brita. "Racial Disparity in Police Shootings Unchanged Over 5 Years." https://news.yale.edu/2020/10/27/racial-disparity-police-shootings-unchanged-over-5-years.

Benkarski, Ashley. "Nashville Music Star Outraged Over Teaching of White Privilege." https://tntribune.com/nashville-music-star-outraged-over-teaching-of-white-privilege/.

Benkler, Yochai, et al. "Study: Breitbart-Led Right-Wing Media Ecosystem Altered Broader Media Agenda." https://www.cjr.org/analysis/breitbart-media-trump-harvard-study.php.

Bensley, Alan D., et al. "The Generality of Belief in Unsubstantiated Claims." *Applied Cognitive Psychology* 34 (2020) 16–28. https://doi.org/10.1002/acp.3581.

Bentz, Leslie. "The Top 10: Facebook 'Vomit' Button for Gays and Other Pat Robertson Quotes." https://www.cnn.com/2013/07/09/us/pat-robertson-facebook-remark/index.html.

Berman, Mark, et al. "Robert Aaron Long: The Atlanta Spa Shooting Suspect's Life Before Attacks." https://www.washingtonpost.com/national/atlanta-shooting-suspect-robert-aaron-long/2021/03/19/9397cdca-87fe-11eb-8a8b-5cf82c3dffe4_story.html.

Bermin, Benjamin A., and R. Key Dismukes. "Pressing the Approach." *Aviation Safety World,* December 2006, 28–33. https://flightsafety.org/wp-content/uploads/2009/07/asw_dec06.pdf.

Bertrand, Marianne, and Sendhil Mullainathan. "Are Emily and Greg More Employable Than Lakisha and Jamal? A Field Experiment on Labor Market Discrimination." National Bureau of Economic Research." July 2003. https://www.nber.org/system/files/working_papers/w9873/w9873.pdf.

Besen, Wayne. "Albert Mohler's Conversion Fraud Factory." https://archive.truthwinsout.org/opinion/2021/04/42405/.

Betancourt, Roland. "What the QAnon of the 6th Century Teaches Us About Conspiracies." https://time.com/5935586/qanon-6th-century-conspiracies/.

Bilevicius, Elena, et al. "Vulnerable narcissism and addiction: The mediating role of shame." *Addictive Behaviors* 92 (2019) 115–21. https://doi.org/10.1016/j.addbeh.2018.12.035.

Bischmann, Alyssa, and Christina Richardson. "Age and Experience of First Exposure to Pornography: Relations to Masculine Norms." https://www.apa.org/news/press/releases/2017/08/pornography-exposure.

Bizumic, Boris, and John Duckitt. "'My Group Is Not Worthy of Me': Narcissism and Ethnocentrism." *Political Psychology* 29 (2008) 437–53. http://dx.doi.org/10.1111/j.1467-9221.2008.00638.x.

Bjork-James, Sophie. "Nearly two centuries ago, a QAnon-like conspiracy theory propelled candidates to Congress." https://theconversation.com/nearly-two-centuries-ago-a-qanon-like-conspiracy-theory-propelled-candidates-to-congress-144838.

Black Lives Matter. "What We Believe." https://uca.edu/training/files/2020/09/black-Lives-Matter-Handout.pdf.

Blevins, Kent. *How to Read the Bible Without Losing Your Mind: A Truth-Seeker's Guide to Making Sense of Scripture.* Eugene: Wipf & Stock, 2014.

Block, Jack, and Jeanne H. Block. "Nursery School Personality and Political Orientation Two Decades Later." *Journal of Research in Personality* 40 (2006) 734–49. https://doi.org/10.1016/j.jrp.2005.09.005.

Blumenthal, Max. "Agent of Intolerance." https://www.thenation.com/article/archive/agent-intolerance/.

Bocian, Konrad, et al. "Moral tribalism: Moral judgments of actions supporting ingroup interests depend on collective narcissism." *Journal of Experimental Social Psychology* 93 (2021) 1–13. https://doi.org/10.1016/j.jesp.2020.104098.

Bolluyt, Jess. "These Are the Most Narcissistic Countries in the World (and How America Stacks Up)." https://www.cheatsheet.com/culture/most-narcissistic-countries-in-the-world-including-america.html/.

Bonam, Courtney M., et al. "Ignoring History, Denying Racism: Mounting Evidence for the Marley Hypothesis and Epistemologies of Ignorance." *Social Psychological and Personality Science* 10 (2019) 257–65. https://doi.org/10.1177/1948550617751583.

Borum, Randy, P. Bartel, and A. Forth. *Manual for the Structured Assessment of Violence Risk in Youth (SAVRY).* Odessa, FL: Psychological Assessment Resources, 2006.

Bouchard, Thomas J., and Matt McGue. "Genetics and Environmental Influences on Human Psychological Differences." *Developmental Neurobiology* 54 (2003) 4–45. https://doi.org/10.1002/neu.10160.

Bowes, Shauna M., et al. "Looking Under the Tinfoil Hat: Clarifying the Personological and Psychopathological Correlates of Conspiracy Beliefs." *Journal of Personality* 00 (2020) 1–15. https://doi.org/10.1111/jopy.12588.

Boyes, Alice. "The Self-Serving Bias: Definition, Research, and Antidotes." https://www.psychologytoday.com/us/blog/in-practice/201301/the-self-serving-bias-definition-research-and-antidotes.

Bradley, Jason D. "3 Reasons Evangelical Christians Fall for Conspiracy Theories." https://www.patheos.com/blogs/jaysonbradley/2020/05/3-reasons-evangelical-christians-fall-for-conspiracy-theories/.

Brandt, Mark J., and Daryl R. Van Tongeren. "People both high and low on religious fundamentalism are prejudiced toward dissimilar groups." *Journal of Personality and Social Psychology* (112) (2017) 76–97. https://doi.org/10.1037/pspp0000076.

Brandt, Mark J., et al. "The Association Between Threat and Politics Depends on the Type of Threat, the Political Domain, and the Country." *Personality and Social Psychology Bulletin* (2020) 1–20. https://doi.org/10.1177/0146167220946187.

Brem, Meagan, et al. "Dispositional Mindfulness, Shame, and Compulsive Sexual Behaviors Among Men in Residential Treatment for Substance Use Disorders." *Mindfulness* 8 (2017) 1552–58. https://doi.org/10.1007/s12671-017-0723-0.

Brenan, Megan. "New Highs Say Black People Treated Less Fairly in Daily Life." https://news.gallup.com/poll/317564/new-highs-say-black-people-treated-less-fairly-daily-life.aspx.

Briñol, Pablo, et al. "Affective and Cognitive Validation of Thoughts: An Appraisal Perspective on Anger, Disgust, Surprise, and Awe." *Journal of Personality and Social Psychology* 114 (2018) 693–718. https://doi.org/10.1037/pspa0000118.

Brody, David. "Franklin Graham Tells CBN News He Thinks Democratic Party is 'Opposed to Faith.'" https://www1.cbn.com/cbnnews/2020/august/exclusive-franklin-graham-tells-news-he-thinks-democrats-are-opposed-to-faith.

Brooks, Khristopher J. "Racism has Cost the U.S. $16 Trillion, Citigroup Finds." https://
www.cbsnews.com/news/us-gdp-growth-missed-16-trillion-systemic-racism-
inequality-report/.

Brotherton, Robert. *Suspicious Minds: Why We Believe Conspiracy Theories*. New York:
Bloomsbury Sigma, 2007.

Brotherton, Robert, and Christopher C. French. "Belief in Conspiracy Theories and
Susceptibility to the Conjunction Fallacy." *Applied Cognitive Psychology* 28 (2014)
238–48. https://doi.org/10.1002/acp.2995.

Brotherton, Robert, and Silan Eser. "Bored to Fears: Boredom Proneness, Paranoia,
and Conspiracy Theories." *Personality and Individual Differences* 80 (2015) 1–5.
https://doi.org/10.1016/j.paid.2015.02.011.

Brotherton, Robert, et al. "Measuring belief in conspiracy theories: the generic
conspiracist beliefs scale." *Frontiers in Psychology* 4 (2013) 279. https://doi.
org/10.3389/fpsyg.2013.00279.

Brown, Anna. "Nearly Half of U.S. Adults Say Dating Has Gotten Harder for Most People
in the Last 10 Years." https://www.pewresearch.org/social-trends/2020/08/20/
nearly-half-of-u-s-adults-say-dating-has-gotten-harder-for-most-people-in-the-
last-10-years/.

Brown, Austin Channing. *I'm Still Here: Black Dignity in a World Made for Whiteness*.
New York: Convergent, 2018.

Brown, Brené. "Listening to Shame." TED2012. https://www.ted.com/talks/brene_
brown_listening_to_shame

Brown, Michael. "Joy Behar, Mike Pence, Donald Trump and the Question of Public
Apologies." https://www.christianpost.com/amp/joy-behar-mike-pence-donald-
trump-and-the-question-of-public-apologies.html.

Brueck, Hilary, and Canela López. "These Key Psychological Differences Can
Determine Whether You're Liberal or Conservative." https://www.businessinsider.
com/psychological-differences-between-conservatives-and-liberals-2018-2.

Brydum, Sunivie. "John Paulk Formally Renounces, Apologizes for Harmful 'Ex-Gay'
Movement." https://www.advocate.com/politics/religion/2013/04/24/john-paulk-
formally-renounces-apologizes-harmful-ex-gay-movement.

Buechner, Bryan M., et al. "Political Ideology and Executive Functioning: The Effects
of Conservatism and Liberalism on Cognitive Flexibility and Working Memory
Performance." *Social Psychological and Personality Science* 12 (2021) 237–47.
https://doi.org/10.1177/1948550620913187.

Bump, Philip. "The Group Least Likely to Think the U.S. Has a Responsibility to
Accept Refugees? Evangelicals." https://www.washingtonpost.com/news/politics/
wp/2018/05/24/the-group-least-likely-to-think-the-u-s-has-a-responsibility-to-
accept-refugees-evangelicals/.

———. "'There is not Systemic Racism' Says a Governor Who Named April as
Confederate Heritage Month." https://www.washingtonpost.com/politics/2021/04
/30/there-is-not-systemic-racism-says-governor-who-named-april-confederate-
heritage-month/.

Burge, Ryan P. "Is 'White Born-Again Christian' Just a Synonym for 'Republican'?"
https://religioninpublic.blog/2019/02/05/is-white-born-again-christian-just-a-
synonym-for-republican/.

———. *The Nones: Where They Came From, Who They Are, and Where They are Going*.
Minneapolis: Fortress, 2021.

Burger, Axel M., et al. "The Role of Motivation in the Association of Political Ideology with Cognitive Performance." *Cognition* 195 (2020) 104124. https://doi.org/10.1016/j.cognition.2019.104124.

Burke, Daniel. "How QAnon Uses Religion to Lure Unsuspecting Christians." https://www.cnn.com/2020/10/15/us/qanon-religion-churches/index.html.

Burke, Kelsy, and Samuel L. Perry. "How pleading 'sexual addiction' protects evangelical men." https://religionnews.com/2021/03/19/how-pleading-sexual-addiction-protects-men-evangelical-men-robert-aaron-long-atlanta-shooting/.

Burns, Ken, Ric Burns, and David G. McCullough. *The Civil War*. 25th commemorative ed. DVD, 2015.

Burton, Tara Isabella. "Study: When It Comes to Detecting Racial Inequality, White Christians Have a Blind Spot." https://www.vox.com/identities/2017/6/23/15855272/prri-study-white-christians-discrimination-blind-spot.

Bussee, Michael. "Michael Bussee." https://bornperfect.org/former-ex-gay-leaders/michael-bussee/.

Butler, Anthea. *White Evangelical Racism: The Politics of Morality in America*. Chapel Hill, NC: The University of North Carolina Press, 2021.

Calhoun, Lawrence G., and Arnie Cann. "Differences in Assumptions About a Just World: Ethnicity and Point of View." *The Journal of Social Psychology* 134 (1994) 765–70. https://doi.org/10.1080/00224545.1994.9923011.

Camara, M'Balou, et al. "Entering Entrepreneurship: Racial Disparities in the Pathways into Business Ownership." https://drive.google.com/file/d/1PKPONU9Wwglun8OOtSlbAaf8BtSan_C5/view.

Cameron, Chris. "In a Speech to a New Hampshire G.O.P. Group, Pence Calls Systemic Racism a 'Left-Wing Myth.'" https://www.nytimes.com/2021/06/03/us/politics/pence-trump-systemic-racism.html.

Camp, Lee C. *Scandalous Witness: A Little Political Manifesto for Christians*. Grand Rapids: Eerdmans, 2020.

Campbell, Colin. "Mike Huckabee: I Wish I Could Have Claimed to Be Transgender to 'Shower With the Girls' in High School." https://www.businessinsider.com/mike-huckabee-i-wish-i-could-have-pretended-to-be-transgender-2015-6.

Campbell, W. Keith. "Narcissism and Romantic Attraction." *Journal of Personality and Social Psychology* 77 (1999) 1254–70. https://www.researchgate.net/publication/232544903_Narcissism_and_romantic_attraction.

Campolo, Tony, and Shane Claiborne. "The Evangelicalism of Old White Men is Dead." https://www.nytimes.com/2016/11/29/opinion/the-evangelicalism-of-old-white-men-is-dead.html.

Cannon, Justin R. *The Bible, Christianity, & Homosexuality*. Scotts Valley, CA: CreateSpace Independent, 2008.

Cantwell, Christopher D. "How the Study of Evangelicalism has Blinded us to the Problems in Evangelical Culture." https://religiondispatches.org/author/c_cantwell/.

Carlson, Adam. "What We Know About the Child Pornography Case Against Josh Duggar, Which He Denies." https://people.com/crime/what-we-know-about-case-against-josh-duggar/.

Carlson, Erika N., et al. "You Probably Think this Paper's About You: Narcissists' Perceptions of their Personality and Reputation." *Journal of Personality and Social Psychology* 101 (2011) 185–201. https://doi.org/10.1037/a0023781.

Carlucci, L., et al. Does a Fundamentalist Mindset Predict a State or Trait Anxiety? The Covariate Role of Dogmatism." *Journal of Religious Health* 60 (2021) 1029–45. https://doi.org/10.1007/s10943-020-01016-5.

Carmon, Ziv, and Dan Ariely. "Focusing on the Foregone: How Value Can Appear So Different to Buyers and Sellers." *Journal of Consumer Research.* 27 (3) (2000) 360–70. https://academic.oup.com/jcr/article-abstract/27/3/360/1796841?redirectedFrom=fulltext&login=false.

Carratala, Sofia, and Connor Maxwell. "Health Disparities by Race and Ethnicity." https://www.americanprogress.org/issues/race/reports/2020/05/07/484742/health-disparities-race-ethnicity/.

Carter, Joe. "The FAQs: What Christians Should Know About QAnon." https://www.thegospelcoalition.org/article/the-faqs-what-christians-should-know-about-qanon/.

Cascio, Christopher N., et al. "Narcissists' Social Pain Seen Only in the Brain." *Social Cognitive and Affective Neuroscience* 10 (2015) 335–41. https://doi.org/10.1093/scan/nsu072.

Cashwell, Craig S., et al. "Spiritual Bypass: A Preliminary Investigation." *Counseling and Values* 54 (2010) 162–74. https://doi.org/10.1002/j.2161-007X.2010.tb00014.x.

Cathey, Dave. "Skewed View of Tulsa Race Massacre Started on Day 1 with 'The Story That Set Tulsa Ablaze.'" https://www.bunkhistory.org/resources/7975.

Cavendish, Steve, et al. "Behind the Nashville Bombing, a Conspiracy Theorist Stewing About the Government." https://www.nytimes.com/2021/02/24/us/anthony-warner-nashville-bombing.html.

CBS Interactive. "Will Smith: My Work Ethic Is 'Sickening.'" www.cbsnews.com/news/will-smith-my-work-ethic-is-sickening/.

Centers for Disease Control and Prevention. *A Closer Look at African American Men and High Blood Pressure Control: A Review of Psychosocial Factors and Systems-Level Interventions.* Atlanta: U.S. Department of Health and Human Services, 2010.

———. "COVID-19 Hospitalization and Death by Race/Ethnicity." https://stacks.cdc.gov/view/cdc/91857.

———. *Infant Mortality.* Atlanta: U.S. Department of Health and Human Services, 2019.

Cesario, Joseph, and David J. Johnson. "Statement on the Retraction of 'Officer Characteristics and Racial Disparities in Fatal Officer-involved Shootings.'" https://psyarxiv.com/dj57k/.

Cha, J. Mijin. "New HUD Report Shows Continued Discrimination Against People of Color." https://www.demos.org/blog/new-hud-report-shows-continued-discrimination-against-people-color.

Chang, Alvin. "We analyzed every QAnon post on Reddit. Here's who QAnon supporters actually are." https://www.vox.com/2018/8/8/17657800/qanon-reddit-conspiracy-data.

Chapman University. "The Chapman University Survey on American Fears, Wave 3." https://blogs.chapman.edu/wilkinson/2016/10/11/what-arent-they-telling-us/#_ftn1.

Chappell, Bill. "'We Are Not Cured': Obama Discusses Racism in America With Marc Maron." https://www.npr.org/sections/thetwo-way/2015/06/22/416476377/we-are-not-cured-obama-discusses-racism-in-america-with-marc-maron.

Chapman, Michael. "Rev. Graham to Bruce Jenner: 'Changing the Outside Doesn't Change the Inside.'" https://www.cnsnews.com/blog/michael-w-chapman/rev-graham-bruce-jenner-changing-outside-doesnt-change-inside-only-god-can.

Charron, Nicholas, and Paola Annoni. "What is the Influence of News Media on People's Perception of Corruption? Parametric and Non-Parametric Approaches." *Social Indicators Research* 153 (2020) 1139–65. https://doi.org/10.1007/s11205-020-02527-0.

Chatard, Armand, et al. "'How good are you in math?' The Effect of Gender Stereotypes on Students' Recollection of Their School Marks." *Journal of Experimental Social Psychology* 43 (2007) 1017–24. https://doi.org/10.1016/j.jesp.2006.10.024.

Chavez, Nicole. "Asian Americans Reported Being Targeted at Least 500 Times in the Last Two Months." https://www.cnn.com/2021/03/16/us/asian-americans-hate-incidents-report/index.html.

Cheatham, Mark R. "Conspiracy Theories Abounded in 19th-Century American Politics." https://www.smithsonianmag.com/history/conspiracy-theories-abounded-19th-century-american-politics-180971940/.

Chen, M. Keith, et al. "Racial Disparities in Voting Wait Times: Evidence from Smartphone Data." https://arxiv.org/pdf/1909.00024.pdf.

Cicero, Marcus Tullius. *On the Orator: Book 3; On Fate; Stoic Paradoxes; Divisions of Oratory.* Translated by Harris Rackham. https://www.hup.harvard.edu/catalog.php?isbn=9780674993846.

Chiwaya, Nigel, and Janell Ross. "The American Dream While Black: 'Locked in a vicious cycle.'" https://www.nbcnews.com/specials/american-dream-while-black-homeownership/

Cho, Diane J. "The History Behind the 1921 Tulsa Race Massacre." https://www.yahoo.com/now/history-behind-1921-tulsa-race-114000338.html.

Choma, Becky, et al. "Right-Wing Ideology as a Predictor of Collective Action: A Test Across Four Political Issue Domains." *Political Psychology* 41 (2020) 303–22. https://doi.org/10.1111/pops.12615.

Chopik, William J., and Kevin J. Grimm. "Longitudinal changes and historic differences in narcissism from adolescence to older adulthood." *Psychology and Aging* 34 (2019) 1109–23. https://doi.org/10.1037/pag0000379.

Chotiner, Isaac. "Is the World Actually Getting . . . Better?" https://slate.com/news-and-politics/2018/02/steven-pinker-argues-the-world-is-a-safer-healthier-place-in-his-new-book-enlightenment-now.html.

Chumley, Cheryl K. "Blacks More Racist than Whites, Say Americans to Rasmussen." https://www.washingtontimes.com/news/2020/jul/24/blacks-more-racist-whites-say-americans-rasmussen/.

Cichocka, Aleksandra, and Aleksandra Cislak. "Nationalism as Collective Narcissism." *Current Opinion in Behavioral Sciences* 34 (2020) 69–74. https://doi.org/10.1016/j.cobeha.2019.12.013.

Cichocka, Aleksandra, et al. "Does Self-Love or Self-Hate Predict Conspiracy Beliefs? Narcissism, Self-Esteem, and the Endorsement of Conspiracy Theories." *Social Psychological and Personality Science* 7 (2016) 157–66. https://doi.org/10.1177/1948550615616170.

Cichocka, Aleksandra, et al. "On Self-Love and Outgroup Hate: Opposite Effects of Narcissism on Prejudice and via Social Dominance Orientation and Right-Wing

Authoritarianism." *European Journal of Personality* 31 (2017) 366–84. https://doi. org/10.1002%2Fper.2114.

Cichocka, Aleksandra, et al. "'They Will Not Control Us': Ingroup Positivity and Belief in Intergroup Conspiracies." *British Journal of Psychology* 107 (2015) 556–76. https://doi.org/10.1111/bjop.12158.

Cineas, Fabiola. "Merriam-Webster has a New Definition of 'Racism.'" https://www. vox.com/identities/2020/6/10/21286656/merriam-webster-racism-definition.

Clark, Noël. "The Etiology and Phenomenology of Sexual Shame: A Grounded Theory Study." PhD diss., Seattle Pacific University, 2017. https://digitalcommons.spu. edu/cpy_etd/25.

Claus, Ronald E., et al. "Racial and Ethnic Disparities in the Police Handling of Juvenile Arrests." *Crime & Delinquency* 64 (2018) 1375–93. https://doi.org/10.1177/00 11128717741615.

Clayton, Katherine, et al. "The Validity of the IAT and the AMP as Measures of Racial Prejudice." https://dx.doi.org/10.2139/ssrn.3744338.

Clementson, David E. "How Web Comments Affect Perceptions of Political Interviews and Journalistic Control." *Political Psychology* 40 (2019) 815–36. https://doi. org/10.1111/pops.12560.

Coaston, Jane. "Does Teaching America It's Racist Make It Less Racist?" https://www. nytimes.com/2021/05/19/opinion/race-theory-us-racism.html?.

Cole, Nicki Lisa. "Definition of Systemic Racism in Sociology." https://www.teamunify. com/mtms/UserFiles/Image/QuickUpload/definition-of-systemic-racism-in-sociology_008947.pdf.

Conversano, Ciro, et al. "Optimism and Its Impact on Mental and Physical Well-Being." *Clinical Practice & Epidemiology in Mental Health* 6 (2010) 25–29. https://doi.org /10.2174/1745017901006010025.

Conway, Bevil. "Why Do We Care About the Colour of the Dress?" https://www. theguardian.com/commentisfree/2015/feb/27/colour-dress-optical-illusion-social-media.

Cook, Corey L., et al. "The world is a scary place: Individual differences in belief in a dangerous world predict specific intergroup prejudices." *Group Processes and Intergroup Relations* 21 (2016) 584–96. https://doi.org/10.1177/1368430216670024.

Cook, John, et al. "Coronavirus, 'Plandemic' and the Seven Traits of Conspiratorial Thinking." https://theconversation.com/coronavirus-plandemic-and-the-seven-traits-of-conspiratorial-thinking-138483.

Cooley, Erin., et al. "Liberals perceive more racism than conservatives when police shoot Black men—But, reading about White privilege increases perceived racism, and shifts attributions of guilt, regardless of political ideology." *Journal of Experimental Social Psychology* 85 (2019). https://doi.org/10.1016/j.jesp.2019.103885.

Cooper, Marjorie J., and Chris Pullig. "I'm Number One! Does Narcissism Impair Ethical Judgment Even for the Highly Religious?" *Journal of Business Ethics* 112 (2013) 167–76. www.jstor.org/stable/23324964.

Costello, Thomas H., et al. "'Escape from Freedom': Authoritarianism-Related Traits, Political Ideology, Personality, and Belief in Free Will/Determinism." *Journal of Research in Personality* 86 (2020) 103957. https://doi.org/10.1016/j. jrp.2020.103957.

Council on Biblical Manhood and Womanhood. "The Nashville Statement." https:// cbmw.org/nashville-statement.

Cox, Daniel. "After the Ballots Are Counted: Conspiracies, Political Violence, and American Exceptionalism." *Survey Center on American Life*, January 2021. https://www.aei.org/wp-content/uploads/2021/02/After-the-Ballots-Are-Counted.pdf?x91208.

Cox, Daniel, Juhem Navarro-Rivera, and Robert P. Jones. "I Know What You Did Last Sunday." https://www.prri.org/academic/study-know-last-sunday-finds-americans-significantly-inflate-religious-participation/.

Cox, Daniel, et al. "Religious Liberty Issues." http://www.prri.org/research/lgbt-transgender-bathroom-discrimination-religious-liberty/.

Crawford, Christian G. "Will Dismukes, the Klan and the Future of Alabama." https://www.al.com/opinion/2020/07/will-dismukes-the-klan-and-the-future-of-alabama.html.

Cree, Bruce A., and Louis H. Weimer. "Sensory System, Overview." *Encyclopedia of the Neurological Sciences* (2003) 234–41. https://doi.org/10.1016/B0-12-226870-9/00897-2.

Crew, Bec. "Here's Why You Can't See All 12 Black Dots in This Crazy Optical Illusion." https://www.sciencealert.com/here-s-why-you-can-t-see-all-12-black-dots-in-this-crazy-optical-illusion.

Crosby, Courtney L., et al. "Six Dimensions of Sexual Disgust." *Personality and Individual Differences* 156 (2020) 109714. https://doi.org/10.1016/j.paid.2019.109714.

D'Amato, Erik. "Mystery of Disgust." https://www.psychologytoday.com/us/articles/199801/mystery-disgust.

Daghigh, Ahmad. "Exploring the Relation Between Religiosity and Narcissism in an Iranian Sample." *Personality and Individual Differences* 139 (2019) 96–101. https://psycnet.apa.org/doi/10.1016/j.paid.2018.10.040.

Daly, Michael, and Eric Robinson. "Anxiety Reported by US Adults in 2019 and During the 2020 COVID-19 Pandemic: Population-Based Evidence from Two Nationally Representative Samples." *Journal of Affective Disorders* 286 (2021) 296–300. https://doi.org/10.1016/j.jad.2021.02.054.

Dates, Charlie. "'We Out': Charlie Dates on Why His Church is Leaving the SBC Over Rejection of Critical Race Theory." https://religionnews.com/2020/12/18/we-out-charlie-dates-on-why-his-church-is-leaving-the-sbc-over-rejection-of-critical-race-theory/.

Davies, Douglas J., and Michael J. Thate, eds. "Religion and the Individual: Belief, Practice, and Identity." www.mdpi.com/journal/religions.

Davis, Joshua. "Enforcing Christian Nationalism: Examining the Link Between Group Identity and Punitive Attitudes in the United States." *Journal for the Scientific Study of Religion* 57 (2018) 300–317. https://doi.org/10.1111/jssr.12510.

Day, Orla. "Adults That Experience Sexual Shame: Effects on Self-Esteem and Sexual Satisfaction." PhD diss., Dublin Business School, 2019.

De Cuyper, Anneleen. "Blame the Outgroup: Can Our Beliefs in a Just World Lead to Prejudice and Racism?" MS diss., Ghent University, 2016.

Decision Lab. "The Similar-to-Me Effect." https://thedecisionlab.com/reference-guide/psychology/the-similar-to-me-effect/.

DeGroat, Chuck. *When Narcissism Comes to Church: Healing Your Community from Emotional and Spiritual Abuse*. Downers Grove, IL: InterVarsity, 2020.

Degruy, Joy. *Post Traumatic Slave Syndrome: America's Legacy of Enduring Injury and Healing*. Milwaukie, OR: Uptone, 2005.

DenHoed, Andrea. "Josh Duggar's Ashley Madison Problem." https://www.newyorker.com/news/news-desk/josh-duggars-ashley-madison-problem.

Denovan, Andrew, et al. "Conspiracist Beliefs, Intuitive Thinking, and Schizotypal Facets: A Further Evaluation." *Applied Cognitive Psychology* 34 (2020) 1394–1405. https://doi.org/10.1002/acp.3716.

DeSilver, Drew. "Black Unemployment Rate is Consistently Twice That of Whites." https://www.pewresearch.org/fact-tank/2013/08/21/through-good-times-and-bad-black-unemployment-is-consistently-double-that-of-whites/.

Dewan, Shalia, and Kay Nolan. "Pharmacist Accused of Tampering with Vaccine was Conspiracy Theorist, Police Say." https://www.nytimes.com/2021/01/04/us/pharmacist-accused-of-tampering-with-vaccine-was-conspiracy-theorist-police-say.html.

Diamant, Jeff. "Half of U.S. Christians Say Casual Sex between Consenting Adults Is Sometimes or Always Acceptable." https://www.pewresearch.org/fact-tank/2020/08/31/half-of-u-s-christians-say-casual-sex-between-consenting-adults-is-sometimes-or-always-acceptable/.

Dias, Elizabeth. "'Christianity Will Have Power.'" https://www.nytimes.com/2020/08/09/us/evangelicals-trump-christianity.html.

Dias, Elizabeth, and Ruth Graham. "How White Evangelical Christians Fused With Trump Extremism." https://www.nytimes.com/2021/01/11/us/how-white-evangelical-christians-fused-with-trump-extremism.html.

Digman, John M. "Personality Structure: Emergence of the Five-Factor Model." *Annual Review of Psychology* 41 (1990) 417–40. https://doi.org/10.1146/annurev.ps.41.020190.002221.

Di Sarno, Marco, et al. "Shame Behind the Corner? A Daily Diary Investigation of Pathological Narcissism." *Journal of Research in Personality* 85 (2020) 103924. https://doi.org/10.1016/j.jrp.2020.103924.

Djupe, Paul A. "Christian Nationalism is about Dominance." https://religioninpublic.blog/2020/12/28/christian-nationalism-is-about-dominance/.

———. "The Inverted Golden Rule: Are Atheists as Intolerant as Evangelicals Think They Are?" https://religioninpublic.blog/2019/12/23/the-inverted-golden-rule-are-atheists-as-intolerant-as-evangelicals-think-they-are/.

———. "What Does Christian Nationalist Democracy Look Like?" https://religioninpublic.blog/2021/02/01/what-does-christian-nationalist-democracy-look-like/.

Djupe, Paul A., and Jacob Dennen. "Christian nationalists and QAnon followers tend to be anti-Semitic. That was seen in the Capitol attack." https://www.washingtonpost.com/politics/2021/01/26/christian-nationalists-qanon-followers-tend-be-anti-semitic-that-was-visible-capitol-attack/.

Djupe, Paul A., and Ryan P. Burge. "A Conspiracy at the Heart of It: Religion and Q." https://religioninpublic.blog/2020/11/06/a-conspiracy-at-the-heart-of-it-religion-and-q/.

Doane, Michael J., et al. "Extrinsic Religious Orientation and Well-Being: Is Their Negative Association Real or Spurious?" Review of Religious Research 56 (2014) 45–60. https://www.jstor.org/stable/43185908.

Dolan, Eric W. "New Study Finds Authoritarian Personality Traits are Associated with Belief in Determinism." https://www.psypost.org/2020/05/new-study-finds-authoritarian-personality-traits-are-associated-with-belief-in-determinism-56805#:~:text=New%20study%20finds%20authoritarian%20personality%20

traits%20are%20associated%20with%20belief%20in%20determinism,-by%20
Eric%20W&text=New%20research%20published%20in%20the,role%20in%20
right%2Dwing%20authoritarianism.

Donaldson-Pressman, Stephanie, and Robert M. Pressman. *The Narcissistic Family: Diagnosis and Treatment.* San Francisco: Jossey-Bass, 1994.

Donohue, Bill. "'Christian Nationalism' is an Invention of Christian Bashers." https://cnsnews.com/commentary/bill-donohue/christian-nationalism-invention-christian-bashers.

Doran, Will. "White Supremacists Took Over a City—Now NC is Doing More to Remember the Deadly Attack." https://www.newsobserver.com/news/politics-government/state-politics/article192202109.html.

Douglas, Erin. "Former Houston Police Captain Accused of Violent Attempt to Prove Election Conspiracy Was Hired by GOP Activist's Group." https://www.texastribune.org/2020/12/15/steven-hotze-texas-election-fraud-Houston-police-arrested/.

Douglas, Karen M., et al. "The Psychology of Conspiracy Theories." *Current Directions in Psychological Science* 26 (2017) 538–42. https://doi.org/10.1177/096 3721417718261.

Douglas, Karen M., et al. "Understanding Conspiracy Theories." *Political Psychology* 40 (2019) 3–35. https://www.researchgate.net/publication/329774882_Understanding _conspiracy_theories.

Downing, Margaret. "Myths and Legends." https://www.houstonpress.com/news/myths-and-legends-6558387.

Drinkwater, Ken, et al. "Reality Testing, Conspiracy Theories, and Paranormal Beliefs." *The Journal of Parapsychology* 76 (2012) 57–77. link.gale.com/apps/doc/A299638703/HWRC?u=tel_a_vanderbilt&sid=bookmark-HWRC&xid=9aa24561.

Dubebdorff, Sarah J., and Andrew Luchner. "Narcissistic Differences in Christian and Nonreligious Individuals." Honors thesis, Rollins College, 2016.

Duckitt, John. "A dual-process cognitive-motivational theory of ideology and prejudice." *Advances in Experimental Social Psychology* 33 (2001) 41–113. https://doi.org/10.1016/S0065-2601(01)80004-6.

Duford, Jerushah. "I'm Billy Graham's granddaughter. Evangelical support for Donald Trump insults his legacy." https://news.yahoo.com/im-billy-grahams-granddaughter-evangelical-160009725.html.

Duffy, Mary E., et al. "Trends in Mood and Anxiety Symptoms and Suicide-Related Outcomes Among U.S. Undergraduates, 2007–2018: Evidence From two National Surveys." *Journal of Adolescent Health* 65 (2019) 590–98. https://doi.org/10.1016/j.jadohealth.2019.04.033.

Dunaetz, David R., et al. "Do Larger Churches Tolerate Pastoral Narcissism More than Smaller Churches?" *Great Commission Research Journal* 10 (2018) 69–89. https://www.researchgate.net/publication/328304835_Do_Larger_Churches_Tolerate_Pastoral_Narcissism_More_than_Smaller_Churches.

Dunn, Thomas. "A Christian Crowdfunding Site has Raised Over $300,000 for the Kenosha Shooter's Legal Defense Fund." https://boingboing.net/2020/09/03/a-christian-crowdfunding-site.html.

Dunning, David. "The Dunning-Kruger Effect: On Being Ignorant of One's Own Ignorance." *Advances in Experimental Social Psychology* 44 (2011) 247–96. https://doi.org/10.1016/B978-0-12-385522-0.00005-6.

Dunning, Eric, et al. "Spectator Violence at Football Matches: Toward a Sociological Explanation." *The British Journal of Sociology* 37 (1986) 221–44. https://doi.org/10.2307/590355.

Duriez, Bart, and Bart Soenens. "Personality, Identity Styles and Authoritarianism: An Integrative Study Among Late Adolescents." *European Journal of Personality* 20 (2006) 397–417. https://doi.org/10.1002/per.589.

Dweck, Carol. "Mindsets and Math/Science Achievement." https://pdf4pro.com/view/mindsets-and-math-science-achievement-growth-mindset-6c7265.html.

———. *Mindset: The New Psychology of Success.* New York: Ballantine.

Dyduch-Hazer, Karolina, et al. "Collective Narcissism and In-Group Satisfaction Predict Opposite Attitudes Toward Refugees via Attribution of Hostility." *Frontiers in Psychology* 10 (2019) 1–12. https://doi.org/10.3389/fpsyg.2019.01901.

Dyer, Jennifer E. "Loving Thyself: A Kohutian Interpretation of a 'Limited' Mature Narcissism in Evangelical Megachurches." *Journal of Religion and Health* 51 (2012) 241–55. https://www.jstor.org/stable/41653766.

Earls, Aaron. "Half of U.S. Protestant Pastors Hear Conspiracy Theories in Their Churches." https://research.lifeway.com/2021/01/26/half-of-u-s-protestant-pastors-hear-conspiracy-theories-in-their-churches/.

———. "Religious Americans See Pandemic as Sign From God." https://lifewayresearch.com/2020/05/20/religious-americans-see-pandemic-as-sign-from-god/.

Eckholm, Erik. "Rift Forms in Movement as Belief in Gay 'Cure' is Renounced." https://www.nytimes.com/2012/07/07/us/a-leaders-renunciation-of-ex-gay-tenets-causes-a-schism.html.

EdBuild. "Education." https://edbuild.org/content/23-billion/full-report.pdf.

Edelman, Gilad. "QAnon Supporters Aren't Quite Who You Think They Are." https://www.wired.com/story/qanon-supporters-arent-quite-who-you-think-they-are/.

Edsall, Thomas B. "The QAnon Delusion Has Not Loosened Its Grip." https://www.nytimes.com/2021/02/03/opinion/qanon-conspiracy-theories.html.

Edwards, David. "Diner patron tells Fox News: 'Like it says in the Bible . . . America is supposed to be the city on the hill.'" https://www.rawstory.com/bible-city-on-the-hill/.

Edwards, Frank, et al. "Risk of being killed by police use of force in the United States by age, race–ethnicity, and sex." *Proceedings of the National Academy of Sciences of the United States* 34 (2019). https://doi.org/10.1073/pnas.1821204116.

Effectiviology. "The Just-World Hypothesis: On the Belief that Everyone Gets What They Deserve." https://effectiviology.com/just-world/.

Efrati, Yaniv, and Meyran Boniel-Nissim. "Parents' Psychopathology Promotes the Adoption of Ineffective Pornography-Related Parenting Mediation Strategies." *Journal of Sex & Marital Therapy* 47 (2021) 117–29. https://doi.org/10.1080/0092623X.2020.1835759.

Eickmeier, Kathrin, et al. "The 5-Factor Disgust Scale: Development and Validation of a Comprehensive Measure of Disgust Propensity." *European Journal of Psychological Assessment* 35 (2019) 403–13. https://doi.org/10.1027/1015-5759/a000401.

Ekehammar, Bo. "What Matters Most to Prejudice: Big Five Personality, Social Dominance Orientation, or Right-Wing Authoritarianism?" *European Journal of Personality* 18 (2004) 463–82. https://doi.org/10.1002/per.526.

Ekstrom, Pierce D., and Calvin K. Lai. "The Selective Communication of Political Information." *Social Psychological and Personality Science* 12 (2020) 789–800. https://doi.org/10.1177/1948550620942365.

Elad-Strenger, Julia, et al. "Is Disgust a 'Conservative' Emotion?" *Personality and Social Psychology Bulletin* 46 (2020) 896–912. https://doi.org/10.1177/0146167219880191.

Eligon, John. "Black Doctor Dies of COVID-19 After Complaining of Racist Treatment." https://www.nytimes.com/2020/12/23/us/susan-moore-black-doctor-indiana. html

Emerson, Michael O., and Christian Smith. *Divided By Faith: Evangelical Religion and the Problem of Race in America.* New York: Oxford University Press, 2000.

Enns, Peter. *The Bible Tells Me So: Why Defending Scripture Has Made Us Unable to Read It.* New York: HarperCollins, 2014.

———. *How the Bible Actually Works.* New York: HarperCollins, 2019.

———. *The Sin of Certainty: Why God Desires Our Trust More Than Our "Correct" Beliefs.* New York: HarperCollins, 2016.

Entringer, Theresa M., et al. "Big Five Facets and Religiosity: Three Large-scale, Cross-cultural, Theory-driven, and Process-attentive Tests." *Journal of Personality and Social Psychology* (2020) 1662–95. https://doi.org/10.1037/pspp0000364.

Escobar, Kathy. *Faith Shift.* New York: Convergent, 2014.

Fagan, Jeffrey A., and Alexis D. Campbell. "Race and Reasonableness in Police Killings." *Boston University Law Review* 100 (2020) 951. https://scholarship.law.columbia. edu/faculty_scholarship/2656.

Fairlie, Robert W., and Alicia M. Robb. "Race and Entrepreneurial Success: Black-, Asian-, and White-Owned Businesses in the United States." http://www.jstor.org/stable/j.ctt5hhhd2.

Farivar, Masood. "Hate Crimes Targeting Asian Americans Spiked by 150% in Major US Cities." https://www.voanews.com/usa/race-america/hate-crimes-targeting-asian-americans-spiked-150-major-us-cities.

Fatfouta, Ramzi, and Michela Schöder-Abé. "A Wolf in Sheep's Clothing? Communal Narcissism and Positive Implicit Self-views in the Communal Domain." *Journal of Research in Personality* 76 (2018) 17–21.

Fea, John. *Believe Me: The Evangelical Road to Donald Trump.* Grand Rapids: Eerdmans, 2018.

———. "An Illuminati Conspiracy Theory Captured American Imaginations in the Nation's Earliest Days—And Offers a Lesson for Now." https://time.com/5892376/early-american-conspiracy-theory/.

Federal Bureau of Investigation. "2017 Crime in the United States." https://ucr.fbi.gov/crime-in-the-u.s/2017/crime-in-the-u.s.-2017/topic-pages/tables/table-1.

Federico, Christopher M., and Agnieszka Golec de Zavala. "Collective Narcissism in the 2016 Presidential Election." *Public Opinion Quarterly* (2018). https://www.researchgate.net/publication/320353260_Federico_C_Golec_de_Zavala_A_in_press_Collective_narcissism_in_the_2016_Presidential_election_Public_Opinion_Quarterly.

Feldman Barrett, Lisa, and Paula R. Pietromonaco. "Accuracy of the Five-Factor Model in Predicting Perceptions of Daily Social Interactions." *Personality and Social Psychology Bulletin* 23 (1997) 1–51. https://doi.org/10.1177/0146167297231005.

Felitti, Vincent J., et al. "Relationship of Childhood Abuse and Household Dysfunction to Many of the Leading Causes of Death in Adults: The Adverse Childhood

Experiences (ACE) Study." *American Journal of Preventive Medicine* 14 (1998) 245–58.

Felton, Emmanuel. "Black Police Officers Describe The Racist Attacks They Faced As They Protected The Capitol." https://www.buzzfeednews.com/article/emmanuelfelton/black-capitol-police-racism-mob.

Fessler, Daniel M. T., et al. "Political Orientation Predicts Credulity Regarding Putative Hazards." *Psychological Science* 28 (2017) 651–60. https://doi.org/10.1177/0956797617692108.

Fiagbenu, Michael Edem, et al. "Of Deadly Beans and Risky Stocks: Political Ideology and Attitude Formation via Exploration Depend on the Nature of the Attitude Stimuli." *British Journal of Psychology* 112 (2021) 342–57. https://doi.org/10.1111/bjop.12430.

Figueroa, Caroline. "The Psychology of Denying Racism." https://medium.com/age-of-awareness/the-psychology-of-denying-racism-7c5948a3ac1.

Firestone, Lisa. "Is Narcissism Shaped by Attachment Style?" https://www.psychologytoday.com/us/blog/compassion-matters/201711/is-narcissism-shaped-attachment-style.

Forbes, Miriam K., and Robert F. Krueger. "The Great Recession and Mental Health in the United States." *Clinical Psychological Science* 7 (2019) 900–913. https://doi.org/10.1177/2167702619859337.

Ford, Tiffany N., et al. "Race Gaps in COVID-19 Deaths are Even Bigger Than They Appear." https://www.brookings.edu/blog/up-front/2020/06/16/race-gaps-in-covid-19-deaths-are-even-bigger-than-they-appear/.

Fortin, Jacey. "Former Houston Officer Investigating 'Fraudulent' Ballots is Charged With Assault." https://www.nytimes.com/2020/12/16/us/houston-police-captain-mark-aguirre.html.

Foster, Caroline. *Narcissistic Parents. The Complete Guide for Adult Children, Including 2 Manuscripts: Narcissistic Mothers & Narcissistic Fathers. How to Handle a Narcissistic Parent and Recover from CPTSD.* Independently Published, 2019.

Frankel, Todd C. "A Majority of the People Arrested for Capitol Riot Had a History of Financial Trouble." https://www.washingtonpost.com/business/2021/02/10/capitol-insurrectionists-jenna-ryan-financial-problems/.

Franks, Bradley, et al. "Beyond 'Monologicality'? Exploring Conspiracist Worldviews." *Frontiers in Psychology* 8 (2017) 861. https://doi.org/10.3389/fpsyg.2017.00861.

Freeman, Rhonda. "How to Tell if You're Dealing with a Malignant Narcissist." https://www.psychologytoday.com/us/blog/neurosagacity/201702/how-tell-youre-dealing-malignant-narcissist.

French, David. "Fact and Fiction About Racism and the Rise of the Religious Right." https://frenchpress.thedispatch.com/p/fact-and-fiction-about-racism-and.

———. "How a Rising Religious Movement Rationalizes the Christian Grasp for Power." https://frenchpress.thedispatch.com/p/how-a-rising-religious-movement-rationalizes.

———. "In a Post-Roe World, Pro-Lifers Would Still Have a Lot of Work Left to Do." https://www.nationalreview.com/2019/07/in-a-post-roe-world-pro-lifers-would-still-have-a-lot-of-work-left-to-do/.

Friedman, Lauren F. "This Chart Showing the Gap Between Black and White Life Expectancy Should Be a National Embarrassment." https://www.businessinsider.com/huge-racial-gap-in-life-expectancy-2014-1.

Froese, Paul, et al. "American Values, Mental Health, and Using Technology in the Age of Trump: Findings from the Baylor Religion Survey, Wave 5." www.baylor.edu/BaylorReligionSurvey.

Fry, Stephen. "Stephen Fry Meets an Ex-Gay Therapist." https://www.youtube.com/embed/WnBBqYFGKB8.

Fryer, Roland G. An Empirical Analysis of Racial Differences in Police Use of Force. Journal of Political Economy (2016), 1.

Fulwood, Sam, III. "America is Plagued by a Chronic Misunderstanding of Slavery and White Supremacy." https://archive.thinkprogress.org/america-is-plagued-by-a-chronic-misunderstanding-of-slavery-and-white-supremacy-89560f69ec4d/.

Funaro, Vincent. "Caitlyn Jenner Transformation Won't Change Who Bruce Was as a Father, Says Franklin Graham." https://www.christianpost.com/news/caitlyn-jenner-transformation-wont-change-who-bruce-was-as-a-father-says-franklin-graham.html.

Furnham, Adrian, and Barrie Gunter. "Just World Beliefs and Attitudes Towards the Poor." British Journal of Social Psychology 23 (1984) 265–69. 2651/j.2044-8309.1984.tb00637.x.

Gagné, Jean-Philippe, and Adam S. Radomsky. "Manipulating beliefs about losing control causes checking behaviour." Journal of Obsessive-Compulsive and Related Disorders 15 (2017) 34–42.

Galston, William A. "Has Trump caused white evangelicals to change their tune on morality?" https://www.brookings.edu/blog/fixgov/2016/10/19/has-trump-caused-white-evangelicals-to-change-their-tune-on-morality/.

Garcia, Sandra E. "Tennessee Pastor Who Is Also a Detective Calls for L.G.B.T. People to Be Executed." https://www.nytimes.com/2019/06/15/us/knoxville-pastor-grayson-fritts.html.

Garfield, Leanna. "The Author of Bill Gates' Favorite Book Suggests 9 Big Reasons the World is Getting Better." https://www.businessinsider.com/bill-gates-steven-pinker-world-is-improving-2018-5.

Garisto, Daniel. "Smartphone Data Show Voters in Black Neighborhoods Wait Longer." https://www.scientificamerican.com/article/smartphone-data-show-voters-in-black-neighborhoods-wait-longer1/.

Garloch, Karen. "Charlotte-Area Transgender Teens' Suicides Rock Community." http://www.charlotteobserver.com/news/local/article16655111.html.

Gawronski, Bertram. "Fundamental Attribution Error." In Encyclopedia of Social Psychology, edited by Roy F. Baumeister and Kathleen D. Vos, 367–69. Thousand Oaks, CA: Sage, 2007.

Gay and Lesbian Alliance Against Defamation. "Conversion Therapy." https://www.glaad.org/conversiontherapy.

Gay and Lesbian Alliance Against Defamation. "Michael Johnston Advertisement." https://www.glaad.org/advertising/library/mom?page=4&response_type=embed.

Gebauer, Jochen E., et al. "Communal Narcissism." Journal of Personality and Social Psychology 103 (2012) 854–78. https://doi.org/10.1037/a0029629.

Gebauer, Jochen E., et al. "Christian self-enhancement." Journal of Personality and Social Psychology 113 (2017) 786–809. https://doi.org/10.1037/pspp0000140.

Gerber, Alan S., et al. "The Big Five Personality Traits in the Political Arena." The Annual Review of Political Science 14 (2011) 265–87. https://www.annualreviews.org/doi/full/10.1146/annurev-polisci-051010-111659.

Geronimus, Arline T., et al. "'Weathering' and Age Patterns of Allostatic Load Scores Among Blacks and Whites in the United States." *American Journal of Public Health* 96 (2006) 826–33. https://doi.org/10.2105/AJPH.2004.060749.

Gerson, Michael. "The Last Temptation." https://www.theatlantic.com/magazine/archive/2018/04/the-last-temptation/554066/.

Ghandour, Reem M., et al. "Prevalence and Treatment of Depression, Anxiety, and Conduct Problems in U.S. Children." *The Journal of Pediatrics* 206 (2019) 256–67. https://doi.org10.1016/j.jpeds.2018.09.021.

Gil de Zúñiga, Homero, et al. "Effects of the News-Finds-Me Perception in Communication: Social Media Use Implications for News Seeking and Learning About Politics." *Journal of Computer-Mediated Communication* 22 (2017) 105–23. https://doi.org/10.1111/jcc4.12185.

Gilliland, Randy, et al. "The Roles of Shame and Guilt in Hypersexual Behavior." *Sexual Addiction and Compulsivity* 18 (2011) 12–29. https://www.researchgate.net/publication/263259085_The_Roles_of_Shame_and_Guilt_in_Hypersexual_Behavior.

Gjelten, Tom. "Evangelical Christians Grapple With Racism As Sin." https://www.npr.org/2020/06/06/871014393/evangelical-christians-grapple-with-racism-as-sin.

———. "White Supremacist Ideas Have Historical Roots In U.S. Christianity." https://www.npr.org/2020/07/01/883115867/white-supremacist-ideas-have-historical-roots-in-u-s-christianity.

Glazzard, Jonathan, and Samuel Stones. "Social Media and Young People's Mental Health and Wellbeing." In *Selected Topics in Child and Adolescent Mental Health*, edited by Samuel Stones, Jonathan Glazzard, and Maria Muzio, 7–20 (2019), *IntechOpen*, https://www.intechopen.com/chapters/68639.

Glover, Julian. "Black CA Couple Lowballed by $500K in Home Appraisal, Believe Race was a Factor." https://abc7news.com/black-homeowner-problems-sf-bay-area-housing-discrimination-minority-homeownership-anti-black-policy/10331076/.

Goertzel, Ted. "Belief in Conspiracy Theories." *Political Psychology* 15 (1994) 731–42. https://doi.org/10.2307/3791630.

Golec de Zavala, Agnieszka. "Collective Narcissism and In-Group Satisfaction Are Associated With Different Emotional Profiles and Psychological Wellbeing." *Frontiers in Psychology* 10 (2019). https://doi.org/10.3389/fpsyg.2019.00203.

———. "Narcissism: not only an individual failing." https://www.academia-net.org/news/narcissism-is-not-only-an-individual-failing/1613960.

———. "Why is Collective Narcissism So Reliably Associated with Conspiratorial Thinking?" https://collectivenarcissism.com/blog/conspiracy_thinking.

Golec de Zavala, Agnieszka, and Aleksandra Cichocka. "Collective Narcissism and Anti-Semitism in Poland." *Group Processes & Intergroup Relations* 15 (2012) 213–29. https://doi.org/10.1177/1368430211420891.

Golec de Zavala, A., A. Chichocka, and I. Iskra-Golec. "Collective Narcissism Moderates the Effect of In-Group Image Threat on Intergroup Hostility." *Journal of Personality and Social Psychology* 104 6 (2013) 1019–39. https://doi.org./10.1037/a0032215.

Golec de Zavala, Agnieszka, and Christopher M. Federico. "Collective Narcissism and the Growth of Conspiracy Thinking Over the Course of the 2016 United States Presidential Election: A Longitudinal Analysis." *European Journal of Social Psychology* 48 (2018) 1011–18. https://doi.org/10.1002/ejsp.2496.

Golec de Zavala, Agnieszka, and Dorottya Lantos. "Collective Narcissism and Its Social Consequences: The Bad and the Ugly." *Current Directions in Psychological Science* 29 (2020) 273–78. https://doi.org/10.1177/0963721420917703.

Golec de Zavala, Agnieszka, and Kinga Bierwiaczonek. "Male, National, and Religious Collective Narcissism Predict Sexism." *Sex Roles* 84 (2021) 1–21. https://www.researchgate.net/publication/345315748_Male_National_and_Religious_Collective_Narcissism_Predict_Sexism.

Golec de Zavala, Agnieszka, et al. "Collective narcissism and its social consequences." *Journal of Personality and Social Psychology* 97 (2009) 1074–96. https://doi.org/10.1037/a0016904.

Golec de Zavala, Agnieszka, et al. "Collective Narcissism Predicts Hypersensitivity to In-group Insult and Direct and Indirect Retaliatory Intergroup Hostility." *European Journal of Personality* 30 (2016) 532–51. https://doi.org/10.1002/per.2067.

Golec de Zavala, Agnieszka, et al. "Collective Narcissism: Political Consequences of Investing Self-Worth in the Ingroup's Image." *Political Psychology* 40 (2019) 37–74. https://doi.org/10.1111/pops.12569.

Golec de Zavala, Agnieszka., et al. "Low Self-Esteem Predicts Out-Group Derogation via Collective Narcissism, but This Relationship Is Obscured by In-Group Satisfaction." *Journal of Personality and Social Psychology* 119 (2020) 741–64. http://dx.doi.org/10.1037/pspp0000260.

Goleman, Daniel. *Emotional Intelligence: Why It Can Matter More Than IQ.* New York: Bantam, 1995.

Gollwitzer, Anton, and Margaret S. Clark. "Anxious attachment as an antecedent of people's aversion toward pattern deviancy." *European Journal of Social Psychology* 49 (2019) 1–17. https://doi.org/10.1002/ejsp.2565.

Gollwitzer, Anton, et al. "Pattern deviancy aversion predicts prejudice via a dislike of statistical minorities." *Journal of Experimental Psychology: General* (2019) 1–27. https://www.researchgate.net/publication/336248041_Pattern_deviancy_aversion_predicts_prejudice_via_a_dislike_of_statistical_minorities.

Goncalves, Felipe, and Emily Weisburst. "Economics Research on Racial Disparities in Policing." https://econofact.org/economic-research-on-racial-disparities-in-policing.

Gonyea, Don. "Majority Of White Americans Say They Believe Whites Face Discrimination." https://www.npr.org/2017/10/24/559604836/majority-of-white-americans-think-theyre-discriminated-against.

González-Ramírez, Andrea. "The Ever-Growing List of Trump's Most Racist Rants." https://gen.medium.com/trump-keeps-saying-racist-things-heres-the-ever-growing-list-of-examples-21774f6749a4.

Goodman, Joseph. "How the Discrimination of Alabama Football Star O.J. Howard Changed a School." https://www.al.com/sports/2016/05/alabama_crimson_tide_oj_howard.html.

Goodrich, Terry. "Evangelicals Have Higher-than-average Divorce Rates, According to a Report Compiled by Baylor for the Council on Contemporary Families." https://www.baylor.edu/mediacommunications/news.php?action=story&story=137892.

Goodstein, Laurie. "He's a Superstar Pastor: She Worked for Him and Says He Groped Her Repeatedly." https://www.nytimes.com/2018/08/05/us/bill-hybels-willow-creek-pat-baranowski.html.

Goodwin, Renee D., et al. "Trends in Anxiety Among Young Adults in the United States, 2008–2018: Rapid Increases Among Young Adults." *Journal of Psychiatric Research* 130 (2020) 441–46. https://doi.org/10.1016/j.jpsychires.2020.08.014.

Goreis, Andreas, and Martin Voracek. "A Systematic Review and Meta-Analysis of Psychological Research on Conspiracy Beliefs: Field Characteristics, Measurement Instruments, and Associations With Personality Traits." *Frontiers in Psychology* 10 (2019). https://doi.org/10.3389/fpsyg.2019.00205.

Gorski, Philip S. *American Covenant: A History of Civil Religion from the Puritans to the Present*. Princeton, NJ: Princeton University Press, 2017.

Gorvett, Zaria. "How the News Changes the Way We Think and Behave." https://www.bbc.com/future/article/20200512-how-the-news-changes-the-way-we-think-and-behave?ocid=ww.social.link.email.

Gothard, Bill. *Wisdom Worksheet (Booklet 49–Preliminary Edition)*. Oak Brook, IL: Institute in Basic Life Principles, 1999.

Gow, Paul, and Joel Rookwood. "Doing it for the team—examining the causes of hooliganism in English football." *Journal of Qualitative Research in Sports Studies* 2 (2008) 71–82. https://api.semanticscholar.org/CorpusID:55999198.

Goyal, Monika K., et al. "Racial and/or Ethnic and Socioeconomic Disparities of SARS-CoV-2 Infection Among Children." https://doi.org/10.1542/peds.2020-009951.

Graeupner, Damaris, and Alin Coman. "The dark side of meaning-making: how social exclusion leads to superstitious thinking." *Journal of Experimental Social Psychology* 69 (2017) 218–22. https://doi.org/10.1016/j.jesp.2016.10.003.

Graham, David A., et al. "An Oral History of Trump's Bigotry." https://www.theatlantic.com/magazine/archive/2019/06/trump-racism-comments/588067/.

Graham, Ruth. "Atlanta Suspect's Fixation on Sex Is Familiar Thorn for Evangelicals." https://www.nytimes.com/2021/03/20/us/evangelical-sex-addiction-atlanta-suspect.html.

———. "The Rise and Fall of Carl Lentz, the Celebrity Pastor of Hillsong Church." https://www.nytimes.com/2020/12/05/us/carl-lentz-hillsong-pastor.html.

Graham, Ruth, et al. "Suspect's Church Calls Spa Attacks 'the Result of a Sinful Heart.'" https://www.nytimes.com/2021/03/19/us/robert-aaron-long-church-atlanta.html.

Gramlich, John. "Black Imprisonment Rate in the U.S. has Fallen by a Third Since 2006." https://www.pewresearch.org/fact-tank/2020/05/06/share-of-black-white-hispanic-americans-in-prison-2018-vs-2006/.

———. "Voters' Perceptions of Crime Continue to Conflict with Reality." https://www.pewresearch.org/fact-tank/2016/11/16/voters-perceptions-of-crime-continue-to-conflict-with-reality/.

———. "What the Data Says (and Doesn't Say) About Crime in the United States." https://www.pewresearch.org/fact-tank/2020/11/20/facts-about-crime-in-the-u-s/.

Green, Emma. "The Unofficial Racism Consultants to the White Evangelical World." https://www.theatlantic.com/politics/archive/2020/07/white-evangelicals-black-lives-matter/613738/.

Green, Ricky. "Conspiracy Belief as a Coping Strategy: An Attachment Theory Perspective." PhD diss., University of Kent, 2021. https://gtr.ukri.org/projects?ref=studentship-2117778.

Green, Ricky, and Karen M. Douglas. "Anxious Attachment and Belief in Conspiracy Theories." *Personality and Individual Differences* 125 (2018) 30–37. https://doi.org/10.1016/j.paid.2017.12.023.

Greenspan, Rachel E. "The Bizarre Origins of the Lizard-People Conspiracy Theory Embraced by the Nashville Bomber, and how it's Related to QAnon." https://www.insider.com/lizard-people-conspiracy-theory-origin-nashville-bomber-qanon-2021-1.

Greenstein, Michael, and Nancy Franklin. "Anger Increases Susceptibility to Misinformation." *Experimental Psychology* 67 (2020) 202–9. https://doi.org/10.1027/1618-3169/a000489.

Gregory, Sara. "Students Brought Story of the Norfolk 17 to Life for a History Class." https://www.pilotonline.com/news/education/article_10850a2a-7e5e-11e9-b245-b393e11cdec6.html.

Greif, Andrew "Doc Rivers: 'It's amazing why we keep loving this country, and this country does not love us back.'" Los Angeles Times, August 25, 2020. https://www.latimes.com/sports/clippers/story/2020-08-25/doc-rivers-loving-this-country-and-does-not-love-us-back.

Grijalva, Emily, and Peter D. Harms. "Narcissism: An Integrative Synthesis and Dominance Complementarity Model." *Academy of Management Perspectives* 28 (2014) 108–27. http://dx.doi.org/10.5465/amp.2012.0048.

Griswold, Eliza. "A Pennsylvania Lawmaker and the Resurgence of Christian Nationalism." https://www.newyorker.com/news/on-religion/a-pennsylvania-lawmaker-and-the-resurgence-of-christian-nationalism.

———. "Evangelicals of Color Fight Back Against the Religious Right." https://www.newyorker.com/news/on-religion/evangelicals-of-color-fight-back-against-the-religious-right.

———. "How Black Lives Matter Is Changing the Church." https://www.newyorker.com/news/on-religion/how-black-lives-matter-is-changing-the-church.

Grubbs, Joshua B., et al. "Addiction or Transgression? Moral Incongruence and Self-Reported Problematic Pornography Use in a Nationally Representative Sample." *Clinical Psychological Science* 8 (2020) 936–46. https://doi.org/10.1177/2167702620922966.

Grubbs, Joshua B., et al. "Status Seeking and Public Discourse Ethics: A Nationally Representative Sample with Longitudinal Follow-Up." https://doi.org/10.17605/OSF.IO/ZBG3D.

Guffey, Robert. "Making Sense of QAnon: What Lies Behind the Conspiracy Theory that's Eating America?" https://www.salon.com/2020/08/30/making-sense-of-qanon-what-lies-behind-the-conspiracy-theory-thats-eating-america/.

———. "What is QAnon? A Not-So-Brief Introduction to the Conspiracy Theory That's Eating America." https://www.salon.com/2020/08/16/what-is-qanon-a-not-so-brief-introduction-to-the-conspiracy-theory-thats-eating-america/.

Gushee, David P. *After Evangelicalism: The Path to a New Christianity.* Louisville: Westminster John Knox, 2020.

———. *Still Christian: Following Jesus Out of American Evangelicalism.* Louisville: Westminster John Knox, 2017.

Guy, Jack. "Black Women with Natural Hairstyles are Less Likely to Get Job Interviews." https://www.cnn.com/2020/08/12/business/black-women-hairstyles-interview-scli-intl-scn/index.html.

Hagerman, Margaret. *White Kids: Growing Up With Privilege in a Racially Divided America*. New York: New York University Press, 2018.

Hagerty, Barbara Bradley. "Evangelicals Fight Over Therapy To 'Cure' Gays." https://www.npr.org/2012/07/06/156367287/evangelicals-fight-over-therapy-to-cure-gays.

Haggag, Kareem, and Devin Pope. "There are Stark Racial Disparities in Voting Times. Here's How to Fix Them." https://www.washingtonpost.com/opinions/there-are-stark-racial-disparities-in-voting-times-heres-how-to-fix-them/2019/12/16/5fb4948a-1c5b-11ea-b4c1-fdod91b60d9e_story.html.

Haidt, Jonathan. *The Righteous Mind: Why Good People Are Divided by Politics and Religion*. New York: Vintage, 2012.

Hall, Ben, and Kevin Sisniewski. "Nashville Bomber's Bizarre Writings Reveal Belief in Aliens and Lizard People." https://www.newschannel5.com/news/newschannel-5-investigates/nashville-bombers-bizarre-writings-reveal-belief-in-aliens-and-lizard-people.

Haltiwanger, John. "The Trump Administration Does Not Believe in Systemic Racism. But It's So Real that Merriam-Webster is Changing the Definition of Racism to Include It." https://www.businessinsider.com/trump-administration-doesnt-believe-in-systemic-racism-its-not-debatable-2020-6.

Hampton, Deon J. "'They Were Killing All the Black People': This 107-year-old Still Remembers Tulsa Massacre." https://www.nbcnews.com/news/us-news/they-were-killing-all-black-people-107-year-old-still-n1268420.

Hanel, Paul H., et al. "Centrality of Religiosity, Schizotypy, and Human Values: The Impact of Religious Affiliation." *Religions* 10 (2019). https://doi.org/10.3390/rel10050297.

Hanks, Angela, et al. "Systematic Inequality: How America's Structural Racism Helped Create the Black-White Wealth Gap." https://www.americanprogress.org/issues/race/reports/2018/02/21/447051/systematic-inequality/.

Hannover, Betina, et al. "Religiosity, Religious Fundamentalism, and Ambivalent Sexism Toward Girls and Women Among Adolescents and Young Adults Living in Germany." *Frontiers in Psychology* 9 (2018) 1–17. https://doi.org/10.3389/fpsyg.2018.02399.

Hardy, Bradley L., et al. "The Historical Role of Race and Policy for Regional Inequality." https://www.hamiltonproject.org/papers/the_historical_role_of_race_and_policy_for_regional_inequality.

Harriot, Michael. "Redlining: The Origin Story of Institutional Racism." https://www.theroot.com/redlining-the-origin-story-of-institutional-racism-1834308539.

Harris, Dan. "Haggard Admits Buying Meth." https://abcnews.go.com/GMA/story?id=2626067&page=2.

Harris, Joshua. *I Kissed Dating Goodbye*. Portland, OR: Multnomah, 1999.

Hart, Joshua, and Molly Graether. "Something's Going on Here: Psychological Predictors of Belief in Conspiracy Theories." *Journal of Individual Differences* 39 (2018) 229–37. https://doi.org/10.1027/1614-0001/a000268.

Harvard Health. "Optimism and Your Health." https://www.health.harvard.edu/heart-health/optimism-and-your-health.

Hatemi, Peter K., et al. "Genetic Influences on Political Ideologies: Twin Analyses of 19 Measures of Political Ideologies from Five Democracies and Genome-Wide

Findings From Three Populations." *Behavior Genetics* 44 (2014) 282–94. https://doi.org/10.1007/s10519-014-9648-8.

Hawkins, J. Russell. *The Bible Told Them So: How Southern Evangelicals Fought to Preserve White Supremacy.* New York: Oxford University Press, 2021.

Hawkins, Stephen, et al. "Hidden Tribes: A Study of America's Polarized Landscape." https://hiddentribes.us/media/qfpekz4g/hidden_tribes_report.pdf.

Healy, Kieran. "America is a Violent Country." https://www.washingtonpost.com/news/monkey-cage/wp/2017/10/03/america-is-a-violent-country/.

Hearon, Sarah. "Josh Duggar's Lawsuits, Scandals, and Controversies Over the Years." https://www.usmagazine.com/celebrity-news/pictures/josh-duggars-lawsuits-scandals-and-controversies-over-the-years/.

Heaven, Patrick C. L., et al. "Cognitive Ability, Right-Wing Authoritarianism, and Social Dominance Orientation: A Five-Year Longitudinal Study Amongst Adolescents." *Intelligence* 39 (2011) 15–21. https://doi.org/10.1016/j.intell.2010.12.001.

Held Evans, Rachel. *Inspired: Slaying Giants, Walking on Water, and Loving the Bible Again.* Nashville: Nelson, 2018.

———. *Searching for Sunday.* Nashville: Nelson, 2015.

Helling, Dave. "Even Before Josh Hawley, Conservative Conspiracy Theories Thrived in Kansas and Missouri." https://www.kansascity.com/opinion/opn-columns-blogs/dave-helling/article248415635.html.

Henao, Luis Andres, et al. "For George Floyd, a Complicated Life and Consequential Death." https://abcnews.go.com/US/wireStory/george-floyd-complicated-life-consequential-death-77199500.

Henderson, Alex. "'The Church of Q Anon': How a Bizarre Conspiracy Theory is Linked to Evangelical Christianity." https://www.salon.com/2020/05/24/the-church-of-qanon-how-a-bizarre-conspiracy-theory-is-linked-to-evangelical-christianity-_partner/.

———. "Nearly 60 Percent of Capitol Riot Arrestees Have Something in Common: A History of Financial Problems: Analysis." https://www.alternet.org/2021/02/capitol-rioters/.

Henderson, Felicia, and Zoe Kinias. "Understanding the Origins of White Denial." https://knowledge.insead.edu/blog/insead-blog/understanding-the-origins-of-white-denial-1528.

Herman, Peter, et al. "Comet Pizza Gunman Anticipated 'Violent Confrontation,' Court Papers Say." https://www.washingtonpost.com/local/public-safety/federal-charges-to-be-filed-against-man-involved-in-dc-pizza-shop-incident/2016/12/13/6c45e14a-c141-11e6-9578-0054287507db_story.html.

Hermann, Anthony, and Robert C. Fuller. "Trait Narcissism and Contemporary Religious Trends." *Archive for the Psychology of Religion* 39 (2017) 99–117. https://www.researchgate.net/publication/318689893_Trait_Narcissism_and_Contemporary_Religious_Trends.

Hiebler-Ragger, Michaela., et al. "Personality Influences the Relationship Between Primary Emotions and Religious/Spiritual Well-Being." *Frontiers in Psychology* 9 (2018). https://doi.org/10.3389/fpsyg.2018.00370.

Hill, Terrence D., et al. "The Blood of Christ Compels Them: State Religiosity and State Population Mobility During the Coronavirus (COVID-19) Pandemic." *Journal of Religion and Health* 59 (2020) 2229–42. https://doi.org/10.1007/s10943-020-01058-9.

Hillier, Amy E. "Redlining and the Home Owners' Loan Corporation." *Journal of Urban History* 29.4 (May 2003) 394–420. https://doi.org/10.1177/0096144203029004002.

History.com Editors. "Jim Crow Laws." https://www.history.com/topics/early-20th-century-us/jim-crow-laws.

———. "Tulsa Race Massacre." https://www.history.com/topics/roaring-twenties/tulsa-race-massacre.

History Makers. "Patricia Turner: Biography." https://www.thehistorymakers.org/biography/patricia-turner-41.

Hodge, Channon, et al. "Burned from the Land: How 60 Years of Racial Violence Shaped America." https://www.cnn.com/interactive/2021/05/us/whitewashing-of-america-racism/.

Hollywood Reporter Staff. "#OscarsSoWhite: How to Win an Oscar if You're Black." https://www.hollywoodreporter.com/movies/movie-news/oscarssowhite-how-win-an-oscar-859613/.

Homan, Patricia, and Amy Burdette. "When Religion Hurts: Structural Sexism and Health in Religious Congregations." *American Sociological Review* 86 (2021) 234–255. https://doi.org/10.1177/0003122421996686.

Hooper, Walter, ed. *The Collected Letters of C. S. Lewis*, vol. 3. San Francisco: HarperCollins, 2007.

Hornor, Gail. "Child and Adolescent Pornography Exposure." *Continuing Education: Journal of Pediatric Healthcare* 34 (2020) 191–99. https://doi.org/10.1016/j.pedhc.2019.10.001.

Horst, Myron. "Bill Gothard: The Biggest Conservative Fraud in Modern Times?" http://www.biblicalresearchreports.com/bill-gothard-biggest-conservative-fraud-modern-times/.

Hostetter, Martha, and Sarah Klein. "In Focus: Reducing Racial Disparities in Health Care by Confronting Racism." https://www.commonwealthfund.org/publications/2018/sep/focus-reducing-racial-disparities-health-care-confronting-racism.

Hotchkiss, Jason T. "The Relationship Between Sexual Compulsivity, Emotional and Spiritual Distress of Religious and Non-Religious Internet Pornography Users." *Journal of Religion and Health* 60 (2021) 1630–51. https://doi.org/10.1007/s10943-020-01152-y.

Howell, Elizabeth A., et al. "Race and Ethnicity, Medical Insurance, and Within-Hospital Severe Maternal Morbidity Disparities." *Obstetrics & Gynecology* 135 (2020) 285–93. https://doi.org/10.1097/AOG.0000000000003667.

Huckabee, Tyler. "Under God: The Rise of Christian Nationalism." https://www.relevantmagazine.com/magazine/under-god-the-rise-of-christian-nationalism/.

———. "Wrestling with Misogyny, Racism, and Toxic Purity Culture in the Wake of the Atlanta Shootings." https://www.relevantmagazine.com/current/nation/wrestling-with-misogyny-racism-and-toxic-purity-culture-in-the-wake-of-the-atlanta-shootings/.

Hughes, Sara, and Laura Machan. "It's a Conspiracy: COVID-19 Conspiracies Link to Psychopathy, Machiavellianism and Collective Narcissism." *Personality and Individual Differences* 171 (2021). https://doi.org/10.1016/j.paid.2020.110559.

Hughes, William. "Morgan Wallen's Sales Quadruple After Getting Caught Using Racial Slur on Camera." https://www.yahoo.com/lifestyle/morgan-wallens-sales-quadruple-getting-230600882.html.

Hune-Brown, Nicholas. "The Marley Hypothesis: Who Actually Sees Racism?" https://hazlitt.net/blog/marley-hypothesis-who-actually-sees-racism.

Hunt, Matthew O. "Status, Religion, and the 'Belief in a Just World': Comparing African Americans, Latinos, and Whites." *Social Science Quarterly* 81 (2000) 325–43. https://www.jstor.org/stable/42864385.

Hurst, Jack. *Nathan Bedford Forrest: A Biography*. New York: Vintage, 1994.

Iati, Marisa. "Conversion Therapy Center Founder Who Sought to Turn LGBTQ Christians Straight Says He's Gay, Rejects 'Cycle of Self Shame.'" https://www.washingtonpost.com/religion/2019/09/03/conversion-therapy-center-founder-who-sought-turn-lgbtq-christians-straight-now-says-hes-gay-rejects-cycle-shame/.

———. "What is Critical Race Theory, and Why Do Republicans Want to Ban It in Schools?" https://www.washingtonpost.com/education/2021/05/29/critical-race-theory-bans-schools/.

Imhoff, Jordyn. "Health Inequality Actually Is a "Black and White Issue," Research Says." https://healthblog.uofmhealth.org/lifestyle/health-inequality-actually-a-black-and-white-issue-research-says.

Inbar, Yoel, et al. "Disgust Sensitivity Predicts Intuitive Disapproval of Gays." *Emotion* 9 (2009) 435–39. https://doi.org/10.1037/a0015960.

Inbar, Yoel, et al. "Disgusting Smells Cause Decreased Liking of Gay Men." *Emotion* 12 (2012) 23–27. https://doi.org/10.1037/a0023984.

Ingraham, Christopher. "Black Men Sentenced to More Time for Committing the Exact Same Crime as a White Person, Study Finds." *Washington Post*, November 16, 2017.

Iqbal, Nosheen. "Academic Robin DiAngelo: 'We Have to Stop Thinking About Racism as Someone Who Says the N-Word.'" https://www.theguardian.com/world/2019/feb/16/white-fragility-racism-interview-robin-diangelo.

Irons, Meghan E. "Researchers Expected 'Outrageously High' Discrimination Against Black Renters. What They Found was Worse than Imagined." https://www.bostonglobe.com/2020/07/01/metro/blacks-voucher-holders-face-egregious-housing-discrimination-study-says/.

Isom, D. A., et al. "Status Threat, Social Concerns, and Conservative Media: A Look at White America and the Alt-Right." *Societies* 11.71 (2021). https://doi.or/10.3390/soc11030072.

Jackson, Joshua Conrad, et al. "The Faces of God in America: Revealing Religious Diversity Across People and Politics." *PLoS One* 13 (2018). https://doi.org/10.1371/journal.pone.0198745.

Jarmolowicz, D. P., et al. "Sunk costs, psychological symptomology, and help seeking." *SpringerPlus* 5 (2016) 1699. https://doi.org/10.1186/s40064-016-3402-z.

Jarrett, Christian. "Three Years of Research into #thedress, Digested—a Lesson in Humility for Perceptual Science." https://digest.bps.org.uk/2018/05/16/three-years-of-research-into-thedress-digested-a-lesson-in-humility-for-perceptual-science/.

Jauk, Emanuel, et al. "The Relationship between Grandiose and Vulnerable (Hypersensitive) Narcissism." *Frontiers in Psychology* 8 (2017). https://doi.org/10.3389/fpsyg.2017.01600.

Jefferies, Philip, and Michael Ungar. "Social Anxiety in Young People: A Prevalence Study in Seven Countries." *PLoS One* 15 (2020) https://doi.org/10.1371/journal.pone.0239133.

Jenkins, Jack. "More Than a Quarter of White Evangelicals Believe Core QAnon Conspiracy Theory." https://www.ncronline.or/news/politics/survey-more-than-a-quarter-white-evangelicals-believe-core-qanon-conspiracy-theory.

Jensen, Michael, and Kane Sheehan. "QAnon Offenders in the United States." National Consortium for the Study of Terrorism and Responses to Terrorism, College Park, MD (May 2021). https://www.start.umd.edu/pubs/START_PIRUS_QAnon_Feb2021.pdf.

Johnson, David J., et al. "Officer characteristics and racial disparities in fatal officer-involved shootings." *Proceedings of the National Academy of Sciences (PNAS)* 116.32 (August 6, 2019) 15877–82. https://pnas.org/doi/full/10.1073/pnas.1903856116.

Johnson, David J., et al. "Retraction for Johnson et al., 'Officer characteristics and racial disparities in fatal officer-involved shootings.'" *Proceedings of the Nationals Academy of Sciences (PNAS)* 117.30 (July 28, 2020) 18130. https://doi.org/10.1073/pnas.2014148117.

Jolley, Daniel, et al. "Belief in Conspiracy Theories and Intentions to Engage in Everyday Crime." *British Journal of Social Psychology* 58 (2019) 534–49. https://doi.org/10.1111/bjso.12311.

Jolley, Daniel, et al. "Exposure to Intergroup Conspiracy Theories Promotes Prejudice which Spreads Across Groups." *British Journal of Psychology* 111 (2020) 17–35. https://doi.org/10.1111/bjop.12385.

Jonas, Eva, et al. "Focus Theory of Normative Conduct and Terror-Management Theory: The Interactive Impact of Mortality Salience and Norm Salience on Social Judgment." *Journal of Personality and Social Psychology* 95 (2008) 1239–51. https://doi.org/10.1037/a0013593.

Jones, Eva, and Peter Fischer. "Terror management and religion: Evidence that intrinsic religiousness mitigates worldview defense following mortality salience." *Journal of Personality and Social Psychology* 91 (2006) 553–67. https://doi.org/10.1037/0022-3514.91.3.553.

Jones, Rachel K., et al. "Abortion Incidence and Service Availability in the United States, 2017." *New York: Guttmacher Institute* (2019). https://doi.org/10.1363/4304111.

Jones, Robert P. "Racism Among White Christians is Higher than Among the Nonreligious. That's No Coincidence." https://www.nbcnews.com/think/opinion/racism-among-white-christians-higher-among-nonreligious-s-no-coincidence-ncna1235045.

———. *White Too Long: The Legacy of White Supremacy in American Christianity.* New York: Simon & Schuster, 2020.

Jost, John T. "Anger and Authoritarianism Mediate the Effects of Fear on Support for the Far Right: What Vasilopoulos et al. (2019) Really Found." *Political Psychology* 40 (2019) 705–11. https://doi.org/ 10.1111/pops.12567.

Jost, John T., et al. "The Politics of Fear: Is There an Ideological Asymmetry in Existential Motivation? *Social Cognition* 35 (2017) 324–53. https://doi.org/10.1521/soco.2017.35.4.324.

Jovančević, Ana, and Nebojša Milićević. "Optimism-pessimism, conspiracy theories and general trust as factors contributing to COVID-19 related behavior—A cross-cultural study." *Personality and Individual Differences* 167 (2020) 110216–22. https://doi.org/10.1016/j.paid.2020.110216.

Just the Facts Coalition. *Just the Facts About Sexual Orientation and Youth: A Primer for Principals, Educators, and School Personnel.* Washington, DC: American

Psychological Association. https://www.apa.org/pi/lgbt/resources/just-the-facts. pdf.

Kabarriti, Rafi, et al. "Association of Race and Ethnicity With Comorbidities and Survival Among Patients With COVID-19 at an Urban Medical Center in New York." *JAMA Network Open* 3 (2020). https://jamanetwork.com/journals/ jamanetworkopen/fullarticle/2770960.

Kahneman, Daniel, and Amos Tversky. "Prospect Theory: An Analysis of Decision under Risk." *Econometrica* 47.2 (1979) 263–91.

Kaminska, Izabella. "The 'Game Theory' in the Qanon Conspiracy Theory." https:// www.ft.com/content/74f9d2of-9ff9-4fad-808f-c7e4245a1725.

Kämmerer, Annette. "The Scientific Underpinnings and Impacts of Shame." https:// www.scientificamerican.com/article/the-scientific-underpinnings-and-impacts-of-shame/.

Kanai, Ryota, et al. "Political Orientations are Correlated with Brain Structure in Young Adults." *Current Biology* 21 (2011) 677–80. https://doi.org/10.1016/j. cub.2011.03.017.

Kanamori, Yasuko, et al. "A Comparison Between Self-Identified Evangelical Christians' and Nonreligious Persons' Attitudes Toward Transgender Persons." *Psychology of Sexual Orientation and Gender Diversity* 4 (2017) 75–86. https://doi.org/10.1037/ sgd0000166.

Kanamori, Yasuko, et al. "Christian Religiosity and Attitudes Toward the Human Value of Transgender Individuals." *Psychology of Sexual Orientation and Gender Diversity* 6 (2019) 42–53. https://doi.org/10.1037/sgd0000305.

Karimi, Faith. "A 911 call, a racial slur, a refusal to cash a check. This is what it's like for some Black bank customers." https://www.cnn.com/2020/07/02/us/banking-while-black-racism-trnd/index.html.

Kashdan, Todd B. "Psychological Flexibility as a Fundamental Aspect of Health." *Clinical Psychology Review* 30 (2010) 865–78. https://doi.org/10.1016/j.cpr.2010.03.001.

Kashima, Emi S. "Culture and Terror Management: What is 'Culture' in Cultural Psychology and Terror Management Theory?" *Social and Personality Psychology Compass* 4 (2010) 164–73. https://doi.org/10.1111/j.1751-9004.2009.00248.x.

Kaur, Harmeet. "These Variables Affect Whether You Live, Die or Get Help During the Pandemic." https://www.cnn.com/2020/08/20/us/systemic-racism-coronavirus-pandemic-trnd/index.html.

Keen, Sam. *The Passionate Life: Stages of Loving.* San Francisco: Harper, 1992.

Kellaway, Mitch. "Trans Teen Activist, Former Homecoming King, Dies in Charlotte, NC." https://www.advocate.com/obituaries/2015/03/24/trans-teen-activist-home coming-king-dies.

Kelly, John. "Analysis of Police Arrests Reveals Stark Racial Disparity in NY, NJ and CT." https://abc7ny.com/police-racial-bias-profiling-disparity-in-arrests-black-arrest -rates/6241175/.

Kerby, Lauren. "White Christian Nationalists Want More Than Just Political Power." https://www.theatlantic.com/ideas/archive/2021/01/white-evangelicals-fixation-on-washington-dc/617690/.

Khazanchi, Rohan, et al. "Racism, Not Race, Drives Inequity Across the COVID-19 Continuum." *JAMA Network Open* 3 (2020) https://jamanetwork.com/journals/ jamanetworkopen/fullarticle/2770954.

Kim, H. Nina, et al. "Assessment of Disparities in COVID-19 Testing and Infection Across Language Groups in Seattle, Washington." *JAMA Network Open* 3 (2020). https://jamanetwork.com/journals/jamanetworkopen/fullarticle/2770951.

Kinnaman, David. "Barna's Perspective on Race and the Church." https://www.barna.com/barnas-perspective-on-race-and-the-church/.

Kinnaman, David, and Brooke Hempell. "U.S. Adults See Evangelicals Through a Political Lens." https://www.barna.com/research/evangelicals-political-lens/.

Kinnaman, David, and Gabe Lyons. *unChristian: What a New Generation Really Thinks About Christianity and Why it Matters.* Grand Rapids: Baker, 2007.

Kiss, Mark J., et al. "A Meta-Analytic Review of the Association Between Disgust and Prejudice Toward Gay Men." *Journal of Homosexuality* 67 (2020) 674–96. https://doi.org/10.1080/00918369.2018.1553349.

Kjærvik, Sophie, and Brad Bushman. "The link between narcissism and aggression: A meta-analytic review." *Psychological Bulletin* 147 (2021) 477–503. https://doi.org/10.1037/bul0000323.

Klain, Hannah, et al. "Waiting to Vote: Racial Disparities in Election Day Experiences." https://www.brennancenter.org/sites/default/files/2020-06/6_02_WaitingtoVote_FINAL.pdf.

Klass, Brian. "Why is it so hard to deprogram Trumpian conspiracy theorists?" https://www.washingtonpost.com/opinions/2021/01/25/why-is-it-so-hard-deprogram-trumpian-conspiracy-theorists/.

Klein, Ezra. "Why Are Liberals More Afraid of the Coronavirus Than Conservatives?" https://www.vox.com/2020/5/21/21262329/coronavirus-liberals-conservatives-polls-afraid-psychology-distacing.

Klein, Joyce A. "Bridging the Divide: How Business Ownership Can Help Close the Racial Wealth Gap." https://www.aspeninstitute.org/wp-content/uploads/2017/01/Briding-the-Divide.pdf.

Klein, Linda Kay. *Pure: Inside the Evangelical Movement that Shamed a Generation of Young Women and How I Broke Free.* New York: Touchstone, 2018.

Kleinberg, Jeffrey. "The Dynamics of Corruptogenic Organizations." *Journal of Group Psychotherapy* 64 (2014) 421–43. https://doi.org/10.1521/ijgp.2014.64.4.420.

Knowles, Hannah. "Number of Working Black Business Owners Falls 40 Percent, Far More Than Other Groups Amid Coronavirus." https://www.washingtonpost.com/business/2020/05/25/black-minority-business-owners-coronavirus/.

Knox, Dean, and Jonathan Mummolo. "A Widely Touted Study Found No Evidence of Racism in Police Shootings. It's Full of Errors." https://www.washingtonpost.com/outlook/2020/07/15/police-shooting-study-retracted/.

Kobes Du Mez, Kristin. *Jesus and John Wayne: How White Evangelicals Corrupted a Faith and Fractured a Nation.* New York: Liveright, 2020.

Kohler, Will. "Gay History—June 19, 1983: Founder of the Moral Majority Jerry Falwell: 'AIDS is God's Punishment for Homosexuals.'" http://www.back2stonewall.com/2021/06/gay-history-june-19-1983-jerry-falwell-aids-gods-punishment-homosexuals.html.

Kolata, Gina. "Social Inequities Explain Racial Gaps in Pandemic, Studies Find." https://www.nytimes.com/2020/12/09/health/coronavirus-black-hispanic.html.

Kortsmit, Katherine, et al. "Abortion Surveillance—United States, 2018." *Morbidity and Mortality Weekly Report Surveillance Summary 2020* 69 (2020) 1–29. http://dx.doi.org/10.15585/mmwr.ss6907a1.

Kraus, Michael W., et al. "The Misperception of Racial Economic Inequality." *Perspectives on Psychological Science* 14 (2019) 899–921. https://doi.org/10.1177 %2F1745691619863049.

Kristian, Bonnie. "QAnon is a Wolf in Wolf's Clothing." https://www.christianitytoday. com/ct/2020/august-web-only/qanon-is-wolf-in-wolfs-clothing.html.

Krouwel, Andre, et al. "Does Extreme Political Ideology Predict Conspiracy Beliefs, Economic Evaluations, and Political Trust? Evidence From Sweden." *Journal of Social and Political Psychology* 5 (2018) 435–62. https://doi.org/10.5964/jspp. v5i2.745.

Kruger, Justin, and David Dunning. "Unskilled and Unaware of It: How Difficulties in Recognizing One's Incompetence Lead to Inflated Self-Assessments." *Journal of Personality and Social Psychology* 77 (1999) 1121–34.

Kteily, Nour S., et al. "Social Dominance Orientation: Cause or 'Mere Effect'? Evidence for SDO as a Causal Predictor of Prejudice and Discrimination Against Ethnic and Racial Outgroups." *Journal of Experimental Social Psychology* 47 (2011) 208–14. https://doi.org/10.1016/j.jesp.2010.09.009.

Kumar, Anugrah. "Are Most Single Christians in America Having Sex?" https://www. christianpost.com/news/are-most-single-christians-in-america-having-sex.html.

Kunst, Jennifer L., et al. "Causal Attributions for Uncontrollable Negative Events." *Journal of Psychology and Christianity* 19 (2000) 47–60. https://psycnet.apa.org/ record/2000-07654-003.

Kurtzleben, Danielle. "Data Show Racial Disparity in Crack Sentencing." https://www. usnews.com/news/articles/2010/08/03/data-show-racial-disparity-in-crack-sentencing.

———. "Seeking Suburban Votes, Trump To Repeal Rule Combating Racial Bias In Housing." https://www.npr.org/2020/07/21/893471887/seeking-suburban-votes-trump-targets-rule-to-combat-racial-bias-in-housing.

Labberton, Mark, ed. *Still Evangelical? Insiders Reconsider Political, Social, and Theological Meaning.* Downers Grove, IL: InterVarsity, 2018.

Lace, John W., et al. "Five-Factor Model Personality Traits and Self-Classified Religiousness and Spirituality." *Journal of Religion and Health* 59 (2020) 1344–69. https://doi.org/10.1007/s10943-019-00847-1.

Ladd, Chris. "The Article Removed from Forbes, 'Why White Evangelicalism Is So Cruel.'" https://www.politicalorphans.com/the-article-removed-from-forbes-why-white-evangelicalism-is-so-cruel/.

LaFrance, Adrienne. "The Prophecies of Q." https://www.theatlantic.com/magazine/ archive/2020/06/qanon-nothing-can-stop-what-is-coming/610567/.

Landor, Antoinette M., and Leslie Gordon Simons. "Why Virginity Pledges Succeed or Fail: The Moderating Effect of Religious Commitment Versus Religious Participation." *Journal of Child and Family Studies* 26 (2014) 1102–13. https://doi. org/10.1007/s10826-013-9769-3.

Lang, Cady. "President Trump Has Attacked Critical Race Theory. Here's What to Know About the Intellectual Movement." https://time.com/5891138/critical-race-theory-explained/.

Lantian, Anthony, et al. "'I Know Things They Don't Know!' The Role of Need for Uniqueness in Belief in Conspiracy Theories." *Social Psychology* 48 (2017) 160–73. https://doi.org/10.1027/1864-9335/a000306.

Lawson, Ronald L. "The Troubled Career of an 'Ex-Gay' Healer: Colin Cook, Seventh-day Adventists, and the Christian Right." https://ronaldlawson.net/2018/06/11/the-troubled-career-of-an-ex-gay-healer-colin-cook-seventh-day-adventists-and-the-christian-right/.

Layne, Nathan, et al. "Details Emerge About Man Arrested in Georgia Shootings." https://www.reuters.com/article/us-crime-georgia-spas-suspect/details-emerge-about-man-arrested-in-georgia-shootings-idUSKBN2B92L3.

Leak, Gary K., and Brandy A. Randall. "Clarification of the Link Between Right-Wing Authoritarianism and Religiousness: The Role of Religious Maturity." *Journal for the Scientific Study of Religion* 34 (1995) 245–52. https://doi.org/10.2307/1386769.

Lee, Lewina O., et al. "Optimism is Associated with Exceptional Longevity in 2 Epidemiologic Cohorts of Men and Women." *Proceedings of the National Academy of Sciences of the United States of America* 10 (2019) 18357–62. https://doi.org/10.1073/pnas.1900712116.

Lee, Morgan. "Christian Nationalism is Worse Than You Think." https://www.christianitytoday.com/ct/podcasts/quick-to-listen/christian-nationalism-capitol-riots-trump-podcast.html.

Lee, Royce J., et al. "Narcissistic and Borderline Personality Disorders: Relationship with Oxidative Stress." *Journal of Personality Disorders* 34 (2020) 6–24. https://doi.org/10.1521/pedi.2020.34.supp.6.

Lemons, Stephen. "Tempe Pastor Hails Orlando Massacre for Leaving '50 Less Pedophiles in This World': Video." https://www.phoenixnewtimes.com/news/tempe-pastor-hails-orlando-massacre-for-leaving-50-less-pedophiles-in-this-world-video-8372346.

Leone, Luigi, et al. "Avoidant Attachment Style and Conspiracy Ideation." *Personality and Individual Differences* 134 (2018) 329–36. https://doi.org/10.1016/j.paid.2018.06.043.

Leone, Luigi., et al. "HEXACO, Social Worldviews and Socio-Political Attitudes: a Meditation Analysis." *Personality and Individual Differences* 53 (2012) 995–1001. http://dx.doi.org/10.1016/j.paid.2012.07.016.

Leong, Yuan C., et al. "Conservative and Liberal Attitudes Drive Polarized Neural Responses to Political Content." *Proceedings of the National Academy of Sciences of the United States of America* 117 (2020) 27731–39. https://doi.org/10.1073/pnas.2008530117.

Leonhardt, David. "Details on the List of Trump's Racist Statements." https://www.nytimes.com/2018/01/15/opinion/donald-trump-racist-statements.html.

Leonhardt, David, and Ian Prasad Philbrick. "Donald Trump's Racism: The Definitive List, Updated." https://www.nytimes.com/interactive/2018/01/15/opinion/leonhardt-trump-racist.html.

Lett, E., et al. "Racial inequity in fatal US police shootings, 2015–2020." *Journal of Epidemiology & Community Health* 75 (2021) 394–97.

Levari, David E., et al. "Prevalence-Induced Concept Change in Human Judgement." *Science* 360 (2018) 1465–67. https://doi.org/10.1126/science.aap8731.

Levin, Michael E., et al. "Examining Psychological Inflexibility as a Transdiagnostic Process Across Psychological Disorders." *Journal of Contextual Behavioral Science* 3 (2014) 155–63. https://doi.org/10.1016/j.jcbs.2014.06.003.

Levine, Amir, and Rachel Heller. *Attached: The New Science of Adult Attachment and How It Can Help You Find and Keep Love.* New York: TarcherPerigee, 2012.

Lewis, Andrew R., and Dana Huyser de Bernardo. "Belonging Without Belonging: Utilizing Evangelical Self-Identification to Analyze Political Attitudes and Preferences." *Journal for the Scientific Study of Religion* 49.1 (2010) 112–26. http://www.jstor.org/stable/40664679.

Lewis, John. "Together, You Can Redeem the Soul of Our Nation." https://www.nytimes.com/2020/07/30/opinion/john-lewis-civil-rights-america.html.

Li, Wei. "Racial Disparities in COVID-19." https://sitn.hms.harvard.edu/flash/2020/racial-disparities-in-covid-19/.

Lieber, Ron, and Tara Siegel Bernard. "The Stark Racial Inequity of Personal Finances in America." https://www.nytimes.com/2020/06/09/your-money/race-income-equality.html.

Lifeway Research. "Evangelical Beliefs and Identity." http://lifewayresearch.com/wp-content/uploads/2017/12/Evangelical-Beliefs-and-Identity.pdf.

Linzer, Drew. "Civics National Politics Survey: September 2020." https://civiqs.com/documents/Civiqs_DailyKos_monthly_banner_book_2020_09_klw74f.pdf.

Lipka, Michael. "Evangelicals increasingly say it's becoming harder for them in America." https://www.pewresearch.org/fact-tank/2016/07/14/evangelicals-increasingly-say-its-becoming-harder-for-them-in-america/.

Lipkusa, Isaac M., et al. "The Importance of Distinguishing the Belief in a Just World for Self Versus Others: Implications for Psychological Well-Being." *Personality and Social Psychology Bulletin* 22 (1996) 666–77. https://doi.org/10.1177/0146167296227002.

Liptak, Adam. "A Vast Racial Gap in Death Penalty Cases, New Study Finds." https://www.nytimes.com/2020/08/03/us/racial-gap-death-penalty.html.

Lofstrom, Magnus, and Brandon Martin. "Toward Understanding Racial Disparities in Arrests." https://www.ppic.org/blog/toward-understanding-racial-disparities-in-arrests/.

Long, Heather, and Andrew Van Dam. "The Black-white Economic Divide is as Wide as It was in 1968." https://www.washingtonpost.com/business/2020/06/04/economic-divide-black-households/.

Lopez, German. "Survey: White Evangelicals Think Christians Face More Discrimination than Muslims." https://www.vox.com/identities/2017/3/10/14881446/prri-survey-muslims-christians-discrimination.

Louis-Jean, James, et al. "Coronavirus (COVID-19) and Racial Disparities: a Perspective Analysis." *Journal of Racial and Ethnic Health Disparities* 7 (2020). https://doi.org/10.1007/s40615-020-00879-4.

Łowicki, Paweł, and Marcin Zajenkowski. "No Empathy for People nor for God: The Relationship Between the Dark Triad, Religiosity and Empathy." *Personality and Individual Differences* 115 (2017) 169–73. https://doi.org/10.1016/j.paid.2016.02.012.

Luckhurst, Toby. "Wilmington 1898: When White Supremacists Overthrew a US Government." https://www.bbc.com/news/world-us-canada-55648011.

Ludden, David. "How Christians React to the Religion-Science Conflict." https://www.psychologytoday.com/us/blog/talking-apes/202007/how-christians-react-the-religion-science-conflict.

Luhby, Tami. "US Black-white Inequality in 6 Stark Charts." https://www.cnn.com/2020/06/03/politics/black-white-us-financial-inequality/index.html.

Luhrmann, T. M. *When God Talks Back: Understanding the American Evangelical Relationship With God*. New York: Vintage, 2012.

Luo, Michael. "American Christianity's White-Supremacy Problem." https://www.newyorker.com/books/under-review/american-christianitys-white-supremacy-problem.

———. "The Wasting of the Evangelical Mind." https://www.newyorker.com/news/daily-comment/the-wasting-of-the-evangelical-mind.

Luo, Yu L.L., and Huajian Cai. "A Behavioral Genetic Study of Intrapersonal and Interpersonal Dimensions of Narcissism." *PLOS One* 9 (2014). https://doi.org/10.1371/journal.pone.0093403.

Lyons, Julie. "Robert Jeffress Wants a Mean 'Son of a Gun' for President, Says Trump Isn't a Racist." https://www.dallasobserver.com/news/robert-jeffress-wants-a-mean-son-of-a-gun-for-president-says-trump-isnt-a-racist-8184721.

Maaß, Ulrike, et al. "Narcissists of a Feather Flock Together: Narcissism and the Similarity of Friends." *Personality and Social Psychology Bulletin* 42 (2016) 366–84. https://doi.org/10.1177/0146167216629114.

MacArthur, John, et al. "The Statement on Social Justice & the Gospel." https://statementonsocialjustice.com/.

Macdonald, Andrew. "Conspiracy Theories in a Time of Coronavirus: How to Address the Problems They Reveal." https://www.christianitytoday.com/edstetzer/2020/april/conspiracy-theories-in-time-of-coronavirus-how-to-address-p.html.

Mahdawi, Arwa. "Jane Roe's Deathbed Confession Exposes the Immorality of the Christian Right." https://www.theguardian.com/commentisfree/2020/may/20/jane-roe-abortion-arwa-mahdawi.

Maher, Bill. *Real Time with Bill Maher*. HBO, August 4, 2017.

Mallory, Christy, et al. "Conversion Therapy and LGBT Youth—Update." *UCLA: The Williams Institute* (2019). https://escholarship.org/uc/item/0937z8tn.

Manji, Irshad. *Don't Label Me: An Incredible Conversation for Divided Times*. New York: St. Martin's, 2019.

Manseau, Peter. "Some Capitol rioters believed they answered God's call, not just Trump's." https://www.washingtonpost.com/outlook/2021/02/11/christian-religion-insurrection-capitol-trump/.

March, Evita, and Jordan Springer. "Belief in Conspiracy Theories: The Predictive Role of Schizotypy, Machiavellianism, and Primary Psychopathy." *PLoS One* 14 (2019). https://doi.org/10.1371/journal.pone.0225964.

Marchese, David. "Rev. William Barber Believes America Is Reaping What It Has Sown." https://www.nytimes.com/interactive/2020/12/28/magazine/william-barber-interview.html.

Marchlewska, Marta, et al. "Populism as Identity Politics: Perceived In-Group Disadvantage, Collective Narcissism, and Support for Populism." *Social Psychology and Personality Science* 9 (2017) 151–62. https://doi.org/10.1177/1948550617732393.

Marcus, George E. "Applying the Theory of Affective Intelligence to Support for Authoritarian Policies and Parties." *Political Psychology* 40 (2019) 109–39. https://doi.org/10.1111/pops.12571.

Margo, Robert A. "Historical Perspectives on Racial Economic Differences: A Summary of Recent Research." https://www.nber.org/reporter/spring05/historical-perspectives-racial-economic-differences-summary-recent-research.

Marino, Brielle A. "The Psychology of Conspiracy Theories." https://www.psychologytoday.com/us/blog/adventures-in-cognition/202009/the-psychology-conspiracy-theories.

Marks, Gene. "Black-owned Firms Are Twice as Likely To be Rejected for Loans. Is This Discrimination?" https://www.theguardian.com/business/2020/jan/16/black-owned-firms-are-twice-as-likely-to-be-rejected-for-loans-is-this-discrimination

Marksjarvis, Gail. "Why Black Homeownership Rates Lag Even as the Housing Market Recovers." https://www.chicagotribune.com/business/ct-black-homeownership-plunges-0723-biz-20170720-story.html.

Marshall, Michael. "US Police Kill Up to 6 Times More Black People than White People." https://www.newscientist.com/article/2246987-us-police-kill-up-to-6-times-more-black-people-than-white-people/.

Martens, W. H. J. "Shame and Narcissism: Therapeutic Relevance of Conflicting Dimensions of Excessive Self Esteem, Pride, and Pathological Vulnerable Self. *Annals of the American Psychotherapy Association* 8.2 (2005) 10–17.

Martens, Willem. "A Multicomponential Model of Shame." *Journal for the Theory of Social Behavior* 35 (2005) 399–411. https://www.researchgate.net/publication/232566252_Shame_and_Narcissism_Therapeutic_Relevance_of_Conflicting_Dimensions_of_Excessive_Self_Esteem_Pride_and_Pathological_Vulnerable_Self.

Martin, George R. R. *A Game of Thrones (Song of Ice and Fire)*. New York: Bantam, 1996.

Martin, Rachel, and Jeffrey Young. "Schema Therapy." In *Handbook of Cognitive-Behavioral Therapies,* edited by Keith S. Dobson, 317–46. New York: Guilford, 2010.

Martin, Jeffery. "Donald Trump Says Critical Race Theory is 'Like a Cancer.'" https://www.newsweek.com/donald-trump-says-critical-race-theory-like-cancer-1534192.

Martin, Nina, et al. "Nothing Protects Black Women From Dying in Pregnancy and Childbirth." https://www.propublica.org/article/nothing-protects-black-women-from-dying-in-pregnancy-and-childbirth.

Martínez, Jessica, and Gregory A. Smith. "How the faithful voted: a preliminary 2016 analysis." https://www.pewresearch.org/fact-tank/2016/11/09/how-the-faithful-voted-a-preliminary-2016-analysis/.

Martino, Elio. "This is Why You Are Attracted to Conspiracy Theories." https://www.psychologytoday.com/us/blog/dark-side-psychology/202010/is-why-you-are-attracted-conspiracy-theories.

Maslow, A. H. "A Theory of Human Motivation." *Psychological Review* 50 (1943) 370–96. https://psycnet.apa.org/doi/10.1037/h0054346.

Mauch, Ally. "Josh Duggar Charged with Receiving and Possessing Child Pornography, Pleads Not Guilty." https://people.com/tv/josh-duggar-pleads-not-guilty/.

May, Charlie. "Trump Pastor on 'Fox & Friends': NFL Players Are Lucky to Not Be 'shot in the head' for protest." *Slate,* September 26, 2017.

Mayfield, D. L. "Why American evangelicals are so tempted by the easy assurance of conspiracy theories." https://religionnews.com/2020/06/05/why-american-evangelicals-are-so-tempted-by-the-easy-assurance-of-conspiracy-theories/.

Mbakwe, Tola. "Bible tops list of books Brits lie about reading." https://premierchristian.news/en/news/article/bible-tops-list-of-books-brits-lie-about-reading.

McAdams, Dan, et al. "What if there were no God? Politically conservative and liberal Christians imagine their lives without faith." *Journal of Research in Personality* 42.6 (2008) 1–5. https://www.sciencedirect.com/science/article/abs/pii/S0092656608001116?via%3Dihub.

McAuliffe, Kathleen. "Liberals and Conservatives React in Wildly Different Ways to Repulsive Pictures." https://www.theatlantic.com/magazine/archive/2019/03/the-yuck-factor/580465/.

McCarthy, Bill. "PolitiFact: QAnon hoax has been linked to violence. Fox News' Greg Gutfeld falsely claimed it hasn't." https://www.tampabay.com/florida-politics/buzz/2020/08/26/politifact-qanon-hoax-has-been-linked-to-violence-fox-news-greg-gutfeld-falsely-claimed-it-hasnt/#.

McCaulley, Esau. *Reading While Black: African American Biblical Interpretation as an Exercise in Hope.* Downers Grove, IL: InterVarsity, 2020.

McDonough, Katie. "Conversion therapy advocate issues formal apology, renounces "ex-gay" past." https://www.salon.com/2013/04/25/conversion_therapy_advocate_issues_formal_apology_renounces_ex_gay_past/.

McKernan, Signe-Mary, et al. "Nine Charts about Wealth Inequality in America (Updated)." https://apps.urban.org/features/wealth-inequality-charts/.

McLaughlin, Matt. "Sodomite Suppression Act: Penal Code Section 39." https://oag.ca.gov/system/files/initiatives/pdfs/15-0008%20%28Sodomy%29_0.pdf.

McLaughlin, Rebecca. *Confronting Christianity: 12 Hard Questions for the World's Largest Religion.* Wheaton, IL: Crossway, 2019.

Meacham, Jon. *His Truth is Marching On: John Lewis and the Power of Hope.* New York: Random House, 2020.

Menasce Horowitz, Juliana, et al. "Views of Racial Inequality." https://www.pewresearch.org/social-trends/2019/04/09/views-of-racial-inequality/.

Menasce Horowitz, Juliana, et al. "Race in America 2019." https://www.pewresearch.org/social-trends/2019/04/09/race-in-america-2019/.

Mendoza, Madalyn. "The Only Black Student: San Antonio Resident and Member of Norfolk 17 Dies." https://www.mysanantonio.com/news/local/history-culture/article/Louis-Cousins-one-of-historic-Norfolk-17-who-15001926.php.

Mentch, Lucas. "On Racial Disparities in Recent Fatal Police Shootings." *Statistics and Public Policy* 7 (2020) 9–18. https://doi.org/10.1080/2330443X.2019.1704330.

Merevick, Tony. "Exclusive: 9 Former Ex-Gay Leaders Join Movement to Ban Gay Conversion Therapy." https://www.buzzfeed.com/tonymerevick/exclusive-9-former-ex-gay-leaders-join-movement-to-ban-gay-c.

Merritt, Jonathan. "How Christians Turned Against Gay Conversion Therapy." https://www.theatlantic.com/politics/archive/2015/04/how-christians-turned-against-gay-conversion-therapy/390570/.

Meyers, Ethan A., et al. "Wronging past rights: The sunk cost bias distorts moral judgment." *Judgment and Decision Making* 14.6 (2019) 721–27.

Meyers, Seth. "Narcissistic Parents' Psychological Effect on Their Children." https://www.psychologytoday.com/us/blog/insight-is-2020/201405/narcissistic-parents-psychological-effect-their-children.

Michaels, Jay L., et al. "Individual Differences in Religious Motivation Influence How People Think." *Journal for the Scientific Study of Religion* 60 (2020) 64–82. https://doi.org/10.1111/jssr.12696.

Milbank, Dana. "Trump's Racist Appeals Powered a White Evangelical Tsunami." https://www.washingtonpost.com/opinions/2020/11/13/trumps-racist-appeals-powered-white-evangelical-tsunami/.

Miller, Joanne M. "Conspiracy Endorsement as Motivated Reasoning: The Moderating Roles of Political Knowledge and Trust." *American Journal of Political Science* 60 (2016) 824–44. https://doi.org/10.1111/ajps.12234.

Miller, Joshua D., et al. "Controversies in Narcissism." *Annual Review of Clinical Psychology* 13 (2017). https://www.researchgate.net/publication/315187414_Controversies_in_Narcissism.

Milloy, Courtland. "The Cure for Racial Disparities in Health Care is Known. It's the Willingness to Fix It that's Lagging." https://www.washingtonpost.com/local/the-cure-for-racial-disparities-in-health-care-is-known-its-the-willingness-to-fix-it-thats-lagging/2020/04/21/1ed28610-83c7-11ea-878a-86477a724bdb_story.html.

Mills, Rosemary S. L. "Taking Stock of the Developmental Literature on Shame." *Developmental Review* 25 (2005) 26–63.

Milton, Daniel, and Andrew Mines. "This is War." https://extremism.gwu.edu/sites/g/files/zaxdzs2191/f/This_is_War.pdf.

Miner Bridges, Maureen. "Psychological Contributions to Understanding Prejudice and the Evangelical Mind." https://christianscholars.com/psychological-contributions-to-understanding-prejudice-and-the-evangelical-mind/.

Mitchell, Amy, et al. "Three Months in, Many Americans see Exaggeration, Conspiracy Theories, and Partisanship in COVID-19 News." https://www.journalism.org/2020/06/29/most-americans-have-heard-of-the-conspiracy-theory-that-the-covid-19-outbreak-was-planned-and-about-one-third-of-those-aware-of-it-say-it-might-be-true/.

Mock, Brentin. "What New Research Says About Race and Police Shootings." https://www.bloomberg.com/news/articles/2019-08-06/race-and-police-shootings-what-new-research-says.

Mohler, Albert. "The Tragedy of Joshua Harris: Sobering Thoughts for Evangelicals." August 1, 2019. https://albertmohler.com/2019/08/01/joshua-harris.

Molina, Alejandra. "Black Lives Matter Co-founder Denounces Pat Robertson for Saying the Movement is 'Anti-God.'" https://religionnews.com/2020/09/12/black-lives-matter-co-founder-denounces-pat-robertson-for-saying-the-movement-is-anti-god/.

Morewedge, Carey K., and Colleen E. Giblin. "Explanations of the endowment effect: an integrative review." *Trends in Cognitive Sciences* 19.6 (2015) 339–48. https://www.cell.com/trends/cognitive-sciences/fulltext/S1364-6613(15)00078-9?_returnURL=https%3A%2F%2Flinkinghub.elsevier.com%2Fretrieve%2Fpii%2FS136461315000789%3Fshowall%3Dtrue.

Morford, Mark. "The Sad, Quotable Jerry Falwell / It's Bad Form to Speak Ill of the Dead. Good Thing This Man's Own Vile Words Speak for Themselves." https://www.sfgate.com/entertainment/morford/article/The-Sad-Quotable-Jerry-Falwell-It-s-bad-form-3302297.php.

Morris, Stephen G. "Empathy and the Liberal-Conservative Political Divide in the U.S." *Journal of Social and Political Psychology* 8 (2020) 8–24. https://doi.org/10.5964/jspp.v8i1.1102.

Moskalenko, Sophai. "Many QAnon Followers Report Mental Health Diagnoses." https://theconversation.com/many-qanon-followers-report-having-mental-health-diagnoses-157299.

———. "Opinion: QAnon Supporters Suffer From Poor Mental Health, Not Radical Extremism." https://www.marketwatch.com/story/qanon-supporters-suffer-from-poor-mental-health-not-radical-extremism-11616703136?mod=search_headline.

Moss, Candida. *The Myth of Persecution: How Early Christians Invented a Story of Martyrdom.* New York: HarperCollins, 2013.

Motiño, Alejandra, et al. "Cross-Cultural Analysis of Spiritual Bypass: A Comparison Between Spain and Honduras." *Frontiers in Psychology* 12 (2021) 658739. https://doi.org/10.3389/fpsyg.2021.658739.

Motta, Matthew, et al. "Knowing Less But Presuming More: Dunning-Kruger Effects and the Endorsement of Anti-Vaccine Policy Attitudes." *Social Science & Medicine* 211 (2018) 274–81. https://doi.org/10.1016/j.socscimed.2018.06.032.

Moulding, Richard., et al. "Better the Devil You Know than a World You Don't? Intolerance of Uncertainty and Worldview Explanations for Belief in Conspiracy Theories." *Personality and Individual Differences* 98 (2016) 345–54. https://doi.org/10.1016/j.paid.2016.04.060.

Moulding, Richard, et al. "Desire for Control, Sense of Control, and Obsessive-Compulsive Checking: An Extension to Clinical Samples." *Journal of Anxiety Disorders* 22 (2008) 1472–79. https://doi.org/10.1016/j.janxdis.2008.03.001.

Mullins, Angela. *Working for Uncle Henry.* Independently published, 2019.

Muñoz-Price, L. Silvia, et al. "Racial Disparities in Incidence and Outcomes Among Patients With COVID-19." *JAMA Network Open* 3 (2020). https://jamanetwork.com/journals/jamanetworkopen/fullarticle/2770961.

Murphy, Paul P. "Born on the Dark Fringes of the Internet, QAnon is Now Infiltrating Mainstream American Life and Politics." https://www.cnn.com/2020/07/03/us/what-is-qanon-trnd/index.html.

Nai, Alessandro, and Emre Toros. "The peculiar personality of strongmen: comparing the Big Five and Dark Triad traits of autocrats and non-autocrats." *Political Research Exchange* 2.1 (2001) 1–19. https://www.tandfonline.com/doi/full/10.1080/2474736X.2019.1707697.

Nash, Elizabeth, and Joerg Dreweke. "The U.S. Abortion Rate Continues to Drop: Once Again, State Abortion Restrictions are Not the Main Driver." *Guttmacher Policy Review* 22 (2019) 41–48. https://www.guttmacher.org/sites/default/files/article_files/gpr2204119.pdf.

Nashrulla, Tasneem, and Jim Dalrymple. "Here's What We Know About the Alleged "Pizzagate" Gunman." https://www.buzzfeednews.com/article/tasneemnashrulla/heres-what-we-know-about-the-pizzagate-gunman.

National Center for Education Statistics. "Indicators of School Crime and Safety: 2019." https://nces.ed.gov/programs/crimeindicators/index.asp.

National Center for Education Statistics. "National Assessment of Educational Progress." https://nces.ed.gov/nationsreportcard/.

National Institute of Mental Health. "Mental Health Information: Any Anxiety Disorder." https://www.nimh.nih.gov/health/statistics/any-anxiety-disorder.

Navarrete, Carlos David, and David M. T. Fessler. "Disease Avoidance and Ethnocentrism: The Effects of Disease Vulnerability and Disgust Sensitivity on Intergroup Attitudes." *Evolution and Human Behavior* 27 (2006) 270–82. https://doi.org/10.1016/j.evolhumbehav.2005.12.001.

Neal, Jennifer, and Donna Frick-Horbury. "The Effects of Parenting Styles and Childhood Attachment Patterns on Intimate Relationships." *Journal of Instructional Psychology* 28 (2001) 178. link.gale.com/apps/doc/A79370572/ITOF?u=tel_a_vanderbilt&sid=bookmark-ITOF&xid=37afbe56.

Nelson, Jessica C., et al. "The Marley Hypothesis: Denial of Racism Reflects Ignorance of History." *Psychological Science* 24 (2013) 213–18. https://doi.org/10.1177/0956797612451466.

Nelson, Samantha. "Paper Finding No Racial Bias in Shootings by Police Criticized." https://www.usatoday.com/story/news/nation-now/2016/07/21/paper-finding-no-racial-bias-shootings-police-criticized/87301632/.

The New York Times. "1619 Project." https://www.nytimes.com/interactive/2019/08/14/magazine/1619-america-slavery.html.

Nicolosi, Joseph, et al. "Retrospective Self-Reports of Changes in Homosexual Orientation: A Consumer Survey of Conversion Therapy Clients." *Psychological Reports* 86 (2000) 1071–88. https://doi.org/10.1177/003329410008600302.2.

Nie, Fanhao. "Adolescent Porn Viewing and Religious Context: Is the Eye Still the Light of the Body?" *Deviant Behavior* (2020) 1382–95. https://doi.org/10.1080/01639625.2020.1747154.

Noll, Mark A. *The Scandal of the Evangelical Mind.* Grand Rapids: Eerdmans, 1994.

Norman, Andy. "The Cause of America's Post-Truth Predicament." https://www.scientificamerican.com/article/the-cause-of-americas-post-truth-predicament/.

Northwestern University. "Political Conservatives Fear Chaos; Liberals Fear Emptiness." https://www.sciencedaily.com/releases/2008/09/080924124549.htm.

NPR. "Black Preschoolers Far More Likely to Be Suspended." https://www.npr.org/sections/codeswitch/2014/03/21/292456211/black-preschoolers-far-more-likely-to-be-suspended.

———. "Ousted Evangelical Reflects on Faith, Future." https://www.npr.org/transcripts/128776382.

NPR et al. "Discrimination in America: Experiences and Views of African Americans." https://media.npr.org/assets/img/2017/10/23/discriminationpoll-african-americans.pdf.

Oesterreich, Detlef. "Flight into Security: A New Approach and Measure of the Authoritarian Personality." *Political Psychology* 26 (2005) 275–97. https://www.jstor.org/stable/3792615.

Ohlheiser, Abby. "Evangelicals are Looking for Answers Online. They're Finding QAnon Instead." https://www.technologyreview.com/2020/08/26/1007611/how-qanon-is-targeting-evangelicals/.

Olito, Frank. "36 of the Most Popular Conspiracy Theories in the U.S." https://www.insider.com/popular-conspiracy-theories-united-states-2019-5.

Olmstead, Molly. "'God Have Mercy on and Help Us All': How Prominent Evangelicals Reacted to the Storming of the U.S. Capitol." https://slate.com/human-interest/2021/01/trump-capitol-riot-evangelical-leaders-reactions.html.

Oppel Jr., Richard A., et al. "The Fullest Look Yet at the Racial Inequity of Coronavirus." https://www.nytimes.com/interactive/2020/07/05/us/coronavirus-latinos-african-americans-cdc-data.html.

Osmundsen, Mathias, et al. "The Psychophysiology of Political Ideology: Replications, Reanalysis, and Recommendations." *Journal of Politics* 84.1 (January 2022). https://www.journals.uchicago.edu/doi/abs/10.1086/714780.

Owens, Ann. "Segregation by Household Composition and Income Across Multiple Spatial Scales." *Handbook on Urban Segregation*, edited by Sako Musterd, 239–53. Cheltenham, UK: Edward Elgar, 2020.

Owens, Ann. "Unequal Opportunity: School and Neighborhood Segregation in the USA." *Race and Social Problems* 12 (2020) 29–41. https://doi.org/10.1007/s12552-019-09274-z.

Oxley, Douglas R., et al. "Political Attitudes Vary with Physiological Traits." *Science* 321 (2008) 1667–70. https://doi.org/10.1126/science.1157627.

Packard, Josh, and Ashleigh Hope. *Church Refugees: Sociologists Reveal Why People are DONE with Church But Not Their Faith*. Loveland, CO: Group, 2015.

Paik, Anthony, et al. "Broken Promises: Abstinence Pledging and Sexual and Reproductive Health." *Journal of Marriage and Family* 78 (2016) 546–61. https://doi.org/10.1111/jomf.12279.

Palma, Sky. "A Simple Experiment Reveals a Stark Difference in How Trump and Biden Perceive Reality." https://www.rawstory.com/2020/09/a-simple-experiment-reveals-a-startling-difference-in-how-trump-and-biden-supporters-perceive-reality/.

Pänkäläinen, Mikko, et al. "Pessimism and risk of death from coronary heart disease among middle-aged and older Finns: an eleven-year follow-up study." *BMC Public Health* 16 (2016) 1124. https://doi.org/10.1186/s12889-016-3764-8.

Parent, Joseph M., and Joseph Uscinski. *American Conspiracy Theories*. New York: Oxford University Press, 2014.

Parent, Mike C., and Kevin Silva. "Critical Consciousness Moderates the Relationship Between Transphobia and 'Bathroom Bill' Voting." *Journal of Counseling Psychology* 65 (2018) 403–12. https://doi.org/10.1037/sgd0000305.

Patterson, Kiahnna. "Hidden History: The Norfolk 17." https://www.wavy.com/news/hidden-history-the-norfolk-17/.

Patton-Bullock, Tylena, and Fred Dews. "Charts of the Week: Racial Wealth Gap, COVID-19, Deaths of Despair." https://www.brookings.edu/blog/brookings-now/2020/07/10/charts-of-the-week-racial-wealth-gap-covid-19-deaths-of-despair/.

Paul Ekman Group. "What is Disgust?" https://www.paulekman.com/universal-emotions/what-is-disgust/.

Pease, Joshua. "The Fundamentalist Trap." https://newrepublic.com/article/151787/bill-gothard-fundamentalist-trap.

Perkins, John M. *One Blood: Parting Words to the Church on Race and Love*. Chicago: Moody, 2018.

Perry, Ryan, et al. "Dangerous and Competitive Worldviews: A Meta-Analysis of their Associations with Social Dominance Orientation and Right-Wing Authoritarianism." *Journal of Research in Personality* 47 (2013) 116–27. http://dx.doi.org/10.1016/j.jrp.2012.10.004.

Perry, Samuel L. *Addicted to Lust: Pornography in the Lives of Conservative Protestants*. New York: Oxford University Press, 2019.

———. "How Pornography Use Reduces Participation in Congregational Leadership: A Research Note." *Review of Religious Research* 61 (2019) 57–74. https://doi.org/10.1007/s13644-018-0355-4.

————. "Not Practicing What You Preach: Religion and Incongruence Between Pornography Beliefs and Usage." *The Journal of Sex Research* 55 (2018) 369–80. https://doi.org/10.1080/00224499.2017.1333569.

————. "Racial Habitus, Moral Conflict, and White Moral Hegemony Within Interracial Evangelical Organizations." *Qualitative Sociology* 35 (2012) 89–108. https://doi.org/10.1007/s11133-011-9215-z.

Perry, Samuel L., and George M. Hayward. "Seeing is (Not) Believing: How Viewing Pornography Shapes the Religious Lives of Young Americans." *Social Forces* 95 (2017) 1757–88. https://doi.org/10.1093/sf/sow106.

Perry, Samuel L., and Andrew L. Whitehead. "Linking Evangelical Subculture and Phallically Insecure Masculinity Using Google Searches for Male Enhancement." *Journal for the Scientific Study of Religion* 60 (2021) 442–53. https://doi.org/10.1111/jssr.12717.

————. "Only Bad for Believers? Religion, Pornography Use, and Sexual Satisfaction Among American Men." *The Journal of Sex Research* 56 (2019) 50–61. https://doi.org/10.1080/00224499.2017.1423017.

————. "Porn as a Threat to the Mythic Social Order: Christian Nationalism, Anti-Pornography Legislation, and Fear of Pornography as a Public Menace." *The Sociological Quarterly* (2020) 313–36. https://doi.org/10.1080/00380253.2020.1822220.

————. "Racialized Religion and Judicial Injustice: How Whiteness and Biblicist Christianity Intersect to Promote a Preference for (Unjust) Punishment." *Journal for the Scientific Study of Religion* 60 (2020) 46–63. https://www.researchgate.net/publication/345774281_Racialized_Religion_and_Judicial_Injustice_How_Whiteness_and_Biblicist_Christianity_Intersect_to_Promote_a_Preference_for_Unjust_Punishment.

Perry, Samuel L., et al. "Culture Wars and COVID-19 Conduct: Christian Nationalism, Religiosity, and Americans' Behavior During the Coronavirus Pandemic." *Journal for the Scientific Study of Religion* 59 (2020) 405–16. https://doi.org/10.1111/jssr.12677.

Perry, Samuel L., et al. "Prejudice and Pandemic in the Promised Land: How White Christian Nationalism Shapes Americans' Racist and Xenophobic Views of COVID-19." *Ethnic and Racial Studies* 44 (2021) 759–772. https://doi.org/10.1080/01419870.2020.1839114.

Perry, Samuel L., et al. "Save the Economy, Liberty, and Yourself: Christian Nationalism and Americans' Views on Government COVID-19 Restrictions." *Sociology of Religion: A Quarterly Review* (2020) 1–21. https://doi.org/10.1093/socrel/sraa047.

Perry, Tod. "Michael Che's Fantastic Take on the Phrase 'Black Lives Matter' is More Relevant Than Ever." https://megaphone.upworthy.com/p/michael-che-black-lives-matter.

Pettigrew, Thomas F. "Social Psychological Perspectives on Trump Supporters." *Journal of Social and Political Psychology* 5 (2017) 107–16. https://doi.org/10.5964/jspp.v5i1.750.

Pew Research Center. "Religious Beliefs and Views of Homosexuality." https://www.pewresearch.org/politics/2013/06/06/section-3-religious-belief-and-views-of-homosexuality/.

————. "Religious Landscape Study." https://www.pewforum.org/religious-landscape-study/.

———. "What Americans Know About Religion." https://www.pewforum.org/2019/07/23/what-americans-know-about-religion/.

Phillips, Morgan. "Trump tells voters who live in suburbs they 'will no longer be bothered' by low-income housing." https://www.foxnews.com/politics/trump-suburban-voters-housing-rule.

Phillips, Scott, and Justin Marceau. "Whom the State Kills." *Harvard Civil Rights–Civil Liberties Law Review* 55 (2020) 2–45. https://harvardcrcl.org/wp-content/uploads/sites/10/2020/08/08.10.2020-Phillips-Marceau-For-Website.pdf.

Philpott, Kent. *The Third Sex? Six Homosexuals Tell Their Stories.* Plainfield, NJ: Logos International, 1975.

Piacenza, Joanna. "Roughly Half the Electorate Views Christian Nationalism as a Threat." https://morningconsult.com/2019/04/02/roughly-half-the-electorate-views-christian-nationalism-as-a-threat/.

Picciotto, Gabriela, and Jesse Fox. "Exploring Experts' Perspectives on Spiritual Bypass: A Conventional Content Analysis." *Pastoral Psychology* 67 (2018) 65–84. https://doi.org/10.1007/s11089-017-0796-7.

Picheta, Rob. "Black Newborns 3 Times More Likely to Die When Looked After By White Doctors." https://www.cnn.com/2020/08/18/health/black-babies-mortality-rate-doctors-study-wellness-scli-intl/index.html.

Pierre, Joe. "How Does QAnon Hook People In?" https://www.psychologytoday.com/us/blog/psych-unseen/202009/how-does-qanon-hook-people-in.

Pinker, Steven. *The Better Angels of Our Nature: Why Violence Has Declined.* New York: Penguin, 2012

———."Is the World Getting Better or Worse? A Look at the Numbers." Filmed April 2018. TED video, 18:23. https://www.ted.com/talks/steven_pinker_is_the_world_getting_better_or_worse_a_look_at_the_numbers?language=en.

Planas, Antonio. "After she concealed her race, Black Indianapolis owner's home value more than doubled." https://www.nbcnews.com/news/us-news/after-concealing-her-race-black-indianapolis-owner-s-home-value-n1267710.

Posner, Sarah. "The Evangelicals Who Are Taking on QAnon." https://www.nytimes.com/2020/09/17/opinion/evangelicals-qanon.html.

———. *Unholy: Why White Evangelicals Worship at the Altar of Donald Trump.* New York: Random House, 2020.

Post, Jerrold M. "Narcissism and the Charismatic Leader-Follower Relationship." *Political Psychology* 7 (1986) 675–88. https://doi.org/10.2307/3791208.

Primack, Brian A., et al. "Use of Multiple Social Media Platforms and Symptoms of Depression and Anxiety: A Nationally Representative Study Among U.S. Young Adults." *Computers in Human Behavior* 69 (2017) 1–9. https://doi.org/10.1016/j.chb.2016.11.013.

Pryor, William H., et al. "Demographic Differences in Sentencing." United States Sentencing Commission, November 2017.

Przeworski, Amy, et al. "A Systematic Review of the Efficacy, Harmful Effects, and Ethical Issues Related to Sexual Orientation Change Efforts." *Clinical Psychology: Science and Practice* 28 (2021) 81–100. https://doi.org/10.1111/cpsp.12377.

Psychologist World. "Authoritarian Personality." https://www.psychologistworld.com/influence-personality/authoritarian-personality.

Public Religion Research Institute. "More Americans, especially White Evangelicals, Now Say Personal Immorality Not Disqualifying for Elected Officials." https://

www.prri.org/research/prri-brookings-oct-19-poll-politics-election-clinton-double-digit-lead-trump/.

———. "Understanding QAnon's Connection to American Politics, Religion, and Media Consumption." https://www.prri.org/research/qanon-conspiracy-american -politics-report/.

Pulliam, Sarah. "Richard Cizik Resigns From the National Association of Evangelicals." https://www.christianitytoday.com/ct/2008/decemberweb-only/150-42.0.html.

Pulliam Bailey, Sarah. "Alabama politician resigns as a Southern Baptist pastor after KKK leader's birthday celebration." *Washington Post*, July 30, 2020. https://www. washingtonpost.com/religion/2020/07/30/alabama-republican-resigns-southern-baptist/

———. "Black and White Evangelicals Once Talked About 'Racial Reconciliation.' Then Trump Came Along." https://www.washingtonpost.com/religion/2020/08/21/ black-and-white-evangelicals-trump-racial-reconciliation/.

———. "New Charges Allege Religious Leader, Who Has Ties to the Duggars, Sexually Abused Women." https://www.washingtonpost.com/news/acts-of-faith/wp/2016/01/06/new-charges-allege-religious-leader-who-has-ties-to-the-duggars-sexually-abused-women/.

———. "Poll Shows a Dramatic Generational Divide in White Evangelical Attitudes on Gay Marriage." https://www.washingtonpost.com/news/acts-of-faith/wp/2017 /06/27/there-is-now-a-dramatic-generational-divide-over-white-evangelical-attitudes-on-gay-marriage/.

Pulliam Bailey, Sarah, and Teo Armus. "Christian Leaders Wrestle with Atlanta Shooting Suspect's Southern Baptist Ties." https://www.washingtonpost.com/ religion/2021/03/17/atlanta-shooting-southern-baptist-pastors-wrestle/.

Puls, Darrell. "Narcissistic Pastors and the Making of Narcissistic Churches." *Great Commission Research Journal* 12 (2020) 67–92.

Putnam, Adam, et al. "Collective Narcissism: Americans Exaggerate the Role of their Home State in Appraising U.S. History." *Psychological Science* 29 (2018) 1414–1422.

Rabb, Nathaniel, et al. "Truths About Beauty and Goodness: Disgust Affects Moral but not Aesthetic Judgements." *Psychology of Aesthetics, Creativity, and the Arts* 10 (2016) 492–500. https://doi.org/10.1037/aca0000051.

Rabin, Roni Caryn. "Why the Coronavirus More Often Strikes Children of Color." https://www.nytimes.com/2020/09/01/health/coronavirus-children-minorities. html.

Raji, Deborah. "How Our Data Encodes Systematic Racism." https://www.technology review.com/2020/12/10/1013617/racism-data-science-artificial-intelligence-ai-opinion/.

Ramirez, Alejandro. "John Rich Is Angry About Lipscomb Academy's Dean of Intercultural Development." https://www.nashvillescene.com/news/pithinthewind/john-rich-is-angry-about-lipscomb-academys-dean-of-intercultural-development/article_ d0e7797a-9a3c-5f86-8e8c-fba6dba38951.html.

Ray, Travis N., and Michele R. Parkhill. "Heteronormativity, Disgust Sensitivity, and Hostile Attitudes Toward Gay Men: Potential Mechanisms to Maintain Social Hierarchies." *Sex Roles* 84 (2021) 49–60. https://doi.org/10.1007/s11199-020-01146-w.

Ream, Todd C., et al., eds. *The State of the Evangelical Mind: Reflections on the Past, Prospects for the Future*. Downers Grove, IL: IVP Academic, 2018.

Reed, Brad. "Mail Ballots Cast by Black Voters in North Carolina Rejected 4 times More than White Voters: Report." https://www.salon.com/2020/09/18/mail-ballots-cast-by-black-voters-in-north-carolina-rejected-4-times-more-than-white-voters-report_partner/.

Relationships in America Survey. "How Common is Premarital Sex?" https://relationshipsinamerica.com/relationships-and-sex/how-common-is-premarital-sex.

Relevant Staff. "This Megachurch Used Its Sunday Service to Spread QAnon Conspiracy Theories." https://www.relevantmagazine.com/culture/this-megachurch-used-its-sunday-service-to-spread-qanon-conspiracy-theories/.

————. "Why Are So Many Christians Falling for QAnon?" https://www.relevantmagazine.com/faith/church/why-are-so-many-christians-falling-for-qanon/.

Religion News Service. "Russell Moore to ERLC Trustees: 'They Want Me to Live in Psychological Terror.'" https://religionnews.com/2021/06/02/russell-moore-to-erlc-trustees-they-want-me-to-live-in-psychological-terror/.

Reneau, Annie. "A former QAnon believer answers all your questions about how the cult really works." https://www.upworthy.com/former-qanon-believer-q-and-a.

Resnick, Brian. "How 'Collective Narcissism' Helps Explain the Election of Trump." https://www.vox.com/science-and-health/2017/1/4/14106088/collective-narcissism-trump-brexit-psychology.

Richardson, Randi. "Tulsa Race Massacre, 100 Years Later: Why It Happened and Why It's Still Relevant Today." https://www.nbcnews.com/news/nbcblk/tulsa-race-massacre-100-years-later-why-it-happened-why-n1268877.

Rieper, Kaitlyn. "Religiosity and Conspiratorial Beliefs Linked in Baylor Religion Survey Findings." https://www.baylor.edu/mediacommunications/news.php?action=story&story=223733.

Rigney, Joe. "The Enticing Sin of Empathy: How Satan Corrupts through Compassion." https://www.desiringgod.org/articles/the-enticing-sin-of-empathy.

Ritchie, Hannah, and Max Roser. "Mental Health." https://ourworldindata.org/mental-health.

Ritter, Ryan S., and Jesse Lee Preston. "Gross Gods and Icky Atheism: Disgust Responses to Rejected Religious Beliefs." *Journal of Experimental Social Psychology* 47 (2011) 1225–30. https://doi.org/10.1016/j.jesp.2011.05.006.

Rivera, Joshua. "Vanished From the Earth." https://slate.com/human-interest/2021/05/rapture-fear-evangelical-americans-church-miller.html.

Roach, David. "SBC Recalls 'Year of Waking Up' Since Abuse Investigation." February 10, 2020. https://www.christianitytoday.com/news/2020/february-sbc-waking-up-houston-chronicle-abuse-investigation.html.

Roberts, Brent, et al. "It Is Developmental Me, Not Generation Me: Developmental Changes Are More Important Than Generational Changes in Narcissism—Commentary on Trzesniewski & Donnellan (2010)." *Perspectives on Psychological Science* 5 (2010) 97–102. https://doi.org/10.1177/1745691609357019.

Roberts, Steven O., and Michael T. Rizzo. "The Psychology of American Racism." *The American Psychologist* 76 (2021) 475–87. https://doi.org/10.1037/amp0000642.

Robertson, Campbell. "A Quiet Exodus: Why Black Worshipers Are Leaving White Evangelical Churches." https://nyti.ms/2De9fnP.

Robertson, John M. *Tough Guys and True Believers: Managing Authoritarian Men in the Psychotherapy Room*. New York: Routledge, 2012.

Robins, Amanda. "Narcissistic Families: Growing Up in the War Zone." https://psychcentral.com/blog/narcissistic-families-growing-up-in-the-war-zone/.

Roddel, Shannon. "Understanding Perceptions of Reputation, Identity Offers Opportunity, Study Shows." https://www.sciencedaily.com/releases/2017/08/170830155458.html.

Roets, Arne, et al. "Does Materialism Predict Racism? Materialism as a Distinctive Social Attitude and a Predictor of Prejudice." *European Journal of Personality* 20 (2006) 155–68. https://psycnet.apa.org/doi/10.1002/per.573.

Rogers, Adam. "The Science of Why No One Agrees on the Color of This Dress." https://www.wired.com/2015/02/science-one-agrees-color-dress/.

Rogers, Kaleigh. "Why QAnon Has Attracted So Many White Evangelicals." https://fivethirtyeight.com/features/why-qanon-has-attracted-so-many-white-evangelicals/.

Rohr, Richard, and John Feister. *Hope Against Darkness*. Cincinnati: Franciscan Media, 2002.

Roney, Marty. "Legislator, businessman and now preacher: Prattsville's Will Dismukes wears many hats." https://www.montgomeryadvertiser.com/story/news/2019/03/12/legislator-businessman-and-now-preacher-prattvilles-dismukes-wears-many-hats/3128731002/.

Roose, Kevin. "What is QAnon, the Viral, Pro-Trump Conspiracy Theory?" https://www.nytimes.com/article/what-is-qanon.html.

Rosenberg, Joyce M., and Justin Myers. "Minority-owned Companies Waited Months for Loans, Data Shows." https://apnews.com/article/technology-small-business-new-york-coronavirus-pandemic-7613e946275f085367b5fc8c9a496aea.

Rosenkrantz, Dani E., et al. "Cognitive-Affective and Religious Values Associated with Parental Acceptance of an LGBT Child." *Psychology of Sexual Orientation and Gender Diversity* 7 (2020) 55–65. https://doi.org/10.1037/sgd0000355.

Roser, Max, and Esteban Ortiz-Ospina. "Global Extreme Poverty." https://ourworldindata.org/extreme-poverty#citation.

———. "Literacy." https://ourworldindata.org/literacy#historical-perspective.

Roser, Max, and Hannah Ritchie. "Homicides." https://ourworldindata.org/homicides#global-long-run-perspective.

Roser, Max, et al. "Life Expectancy." https://ourworldindata.org/life-expectancy#life-expectancy-has-improved-globally.

Ross, Bobby. "Tulsa Race Massacre Prayer Room Highlights Churches' 1921 Sins, Seeks Healing." https://religionunplugged.com/news/2021/5/26/tulsa-race-massacre-prayer-room-highlights-churches-1921-sins-seeks-healing.

Rothwell, Jonathan D., and Pablo Diego-Roswell. "Explaining Nationalist Political Views: The Case of Donald Trump." http://dx.doi.org/10.2139/ssrn.2822059.

Routledge, Clay, et al. "Death and End Times: The Effect of Religious Fundamentalism and Mortality Salience on Apocalyptic Beliefs." *Religion, Brain, & Behavior* 8 (2018) 21–30. https://doi.org/10.1080/2153599X.2016.1238840.

Rozsa, Matthew. "Watching Far-Right TV is Single Largest Predictor of Falling for QAnon Conspiracy Theory: Report." https://www.rawstory.com/qanon-newsmax-oann/.

Rubin, Jennifer. "How White Supremacy Infected Christianity and the Republican Party." https://www.washingtonpost.com/opinions/2020/08/03/how-white-supremacy-infected-christianity-republican-party/.

Ryan, Caitlin, et al. "Family Acceptance in Adolescence and the Health of LGBT Young Adults." *Journal of Child and Adolescent Psychiatric Nursing* 23 (2010) 205–13. https://doi.org/10.1111/j.1744-6171.2010.00246.x.

Ryan, Caitlin, et al. "Parent Initiated Sexual Orientation Change Efforts with LGBT Adolescents: Implications for Young Adult Mental Health and Adjustment." *Journal of Homosexuality* 67 (2020) 159–73. https://doi.org/10.1080/00918369.2018.1538407

Saad, Lydia. "U.S. Perceptions of White-Black Relations Sink to New Low." https://news.gallup.com/poll/318851/perceptions-white-black-relations-sink-new-low.aspx.

Saiya, Nilay, and Stuti Manchanda. "Paradoxes of Pluralism, Privilege, and Persecution: Explaining Christian Growth and Decline Worldwide." *Sociology of Religion* (2021) 60–78. https://doi.org/10.1093/socrel/srab006.

Sakala, Leah. "Breaking Down Mass Incarceration in the 2010 Census: State-By-State Incarceration Rates by Race/Ethnicity." https://www.prisonpolicy.org/reports/rates.html.

Salcedo, Andrea. "Wisconsin Pharmacist Who Destroyed More Than 500 Vaccine Doses Believes Earth is Flat, FBI Says." https://www.washingtonpost.com/nation/2021/02/01/wisconsin-pharmacist-vaccine-flatearth/.

Samuels, Elyse, et al. "Surveillance Video Shows Atlanta Suspect Entered First Spa More than an Hour Before Shooting." https://www.washingtonpost.com/investigations/2021/03/19/surveillance-video-atlanta-shooting/.

Sands, Geneva. "White Supremacy is 'Most Lethal Threat' to the US, DHS Draft Assessment Says." https://www.cnn.com/2020/09/08/politics/white-supremacy-dhs-draft-assessment/index.html.

Sasaki, Natsu, et al. "Exposure to Media and Fear and Worry About COVID-19." *Psychiatry and Clinical Neurosciences* 74 (2020) 496–512. https://doi.org/10.1111/pcn.13095.

Sauls, Scott. *Jesus Outside the Lines: A Way Forward for Those Who are Tired of Taking Sides.* Carol Stream, IL: Tyndale House, 2015.

Schaffer, Lisa. "Georgia's Exact Match Voter-ID Law Tossed by Federal Judge." https://www.findlaw.com/legalblogs/courtside/georgias-exact-match-voter-id-law-tossed-by-federal-judge/.

Schermerhorn, Calvin. "Why the Racial Wealth Gap Persists, More than 150 Years After Emancipation." https://www.washingtonpost.com/outlook/2019/06/19/why-racial-wealth-gap-persists-more-than-years-after-emancipation/.

Schleiden, Cydney, et al. "Racial Disparities in Arrests: A Race Specific Model Explaining Arrest Rates Across Black and White Young Adults." *Child and Adolescent Social Work Journal* 37 (2020) 1–14. https://doi.org/10.1007/s10560-019-00618-7.

Schowalter, Brandon. "John Piper Warns Christians Against Critical Race Theory that Makes God of Self." https://www.christianpost.com/news/john-piper-warns-christians-critical-race-theory-makes-god-of-self.html.

Schrauf, Michael, et al. "The Scintillating Grid Illusion." *Vision Research* 37 (1997) 1033–38. https://doi.org/10.1016/S0042-6989(96)00255-6.

Schroeder, George. "Seminary Presidents Reaffirm Baptist Faith and Message, Declare Critical Race Theory Incompatible." https://www.baptistpress.com/resource-library/news/seminary-presidents-reaffirm-bfm-declare-crt-incompatible/.

Schulz, Lion, et al. "Dogmatism Manifests in Lowered Information Search Under Uncertainty." *Proceedings of the National Academy of Sciences of the United States of America* 117 (2020) 31527–34. https://doi.org/10.1073/pnas.2009641117.

Schwartz, Allan. "The Narcissist Versus the Narcissistic Personality Disorder." https://www.mentalhelp.net/blogs/the-narcissist-versus-the-narcissistic-personality-disorder/.

Schwartz, Gabriel L., and Jaquelyn L. Jahn. "Mapping Fatal Police Violence Across U.S. Metropolitan Areas: Overall Rates and Racial/ethnic Inequities, 2013–2017." *PLOS One* 15 (2020). https://doi.org/10.1371/journal.pone.0229686.

Scott, Elizabeth. "Ed Sheeran: Hard Work As Crucial As Education." https://news.sky.com/story/ed-sheeran-hard-work-as-crucial-as-education-10384257.

Scott, Elizabeth, and Rachel Goldman. "What is Optimism?" https://www.verywellmind.com/the-benefits-of-optimism-3144811.

Scott, Eugene. "More than Half of White Evangelicals Say America's Declining White Population is a Negative Thing." https://www.washingtonpost.com/news/the-fix/wp/2018/07/18/more-than-half-of-white-evangelicals-say-americas-declining-white-population-is-a-negative-thing/.

The Sentencing Project. "Criminal Justice Facts." https://www.sentencingproject.org/criminal-justice-facts/.

Serwer, Adam. "The Fight Over the 1619 Project is Not About the Facts." https://www.theatlantic.com/ideas/archive/2019/12/historians-clash-1619-project/604093/.

Sevi, Baris. "Brief Report: Tinder Users are Risk Takers and Have Low Sexual Disgust Sensitivity." *Evolutionary Psychological Science* 5 (2019) 104–8. https://doi.org/10.1007/s40806-018-0170-8.

Sharkey, Patrick, et al. "The Gaps Between White and Black America, in Charts." https://www.nytimes.com/interactive/2020/06/19/opinion/politics/opportunity-gaps-race-inequality.html.

Shear, Michael D. "Pence Won't Say the Words 'Black Lives Matter' in an Interview." https://www.nytimes.com/2020/06/19/us/politics/mike-pence-black-lives-matter.html.

Shellnut, Kate. "After Major Investigation, Southern Baptists Confront the Abuse Crisis They Knew Was Coming." https://www.christianitytoday.com/news/2019/february/southern-baptist-abuse-investigation-houston-chronicle-sbc.html.

———. "Two Prominent Pastors Break With SBC After Critical Race Theory Statement." https://www.christianitytoday.com/news/2020/december/charlie-dates-ralph-west-southern-baptist-sbc-crt.html.

Shenvi, Neil. "The Worldview Behind White Fragility." https://shenviapologetics.com/the-worldview-of-white-fragility-2/.

Sherwood, Harriet. "Author of Christian Relationship Guide Says He Has Lost His Faith." https://www.theguardian.com/world/2019/jul/29/author-christian-relationship-guide-joshua-harris-says-marriage-over.

Shook, Natalie J., et al. "'Dirty Politics': The Role of Disgust Sensitivity in Voting." *Translational Issues in Psychological Science* 3 (2017) 284–97. https://doi.org/10.1037/tps0000111.

Shpancer, Noam. "Systemic Racism Doesn't Rely on Racist People." https://www.
    psychologytoday.com/us/blog/insight-therapy/202006/systemic-racism-doesnt-
    rely-racist-people.
Sibley, Chris G., and John Duckitt. "Personality and Prejudice: A Meta-Analysis and
    Theoretical Review." *Personality and Social Psychology Review* 12 (2008) 248–79.
    https://doi.org/10.1177/1088868308319226.
Sidanius, Jim, et al. "You're Inferior and Not Worth Our Concern: The Interface
    Between Empathy and Social Dominance Orientation." *Journal of Personality* 81
    (2013) 313–23. https://doi.org/10.1111/jopy.12008.
Sider, Ronald J., ed. *The Spiritual Danger of Donald Trump*. Eugene, OR: Cascade, 2020.
Silk, Mark. "Of Pastors and Presidents." https://www.redletterchristians.org/of-pastors-
    and-presidents/.
Silliman, Daniel, and Kate Shellnutt. "Ravi Zacharias Hid Hundreds of Pictures
    of Women, Abuse During Massages, and a Rape Allegation." https://www.
    christianitytoday.com/news/2021/february/ravi-zacharias-rzim-investigation-
    sexual-abuse-sexting-rape.html.
Slee, April, et al. "Trends in Generalized Anxiety Disorders and Symptoms in Primary
    Care: UK Population-Based Cohort Study." *The British Journal of Psychiatry* 218
    (2021) 158–64. https://doi.org/10.1192/bjp.2020.159.
Smallpage, Steven M., et al. "The Partisan Contours of Conspiracy Theory Beliefs."
    Research and Politics (2017) 1–7. https://doi.org/10.1177/2053168017746554.
Smedley, Brian D., et al. *Unequal Treatment: Confronting Racial and Ethnic Disparities
    in Health Care*. Washington, DC: The National Academies, 2003.
Smith, James K.A. "What White Evangelical Christians Can't See When They See
    Racism." https://religionnews.com/2020/08/06/what-white-evangelical-christians
    -cant-see-when-they-see-racism/.
Smith, Timothy W., et al. "Optimism and Pessimism in Social Context: An Interpersonal
    Perspective on Resilience and Risk." *Journal of Research in Personality* 47 (2013)
    553–62. https://doi.org/10.1016/j.jrp.2013.04.006.
Sochos, Antigonos. "Authoritarianism, Trauma, and Insecure Bonds During the Greek
    Economic Crisis." *Current Psychology* 40 (2021) 1923–35. https://doi.org/10.1007/
    s12144-018-0111-5.
Sollenberger, Roger. "Tucker Carlson: 'If We're Going to Survive as a Country, We Must
    Defeat' Black Lives Matter." https://www.salon.com/2020/09/11/tucker-carlson-
    if-were-going-to-survive-as-a-country-we-must-defeat-black-lives-matter/.
Solomon, Danyelle, et al. "Systematic Inequality and American Democracy." https://
    www.americanprogress.org/issues/race/reports/2019/08/07/473003/systematic-
    inequality-american-democracy/.
Somers, Julian M., et al. "Prevalence and Incidence Studies of Anxiety Disorders: A
    Systematic Review of the Literature." *Canadian Journal of Psychiatry* 51 (2006)
    100–113. https://doi.org/10.1177%2F070674370605100206.
Sorokowski, Piotr, et al. "Sex Differences in Human Olfaction: A Meta-Analysis."
    Frontiers in Psychology 10 (2019). https://doi.org/10.3389/fpsyg.2019.00242.
Sosa, Chris. "How Evangelicals Support White Supremacy — Even Though They Reject
    Racism." https://www.salon.com/2017/08/21/how-evangelicals-support-white-su
    premacy-even-though-they-reject-racism_partner/.
Spellman, Jim, and Eric Marrapodi. "New Haggard Accuser: 'He Really Thought he Was
    Invincible.'" https://www.cnn.com/2009/CRIME/01/28/colorado.church.haggard/.

Stanton, Zack. "It's Time to Talk About Violent Christian Extremism." https://www. politico.com/news/magazine/2021/02/04/qanon-christian-extremism-nationalism-violence-466034?fbclid=IwAR3jrz1QU1abqyUH7vkspSwWZy6Vi_Ya-Zv_OgRWyX5MpKWv5iryD4hIT8s%23.

Starbird, Aspen D., and Paul A. Story. "Consequences of Childhood Memories: Narcissism, Malevolent, and Benevolent Childhood Experiences." *Child Abuse & Neglect* 108 (2020) 1–8. https://doi.org/10.1016/j.chiabu.2020.104656.

Stark, Rodney. "What Americans Really Believe: New Findings from the Baylor Surveys of Religion." http://www.isreligion.org/research/surveysofreligion.

Statistica Research Department. "Number of People Shot to Death by the Police in the United States from 2017 to 2021, By Race." https://www.statista.com/statistics/585152/people-shot-to-death-by-us-police-by-race/.

Steffen, Patrick R., and Kevin S. Masters. "Does Compassion Mediate the Intrinsic Religion-Health Relationship?" *Annals of Behavioral Medicine* 30 (2005) 217–24. https://doi.org/10.1207/s15324796abm3003_6.

Stelter, Brian. "QAnon is Conspiratorial, Dangerous, and Growing. And We're Talking About it all Wrong." https://www.cnn.com/2020/08/14/media/qanon-news-coverage/index.html.

Sterniskol, Anni, et al. "Collective Narcissism Predicts the Belief and Dissemination of Conspiracy Theories During the COVID-19 Pandemic." *Medical Letter on the CDC & FDA* (2020) 154. https://doi.org/10.31234/osf.io/4c6av.

Stevens, Ashlie D. "How Evangelicalism's Racist Roots and Purity Culture Teachings Catalyzed the Atlanta Killings." https://www.salon.com/2021/03/20/evangelical-purity-culture-racism-atlanta-shooter/.

————. "How the religious right's purity culture enables predatory behavior." https://www.salon.com/2020/08/27/jerry-falwell-predator-purity-culture/.

Stewart, Patrick A., et al. "The Effect of Trait and State Disgust on Fear of God and Sin." *Frontiers in Psychology* 11 (2020) 51. https://doi.org/10.3389/fpsyg.2020.00051.

Stojanov, Ana, et al. "Does Perceived Lack of Control Lead to Conspiracy Theory Beliefs? Findings from an online MTurk sample." *PLoS ONE* 15 (2020) 0237771. https://doi.org/10.1371/journal.pone.0237771.

Strauss, Valerie. "No Systemic Racism? Look at Student Achievement Gaps in Reading." https://www.washingtonpost.com/education/2021/06/19/systemic-racism-reading-scores/.

Strickhouser, Jason E. "Ignorance of History and Perceptions of Racism: Another Look at the Marley Hypothesis." *Social Psychological and Personality Science* 10 (2019) 977–85. https://www.researchgate.net/publication/328440107_Ignorance_of_History_and_Perceptions_of_Racism_Another_Look_at_the_Marley_Hypothesis.

Stringer, Heather. "5 Questions for Michael Kraus." *APA Monitor*, March 1, 2021, 27.

Strömwall, Leif A., et al. "Rape Victim and Perpetrator Blame and the Just World Hypothesis: The Influence of Victim Gender and Age." *Journal of Sexual Aggression* 19 (2013) 207–17. https://doi.org/10.1080/13552600.2012.683455.

Stronge, Samantha, et al. "Are People Becoming More Entitled Over Time? Not in New Zealand." *Personality and Social Psychology Bulletin* 44 (2017). https://www.researchgate.net/publication/320269069_Are_People_Becoming_More_Entitled_Over_Time_Not_in_New_Zealand.

Stroop, Christopher. "White Evangelicals Have Turned on Refugees." https://foreignpolicy.com/2018/10/29/white-evangelicals-have-turned-on-refugees/.

Sutin, Angelina R., et al. "Turning points and lessons learned: Stressful life events and personality trait development across middle adulthood." *Psychology and Aging* 25 (2010) 524–33. https://doi.org/10.1037/a0018751.

Sutton, Robbie M., and Karen M. Douglas. "Conspiracy Theories and the Conspiracy Mindset: Implications for Political Ideology." *Current Opinion in Behavioral Sciences* 34 (2020) 118–22. http://dx.doi.org/10.1016/j.cobeha.2020.02.015.

Swami, Viren, et al. "Putting the Stress on Conspiracy Theories: Examining Associations Between Psychological Stress, Anxiety, and Belief in Conspiracy Theories." *Personality and Individual Differences* 99 (2016) 72–76. https://doi.org/10.1016/j.paid.2016.04.084.

Swift, Art. "Majority in U.S. Still Believe JFK Killed in a Conspiracy." https://news.gallup.com/poll/165893/majority-believe-jfk-killed-conspiracy.aspx.

Taylor, Steve. "Spiritual Conspiracists: Why Are Spiritual People Attracted to Conspiracy Theories?" https://www.psychologytoday.com/us/blog/out-of-the-darkness/202101/the-appeal-conspiracy-theories-spiritual-people.

Taylor, Victoria. "Evangelicals are the least faithful when it comes to spouses, survey suggests." *New York Daily News*, June 3, 2014. https://www.nydailynews.com/lifestyle/survey-reveals-faiths-unfaithful-article-1.1815733.

Tangherlini, Timothy R. "An automated pipeline for the discovery of conspiracy and conspiracy theory narrative frameworks: Bridgegate, Pizzagate and storytelling on the web." *PLoS One* 15 (2020) 0233879. https://doi.org/10.1371/journal.pone.0233879.

Tangney, June Price. "Moral Affect: The Good, the Bad, and the Ugly." *Journal of Personality and Social Psychology* 61 (1991) 598–607. https://doi.org/10.1037/0022-3514.61.4.598.

Tangney, June Price, et al. "Relation of Shame and Guilt to Constructive versus Destructive Responses to Anger Across the Lifespan." *Journal of Personality and Social Psychology* 70 (1996) 797–809. https://doi.org/10.1037/0022-3514.70.4.797.

Tatum, Beverly Daniel. *Why Are All the Black Kids Sitting Together in the Cafeteria?* New York: Basic, 2017.

Taylor, Don. "Telling the Truth About Race." https://donaldhtaylorjr.wordpress.com/2020/05/29/telling-the-truth-about-race/.

Taylor, Steve. "The Appeal of Conspiracy Theories for Spiritual People." https://www.psychologytoday.com/us/blog/out-the-darkness/202101/the-appeal-conspiracy-theories-spiritual-people.

———. "The Psychology of Nationalism." https://www.psychologytoday.com/us/blog/out-the-darkness/202012/the-psychology-nationalism.

Tedeschi, Richard G., and Lawrence G. Calhoun. *Trauma and Transformation: Growing in the Aftermath of Suffering.* New York: Sage, 2020.

Terlizzi, Emily P., and Maria A. Villarroel. "Symptoms of Generalized Anxiety Disorder Among Adults: United States, 2019." *NCHS Data Brief* 378 (2019).

Terrizzi, John A. "On the Origin of Shame: Feelings of Disgust Toward the Self." PhD diss., West Virginia University, 2013. https://researchrepository.wvu.edu/etd/134.

Terrizzi, John A., and Natalie J. Shook "On the Origin of Shame: Does Shame Emerge From an Evolved Disease-Avoidance Architecture?" *Frontiers in Behavioral Neuroscience* 14 (2020) 19. https://doi.org/10.3389/fnbeh.2020.00019.

Terrizzi, John A., et al. "Disgust: A Predictor of Social Conservativism and Prejudicial Attitudes Toward Homosexuals." *Personality and Individual Differences* 49 (2010) 587–92. https://doi.org/10.1016/j.paid.2010.05.024.

Thaler, Richard. *Misbehaving: The Making of Behavioral Economics.* New York: W. W. Norton.

Thomas, Alexander, and Stella Chess. "The New York Longitudinal Study: From Infancy to Early Adult Life." In *The Study of Temperament: Changes, Continuities, and Challenges,* edited by Robert Plomin and Judith Dunn, 39–52. Hillsdale, NJ: Lawrence Erlbaum Associates, 1986.

Thomas, Naomi. "Coronavirus stresses Americans more than others, study finds." https://www.cnn.com/2020/08/06/health/us-coronavirus-mental-health-problems-wellness/index.html.

Thomas, Pierre, et al. "Driving While Black: ABC News Analysis of Traffic Stops Reveals Racial Disparities in Several US Cities." https://abcnews.go.com/US/driving-black-abc-news-analysis-traffic-stops-reveals/story?id=72891419.

Thompson, Clive. "QAnon Is Like a Game—a Most Dangerous Game." https://www.wired.com/story/qanon-most-dangerous-multiplatform-game/.

Throckmorton, Warren. "First study to refer to ex-gays discredited." https://www.wthrockmorton.com/2011/11/11/first-study-to-refer-to-ex-gays-discredited/.

————. "New Sexual Reorientation Study Off to a Shaky Start; Michael Mailey's Brain Scan Offer is Still Good." https://www.wthrockmorton.com/2017/03/07/new-sexual-reorientation-study-off-shaky-start-michael-baileys-brain-scan-offer-still-good/.

Timm, Jane C. "A white person and a Black person vote by mail in the same state. Whose ballot is more likely to be rejected?" https://www.nbcnews.com/politics/2020-election/white-person-black-person-vote-mail-same-state-whose-ballot-n1234126.

Tisby, Jemar. *The Color of Compromise: The Truth About the American Church's Complicity in Racism.* Grand Rapids: Wolgemuth & Associates, 2019.

————. "Southern Baptist Seminary Presidents Reaffirm Their Commitment to Whiteness." https://thewitnessbcc.com/southern-baptist-seminary-presidents-reaffirm-their-commitment-to-whiteness/.

Todd, Andrew R., et al. "Does Seeing Faces of Young Black Boys Facilitate the Identification of Threatening Stimuli?" *Journal of Psychological Science* 27 (2016) 384–93. https://doi.org/10.1177/0956797615624492.

Torchia, Christopher. "9/11 Conspiracy Theories Rife in the Muslim World." https://www.washingtonpost.com/wp-dyn/content/article/2010/10/02/AR2010100200663.html.

Tracy, Jessica L., et al. "The Physiological Basis of Psychological Disgust and Moral Judgements." *Journal of Personality and Social Psychology* 116 (2019) 15–32. https://doi.org/10.1037/pspa0000141.

Travers, Mark. "Five Charts That Will Change The Way You Think About Racial Inequality." https://www.forbes.com/sites/traversmark/2019/10/01/five-charts-that-will-change-the-way-you-think-about-racial-inequality/.

Truth Wins Out. "History of the Ex-Gay Ministries." https://archive.truthwinsout.org/history-of-the-ex-gay-ministries/.

Trzesniewski, Kali, and Richard Robins. "An Emerging Epidemic of Narcissism or Much Ado About Nothing?" *Journal of Research in Personality* 43 (2009) 498–501.

https://www.researchgate.net/publication/228079535_An_Emerging_Epidemic_
of_Narcissism_or_Much_Ado_About_Nothing.

Tuente, Stéphanie Klein, et al. "Hostile Attribution Bias and Aggression in Adults—A
Systematic Review." *Aggression and Violent Behavior* 46 (2019) 66–81. https://doi.
org/10.1016/j.avb.2019.01.009.

Turken, Sam. "Little Soldiers: Members Of Norfolk 17 Discuss Their Experiences
During School Integration." https://whro.org/news/local-news/7199-we-were-
the-soldiers-two-members-of-norfolk-17-discuss-their-experiences-during-
integration.

Turner, Patricia, and Stephanie Stockdale. *Today I Met a Rainbow*. Bloomington, IN:
AuthorHouse, 2013.

Twenge, Jean M., and Joshua D. Foster. "Mapping the Scale of the Narcissism Epidemic:
Increases in Narcissism 2002–2007 Within Ethnic Groups." *Journal of Research in
Personality* 42 (2008) 1619–22. https://doi.org/10.1016/j.jrp.2008.06.014.

Twenge, Jean M., and Thomas E. Joiner. "U.S. Census Bureau-Assessed Prevalence
of Anxiety and Depressive Symptoms in 2019 and During the 2020 COVID-19
Pandemic." *Depression & Anxiety* (2020) 1–3. https://doi.org/ 10.1002/da.23077.

Twenge, Jean M., et al. "Birth Cohort Increases in Psychopathology Among Young
Americans, 1938–2007: A Cross-Temporal Meta-Analysis of the MMPI." *Clinical
Psychology Review* 30 (2010) 145–54. https://doi.org/10.1016/j.cpr.2009.10.005.

Twenge, Jean M., et al. "Egos Inflating Over Time: A Cross-Temporal Meta-Analysis of
the Narcissistic Personality Inventory." *Journal of Personality* 76 (2008) 875–902.
https://doi.org/10.1111/j.1467–6494.2008.00507.x.

Tyson, Peter. "Dogs' Dazzling Sense of Smell." https://www.pbs.org/wgbh/nova/article/
dogs-sense-of-smell/.

Tyson, Timothy B. "The Ghosts of 1898: Wilmington's Race Riot and the Rise of
White Supremacy." https://media2.newsobserver.com/content/media/2010/5/3/
ghostsof1898.pdf.

Ulrich, Orth, et al. "Tracking the Trajectory of Shame, Guilt, and Pride Across the Life
Span." *Journal of Personality and Social Psychology* 99 (2010) 1061–71. https://doi.
org/10.1037/a0021342.

UNICEF Data. "Under-Five Mortality." https://data.unicef.org/topic/child-survival/
under-five-mortality/.

United States General Accounting Office. "Racial Differences in Arrests." https://www.
gao.gov/assets/ggd-94–29r.pdf.

University of Michigan. "Pray tell: Americans stretching the truth about church
attendance." https://www.sciencedaily.com/releases/2010/12/101201124353.htm.

University of North Carolina Charlotte. "The Racial Wealth Gap: Business Ownership
& Entrepreneurship." https://ui.uncc.edu/story/racial-wealth-gap-business-owner
ship-entrepreneurship.

Unterrainer, Human-Friedrich, et al. "Vulnerable Dark Triad Personality Facets Are
Associated with Religious Fundamentalist Tendencies." *Psychopathology* 49 (2016)
47–52. https://doi.org/10.1159/000443901.

Uscinski, Joseph E. "The Study of Conspiracy Theories." *Argumenta* 3 (2018) 233–45.
https://doi.org/10.23811/53.arg2017.usc.

Uscinski, Joseph E., and Joseph M. Parent. *American Conspiracy Theories*. Oxford:
Oxford University Press, 2014.

van Leeuwen, Florian, et al. "Disgust Sensitivity Relates to Moral Foundations Independent of Political Ideology." *Evolutionary Behavioral Sciences* 11 (2017) 92–98. https://doi.org/10.1037/ebs0000075.

van Prooijen, Jan-Willem. "Connecting the Dots: Illusory Pattern Perception Predicts Belief in Conspiracies and the Supernatural." *European Journal of Social Psychology* 48 (2018) 320–35. https://doi.org/10.1002/ejsp.2331.

———. "An Existential Threat Model of Conspiracy Theories." *European Psychologist* 25 (2020) 16–25. https://doi.org/10.1027/1016-9040/a000381.

———. *The Psychology of Conspiracy Theories*. New York: Routledge, 2018.

———. "Why Education Predicts Decreased Belief in Conspiracy Theories." *Applied Cognitive Psychology* 31 (2016) 50–8. https://doi.org/10.1002/acp.3301.

van Prooijen, Jan-Willem, and Karen M. Douglas. "Belief in Conspiracy Theories: Basic Principles of an Emerging Research Domain." *European Journal of Social Psychology* 48 (2018) 897–908. https://doi.org/10.1002/ejsp.2530.

van Prooijen, Jan-Willem, and Mark van Vugt. "Conspiracy Theories: Evolved Functions and Psychological Mechanisms." *Perspectives on Psychological Science* 13 (2018) 770–88. https://doi.org/10.1177/1745691618774270.

van Prooijen, Jan-Willem, and Mengdi Song. "The Cultural Dimensions of Intergroup Conspiracy Theories." *British Journal of Psychology* 112 (2021) 455–73. https://doi.org/10.1111/bjop.12471.

van Prooijen, Jan-Willem, and Michele Acker. "The Influence of Control on Belief in Conspiracy Theories: Conceptual and Applied Extensions." *Applied Cognitive Psychology* 29 (2015) 753–61. https://doi.org/10.1002/acp.3161.

van Prooijen, Jan-Willem, et al. "Social-Cognitive Processes Underlying Belief in Conspiracy Theories." In *Handbook of Conspiracy Theories*, edited by Michael Butter and Peter Knight, 168–80. Oxon, UK: Routledge.

Van Schie, Charlotte C., et al. "Narcissistic Traits in Young People: Understanding the Role of Parenting and Maltreatment." *Borderline Personality Disorder and Emotional Dysregulation* 7 (2020) 1–10. https://doi.org/10.1186/s40479-020-00125-7.

Vandermaas-Peeler, Alex, et al. "Partisan Polarization Dominates Trump Era: Findings from the 2018 American Values Survey." https://www.prri.org/research/partisan-polarization-dominates-trump-era-findings-from-the-2018-american-values-survey/#page-section-5.

Vanderminden, Jennifer, and Jennifer J. Esala. "Beyond Symptoms: Race and Gender Predict Anxiety Disorder Diagnosis." *Society and Mental Health* 9 (2019) 111–25. https://doi.org/10.1177/2156869318811435.

Vannucci, Anna, et al. "Social Media Use and Anxiety in Emerging Adults." *Journal of Affective Disorders* 207 (2017) 163–66. https://doi.org/10.1016/j.jad.2016.08.040.

Vater, Aline, et al. "Does a Narcissism Epidemic Exist in Modern Western Societies? Comparing Narcissism and Self-esteem in East and West Germany." *PLOS ONE* 13 (2018) 0198386. https://doi.org/10.1371/journal.pone.0188287.

Vij, Sarina. "Why Minority Voters Have a Lower Voter Turnout: An Analysis of Current Restrictions." https://www.americanbar.org/groups/crsj/publications/human_rights_magazine_home/voting-in-2020/why-minority-voters-have-a-lower-voter-turnout/.

Vilsaint, Corrie L., et al. "Racial/Ethnic Differences in 12-month Prevalence and Persistence of Mood, Anxiety, and Substance Use Disorders: Variation by Nativity and Socioeconomic Status." *Comprehensive Psychiatry* 89 (2019) 52–60. https://doi.org/10.1016/j.comppsych.2018.12.008.

Vogels, Emily. "10 Facts About Americans and Online Dating." https://www.pewresearch.or/fact-tank/2020/02/06/10-facts-about-americans-and-online-dating.

Von Grember, Klaus, et al. "2017 Global Hunger Index: The Inequalities of Hunger." https://ebrary.ifpri.org/utils/getfile/collection/p15738coll2/id/131422/filename/131628.pdf.

Vospernik, Petra. "The Relationship of Adaptive and Pathological Narcissism to Attachment Style and Reflective Functioning." PhD diss., The City University of New York, 2014.

Vought, Russ. "Is There Anything Actually Wrong With 'Christian Nationalism'?: Opinion." https://www.newsweek.com/there-anything-actually-wrong-christian-nationalism-opinion-1577519.

Vrbicek, Benjamin. "The Many Faces of Narcissism in the Church." https://www.christianitytoday.com/ct/2020/march/chuck-degroat-narcissism-comes-church.html.

Wadsworth, Nancy D. "The Racial Demons That Help Explain Evangelical Support for Trump." https://www.vox.com/the-big-idea/2018/4/30/17301282/race-evangelicals-trump-support-gerson-atlantic-sexism-segregation-south.

Wagemans, Fieke M. A., et al. "Disgust Sensitivity is Primarily Associated with Purity-Based Moral Judgements." *Emotion* 18 (2018) 277–89. https://doi.org/10.1037/emo0000359.

Wagner-Egger, Pascal, et al. "Creationism and Conspiracism Share a Common Teleological Bias." *Current Biology* 28 (2018) 847–70. https://doi.org/10.1016/j.cub.2018.06.072.

Wallin, David J. *Attachment in Psychotherapy*. New York: Guilford, 2015.

Wallis, Jim. "Southern Baptist Seminary Presidents Double Down on Bad Theology on Race." https://religionnews.com/2020/12/10/southern-baptist-seminary-presidents-double-down-on-bad-theology-on-race/.

Wallisch, Pascal. "Two Years Later, We Finally Know Why People Saw 'The Dress' Differently." https://slate.com/technology/2017/04/heres-why-people-saw-the-dress-differently.html.

Walsh, Matt. "Bruce Jenner Is Not A Woman. He Is A Sick And Delusional Man." https://www.theblaze.com/contributions/bruce-jenner-is-not-a-woman-he-is-a-sick-and-delusional-man.

Wang, Ruile, et al. "The Association Between Disgust Sensitivity and Negative Attitudes Toward Homosexuality: The Mediating Role of Moral Foundations." *Frontiers in Psychology* 10 (2019) 1229. https://doi.org/10.3389/fpsyg.2019.01229.

Wang, Yueyue, et al. "Hostile Attribution Bias and Angry Rumination: A Longitudinal Study of Undergraduate Students." *PLoS One* 14 (2019) 0217759. https://doi.org/10.1371/journal.pone.0217759.

Warzel, Charlie. "How QAnon Creates a Dangerous Alternate Reality." https://www.nytimes.com/2020/08/04/opinion/qanon-conspiracy-theory-arg.html.

Washington's Blog and Global Research. "The Terrorism Statistics Every American Needs to Hear." https://www.globalresearch.ca/the-terrorism-statistics-every-american-needs-to-hear/5382818.

Watson, Denise M. "The Norfolk 17 Face a Hostile Reception as Schools Reopen." https://www.pilotonline.com/projects/massive-resistance/article_05745bcd-a24e-5d1d-9c5c-ce22313d963d.html.

The Week Staff. "Black Wealth Gap." https://theweek.com/articles/939413/black-wealth -gap.

———. "QAnon Goes Mainstream." https://theweek.com/articles/929707/qanon-goes-mainstream.

Wehner, Peter. "The Scandal Rocking the Evangelical World." *The Atlantic*, June 7, 2021. https://wwwtheatlantic.com/ideas/archive/2021/06/russell-moore-sbc/619122/.

———. "There is no Christian case for Trump." https://www.theatlantic.com/ideas/ archive/2020/01/there-no-christian-case-trump/605785/.

Weiler, Jonathan D., and Marc J. Hetherington. *Prius or Pickup? How the Answers to Four Simple Questions Explain America's Great Divide*. New York: Mariner, 2018.

Weinberger, Adam B., et al. "Implicit Pattern Learning Predicts Individual Differences in Belief in God in the United States and Afghanistan." *Nature Communication* 11 (2020) 1–12. https://www.nature.com/articles/s41467-020-18362-3#citeas.

Wellman, David. *Portraits of White Racism*. New York: Cambridge University Press, 1977.

Welwood, John. *Toward a Psychology of Awakening: Buddhism, Psychotherapy, and the Personal and Spiritual Transformation*. Boston: Shambhala, 2000.

Wen, Tiffanie. "A Sociological History of Soccer Violence." https://www.theatlantic. com/health/archive/2014/07/a-sociological-history-of-soccer-violence/374396/.

Wenner Moyer, Melinda. "People Drawn to Conspiracy Theories Share a Cluster of Psychological Features." https://www.scientificamerican.com/article/people-drawn -to-conspiracy-theories-share-a-cluster-of-psychological-features/.

Wenzel, Kristin, et al. "General Belief in a Just World Is Positively Associated with Dishonest Behavior." *Frontiers in Psychology* (8) (2017). https://doi.org/10.3389/ fpsyg.2017.01770.

West, Candace E. "Election Survey: White Evangelicals Remain Cultural Outliers on Race, Trump, Immigration." https://religiondispatches.org/election-survey-white-evangelicals-remain-cultural-outliers-on-race-trump-immigration/.

West, Keon, and Asia A. Eaton. "Prejudiced and Unaware of It: Evidence for the Dunning-Kruger Model in the Domains of Racism and Sexism." *Personality and Individual Differences* 146 (2019) 111–19. https://doi.org/10.1016/j.paid.2019.03.047.

Wetzel, Eunike, et al. "The Narcissism Epidemic Is Dead; Long Live the Narcissism Epidemic." *Psychological Science* 28 (2017) 1833–47. https://doi.org/10.1177 /0956797617724208.

What We Know: The Public Policy Research Portal. "What Does Scholarly Research Say About Whether Conversion Therapy can Alter Sexual Orientation Without Causing Harm?" https://whatweknow.inequality.cornell.edu/wp-content/uploads /2018/04/PDF-Conversion-therapy.pdf.

Whitehead, Andrew L., and Samuel L. Perry. "The Growing Anti-Democratic Threat of Christian Nationalism in the U.S." https://time.com/6052051/anti-democratic-threat-christian-nationalism/.

Whitehead, Andrew L., and Samuel L. Perry. *Taking America Back for God: Christian Nationalism in the United States*. New York: Oxford University Press, 2020.

Whitfield, John B., et al. "Pessimism is Associated with Greater All-Cause and Cardiovascular Mortality, but Optimism is not Protective." *Scientific Reports* 10 (2020) 1–7. https://doi.org/10.1038/s41598-020-69388-y.

Wilcock, Evelyn. "Negative Identity: Mixed German Jewish Descent as a Factor in the Reception of Theodor Adorno." *New German Critique* 81 (2000) 169–87. https://www.jstor.org/stable/488552.

Wilkerson, Isabel. "America's Enduring Caste System." https://www.nytimes.com/2020/07/01/magazine/isabel-wilkerson-caste.html.

Wilkins, Vicky M., and Jeffrey B. Wenger. "Belief in a Just World and Attitudes Toward Affirmative Action." *Policy Studies Journal* 42 (2014) 325–43. https://doi.org/10.1111/psj.12063.

Williams, David R., and Toni D. Rucker. "Understanding and Addressing Racial Disparities in Health Care." *Health Care Financing Review* 21 (2000) 75–90. https://www.ncbi.nlm.nih.gov/pmc/articles/PMC4194634/#/.

Williams, Sarah C. P. "Human Nose Can Detect a Trillion Smells." https://www.sciencemag.org/news/2014/03/human-nose-can-detect-trillion-smells.

Williams, Vanessa. "Closing the Racial Wealth Gap Requires Heavy, Progressive Taxation of Wealth." https://www.brookings.edu/research/closing-the-racial-wealth-gap-requires-heavy-progressive-taxation-of-wealth/.

Wills, Matthew. "Is the Authoritarian Personality a Legitimate Concept?" https://daily.jstor.org/is-the-authoritarian-personality-a-legitimate-concept/.

———. "What Links Religion and Authoritarianism?" https://daily.jstor.org/what-links-religion-and-authoritarianism/.

Wink, Paul, et al. "Religiousness, Spiritual Seeking, and Authoritarianism: Findings from a Longitudinal Study." *Journal for the Scientific Study of Religion* 46 (2007) 321–35. https://www.jstor.org/stable/4621983.

Wolff, Joshua R., et al. "Evangelical Christian College Students and Attitudes Toward Gay Rights: A California University Sample." *Journal of LGBT Youth* 9 (2012) 200–24. https://doi.org/10.1080/19361653.2012.652892.

Wolfinger, Nicholas H. "Counterintuitive Trends in the Link Between Premarital Sex and Marital Stability." https://ifstudies.org/blog/counterintuitive-trends-in-the-link-between-premarital-sex-and-marital-stability.

Wong, Janelle S. *Immigrants, Evangelicals, and Politics in an Era of Demographic Change.* New York: Russell Sage Foundation, 2018.

Wood, Daniel. "As Pandemic Deaths Add Up, Racial Disparities Persist—And In Some Cases Worsen." https://www.npr.org/sections/health-shots/2020/09/23/914427907/as-pandemic-deaths-add-up-racial-disparities-persist-and-in-some-cases-worsen.

Wood, Michael J., and Debra Gray. "Right-Wing Authoritarianism as a Predictor of Pro-Establishment versus Anti-Establishment Conspiracy Theories." *Personality and Individual Differences* 138 (2019) 163–66. https://doi.org/10.1016/j.paid.2018.09.036.

Wood, Michael J., and Karen Douglas. "Are Conspiracy Theories a Surrogate for God?" In *Handbook of Conspiracy Theory and Contemporary Religion* edited by Asbjørn Dyrendal, David G. Robertson, and Egil Asprem, 87–205. Boston: Brill, 2018.

Wood, Michael J., and Karen M. Douglas. "Conspiracy Theory Psychology: Individual Differences, Worldviews, and States of Mind." in *Conspiracy Theories and the People Who Believe Them*, edited by Joseph E. Uscinski, 245–56. New York: Oxford University Press. https://doi.org/10.1093/oso/9780190844073.003.0016.

Workman, Clifford I., et al. "Morality is in the Eye of the Beholder: the Neurocognitive Basis of the 'Anomalous-is-Bad' Stereotype." *Annals Reports* 1494 (2021) 3–17. https://doi.org/10.1111/nyas.14575.

Worland, Justin. "America's Long Overdue Awakening to Systemic Racism." https://time.com/5851855/systemic-racism-america/.

World Population Review. "Most Racist Cities in America 2021." https://worldpopulationreview.com/us-city-rankings/most-racist-cities-in-america.

Xiao, H., et al. "Are we in crisis? National mental health and treatment trends in college counseling centers." *Psychological Services* 14 (2017) 407–15. http://dx.doi.org/10.1037/ser0000130.

Xiaowen, Xu, et al. "An Orderly Personality Partially Explains the Link Between Trait Disgust and Political Conservatism." *Cognition and Emotion* 34 (2020) 302–15. https://doi.org/10.1080/02699931.2019.1627292.

Yalch, Matthew M. "Dimensions of Pathological Narcissism and Intention to Vote for Donald Trump." *PLOS ONE* 16 (2021) 1–13. https://doi.org/10.1371/journal.pone.0249892.

Yoder, Anne M., et al. "The Word *Disgust* May Refer to More Than One Emotion." *Emotion* 16 (2016) 301–8. https://doi.org/10.1037/emo0000118.

Young, Everett H. "Why We're Liberal, Why We're Conservative: A Cognitive Theory on the Origins of Ideological Thinking." PhD diss., Stony Brook University, 2009.

Yun, Lawrence, et al. "Snapshot of Race and Home Buying in America." https://cdn.nar.realtor/sites/default/files/documents/2021-snapshot-of-race-and-home-buying-in-the-us-report-02-17-2021.pdf.

Yustisia, Whinda, et al. "The Role of Religious Fundamentalism and Tightness-Looseness in Promoting Collective Narcissism and Extreme Group Behavior." *Psychology of Religion and Spirituality* 12 (2020) 231–40. http://dx.doi.org/10.1037/rel0000269.

Zaromb, Franklin M., et al. "We Made History: Citizens of 35 Countries Overestimate Their Nation's Role in World History." *Journal of Applied Research in Memory and Cognition* 7 (2018) 521–28. https://doi.org/10.1016/j.jarmac.2018.05.006.

Zentner, Marcel, and John E. Bates. "Child Temperament: An Integrative Review of Concepts, Research Programs, and Measures." *European Journal of Development Science* 2 (2008) 7–37. https://www.researchgate.net/publication/228368866_Child_Temperament_An_Integrative_Review_of_Concepts_Research_Programs_and_Measures.

Zhao, Christina. "Pro-Trump Pastor Says 'Thou Shall Not Have Sex With a Porn Star' is 'Totally Irrelevant' For the President." https://www.newsweek.com/pro-trump-pastor-says-thou-shall-not-have-sex-porn-star-totally-irrelevant-838017.

Zmigrod, Leor, et al. "Cognitive Inflexibility Predicts Extremist Attitudes." *Frontiers in Psychology* 10 (2019) 989. https://doi.org/10.3389/fpsyg.2019.00989.

Zmigrod, Leor, et al. "Cognitive Underpinnings of Nationalistic Ideology in the Context of Brexit." *Proceedings of the National Academy of Sciences* 115 (2018) 4532–40. https://doi.org/10.1073/pnas.1708960115.

Zuckerman, Phil. "COVID-19 and Christian Nationalism." https://www.psychologytoday.com/us/blog/the-secular-life/202012/covid-19-and-christian-nationalism.

Index

Made in the USA
Coppell, TX
29 August 2023

20957928R00187